Please Please Me

PLEASE PLEASE ME

Sixties British Pop, Inside Out

GORDON THOMPSON

OXFORD
UNIVERSITY PRESS
2008

OXFORD
UNIVERSITY PRESS

Oxford University Press, Inc., publishes works that further
Oxford University's objective of excellence
in research, scholarship, and education.

Oxford   New York
Auckland   Cape Town   Dar es Salaam   Hong Kong   Karachi
Kuala Lumpur   Madrid   Melbourne   Mexico City   Nairobi
New Delhi   Shanghai   Taipei   Toronto

With offices in
Argentina   Austria   Brazil   Chile   Czech Republic   France   Greece
Guatemala   Hungary   Italy   Japan   Poland   Portugal   Singapore
South Korea   Switzerland   Thailand   Turkey   Ukraine   Vietnam

Published by Oxford University Press, Inc.
198 Madison Avenue, New York, New York 10016

www.oup.com

Oxford is a registered trademark of Oxford University Press

Library of Congress Cataloging-in-Publication Data
Thompson, Gordon Ross, 1949–
Please please me : sixties British pop, inside out / Gordon Thompson.
p.   cm.
Includes bibliographical references, discography, and index.
ISBN 978-0-19-533318-3; 978-0-19-533325-1 (pbk.)
1. Popular music—Great Britain—1961–1970—History and criticism.   2. Sound
recording industry—Great Britain—History—20th century.   I. Title.
ML3492.T56 2008
781.640941'09046—dc22   2007047545

3   5   7   9   8   6   4   2

Printed in the United States of America
on acid-free paper

Preface

A common joke among adults of a certain age insists that if you remember the sixties, you weren't there. Like many effective one-liners, this one plays on various kinds of truth. The primary premise of this gag references the substance abuse of the era, suggesting widespread brain damage and the inability to remember. However, the sixties transformed Western culture such that, in many ways, the people we are today *weren't* there: we *are* different.

My first experiences of sixties British pop and rock arrived via the radio as my family sat in our kitchen and then, more vividly, via *The Ed Sullivan Show* one Sunday night as the family gathered around the flickering black-and-white televised images of the Beatles. I already held an intuitive knowledge of music and a rudimentary ability to read notation from singing in a church choir, but hearing the Beatles and then the Dave Clark Five, Gerry and the Pacemakers, the Rolling Stones, the Animals, the Kinks, and others connected with me. I had to know more.

Now, in the present, I contemplate my compromised ethnomusicological role. Sixties British rock and pop shaped me as a musician and as an individual. Can chronological distance provide me with the cultural distance I need to deal with this milieu objectively? Is my study ethnography or history? Could it be both? Even the postmodernist stance that underlies my approach emerged in the sixties.

Before I undertook this work, my research background had taken me to Gujarat, India, but in 1996, the opportunity came to teach American students in London. I needed to find a topic that reflected the location of the class. With some trepidation, I volunteered to teach a course on sixties British rock and pop, reflecting both my own interests and those of my students. Building on what I thought I knew, I began the process of researching the music of this era by indulging in the kind of thing fans do: I became a gatherer of facts.[1] At first, discographic trivia (release dates, chart action, labels, etc.) occupied my attention, then biographical details, and, soon, I wanted to know about instruments, amplification, microphones, and tape recorders. I had evolved into a data glut-

---

[1] A chronology of essential data relating to British rock and pop in the sixties can be found at Thompson 1995.

ton. But the weft and weave of ethnography and history require more than just threads of fact. Details need ideational patterns for connective tissue. One can have all the facts right and still get the story wrong.

As I delved into the music, my ethnomusicological instincts engaged. I began talking with musicians and then with songwriters, producers, music directors, engineers, press agents, and others. First, I found a disparity between what people told me and what I had read in various sources. Some musicians told me that their managements had purposefully changed their birth years and had invented interests for profiles in trade papers to construct a younger and hipper image. For others, the distance that celebrity fosters made them simply impossible to reach; nevertheless, one interview tended to lead to another, and another and another. Discographically, one could generally deduce when companies had released recordings, but the specifics of who was actually playing on a disk seldom received attention. The complexity that emerged from my conversations demanded a way to make sense of the patterns and connections among the people, history, technology, and music. The more you know, the more you know that you don't know.

Research on sixties British pop reflects the specialized knowledge bases behind almost every recording. Musicians know best their particular areas of performance, be it the voice, guitar, drums, keyboard, or any of the other numerous instruments. Engineers know engineering, songwriters songwriting, etc. Members of each category provided valuable insights into both their own work and that of others, such that a textured and nuanced story emerged.

I regret my inability to interview some of the most noted personages of the era, which led me to rely on other people's interviews and biographies or on autobiographies. In the end, it is likely that "mistakes were made," but I have always endeavored to get the story right. The process of getting it right revealed the complex underlying, overlapping, decentered realities of these scenes within scenes. Each individual saw his or her part of the industry differently. Indeed, disputes between them continue as they attempt to reconcile their memories with those of others and with the ephemera of fact. I have attempted to reflect the multilinear quality of this story through the multiple voices of these individuals, grouping them into categories that they recognize, even as they may disagree about definitions.

Getting it right for an ethnomusicologist usually involves understanding how a culture thinks about music. In this case, I have sought to understand British perspectives of the era, which includes avoiding the American tag line of "the British invasion." Indeed, the British had already experienced an American invasion, both during and after the Second World War and subsequently in music and culture. I have attempted to understand how British musicians, songwriters, music directors, producers, and engineers understood their scenes, while at the same time recognizing that their memories of the era have been shaped by the intervening years.

Interviewing musicians and others seemed daunting at first, but almost all proved ultimately to be warm, open, and generous. Every time we talked, I learned things that changed how I understood this cultural milieu. At the mundane level, the people I interviewed provided me with the "who, what, where, when, and why." More important, Malcolm Addey, Eric Allen, James Baring, Stan Barrett, Dave Berry, Charlie Blackwell, Joe Brown, Stephen Candib, John Carter, Clem Cattini, Bill Covington, Bryan Daly, Arty Davies, Roger Dean, Bob Efford, Matthew Fisher, Vic Flick, Herbie Flowers, Mo Foster, Bobby Graham, Arthur Greenslade, Bill Harry, Les Hurdle, Nazir Jairazbhoy, Viram Jasani, Peter Knight, Jr., Derek Lawrence, Spencer Leigh, Mark Lewisohn, Carlo Little, Joe Moretti, Mitch Murray, Tony Newman, Peter O'Flaherty, Margot Quantrell, Les Reed, Norman Smith, Geoff Stephens, Big Jim Sullivan, Shel Talmy, Ronnie Verrell, Pip Wedge, Allan Weighell, Michael Weighell, and Andy White shaped how I think about this milieu. Many others contributed to my research (including John Warburg, Dawn Eden, and Brenda Tseunis) and helped me to better annotate the story. I regret that I have not been able to use everything I learned and that I have been unable to give everyone more attention in this text. Nevertheless, what I have learned has been invaluable.

Several individuals have read portions of the manuscript and have provided precious advice on my descriptions of the era and pertinent critiques of my approaches. These include Walter Everett, Allan Kozinn, Fred Lieberman, Vic Flick, Jim Sullivan, Les Reed, Dave Maswick, Malcolm Addey, Geoff Stephens, John Carter, Margot Quantrell, Andy White, Mitch Murray, John Carter, and Norman Smith. Paul Rapp provided beneficial legal advice both on the clock and off. My student assistant L. J. Negro—who transcribed most of the interviews—suffered through hours of tape, listening to me asking the same questions, individual after individual. And my editor, Suzanne Ryan; her assistant, Lora Dunn; and the other folks at Oxford University Press (including Norman Hirschy, Christi Stanforth, and Merryl Sloane) have persistently supported and shepherded this book through its various stages. Hunt Conard at Skidmore College provided assistance in preparing photos. Less obviously, the owner and staff of Uncommon Grounds, a coffee shop in Saratoga Springs, provided an environment in which I was able to write for several hours every day with Internet access and a hot cup of coffee. Finally, my wife of thirty-two years, Jane Thompson, selflessly proofread drafts and provided moral support in this expensive and time-consuming obsession. Sabbaticals without grant money focus the mind and empty the pocket.

And you cannot do this without money: that goes both for making music and for researching music. Skidmore College supported and encouraged my research and teaching through both faculty development grants and a project completion grant. Regents College, London, provided me with my first chance to explore this subject in the classroom and I thank them, and Dean David Morgan in particular, for being open-minded and supportive. Finally, a research grant from Advanced Studies in England helped me to get to London in the summer of 2000 to do some of my first interviews.

Contents

A photo gallery follows p. 130.

Credits

For permission to quote copyrighted material, acknowledgments are due to the following:

Excerpts from *The Legendary Joe Meek: The Telstar Man,* copyright © by John Repsch (London: Cherry Red Books, 2000), www.cherryred.co.uk

Excerpts from *Paul McCartney: Many Years from Now,* copyright © by Barry Miles (New York: Holt, 1997)

Excerpts from "New Sounding Kinks," copyright © by Keith Altham, *New Musical Express* (24 December 1965): 10

Excerpts from "Kinks Don't Mind 'Formby Quartet' Tag," copyright © by Keith Altham, *New Musical Express* (18 March 1966): 3

Excerpts from *Stoned: A Memoir of London in the 1960s,* copyright © by Andrew Loog Oldham (New York: St. Martin's, 2000)

Excerpts from *All You Need Is Ears,* copyright © by George Martin (New York: St. Martin's, 1979)

Numerous attempts to reach Chris Roberts[1] for permission to use excerpts from "Lennon and McCartney Tell You How to Write a Hit!" which was published in *Melody Maker* (1 February 1964), failed.

For permission to quote interview material, acknowledgments are due to the following: Malcolm Addey, Eric Allen, James Baring, Stan Barrett, Charlie

---

[1] Not to be confused with the Chris Roberts who also wrote for *Melody Maker* beginning in the 1980s. *Melody Maker* ceased publication in 2000.

Blackwell, Joe Brown, John Carter, Clem Cattini, Bill Covington, Bryan Daly, Matthew Fisher, Vic Flick, Bobby Graham, Les Hurdle, Joe Moretti, Mitch Murray, Tony Newman, Margot Quantrell, Les Reed, Norman Smith, Geoff Stephens, Jim Sullivan, Shel Talmy, Michael Weighell, and Andy White and the estates of Arthur Greenslade, Ronnie Verrell, Carlo Little, Allan Weighell, and Peter Knight, Sr.

Please Please Me

1

Introduction

Approaches and Material

On 11 January 1963, while mainstream American popular music slumbered in the comfort of predictable stars and assured cultural and industrial hegemony, something caught the ear of a London record reviewer. Keith Fordyce (1963: 4), in his weekly contribution to the musical trade paper the *New Musical Express*, commented on a new recording by a group that had first appeared on the charts during the previous fall. With the Beatles' management promoting the release of "Please Please Me," he critiqued the claim that this single would be "the record of the year."[1] Expressing disdain for the advertising and exhibiting well-founded skepticism, Fordyce comments that he has "just the slightest nagging doubt that, with fifty weeks of releases yet to come this year, it may prove to be a teensy weensy exaggeration!"

He had good reason to doubt the hyperbole routinely sent to the paper by public relations offices. Could they really mean "the record of the year"? In Britain? In the world? He had heard it all before. Nevertheless, the disk did catch

---

[1] This is from Brian Epstein's press release, written by Tony Barrow and Andrew Oldham, which appears in Lewisohn (1988: 25).

his attention. He notes first that a "vocal *and* instrumental quartet" (the emphasis is mine) recorded this disk, distinguishing them from most of the solo male heartthrobs whom record labels routinely promoted. He then continues by congratulating the group, describing the record as a "really enjoyable platter, full of beat, vigour and vitality—and what's more, it's different." Emphasizing their uniqueness, he observes that he "can't think of any other group currently recording in this style" (ibid.). Over the next year, Britain would succumb to this difference and to a flood of derivative "beat groups." America would eventually surrender too.

A year later, on 9 February 1964, as millions watched the Beatles on CBS's *The Ed Sullivan Show,* rock 'n' roll ceased to be an exclusively American art form. By the end of the decade, having overcome considerable political, economic, and technological hurdles, British performers and production teams were fixtures in an internationalized pop music industry. Indeed, London's pop music recording industry came from being a colony of a distinctly American idiom to a major creative center in its own right in a few short years. What's more, Britain's participation changed the music. Remarkably, some American performers began to emulate British models, wearing similar clothes and importing British instruments so that they would look "English." This equivalent of cultural surrender emboldened London to take the music in directions that neither Bill Haley nor Little Richard had ever imagined.

Lacking the economic and technological advantages of their American counterparts, British studios succeeded in the sixties partly through skill, hard work, and determination and partly through luck. The North American market dwarfed the British isles in terms of both population and disposable income. Major American record companies knew that a top-selling disk assured them substantial domestic profits with the potential for international sales serving as icing on the cake. If a British recording became an American hit, the British company stood to reap a bounty, not only because of the greater size of the market, but also because of the postwar power of the dollar. In either case, performers stood to gain a second chance at recording and perhaps a new circuit of concerts. Nevertheless, British hit recordings in the American market were few, with the Beatles being the first British performers to tour successfully.

The 1950s' American media markets, flush with cash and optimistic about the future, had encouraged corporations like Ampex and RCA to pour resources into developing recording technology, benefiting not just the music industry, but also television and film. (See Ampex 2006.) Moreover, American studios purchased equipment in such quantities that they often established international industry standards. Consequently, the British recording industry generally reacted to the musical tastes and technological approaches set by Americans. Furthermore, Britain's sustained financial crisis in the postwar years resulted in government currency restrictions that impeded the importation of foreign (and particularly American) equipment, fostering the development of competitive domestic technologies.

Musically, postwar nationalism worked to London's advantage with British audiences commonly preferring homegrown versions to the American originals. The British pop music industry actively sought American disks for indigenous artists to imitate, copying the original arrangements and interpretive ticks. Moreover, British artists could tour the United Kingdom to promote their versions, while the British Musicians' Union successfully blocked visits by many American performers.[2] European promoters often found British rockers cheaper to hire, both because they were closer and because they would work for less money than Americans (perhaps one reason that Bruno Koschmider hired the Beatles for his Hamburg clubs).

Given that African American performers figured prominently in early sixties pop (e.g., the Shirelles and the Miracles), the preference of white British audiences for performers who looked like themselves added a racist dimension to consumer patterns. Mick Jagger (1963: 3) of the Rolling Stones—commenting on why their versions of African American blues and rhythm-and-blues were successful in London's clubs—observed in early 1963, "Girl fans, particularly, would rather have a copy by a British group than the original American version— mainly I suppose because they like the British blokes' faces, and they feel nearer them." In an era when Commonwealth immigration issues played an important role in British politics and life, Jagger's statement hints at the underlying racism of the era.

The British pop music industry in the mid-fifties scrambled to react to rock 'n' roll when it arrived from America. British musicians could imitate the histrionics of Johnny Ray's "Cry" (1951), but Elvis and Chuck Berry were something entirely different. Copying those Americans who managed to tour Britain (e.g., Eddie Cochran), British artists by the early sixties had garnered enough experience to be able to occasionally crack the American market, which remained the grail. America represented not only a huge and lucrative market, but, as the center of pop culture, offered the fastest path to global success. British artists needed a break, and the cold war set the stage for their dramatic entry. The early sixties

---

[2] The American Federation of Musicians similarly restricted British performers from touring the United States.

witnessed geopolitical standoffs in Berlin and a near nuclear war over missiles in Cuba, followed by the assassination of a popular young American president. The tensions of teens in the Western world found expression through fashion, films, and music.

If anything characterized British pop music between 1962 and 1964, optimism seemed to underlie even the most tragic songs, and the Beatles came to play the principal jesters in the court of teen anxiety. What transpired next offers a cautionary tale about the problems of unexpected success. The sudden international demand for British pop music outstripped its supply of fresh faces and taxed the resources of London's recording industry. Groups that had been satisfactory dance hall entertainers were hustled into the studio and promoted as the next great discovery. Small studios flourished as they satisfied the adolescent hunger for new music, providing independent producers with the microphone time that corporations were increasingly unable to provide. An extensive city-wide infrastructure of studios, producers, engineers, music directors, contractors, agents, and session musicians emerged to create and record music quickly and efficiently. To be sure, competition continued between different parts of this community, but within subgroups, some reciprocal cooperation ensured survival.

At the same time, corporations began giving top artists (e.g., the Beatles) unprecedented access to their studios, allowing them to occupy and control these valuable resources for longer uninterrupted periods. As the sixties unfolded, other artists (e.g., the Rolling Stones and the Who) began routinely recording in the better-equipped studios of New York and Los Angeles. The increased availability and efficiency of transatlantic air travel made access to these studios and the American market a practical option for the best-known British acts. By the end of the sixties, with the growth of independent studios (and the willingness and ability of British artists to travel to the United States to record), the old system gave way, releasing musicians and production crews. Session musicians, music directors, engineers, and producers ventured out into the English-speaking world to explore their visions of how the industry should work. And an era came to an end.

AN ETHNOMUSICOLOGY OF SIXTIES BRITISH POP

Several questions about cultural and musical change arise in the context of understanding the sixties London recording scene. What set off the explosion of pop music that the British called the "beat boom" and the Americans called the "British invasion"? What did participants identify as "British" in this music? What social, economic, technological, political, and historical forces influenced the evolution of this music and the recordings? How did individuals adapt to the changes in their artistic environment? London, operating at a technological and economic disadvantage in relation to its American counterparts in the sixties, changed the direction of popular music. How and why did this happen? More broadly, when discussing this era, should we talk about *a* history of British rock and pop, or should we be discussing multiple parallel histories?

Perhaps the most important sources available to us are the memories of those who participated in the creation of this music. Some (e.g., Andrew Loog Oldham, George Martin, and Geoff Emerick) have written autobiographies. Others (e.g., Alan Clayson and Mo Foster) have compiled recollections of the era. The present study draws upon these sources as well as original interviews conducted between 1999 and 2007 with musicians, producers, music directors, engineers, and others who were active in London between 1956 and 1968. The memories of these individuals, while often attempting to establish reputations, preserve personal accounts of an era and an industry that often hid details of its infrastructure from consumers.

Although ethnomusicologists commonly work in the relative present, we deal with artifacts clearly situated in a cultural context defined by time and place, even if they have audiences far beyond their origins (see Appadurai 1991). We acknowledge that cultural distance informs our perspectives on music; thus, time too presents a vantage point which contextualizes human actions. All of these distances have consequences. Outsiders can easily miss the subtle and evolving nuances of an adopted culture, and oral historians (e.g., Ritchie 2003) have noted how we remember the past fluidly. Nevertheless, outsiders can play important roles in providing new perspectives.

British session musicians, music directors, engineers, and producers participated in thousands of recordings during the sixties. The busiest of them at their busiest times commonly worked on three or more sessions, five or six days a week, for years, producing two or three recordings every session. Their memories of individual sessions, although sometimes cloudy, overlap substantially; some events stand out dramatically in their minds, and others have dissolved into the haze of everyday routine. Their combined recollections contribute valuable complements and alternatives to other kinds of historical and ethnographic documentation. Given that these recording sessions came early in the careers of these individuals, and that many of these events were pivotal in their lives, their memories are likely to have a degree of accuracy. (See Ritchie 2003: 33.) A number of the principals left this milieu (if not the United Kingdom) when the industry underwent significant changes at the end of the sixties and into the seventies, many relocating to the United States, Canada, Australia, and South Africa. Consequently, some have not had many opportunities to compare their stories and to alter them through collective modification of their memories, as in the story of Luigi Trastulli, an Italian steelworker who died in a confrontation with police, but whose myth locals have reimagined through repeated retelling (see Portelli 1991).[3]

The most important artifacts of this era, the recordings provide bundled musical, textual, structural, emotive, technological, and cultural evidence of the communities that came together in London's studios. The musical aspects of song recording include the melody and harmony, and the lyrics constitute the text. The structure includes the form of the arrangement (i.e., verses, choruses, refrains, bridges, etc.), the instrumentation, and the voice ranges of the singers. The emotive component resides in the conviction of the performance, the energy the musicians bring, and how firmly in the rhythmic-metric "groove" they play. The technological quality of the recording includes the audio clarity, dynamic consistency, general frequency range, balance (how well all of the parts of the performance can be heard), and the manipulation of the sound by boosting particular frequencies, selectively damping or amplifying parts of the sound envelope, and the addition of echo or reverberation. Finally, the cultural component describes the people who composed, performed, and recorded the music, the people either for whom the song recording was created or who adopted it on their own, and the environments in which all of this happened. Live performance proved important in the development of and the experimentation with musical ideas, if not as a way of directly experiencing how audiences react. But, as far as the recording industry was concerned, the purpose of performance was to promote record sales. Indeed, this volume takes the intersections between the music and the recording industries as its subject matter.

The terms "rock 'n' roll," "rock," and "pop" appear here somewhat interchangeably, as clear definitions with hard-and-fast borders have evaded most authors. Recognizing that, in many people's minds, these musical terms carry significant orientation differences, musicians in the sixties nevertheless often ignored (or at best tolerated) polarized views. Most groups would have acknowledged that their repertoires included both blues- and rhythm-and-blues-oriented rock 'n' roll songs (e.g., Chuck Berry) and pop songs (e.g., Gerry Goffin and Carole King). The Beatles provide one of the best examples of a band with a heterogeneous repertoire, including everything from show tunes to rockabilly

---

[3] Portelli (1991) discovered that Trastulli died during a protest against Italy joining NATO in 1947. Town and union representatives told a story of how Trastulli had died during an industrial strike in 1949. Portelli describes how change entered during the story's retelling.

rants on their programs. Naturally, some musicians took musical style religiously, such as Eric Clapton, who left the Yardbirds when they recorded one of their biggest hits, "For Your Love," ostensibly because he felt the song was too "commercial." Nevertheless, one of the successes of this era came with the merging of these stylistic preferences such that a "pop" recording could have a secure rock 'n' roll underpinning and vice versa. Indeed, Graham Gouldman's song "For Your Love" and Georgio Gomelsky's production amply illustrates a song mixing rock 'n' roll rhythms, rhythm-and-blues progressions, and pop textures.

The notion of "authenticity" emerges as an important and problematic semiotic quality in the music of this era. Part of the authenticity of the Beatles lies in the perception that they wrote, recorded, and performed much of their own music. While few others could match the ability and success of John, Paul, George, and Ringo (and their production crews), the Beatles set the standard to which others aspired. Indeed, public relations agents devoted considerable attention to projecting their clients as possessing the same kinds of authenticity despite the infrastructure of songwriters, music directors, and session musicians, who ensured that novices could have their names on successful records.

CULTURES OF MUSIC CREATION

In February 1965 (one year after the Beatles made their triumphant first appearance in the United States on *The Ed Sullivan Show*), the pop group Herman's Hermits toured the United Kingdom to promote their most recent release, a 45-rpm disk with the song "Silhouettes" on side A and "Can't You Hear My Heartbeat" on the reverse. When they appeared on programs such as the BBC's *Top of the Pops* (e.g., 11 February 1965), the singer, Peter Noone, stood in front of the rest of the band—consisting of Karl Green (bass), Keith Hopwood (guitar), Derek "Lek" Leckenby (guitar), and Barry Whitman (drums)—and usually mimed to the recording. Television performances were often a mix of prerecorded music (usually the instrumental parts) and live performance (the vocals).

On rare occasions, such as when the Musicians' Union tried to ban the broadcast of mimed performances, groups would perform arrangements of their own recordings.[4] Even in these situations, stage managers and art directors sometimes hid the amplifiers off stage, impeding the musicians' ability to hear what they were playing. On package tours, which could last for weeks with only one or two

---

[4] The British Musicians' Union in 1966, as part of its Keep Music Live campaign, briefly forced broadcasters to drop miming from their programs.

days in each location, groups would perform in theaters and dance halls before ecstatic audiences, who commonly could not hear the music for the screaming. Indeed, the musicians frequently could not even hear each other. Worse, they often ended tours with little in the way of monetary rewards to show for their labors, promoters and agents having skimmed off most of the money to cover transportation, housing, clothing, and a host of other (often phantom) expenses.

During 1964, British bands had won international renown, largely on the success of the Beatles, who had broken the precedent of bands like the Shadows. The model had been a detachable ensemble supporting a vocalist (in the Shadows' case, Cliff Richard), that role commonly justifying the ensemble's existence in the public mind. The Beatles constituted a "group," four personalities, each integral to the identity of the band. They also appeared to be self-contained and -sustaining, writing and recording their own music. Other bands might accompany several singers, as the Tornados did when they went on tour, providing music for many of the acts on a program. Both the Shadows and the Tornados had their own hit instrumental recordings (e.g., "Apache" for the Shadows and "Telstar" for the Tornados), which were largely separate from the singers; however, even then, their management still apparently considered them something of a musical convenience.

Unlike the Beatles and most of the bands of the so-called beat boom, the Shadows and the Tornados rarely sang. They were instrumentalists, electric versions of the horn-based big bands that had dominated dance halls only a few years previously. As in that previous age, they provided danceable music between appearances by crooners, who would step into the spotlight for a few numbers and then retreat, probably followed by other crooners. The Beatles succeeded in breaking that stereotype. The combination of instrumental and vocal proficiency, with the consistent ability to generate their own material, made the Beatles the gold standard for pop music in the mid-1960s, to which many aspired but few could match. Other bands covered American records or obtained new songs from British songwriters. Lacking the experience, determination, and managerial support that the Beatles had, these performers relied upon the recording industry's network of session musicians and music directors. In many cases, they had no choice.

The only member of Herman's Hermits to perform "Silhouettes" and "Can't You Hear My Heartbeat" both on stage and on the recording was Peter Noone, the one-time child actor whose photogenic grin made him a television natural. The producer of the recording, Mickie Most, employed a common practice in the industry: he used session musicians who learned arrangements quickly, played nearly flawlessly, and usually could read music (when provided). Almost as important, in a world where recordings took place in strictly limited three-hour sessions, musicians like Vic Flick and Clem Cattini did not panic when tapes were rolling.

Furthermore, no one in Herman's Hermits composed the songs they recorded. Americans (Frank C. Slay, Jr., and Bob Crewe) composed and first recorded (with the Rays and others in 1957) side A of the disk, "Silhouettes." Side B, "Can't You Hear My Heartbeat," represented a British composition by two aspiring professional songwriters. Indeed, the backup singers (who also provided hand claps) on the Herman's Hermits recordings include the composers, John Carter and Ken Lewis. Their voices also appear on at least two other hit recordings of the time: backing vocals on the Who's first single, "I Can't Explain," and lead vocals on their own "Funny How Love Can Be" as the Ivy League.

The reliance on session musicians and professional songwriters fundamentally contributed to the success of the British and American recording industries in this era. Even the Beatles used a session drummer for their first recordings ("Love Me Do" and "P.S. I Love You"), and they had to plead with their producer, George Martin, to be able to use their own songs instead of Mitch Murray's "How Do You Do It?" (eventually recorded by Gerry and the Pacemakers). However, recording contracts provided so little money that a band such as Herman's Hermits needed to tour because most of their income came from live performances. In the days before arenas and suitable amplification, touring meant small theaters seating at best several hundred people, rarely more. Record companies needed touring groups to sell records, and musicians needed a steady income, even if it meant sleeping in buses. With only a handful of studios and a few hours in which to turn out potential hits, London's resident session musicians proved logical choices for producers looking to make the most of their recording time.

The continuous search for new and salable musical material meant that British publishers developed domestic talent, such that the sixties saw a steady growth in confidence on the part of British songwriters, due in no small measure to the success of Lennon and McCartney, but also because of their discovery of a distinctive voice. In addition, the production of British records—everything from the quality of the performances to the quality of the sound—improved steadily between 1956 and 1968, when they began to approach parity with American studios. Ultimately, the production of every recording relied on contributions from a pool of competing and collaborating individuals and their ideologies.

Community

When the first British rock star, Tommy Steele, rose to prominence seemingly overnight in 1956, the press fabrication held that aspiring impresarios (clothier Larry Parnes and photographer John Kennedy) had recognized the theatrical potential of a mere cabin boy (Tom Hicks) performing in the 2i's coffee bar and transformed him into a star. The conceit even had its own fictional depiction in

Expresso Bongo,[5] the story of hustler Johnny Jackson (Lawrence Harvey) who discovers Bert Rudge (Cliff Richard) in a coffee bar and transforms him into teen sensation Bongo Herbert. The creators of Tommy Steele's and Bongo Herbert's stories wove a fabric of fact and fantasy that clothed the industrial infrastructure and not only enabled the heroes to succeed, but also generated their stories. The nonfictional realization of Tommy Steele's ascendance took much longer to unfold than the story suggested, with Hicks sanguinely involved in the transformation of his image, including the hiring of session musicians. The record company (Decca)[6] sought a fast buck on what it perceived as the transient popularity of rock 'n' roll, but soon found itself with an unexpected phenomenon. Fiction became reality, and soon the British charts had a number of aspiring Bongo Herberts, many of them under the charge of Larry Parnes.

The inequalities and deceptions of the sort that were part of Tommy Steele's and Bongo Herbert's plots have their parallels (e.g., Meintjes 1990 describes the intercultural complications of Paul Simon's *Graceland*). Ethnomusicologists and other scholars have considered music communities formed around both musical creation and consumption in a variety of ways. For example, Mark Slobin (1993: 11), inspired by Arjun Appadurai, considers different kinds of "micromusics," by which he means "small units within big music cultures." And articles in Andy Bennett and Richard Peterson's *Music Scenes: Local, Translocal, and Virtual* (2004) examine how people find different kinds of music, venues, and media through which to bond socially.

One of the most successful attempts at holistically examining the interconnecting elements of an urban music culture remains Daniel Neuman's *The Life of Music in North India* (1980). In particular, Neuman applies the interpretive paradigm of cultural ecology, drawing inspiration from Archer (1964) and method from Steward (1955) to gain a structural overview of North Indian classical musicians living and performing in and around Delhi. He creates a convincing explanation of the changes in the musical system through the years since independence in 1947, identifying the most important factors within this musical ecology as the producers of music, the consumers of music, the contexts of music performance, and the impact

---

[5] Based on a story by Wolf Mankowitz and Julian More with music written by David Heneker and Monty Norman (Julian More serving as co-lyricist). The musical version first appeared at the Saville Theatre, London, on 23 April 1958. The film premiered in London on 20 November 1959.

[6] Decca labels included Decca Records, Brunswick Records, London Records, RCA/RCA Victor Records, and (in 1966) Deram Records with U.S. distribution through London Records.

of technology. An important part of his study resides in a series of dichotomies, the most important of which are rural/urban, hereditary/nonhereditary, soloist/accompanist, Hindu/Muslim, and professional/amateur. Notably, Neuman finds that the relationship between soloists and accompanists in modern Delhi reflects both traditional social patterns and the emerging reality of a modern, democratic, technological, and capitalist India.

London's recording industry—with its producers, music directors, arrangers, songwriters, contractors, and classical, folk, jazz, and popular artists—borrowed directly from the BBC's infrastructure. Naturally, recording corporations developed their own models, and a more extensive overview would have to include the publishing industry and the network of clubs, pubs, and ballrooms that provided a direct link between artists and their publics. This community functioned as an integrated ecology with vertical inequality (e.g., class) and horizontal differentiation (role) in which individuals struggled for success in part through their own talents and initiative and in part by establishing relationships with other individuals in the system. An examination of this ecosystem will reveal it to have been brutal to some while generating significant rewards for others.

A Networked Ecology

The communities that contributed to the dramatic changes in the sixties British popular music industry transformed an often pale imitation of Americana into a robust culture of their own making. From Lonnie Donegan's imitations of American folk music in the mid-fifties to King Crimson's experiments in mode and meter in the late sixties, British musicians were keen both to imitate their idols and to experiment. Moreover, the contexts in which individuals competed also defined them. In London, musicians, music directors, engineers, and producers explored their evolving environment through various kinds of musical adaptations. Musicians such as Jimmy Page developed the ability to play in different styles and to improvise, making them attractive to producers for specific recordings. Another approach was for a studio or a musician to obtain special pieces of musical equipment, which gained them a competitive advantage over others, as when Trident became the first studio in London to import an eight-track recording deck.[7]

Ultimately, an individual's continued importance to the community derived from the number and kinds of relationships he or she had as well as his or her adap-

---

[7] Curiously, when they installed the American Ampex tape decks, they did not allow for the alternating current differences between the United States (60 cycles) and Britain (50 cycles) so that their decks ran slower than their competitors. The result was that recordings made at Trident could only be mastered at Trident. See Ryan and Kehew 2006: 332.

tive abilities as musical tastes and technology evolved. Big Jim Sullivan could read music and play in a variety of styles, but he still sought advantages over other guitarists as a way to maintain his competitive edge. For example, in order to be the first choice of a music director or producer, he routinely tried out electronic devices (such as the D'Armond pedal he used on Dave Berry's "The Crying Game") to alter the sound of his guitar. He was also one of the first to own and learn to play a sitar, an advantage that led producer John Barry to hire him for seven full days of session work (at five times the normal session rate) to play for only five minutes of a James Bond film score. Sullivan also networked with other guitarists, coming to musical compromises, sharing equipment, and covering for them when they were double-booked so that they would return the favor when the same happened to him.

Network analysis (see Wasserman and Faust 1994) considers social actors in terms of dyads, triads, subgroups, and groups, which would include the kinds of interrelationships musicians forged during long and stressful hours of recording and touring. Guitarists like Sullivan, Flick, and Joe Moretti not only had common interests, they also developed relationships with performers on other instruments. Guitarists and bass players, bass players and drummers, drummers and guitarists: each is a kind of dyad. Guitarists and bassists need to interact at a harmonic level: the guitarist's chords are underpinned and directed by the bass lines. The bassist and the drummer establish both the harmonic tempo and the metric matrix (groove) over which the others will apply melody and harmony. And finally, the rhythm guitarist and the drummer establish a rhythmic matrix that defines much of the accompaniment's character. Moreover, these three dyadic relationships form a triad of interacting dyads: the rhythm section.

Producers functioned as critical network hubs, working individually with engineers, music directors, songwriters, and musicians, while contact between each of these other parts varied. Producers often mediated contact between engineers and musicians, making final decisions on the sound in a recording. Music directors and engineers usually had nominal casual contact. Music directors and musicians, on the other hand, could have intense contact, the MD commonly functioning as the producer's representative on the floor of the studio. These relationships would change over the course of the sixties as musicians increased their say in the production process. In particular, with the rise of songwriting performers, the role of the professional songwriter became rather more complex, as did the relationship between his or her composition and the musicians who ultimately performed the music. At one extreme, songwriters only had contact with the producer (or, sometimes, the producer's assistant); however, songwriters in a group increasingly and communally developed their music, with the producer a late addition to the process.

Members of the rhythm section—particularly in 1960s British recording sessions, where they were often physically separate from the classically oriented string players and the jazz-oriented horn players—formed a distinct subgroup of the group "musicians." The guitarists, bassists, keyboard players, and drummers who played in touring bands and recorded in studios had a particular advantage over most orchestral players: they usually understood and had played rock music. Some were jazz musicians who turned up their noses at music they saw as unchallenging and base, but the most successful rhythm section musicians played rock and pop with passion. Two groups of musicians evolved to meet the almost insatiable demand for British pop and rock. Touring musicians were certainly aware of the prowess of session musicians, as when George Harrison identified Big Jim Sullivan as one of his favorites (Coleman 1964) and *Melody Maker* included Sullivan as one of Britain's best guitarists (Coleman 1965). All session musicians started as stage performers, and many went back to touring, just as John Paul Jones and Jimmy Page did in 1968, when they left session work to found Led Zeppelin.

Very real but difficult to measure qualities in "musicianship" lie in a musician's relationships with other musicians and in his or her monetary ties with other music professionals. As a networked community of actors (in this case, musicians) evolves through time—that is, as an ecology of actors adapts to technological, social, and musical change—the financial ties between employers and employees holds stronger than the presence or absence of any one individual. The triadic socio-musical structure of the rhythm section remains, even while individuals take different roles, as musical styles change, and as technological innovations eventually render musical interactions asynchronous. In other words, these musical institutions had their own self-sustaining, -regulating, and -directing qualities that ensured that the institutions survived, while individual musicians, producers, engineers, etc., came and went.

Neuman's ecological description of Delhi's classical music milieu emphasizes what Indian musicians considered to be important. The priorities of London's session musicians predictably differed from Delhi's emphasis on practice, the student-teacher relationship, and the divine. London's sessioneers repeatedly emphasize that musicianship—in particular, stylistic flexibility and the ability to read—formed an essential component of their survival and success, skills usually gained both from long hours of adolescent practice and the combined tedium and unpredictability of touring. Sessioneers also maintain that humor sustained them through the often demeaning treatment they received from producers, contractors, and artists, who sometimes saw the musicians as "dumbo robots who simply went through the mechanical motions of making music" (as one musician complained).

In the hotbed of 1960s British popular musical change, participants endorsed experimentation predicated on the idea that "new" equaled "good," with "old" only being "good" if it seemed so old that they could reinterpret it as new. In some parts of the industry (notably, the touring side), a high turnover of musicians allowed for dramatic changes in musical style or, in another view, a period of fast musical evolutionary development. Musical style constituted a resource that producers mined with creativity. In other parts (such as the studio), where relative personnel stability prevailed, musicians, music directors, engineers, and producers still scrambled to gain the upper hand on their competition.

The gluttonous consumption of British popular music by the Western world in the sixties not only provided considerable work for sessioneers and recording stars, but also precipitated their eventual obsolescence. An industry rooted in the sale of "new" ideas employed individuals (particularly songwriters) only as long as they could provide the "new." Most adapted and moved on to new challenges. Consequently, both technology and success undermined the stability of the session world. As independent studios opened and studio time became cheaper and more readily available, the efficient reading and recording skills of a session musician became less valuable to some producers than the spontaneously created accidents of a disposable neophyte. In turn, producers, engineers, and music directors survived only as long as they could adapt to changes in technology and musical tastes.

Network analysis in its most effective applications relies upon rich data sources that document in detail the number and qualities of contacts between individuals in a social environment. Given the secrecy that surrounded most sixties recording sessions, where only those invited and necessary to the process could be present, we lack sufficient data to construct elaborate descriptions. However, by understanding the underlying principles of network analysis as part of an ecological orientation, we can generate nuanced descriptions of selected individuals involved in the creation of this music. Each of the producers, engineers, music directors, songwriters, and musicians described in this book represents a different model for understanding how this networked ecology functioned. Their backgrounds shaped how they came to function the way they did, providing a nuanced and textured description of this music and era.

HISTORICAL, ECONOMIC, POLITICAL, AND SOCIAL CONTEXTS

The Second World War and deprivation reshaped Britain, fomenting a cohort of war-born iconoclasts, generating technology with which this generation attempted to reimagine civilization, and igniting dramatic changes more than a decade after hostilities in Europe and Asia had ended. The generation that created the British beat boom had neither fought in the war nor played any role in establishing the postwar economic policies that seemed ready to entomb it in the late forties and early fifties. Britain's considerable economic and cultural duress led this generation of war babies to believe that the wheels had come off the system. Born both during the war and in the years immediately following, they were determined to do better than their parents, or at least to do differently. The cycles of selective economic prosperity and collapse and the political movements and wars that plagued the first half of the century had set populations in motion and destabilized social hierarchies, not only in the Western world, but in Asia and Africa as well. Britain, the most important world power of the late nineteenth and early twentieth centuries, was a bellwether of these changes primarily because it had so thoroughly integrated itself economically and politically through its global empire.

Psychologically and economically, postwar Britain dealt with devastating bomb damage to its major urban centers and ports, and waging war had meant incurring a massive war debt of about £3 billion, primarily to the United States. Consequently, the U.S. economy recovered relatively quickly, while Britain's war debt led to the weakness of the pound and decades of financial recuperation. Having expended over £1 billion in foreign investments, Britain's control over its empire evaporated, and London hastily began ceding independence to colonies. With widespread hardship, the Labour government of Clement Attlee (1945–1951) that replaced Churchill and the Conservatives in the first postwar election instituted necessary but expensive social safety nets, including universal health care. Subsequent Labour and Conservative governments placed import restrictions on foreign goods, especially from Britain's primary creditor, the United States. Finally, the over 360,000 British war dead meant both opportunities and a sense of entitlement for those who had survived. Britannia no longer ruled the waves and, while not slaves, many Britons were nevertheless ready for change.

Growing up in postwar Britain meant a life dependent on ration books for everything from soap (rationing ended on 9 September 1950) and sugar (12 September 1953) to petrol (26 May 1950), with materials like steel re-rationed (16 August 1951 to 5 May 1953). Some rationing continued until 1954. Furthermore, this economic vacuum allowed the United States an opportunity to spread its cultural (and political) influence, undermining Britain's cultural systems. The British adage about Americans being "overpaid, oversexed, and over here" had sprung from the reality that Britain was unable to compete economically with its wartime ally. Americans demonstrated how initiative and money could purchase position and privilege while, for some, Britain "played a confident Greece to the

American Rome" (Morgan 2001: 109). In the late fifties and early sixties, many eager young British aspirants saw an opportunity to succeed where birthright and class might have previously denied them access.

The members of this postwar generation (composed of several subgenerations and regional variants) changed everything they touched, if for no other reason than their sheer numbers. Whether in clothing, food, transportation, or music, the extent of "the bulge" (the British equivalent of the American "baby boom") generation meant that not only were their tastes important economically, but their disproportionate numbers encouraged diversification. More specifically, their magnitude and genetic disposition to socialize meant that music functioned as a magnet, attracting new listeners to clubs and concerts. A relatively new phenomenon in British history, this audience consisted largely of "teenagers." With the abolition of mandatory military service in 1957 and the last conscripts called up in mid-November 1960, more men than ever before entered the workforce without having undergone conformity-enhancing induction into the armed services. For women, the growing availability of birth control in the sixties meant more independence.

In this relatively unprecedented situation, the age group between sixteen and twenty-five—beginning with the birth year 1940—had their adolescence extended. Several authors (notably Colin MacInnes in *Absolute Beginners*) have commented on the emergence of teenagers as a new class of consumer in the late fifties. As they increased their buying power, they began to dominate mainstream culture, particularly clothing and music. These culture consumers sought symbols of their newfound and growing power, often seizing upon American and European consumables that both distinguished them from their parents' patriotic tastes and epitomized wealth and access, as purchases were often both expensive and difficult to obtain. This trend decentered authority on topics as diverse as music and clothes and challenged the influence of both the older generations and the upper classes.

In *A Hard Day's Night* (1964), the Richard Lester film starring the Beatles, a conservatively suited, middle-aged man enters their train compartment, closes the window, and turns off their music. He declares that he rides the train regularly and knows his rights; moreover, he declares that his generation had fought a war for them, to which writer Alun Owen has the laconic Ringo reply, "I'll bet you're sorry you won." The scene encapsulates some of the tension between generations that the Beatles and others in the sixties embodied and celebrated. Notably, the Beatles leave the compartment to invade another part of the train, transforming it into their own space through music and capturing a classic trophy of male success: young women.

My Generation

The culture that the Beatles and their generation sought to displace controlled more than train cars: they owned the music industry, from EMI's[8] executive suites in Manchester Square to ballrooms in Brighton. Groups like the Beatles and the Rolling Stones won success first in community dance halls and small independent establishments like the Cavern Club in Liverpool or the Crawdaddy Club in Richmond. Enterprising promoters and fans of pop found places for the music they loved to flourish and, in the process, they created a micro-economy that would eventually help Britain to recover economically.

The revolution may have begun in 1956 when the British adopted an imitation of American folk music as a substitute for the American rock 'n' roll that teens were beginning to hear. Lonnie Donegan had covered Huddie Ledbetter's "Rock Island Line" in 1954, at which point Donegan referred to the genre as "skiffle." In general, British skiffle denoted a folk song performed with a combination of guitars and found instruments, particularly washboards, but also often including a "tea chest" bass made from a tea storage box, a broomstick, and a string or wire. Not surprisingly, few at the 1954 recording session took Donegan's performance seriously, including possibly Donegan and the producer, Hugh Mendl. Decca resurrected the recording in late 1955 when Bill Haley's "Rock around the Clock" topped the British charts. Surprisingly, the Donegan's skiffle experiment became a hit, not only in the United Kingdom, but also in the United States.

Some at the time recognized the reality that the British were substituting skiffle for rock 'n' roll. Bandleader Jack Payne, writing in *Melody Maker* in 1957, states, "In my opinion—though skiffle artists would rather die than admit the truth—this huge appeal lies in the fact that a large proportion of these audiences are Rock-'n'-roll fans." He also notes that, in his mind, rock 'n' roll and skiffle share "three distinctive traits, . . . an exaggerated use of guitars, a heavy exaggerated off-beat, and an exaggerated style of mouthing of words" (1957: 5). His suspicions were well founded. On 21 June 1956, at the Fox Theater in Detroit, Lonnie Donegan and the Johnny Burdette Rock 'n' Roll Trio teamed up to put the "rock" in "Rock Island Line." Less than a year later, in Donegan's recording of "Cumberland Gap," guitarist Denny Wright would imitate Scotty Moore (Elvis's guitarist), and a drum kit would replace the washboard.

---

[8] EMI labels included Columbia Records, HMV Records (His Master's Voice), Parlophone Records, Capitol Records, and (in 1969) Harvest Records with American distribution by Capitol Records.

Jazz bands and artists such as Tony Crombie endeavored to reinvent themselves as rock 'n' roll artists in mid-1956, but performed music closer to the jump jazz of Louis Jordan than to Bill Haley's early country experiments. Evidence of British demand for rock 'n' roll appears in a July 1956 issue of *Melody Maker*: "Rock 'n' roll clubs are opening throughout the country, and record sales are soaring" (N.A. 1956: 2). EMI producer Norrie Paramor emerged from among those looking for a successful British rock recording. Crombie remembers Paramor several times asking him, "Can you come into the studio and do four titles next Wednesday?" Crombie and bandmate guitarist Jimmy Currie (who would go on to perform with Lonnie Donegan) would "knock out pieces like 'Brighton Rock.' They were all very similar, 12-bar blues with a simple melody line, which I would usually do and Jimmy would write straight forward lyrics" (Leigh with Firminger 1996: n.p.).

Although Tommy Steele had the first rock success in Britain in 1956 with "Rock with the Caveman," the United Kingdom waited until 1958 for its first bona fide rock-and-roller when Paramor finally struck pay dirt with Cliff Richard's "Move It." Other British musicians took up the charge. In particular, Johnny Kidd and the Pirates created the rock classic "Shakin' All Over" (1960). British artists also began to have hits on the American side of the Atlantic, notably the Tornados with Joe Meek's production of "Telstar."[9] British musicians had learned how to copy American pop and rock, sometimes directly from American musicians, such as Eddie Cochran and Gene Vincent. By late 1962, as "Telstar" was beginning to slide back down both British and American charts, perhaps the most singular event in modern British pop music history began to unfold when the Beatles' "Love Me Do" had reasonable success on British charts. In 1963, the band's image would blanket Britain, so that, by the end of that year, even American television was running film of the peculiar mass hysteria that was gripping British youth.

Some would argue that British popular music would have flourished regardless of the Beatles' success; nevertheless, this group brought a number of important elements together in their music. The British imitated American models, perennially reacting after the fact to American tastes and technology. Indeed, the Beatles worked with a mode of performance that mainstream America had largely abandoned (the guitar-based rockabilly band) and applied it to the contemporary pop music they heard emerging from the United States. Specifically, the Beatles enfolded girl group pop (e.g., the Shirelles) and Motown rhythm-

---

[9] Remarkably, the recordings of "Shakin' All Over" and "Telstar" share two musicians: guitarist Alan Caddy and drummer Clem Cattini.

and-blues (e.g., the Marvelettes) into an ensemble designed for country music (Carl Perkins) and country rock (Chuck Berry).

That Lennon and McCartney were able to internalize this heterogeneous amalgam and successfully create songs like "I Saw Her Standing There," combining rock elements (a bass line from Chuck Berry's "I'm Talking about You"), girl group touches (prominent hand clapping), and country (Everly Brothers–style open fourth and fifth vocal harmonies) testifies to their musical ears and determination. Perhaps equally important to the rise of the Beatles, George Martin and his production team at Parlophone proved sympathetic but critical listeners with the essential skills to produce successful recordings. Moreover, both the Beatles and Martin's team continued to evolve over the sixties, experimenting with musical materials and the mechanics of production to create recordings that met the expectations of their audience while challenging the limits of what they would accept.

The Beatles were part of an already vibrant British music scene in which songwriters and performers were beginning to blossom and to capture something more than a theatrical snarl. Other bands of the era imitated the example of the Beatles, moving away from covers of American records and developing songwriting skills; incorporating new, old, and exotic musical elements; and pushing the technology that was available in British studios. The Rolling Stones, for example, began their recording career by limiting themselves almost exclusively (and proudly) to covers of American songs and working with a producer who knew little about the mechanics of recording. However, Jagger and Richards quickly developed their compositional skills, writing strong, straightforward rock tunes. When they began recording in American studios, the expertise of American engineers (and the advanced equipment that British studios lacked) gave them an edge.

As British musicians began to master rock and blues, they often redefined the genres in both style and sound, their phrasing becoming iconic of the genres. British pop songwriters flourished, some largely creating material for others, while some performed themselves. British studios, even though they still often lacked the cutting-edge technology used in America, gradually increased in number, sometimes developing their own equipment. By the mid-sixties, musicians and producers came from all over the world to use British studios in the hope of capturing some of the magic. Similarly, American and European musicians sought the sounds produced by homegrown British amplifiers like Marshall and Vox.

Newcomers to this ecology sought advantages in a system already occupied by others. Whether in securing club dates or record sales, they were in competition with each other for a valuable and limited resource: the disposable income of young adults. Moreover, they sought to displace a generation that had largely dominated British culture since the end of the Second World War. Groups such as the Beatles and the Rolling Stones often had to dislodge British bands playing American jazz characteristic of an earlier Chicago or New Orleans. And sometimes, they misrepresented themselves to secure a gig. For example, Mick Jagger notoriously declared in *Jazz News* on 11 July 1962 that the Rolling Stones were not a rock 'n' roll band, in the hope that the managers of the Marquee Club would rehire them (Charlesworth 1994: 10). But with tunes like Wilbert Harrison's "Kansas City" and Chuck Berry's "Back in the U.S.A." on their play list that night, the managers rightly concluded otherwise.

Musical Change

In the sixties, everyone understood that a musical revolution was under way. George Melly, writing in 1966, distinguishes between the popular music of the upper class (he describes it as "high culture") and the music of pop culture (presumably meaning the working class) (1970: 3–4).[10] The "enemies" of pop music, he claims (not entirely unsympathetically), condemn promoters determined to apply a "deliberate psychological harnessing of adolescent sexual feelings to pop music." Moreover, he describes pop as "a cynical method of turning mass-hysterical masturbation to profitable account" (6). Cynical or not, few in Britain (and certainly not those in the music business) could deny the energy of the era.

The two largest British recording corporations in the sixties were EMI (originally Electric and Musical Industries, Ltd.) and Decca. Smaller companies like Pye[11] competed for the lucrative teen market, but lacked the reach of the two majors. EMI's organizational structure (a partial consequence of its history of acquiring smaller companies) featured a number of competing labels, including Columbia, HMV, and Parlophone, each with its own production staff and philosophies, rather than a single eponymous label.[12] Decca, on the other hand, was both the name of the corporation and its largest record label, seldom allow-

---

[10]   Melly observes in his book that he is writing in 1966. The publication date is, however, 1970.

[11]   Philips purchased a controlling interest in Pye in 1966. Pye labels included Pye Records, Pye-Nixa Records, Piccadilly Records, Ember Records, Golden Guinea Records, and Congress Records, as well as distributing American labels Chess Records and King Records. Philips released on the Philips Records and Fontana Records labels. It also distributed American disks by Columbia.

[12]   Both EMI and Decca had American branches—the former by purchasing Capitol in 1955 and the latter by launching an American Decca in 1934—and other international labels (e.g., in Italy, India, and Australia).

ing its subsidiary companies (like Brunswick) to compete on the same footing. Corporations provided recording studios, the manufacturing process that pressed records and printed the labels and sleeves, the distribution system that put disks into stores, and a marketing division to advertise the new releases.

In the late fifties and early sixties, the British recording industry concentrated itself in London, with only a few independent studios, such as IBC and Olympic, offering alternatives to corporate studios. Time was precious, and companies generally restricted recording in their studios to three-hour sessions with three principal slots every day: 10:00 a.m. to 1:00 p.m., 2:30 to 5:30 p.m., and 7:00 to 10:00 p.m. On weekdays, EMI and Decca auditioned new artists and recorded existing contracts, which could include anyone from comedians and Scottish ballad singers to symphony orchestras and pop stars. Weekends and off hours (midnight to 9 a.m.), they recorded theater casts, and last-minute additions to the schedule, and they sold studio time to independent producers (with limitations). Given the restricted resources of this environment, corporations placed a premium on the time-effective use of their studios and usually expected producers in a single three-hour session (which included a short tea break) to have both sides of a single ready for mastering. One of the best-known examples of this regimented artistry is the marathon effort of the Beatles and George Martin on 11 February 1963, during which they recorded ten of the fourteen tunes on their first album, *Please Please Me,* including "I Saw Her Standing There" and "Twist and Shout." Parlophone's Martin booked the Beatles for three consecutive sessions (and the time between) in studio two at EMI's Abbey Road facilities to capitalize quickly on the success of their first two singles. Independent studios picked up commercials and film scoring in addition to pop and jazz sessions.

In order for a session to be this efficient, musicians needed to arrive very well rehearsed and/or able to read music, and play flawlessly on the spot. The Beatles brought their experiences in a stage show they had been rehearsing for months to George Martin (who had also considered recording one of their shows live). The recording industry's infrastructure commonly ignored performers with less experience. Most of the producers of the era relied upon session musicians to get the performance right with precious little time wasted on correcting mistakes or waiting for inspiration to inhabit the soul of a nervous adolescent. They also relied upon engineers who knew exactly where to place microphones and how to get fleeting moments of musical inspiration on tape. The corporation ultimately held the producer responsible for bringing successful recordings to the market, which meant ensuring that the right performance went to the pressing plant, that there was a good master disk (from which the plant would generate other disks), and sometimes that the BBC heard the recording.

Fortunate artists had people who promoted their recordings and performances to influential media outlets. The most important musical papers of the era in Britain were *Melody Maker* and the *New Musical Express,* with other publications like *Record Retailer and Music Industry News* standard reading in the business. Occasional coverage in the *Times* of London, the *Telegraph,* the *Evening Standard,* or even the *News of the World* could also help in building record sales. Finally, a producer and a performer's management would lobby to get their record on one of the British Broadcasting Corporation's channels and their artist on television, which could be a challenge given the government's control over the media. In the early sixties, everyone knew that you needed to get your record on the BBC if the teens whom you wanted to buy your work were to hear your recording.

Defining an Era

In such a competitive environment, people sought ways to circumvent both the corporations and the government. The number and sophistication of independent studios grew through the sixties, so that by 1968 their facilities and equipment were, in some selected instances, superior to corporate installations. Musicians, producers, and management, in order to gain better control over the production and release of their recordings, sometimes resorted to establishing their own record companies, including the Beatles' Apple Records (1968). And, while the government had allowed an independent television network to operate in selected markets beginning in 1955, pirate radio stations had set up shop on offshore boats and abandoned gunnery platforms in the early sixties, circumventing Auntie Beeb's (the BBC) absolute control of the airwaves. The pirates triumphed until August 1967, when the Marine Broadcasting Offences Act shut almost all of these stations down.

Although the face of popular music in the sixties would include a host of young working-class heroes managed by upper-class patrons, the era began with slightly older artists taking the lead. The year 1956 opened with thirty-year-old Bill Haley's "Rock around the Clock" at the top of British charts and, in the summer of 1956, a thirty-one-year-old drummer formed Britain's first official rock band, Tony Crombie and the Rockets. By the end of the year, Jeff Kruger, who had been promoting Crombie's concerts, complained that the television networks were suppressing the cultural groundswell. "The BBC and ITV can't see further than the ends of their noses. Rock 'n' Roll has an enormous following here, but neither will give it a showing. They are just a bunch of stuffed shirts. They and the cinema managers, who are scared of the name, are not giving the music a fair deal" (Dawbarn 1956: 3). That year also saw twenty-five-year-old John Osborne's play *Look Back in Anger* open in London and the press applying the epithet of "angry young men" to anyone who challenged cultural norms.

Clear beginning and ending dates for eras always present difficulties, although we commonly assume that clusters of events suggest cultural trends. Depending on which precedents we might find to be compelling indicators of transformation, the road to the musical sixties began between 1956 and 1958 with the first British attempts at imitating rock 'n' roll. During the second half of 1956, the United Kingdom and France suffered an embarrassing turnabout in their military and political fortunes when Egypt seized the Suez Canal; these former colonial powers found themselves unable to retake this valuable passageway and faced a rebuke from the United Nations (plus an American threat to undermine the pound sterling). Marwick (2003) and Morgan (2001) see the political and social movements of 1957 and 1958 as harbingers of change, although each describes the consequences through distinctly different lenses. The omens of 1958—race riots, new technology, and pivotal political events—suggest profound developments afoot. Changes in the arts, and particularly pop music, reflect the economic, political, and social divisions—and the adaptations to the forces operating in these cultural realms—within British life in the following decade.

SOCIAL PARAMETERS

If 1960s British pop evolved as a cultural ecosystem, what relevant frames of reference define the interactions between individuals? In London at that time, the competition for limited resources prominently focused on the growing disposable income of young adults, especially their purchase of records and admissions to live performances. In many ways, the two mediums (record and ticket sales) were mutually beneficial: performers needed to appear in live venues in order to promote records, which in turn could boost the number of concert tickets sold to patrons. The most significant returns from record sales went to the corporations that provided the recording studios, pressed the records, delivered them to shops, and ultimately held the purse strings.

Songwriters earned royalties, but musicians often received either a flat session fee set by the Musicians' Union (which also got a cut) or, if well represented, pennies from each record sale. Similarly, agents commonly took a percentage off the top of any bookings they arranged (or even bookings they hadn't arranged), often leaving touring musicians to pay for all of the expenses they incurred on the road, including housing, wardrobe, cleaning, food, and transportation, from the meager remains of what a local promoter was willing to pay. Musicians could easily have a hit record, return from a successful tour, and still struggle to pay the bills. Sometimes, they lost their earnings in gambling on the bus, but more often the illusion of stardom had consumed the money even before they set foot on stage.

Musicians found themselves in direct competition with an "establishment" that held significant advantages over them in several relevant social parameters. Much of the dramatic social, musical, and cultural changes that transpired in this environment directly relate to the overlapping social distinctions expressed in terms of working class versus upper class, local versus national, young versus old, and amateur versus professional. Furthermore, individuals commonly found themselves also confronting the establishment's presumptions defining gender and ethnicity. The sixties witnessed the beginnings of a decentering of authority that continues to this day.

Class

One of the most important and lingering determinants of British social life has been the notion that birthright and position privileges individuals, which is often summarized by the concept of "class"; however, social mobility empowered by wealth has also demonstrated the fluidity of class membership. Britain's history of hereditary privilege illustrates the advantages that ruling and upper middle-class families (commonly grouped together as the "upper class") have enjoyed over lower middle-class families and working-class families (generally subsumed under the rubric "working class"). Marwick (1998: 272–273) describes these fundamental divisions in society as "broad aggregates . . . distinguished from each other by inequalities in wealth, income, power (or at least access to it), authority, prestige, freedom, lifestyles, and life chance." Access to education and employment has had a direct correlation with these classes, and individuals have commonly self-identified with one class or the other. Marwick (2003: 25) simplifies this class division to ruling and working class, with the middle class functioning as a transitional social stage.

A major disturbance in this system came in the wake of the First World War when many Britons raised questions about both the purpose of the war and the competence of its leaders. The Second World War reinforced criticisms of class-based discrimination. The economic deprivations of the twentieth century both exacerbated this discontent and opened to the possibility of change, with individuals challenging their economic and social predestinations and redefining their identities. A subtext of the sixties found working-class youth at once celebrating their humble origins and craving an existence free of want. Most important, they espoused an open contempt for privilege, even as they sought its benefits. John Lennon was right: a working-class hero was indeed something to be.

Accent, vocabulary, and grammar have long been important markers of class and regional orientation, and education has been the avenue to the acquisition of those skills. Individuals aspiring to move up the social ladder have usually assumed a certain accent as a marker of their membership in a privileged segment of society. The hierarchical implications of accent have applied to many different expectations in life and certainly to the music industry, historically perhaps one of the most obvious and promising opportunities for social advancement. Musicians and others have described at least one prominent British producer as having adopted a passing version of "received pronunciation" as he moved up the corporate ladder.

Britain has long recognized regional accents as reflecting more than place of birth, stereotyping cultural behavior based on language. A Liverpool (or "Scouse") accent, for example, had associations with hardscrabble working-class origins, and in the late fifties the emergence of cockney rock star Joe Brown helped to celebrate both a local London accent and working-class origins. Brown's band was not the "Brothers," but rather the "Bruvvers," playing on East London slang.

Perhaps even more interesting than the celebration of plebeian roots (and often the accompanying malapropisms), the appearance of American pronunciations—particularly in the performance of rock 'n' roll and blues—provided a benchmark for change. For example, Mick Jagger's pronunciations could shift between a Southside Chicago drawl in "Little Red Rooster" and a more pronounced London accent in "Lady Jane." Presumably, he adopted singing accents depending on his models and primary audiences. He probably learned "Little Red Rooster" from Howlin' Wolf's recording of the song ("The Red Rooster"), while "Lady Jane" imitated Elizabethan art song. Just as important, Jagger secured his blues authenticity for a primarily British audience with the first recording, while in the case of the latter an American audience would have eagerly bought the Englishness of the performance. Indeed, Chris Roberts (1963) comments that English performers copied American diction to ensure hit records.

When Liverpool's Beatles rose to national prominence in 1963, their Scouse inflections arrived with them, and suddenly it seemed that to be a successful pop artist one had to speak as though raised in Merseyside. However, they also mixed contemporary jargon into their speech, signaling language's function as a generational marker as well as signifying class, professional status, and ethnicity. Neologisms such as "grotty" (derived from "grotesque" and implying something distasteful), "fab" (an abbreviation of "fabulous"), and "gear" (an adjective meaning "wonderful") served to separate the newcomers from the educated upper class (who by definition used standard English). This strategic use of language parallels that of jazz musicians who long before had their specialized language adopted by fans for everyday usage; however, 1960s British pop brought this mix of Scouse and teen jargon to a much broader audience. With the phenomenal success of the Beatles and their film *A Hard Day's Night*, both American and British teens were soon aping Scouser youths.

Curiously, the biggest challengers to the working-class Lennon and McCartney of the Beatles were Mick Jagger and Keith Richards of the Rolling Stones, who came from Kent (the origin of received pronunciation) and solid upwardly mobile middle-class backgrounds. Jagger, a student at the London School of Economics, had been on the path to a business career and an establishment accent. Manager Andrew Oldham's strategy to paint them as challengers of the establishment had them contesting their middle-class roots (at least for Jagger, Richards, and Brian Jones), and for many in the United Kingdom, the sixties were about transcending your origins and reinventing yourself. Oldham's vision for the Stones and their own inclinations accomplished this goal handily.

Age

The wave of war and postwar births opened a chasm between those who had experienced the conflict and those too young to fully appreciate it. However, the divide was between more than merely young and old; legal maturity limited who could sign contracts and have licenses, thus defining those who could exploit opportunities and those who would be the exploited. The legal line between young and old—minor and age of majority—was twenty-one years; however, the notion of maturity to war and postwar babies started somewhere in their late twenties. Not surprisingly, as the war-born generation matured both economically and intellectually, their perception of the age of cultural vesting and responsibility slid. If a musician was not quite as young as young fans might presume, his management commonly took a few years off his age in order to have him appear younger. This notwithstanding, rock and pop musicians often were minors. A common phenomenon of the era was the pop musician who was under twenty-one and needed his or her parents to sign a contract with a record company. For example, the members of the Zombies (Rod Argent was eighteen) had to have their parents sign for them when they won a Hertfordshire contest and earned an audition with producer Dick Rowe of Decca. Similarly, Andrew Oldham needed Eric Easton as a partner to manage the Rolling Stones, not just because of his experience and his office but because Easton had an agent's license and Oldham was only nineteen.

Generational conflict in the postwar era combined with the sheer numbers and economic independence of the bulge, empowering and emboldening teens as they increasingly captured significant portions of British culture (Bennett 2000: 11–14). Encouraged by the mobilization of the working and lower middle class, Britain's youth developed an entrenched resentment against the vested interests that stood between them and their anticipated success. The term "establishment" came to apply broadly to the generation that had controlled British life from the end of the Second World War until the end of the sixties, and dominated Britain's industries and cultural life. Thus, the cultural conflict between the establishment and Britain's youth enfolds notions of both class and age.

Rejecting the cultural prerogatives of the establishment and the ambivalence of the middle class became a theme of the era's literature, and popular music became the vehicle through which teens expressed their contempt for the status quo. Musical proponents of the establishment framed the interest in rock 'n' roll by Britain's youth as a consequence of history. Notably, bandleader Vic Lewis (1958) describes a generation of teenagers evacuated from cities, separated from their parents, and undereducated. Similarly, George Melly (1970: 11) observes that pop music was a "reflection of that section of our society which has produced and supported it" (by implication, working-class teenagers). Tony Brown, in an article in *Melody Maker* (1960a: 3), interviews "scores" of individuals to try to understand the teenage passion for rock 'n' roll and to explain this phenomenon to an audience he presumed found the genre repugnant. He starts with a club where he believed rock was essential to local activities. The manager, while observing how popular the music is, apologizes, saying, "Mind you, we have to keep it under control, otherwise, the members wouldn't want to do anything else but jive and play." He notes that music is "far more important to [young people] than to adults," that their earning power exhibits the key to their identity, and that they express their independence through purchasing. One fifteen-year-old male explains, "In our crowd . . . you have to like rock or you're dead." Brown may have been building on Colin MacInnes's observations in *Absolute Beginners* (1980), originally published in 1959, but he does seem to have found evidence of a generational divide.

Professional Status

The path to professionalism is intentionally inhibiting, the purpose of the process being to indoctrinate individuals, whether through a guild's apprenticeships or a university's sequence of degrees. Mentors have the responsibility of guiding young would-be professionals into the trade while at the same time gaining the benefit of an assistant's labor. Legal maturity ensures that individuals have undergone socialization and understand a culture's customs and often unspoken strictures. Governments intend the laws pertaining to legal maturity to protect those too young to understand the binding implications of a legal act; however, in the context of 1960s British rock and pop, that protection was often waived in the name of personal ambition.

In London in the late fifties and early sixties, the Musicians' Union determined access to important parts of the profession of music as well as relations with club owners and studio producers. They usually provided little in the way of education for their members, but they did help to protect selected groups of musicians. Notably, they were aggressive in representing symphonic and pit orchestras while less concerned with the pop bands that began to flourish and whose members were less likely to be union members. In other areas of the industry, professional admission (while perhaps less systematic) still commonly involved a mentor who initiated newcomers. Professional status, thus, arrived in stages. One first learned his or her art through practice and experience: months and years of daily performance in diverse musical styles and often working under trying circumstances. If, as a performer, you gained recognition, you might have a few fleeting experiences in the studio and, if one of those recordings sold, then you might be engaged to help make someone else's work successful. The industry often seemed to believe in magic when musicians had a hit recording, at least until the magic failed. If those experiences were positive and you had impressed the contractors, the calls for work in the studio would become more and more numerous. Similarly, many engineers worked their way up in the studio through diligence and, sometimes, a hit recording.

One consequence of this process was that a gulf opened between aspiring young musicians and the record companies, each of which needed the other to attract audiences. When the beat boom attracted thousands of young men and women to the idea of being a performer, the music industry placed substantial barriers between the newcomers and financial rewards. Even a successful musician-songwriter like Ray Davies of the Kinks repeatedly ran into barriers involving the ownership of his songs and the income from his tours. And the Beatles and Rolling Stones resorted to hiring Allen Klein to renegotiate their contracts with EMI and Decca, respectively, seeking back compensation for what they believed to have been poorly negotiated initial contracts. The inexperience (or, worse, deceit) of managers often meant bucking an industry based on the quick exploitation of naïve young performers, usually through an obfuscation of the contract process. The purpose of the industry was not to invest and develop talent. No wonder these musicians learned to suspect the corporations and their representatives, who were often older professionals living comfortable middle-class lives.

Gender

Gender and sexual identity played important (if unstated) roles in the recording industry as the fifties evolved into the sixties. Being male or female governed not only which musical options individuals had, but also how others interpreted their performance in that role. That is, if you were a male, you could do almost anything musical: guitarist or drummer, bandleader or producer. If you were a female, you could be a singer, but even then the contexts had normative limits. Very few women in this milieu achieved success as drummers, keyboard players, or bass players, and the only ones who played guitar accompanied themselves simply: they almost never appeared in any sort of virtuosic role. The two individual exceptions that routinely come to mind are drummer Ann "Honey" Lantree of the Honeycombs and bassist Megan Davies of the Applejacks, but their prominence indicates how rare they were in this world. Dusty Springfield and Mary Hopkin could accompany themselves on guitar, but most singers (e.g., Sandie Shaw or Lulu) had only the microphone. Similar limits also applied to the business side of music with Shaw's manager, Eve Taylor, and Lulu's manager, Marion Massey, being the rare exceptions of women managers in an industry dominated by men.

Sexual orientation and gender significantly affected the industry as well. The Sexual Offences Act would not decriminalize sexual acts between consenting adults in private until 28 July 1967, and even then gay and lesbian relationships remained hidden. Consequently, even though some of the most notable figures of the era were homosexual, they disguised their identity from the music public. The toll of this cloaked persona on the Beatles' manager Brian Epstein provides but one example of the angst in this community and may have contributed to his abuse of sedatives. Both he and Larry Parnes (manager of performers like Tommy Steele, Billy Fury, and others) seem to have had a special aptitude for successful management, and both found themselves subject to threats. Nevertheless, Epstein's dedication to the Beatles defied the model established by Parnes, who treated his stars more like precious possessions. Joe Meek's sexual orientation probably contributed to his isolation and exacerbated his paranoia. Dusty Springfield had the ironic role of both being a sex symbol for many young men and having a complicated sexuality that favored women. And Andrew Oldham's descriptions of his own sexual identity suggest that, while he was predominantly heterosexual, he adopted stereotypically homosexual behaviors in part as a form of social aggression. He found the straight men he encountered in the business to be intimidated by overt gayness.

Ethnicity

For want of another word, various kinds of ethnic identity played significant roles in 1960s British rock and pop. Perhaps the most obvious but complicated aspect of this milieu was the notion of "British." The idea itself may have been an eighteenth-century product of the Scottish Enlightenment, subsuming a regional (and hitherto separatist and clannish) identity into a larger supranational scheme (Herman 2001). In the mid-sixties, as the so-called British invasion began to dominate Western consciousness, a number of regional identities found a new plane on which to collide. The most important, of course, was the notion of "Englishness," in contrast to Scottish, Irish, or Welsh identity, not to mention the growing heterogeneity of British cosmopolitan life. Moreover, the quality of Englishness remains a deeply contested identity. Who ideally represents Englishness? Which class? Which county?

Issues of insider versus outsider apply in this parameter, especially in regional considerations. When the Beatles came to London to record, they were not only fighting the stereotypes of working-class youth, but they came from a region (Merseyside) more noted for its underemployment and tough life (and the comedians such a life might nurture) than for successful artists. Only one Merseyside rock artist, Billy Fury, had any success, and London doubted that much of value could come from the region. One Londoner, Tony Brown (1960b), went to Liverpool to sample opinions about teenagers in Merseyside. He begins his article by interviewing Cyril Isherwood, the manager of the Liverpool Locarno dance hall. Isherwood admits that he had trouble understanding the speech patterns of Liverpool and Newcastle, sarcastically suggesting that his "coarse ear" took time to grow accustomed "to local inflections of speech" (3). The theater manager suggests that interest in music among teens is "superficial," while qualifying that he has also known "educated adults—schoolteachers and parsons—who had no ear for music" (3). As an illustration of his own superiority and affiliation with the London-based reporter for *Melody Maker*—itself a mouthpiece for the musical establishment—Brown recalls how he asked two Liverpool "girls to name the best singer in Britain." When they responded with "Cliff Richard," he condescendingly replied, "No . . . , I mean the best singer."

Nevertheless, Brown observes how "coffee clubs" in Liverpool have grown dramatically, citing one of the Beatles' old venues, the Jacaranda, and their first manager, Allan Williams. Brown makes no mention of the Beatles, instead describing the Royal Caribbean Steel Band as reflecting an aspect of Liverpool's growing ethnic diversity (see Cohen 2007). Williams indicates that teens are deeply involved with the music, but that "[y]ou have to control it," in his case by shining "a powerful spotlight on any couple carried away by the seductive music." Nevertheless, Brown notes, "Liverpool is well ahead in catering for the non-conformist tastes of the young" (1960b: 3, 17). Drummer Carlo Little, who toured extensively in this era with Screaming Lord Sutch and the Savages, similarly recalls his reaction to Merseyside: "Everyone in Liverpool's playing Chuck Berry and Bo Diddley and all round the rest of the country everyone's playing

Cliff Richard and the Shadows." At one point early in the beat boom, Mersey-side performers were so important that Ralph Horton (manager of Birmingham's Denny Laine and the Diplomats) complained that promoters only wanted acts with Scouse accents (N.A. 1963).

The success of the Beatles brought to national attention Merseyside, as well as nearby Manchester and the more northerly Newcastle. London cathartically transformed performers from other parts of the British Isles into a form acceptable for national and international consumption. Bands like Herman's Hermits and Freddie and the Dreamers from Manchester, or the Animals or Shadows members Hank Marvin and Bruce Welch from Newcastle, came to London because that was where the money was. London also sucked in all manner of performers from the surrounding towns and counties: Jagger and Richards from Kent, the Zombies from Hertfordshire, and the Nashville Teens from Surrey. And then there were performers like Paul Harvey and Lulu emerging from Glasgow and Van Morrison from Belfast contesting the English authority of the industry and encountering forces intent on neutering their ethnicity.

Even Cliff Richard experienced racial discrimination when his family immigrated to the United Kingdom from India, where he had been born. He commented to *Melody Maker* (N.A. 1960b: 15) that school kids had called him "nigger" when he first moved to England (probably because of his dark hair and birth in India). With the continuing collapse of the British Empire in the forties, fifties, and sixties, not only did British civil servants and other colonialists return to the homeland, but a flood of immigrants arrived to claim their legal right to British residency and citizenship. Indians, Pakistanis, Jamaicans, South Africans, and many, many others changed the face of everyday life in the United Kingdom, if not the cultural base of British life. These immigrants from the West Indies, Africa, and South Asia transformed the United Kingdom and quickly made their influence felt musically, as recordings like Millie Small's ska tune "My Boy Lollipop" invaded the top reaches of the charts in 1964. And around the same time, British pop and folk musicians were becoming enamored of Indian and Arabic music, with performers like Davy Graham imitating a North African *nauba* ensemble in his recordings and Ray Davies attempting to incorporate the feel of a Bombay fisherman's song into his work.

Outright racism in Britain first burst the imperial façade of tolerance in August 1958, when whites in Nottingham and, later, London's Notting Hill Gate attacked African, Caribbean, and Asian immigrants. Dance musicians, so much of whose music derived from African American models, both supported racial integration and agitated against it. The Musicians' Union first took a public stand in April 1960 when it banned musicians from performing in South Africa to protest that country's apartheid policies. (See N.A. 1960a.) However, in December 1961, when the MU blacklisted the Bradford Locarno Ballroom for its policy of refusing admission to single black males, seven bandleaders formed a competing union, the British Federation of Musicians (N.A. 1961 and 1962a). Nevertheless, by the end of the month, the Bradford Locarno organization had dropped its policies and the British Federation of Musicians dissolved in September of the next year (N.A. 1962b). Bandleaders may have initially felt that the Musicians' Union seemed unable to protect them and, thus, sided with the owners of the dance hall (Brand 1962a). Interestingly, the dance hall owners changed their policies quickly, but the musicians remained at odds with the union for some time (Brand 1962b). These bandleaders' willingness to support racially discriminating policies by forming an alternative union illustrates how close to the surface racism was in this industry.

Although perfectly comfortable supporting programming that promoted upper- and middle-class culture, the BBC's approach to the era's racial tensions included banning songs that it thought might both offend the new residents of Britain and encourage hatred. In May 1958, it banned Lonnie Donegan's "Nobody Loves like an Irishman," not because of its portrayal of the Irish (a common target of English ridicule), but rather because the song included a line about a man "praying all night with his el Koran." Donegan removed the line in subsequent live performances.

One of the most important and complicated ethnic identities in 1960s Britain was "American." The two countries had fought together in the war, but the Americans had waited before entering the fray, leaving Britain to sustain significant losses while holding off the Germans from 1939 to late 1941. The economic power that the United States accrued supplying the British meant that, when it entered the war, it did so with no damage to its own infrastructure and, ultimately, emerged with a solid financial base. By the 1950s, American popular culture dominated cosmopolitan life in the West, including the various kinds of popular music (rock 'n' roll, blues, pop, and jazz) that the British imported and imitated. When American artists like Eddie Cochran or Buddy Holly toured the United Kingdom, they had a huge impact. More oblique, but with challenging national identities, are those pop icons who were British but had North American military fathers who did not remain in Britain (e.g., Eric Clapton, whose father was Canadian, and Andrew Loog Oldham, whose father was American).

Perhaps the most insidious biases in the music world were religious. The default religion, and thus the religion associated with the establishment, was Christianity, even if in the British Isles the distinction between Protestant and Catholic could be a matter of life and death. Unsurprisingly, many in the recording industry were not particularly religious. Nevertheless, a number commented if their colleagues were Jewish. In particular, some of the most important contractors (called "fixers" by musicians) and string players were Jewish. Sid Sax, Charlie Katz, and others booked most of the session musicians on the most important recording sessions, including those of the Beatles. Session musicians were suspicious of the intentions of contractors and their perceived condescension toward pop music, which was fueled by the reality that string-playing contractors were commonly proponents of classical music (the most established of establishment musics). For many in the industry, religious beliefs served as a convenient marker for differences they had with others. Unsurprisingly, many London Jews chose to change their names, not just as a professional move, but to better blend into British society.

Other British identities included (but were not limited to) Italian, French, and German Britons, whose families had sometimes been in the United Kingdom for generations. Nevertheless, as World War Two began, British police knocked on drummer Clem Cattini's family door to incarcerate his father because he had been born in Italy. When the two-year-old Clemente struck out as they took his father away, one of the officers described the boy as a "right blinking Mussolini." In the world of 1960s British pop, with its strong emphasis on British (particularly English) identity, an Italian British identity could be a complicating detriment to a performer's career. On the other hand, some of the most successful session musicians were Italian British, including Cattini and guitarist Joe Moretti.

TECHNOLOGY

The individuals who created British pop music and who drove its insatiable hunger for innovation operated in an environment ripe for change. In addition to the social parameters mentioned previously, the postwar era glowed with optimism. Technological advances, notably in the areas of electronics and chemistry, emerged from a variety of sources, both unlikely and anticipated. When combined with the most important factor for change in the music and recording industries—a willingness to experiment—British pop music began a period of dramatic revolution and evolution.

Recording Technology

The Second World War may have married misery and violence, but its technological experiments fathered musical changes that would startle their inventors. Notably, the occupation of Germany provided one of the most important contributions to music in the twentieth century: the tape recorder. In the lead-up to the war, the Germans had developed a method of prerecording programs for later broadcast that relied upon a ferric oxide compound applied to cellulose acetate tape. The oxide required a lower magnetic field to record than did wire, the tape facilitated splicing, the material was lighter, and the signal was clearer. Badische Anilin- und Soda-Fabrik (BASF) produced the tape and the Allgemeine Elektrizitäts-Gesellschaft (AEG) produced the tape recorder: the Magnetophon. Ironically, they made their first public recording demonstration with a performance by the London Philharmonic conducted by Thomas Beecham on 19 November 1936 in BASF's hall in Ludwigshaven. They used another technological device that would later become important to the British recording industry: a Neumann condenser microphone. The Germans made significant improvements to the system during the war, developing a way of making relatively clean recordings that they could broadcast at their convenience.

When American troops overran German positions around Frankfurt in 1944, two servicemen—Jim Mullen and Colonel Richard Ranger—obtained Magnetophons, returned with them to the United States, and modified them (with financial support from Bing Crosby) into a device that they would eventually manufacture commercially. Ampex machines would become an industry standard, including in the United Kingdom, where the Ampex 350–2 served as a mainstay of many recording studios, including Decca (Nichols 2001). AEG underwent reconstruction in the postwar years, and its subsidiary Telefunken would eventually provide EMI with one of its first tape recorders. EMI would also purchase the Swiss version of the Magnetophon recorders from Studer and build its own machines both to comply with Britain's currency concerns and to save money. Although EMI's BTR/2 (British Tape Recorder) proved a reliable machine, the engineers usually preferred the Ampex machines that they had managed to obtain.[13] The BBC, on the other hand, as a government agency seems to have been limited to using EMI's BTRs (Hughes 2004).

A significant improvement in tape recording came in the 1950s with the creation of biaxially oriented polyethylene terephthalate polyester film (better known by one of its trade names: Mylar), which replaced the unreliable plastic tape backings that had been in use. Mylar was less likely to tear and allowed for longer recordings and cleaner splices. Mylar also dramatically improved drumheads, replacing calfskin, which had always been subject to changes in humidity and heat.[14] The new drumheads were louder and brighter in sound, and manufacturers had more control over the process.

---

[13] Obtaining American equipment involved going before the Board of Trade to argue either that British manufacturers could not match the American product (a difficult argument for EMI, which manufactured recording equipment and professed its products to be superior to foreign producers) or that the device had some quality that the British company wished to study.

[14] Evans and Remo produced the first Mylar heads around 1958.

Until the war, British companies like Decca and EMI manufactured most disks with shellac, a natural plastic obtained from insect excretions and harvested primarily in Southeast Asia. With Japan's wartime control of this region, the production of these disks became problematic. To produce new recordings, corporations often pulverized and recycled old disks in order to accommodate new pressings (Martland 1997: 148). Sales of disks had already fallen off sharply during the economic depression of the early 1930s with audiences drawn to the new technologies of radio and sound films. Recording companies now came into competition with government agencies, which required shellac disks to produce broadcasts and to record meetings. Broadcasters had been playing disks almost since the beginning of radio,[15] but in wartime Britain, disk "jockeys" entertained with portable systems in residential communities and on military bases, providing music in contexts where musicians were unavailable. Almost as important, with the rationing of fuel, performances by big bands grew to be exorbitantly expensive. In postwar Britain, Decca and EMI continued to produce music, but they had much less shellac for disks and fewer customers who could afford to purchase the equipment to play them.

By the conclusion of the war, chemists in search of a shellac replacement had rediscovered vinyl (polyvinyl chloride) and had developed a durable version of this medium for disks. Vinyl was on its way to becoming the standard, aided by improvements to playback and amplification systems and a smaller recording groove (called a microgroove). For about twenty years, the U.S. industry (and consequently the world) engaged in a battle of speeds with Columbia Records introducing the $33\frac{1}{3}$-rpm, twelve-inch long-play (LP) disk in 1948 and RCA promoting the 45-rpm, seven-inch single in 1949. The slower playback speed and softer medium than the shellac 78-rpm disk allowed for lower surface noise and provided a better reproduction of the music. Consequently, these improvements in the recording process helped to create a new market for popular music. Indeed, the combination of the better recordings made possible by tape and tape recorders and the improved reproduction of these sounds on microgroove vinyl disks created a situation that focused consumer attention on music.

Producers and musicians learned to adapt the available technologies in order to obtain cleaner and more distinct recordings. For example, guitarist Les Paul recognized that one could use tape recorders to layer sounds, recording a guitar

---

[15] Christopher Stone became the first radio "disk jockey" on the new BBC on 7 July 1927, when he played a recording on the BBC (LaborLawTalk 2006). Arnold (2008) claims that the first disk recordings were played in the United Kingdom in 1924.

part with one tape recorder, playing that back, and both re-recording that part and adding an accompanying guitar part on a second tape recorder. The quality of the sound degraded with each subsequent generation, but the flexibility it provided musicians meant a seismic shift in the industry. Soon, audio companies like Ampex developed both smaller recording heads and wider tape, which enabled studios to record multiple tracks, not only resulting in cleaner sounds, but also allowing for the creation of stereo recordings. With the introduction of stereo separation on disks in 1958 (by Audio Fidelity in the United States and by Pye in the United Kingdom), the listening experience improved dramatically.

Corporations also developed technologies that took advantage of the added frequency spectrums. Decca had produced marine radar equipment both during and after the war, and its laboratories learned how to apply that technology to enhance the playback capacity of its disks, calling the approach "full frequency response range" (FFRR). Other issues that had to be resolved included the equalization of the recorded sounds so that consumer amplifiers could reliably reproduce the sounds on the disks. Ever since the industry's adoption of electrical recording in 1925, the quality of recordings had been improving and, with better microphones (again, German) and playback systems, consumers now had a product that could recreate sounds they had never before heard. Of course, stereo turntables and amplifiers were still a rarity and were commonly out of the average consumer's budget, especially in the United Kingdom, but the die had been cast: change was afoot.

Through the war years, families had gathered around their radio sets for news broadcasts and music. Indeed, for many, this was the principal way they listened to music, while the purchase of the relatively expensive and brittle shellac disks was a preserve for wealthier families and, even then, was limited to favorites. Listening tended to be communal. Personal radios were rare until the 1960s, when the catalyst for change was yet another offshoot of wartime research: the transistor. Bell Laboratories in New Jersey, like many others, had been researching how to make radar more effective. One consequence of its work was the first transistor radio, which Regency (underwritten by Texas Instruments) produced in 1954. By 1960, inexpensive Japanese and Chinese radios and earphones began to flood the market, allowing teens to listen to music without parental regulation. Domestically, the use of radios to disseminate music had always been important, but that role now became the norm. The transistor also made its way into corporate tape recorders, such as Studer's fully transistorized A62, which appeared in 1963, replacing maintenance-heavy vacuum-tube[16] machines.

---

[16] The British refer to vacuum tubes as "valves."

Musical Instruments

Of course, one of the most important changes to take place in popular music in this era was the introduction of the electric guitar and its near relative, the electric bass; however, electric guitars seem not to have reached the United Kingdom in any meaningful way until the late fifties. Electronic amplification had been around since the 1920s, when Al Jolson's *The Jazz Singer* (1928) transformed the film industry with an integrated soundtrack. Rickenbacker in 1931 manufactured the first electric guitar, which introduced a primitive magnetic pickup for a steel-stringed "Hawaiian" guitar played either on the lap or on a stand. Its first "Spanish" six-string guitar, the Bakelite Model B, appeared in 1935, although it weighed so much that some players needed a stand to hold it. The next year (1936), Gibson produced its first guitar, the ES 150 ("Electric Spanish"), a hollow-body archtop guitar with f-holes. In 1939, Charlie Christian brought this guitar to much wider American attention when he began playing it in Benny Goodman's sextet.

Despite the growing importance of electric guitars in the United States, Britain was about to enter the Second World War. With Germany bombing its cities and Commonwealth troops driven from the European mainland, the nation focused on survival: electric guitars would have to wait to enter the British consciousness until the 1950s. Even in the United States, companies developing electric guitars slowed their production when Franklin D. Roosevelt committed the nation to war in late 1941, as the metal in these guitars was of strategic importance.

In the postwar years, American companies like Gibson resumed their production and, in 1950, Fender introduced its first six-string standard guitars—the Esquire and the Broadcaster (soon renamed the Telecaster). Even then, American electric guitars were rare in Britain, only officially entering that market in 1959, when the government lifted a ban on American imports. Meanwhile, young British guitarists improvised amplification devices, found ways to import equipment from the United States, or bought European versions. Guitarist Vic Flick—who would play with the John Barry Seven on many of the early pop television shows and would become a sought-after session musician (recording, among other things, the "James Bond Theme")—attached war-surplus equipment to his acoustic guitar around 1950–1951. His instrument was "a round sound hole, Gibson Kalamazoo."[17] However, in the context of the family band, he com-

[17] The Kalamazoo was Gibson's budget-line guitar, which was sold separately from Gibson's usual dealer network. This particular guitar may have come to the United Kingdom either with an American serviceman or through someone who worked on one of the transatlantic ocean liners.

plained, you "couldn't hear it, so we got this tank commander's mike, strapped it onto the machine head, and played it through my dad's big radio so that it was amplified. I mean, it was quite a strange setup." Lonnie Donegan tells a similar story, claiming (characteristically) that he was the first to put a war-surplus microphone on his guitar, although his was a pilot's microphone: "The surplus stores were selling everything from the army in those days, and we used it as a contact mike. We strapped it to the front of the guitar—it was all rubber—and we played through the radio because we didn't know anything about amplifiers. In fact, I doubt if you could have even bought one then. We certainly couldn't afford one" (Foster 2000: 23).

With American musical equipment so difficult to obtain in the fifties, British musicians most often turned to European instruments, commonly those made by the German companies Höfner and Framus. Höfner probably offered the option of electric pickups on its President and Committee guitars around 1954; however, amplifiers would have been both difficult and expensive to obtain. American amplifiers, running with an alternating current of 110 cycles, would have been incompatible with the British 220-cycle standard, even if they were available. In the early 1950s, Britain was in the midst of major reconstruction, rebuilding the infrastructure destroyed by the Germans during the war. About 1954, Flick remembers that he had outgrown the Kalamazoo and now his "big dream was to get a Höfner President guitar.[18] I worked all one summer season, laying concrete—which I'm not quite good at. I saved all the money up for this Höfner President, which was covered in white pearl and, oh my goodness, I was so proud of this guitar."

Another young guitarist of this era, who would play with Marty Wilde's Wildcats and accompany Eddie Cochran during his fatal April 1960 British tour, Big Jim Sullivan remembers that he had a "Framus Black Rose from about 1955 to '57. It had a little Höfner pickup on it with a little slit on the top with a wheel that was the volume control. I remember Denny Wright had the same pickup on his Höfner Committee." Framus advertising in this era shows both Wright (who recorded and played with Lonnie Donegan) and the best-known session musician of the fifties, Bert Weedon, holding Höfner Committees.

Joe Moretti (who plays the iconic riff on Johnny Kidd and the Pirates' "Shakin' All Over") had even more humble guitar beginnings. His first instrument was "a little Swedish boxwood guitar called a Herdin. Terrible thing. It was just painted with brown varnish, but I could pick out notes on it." He soon identified the gui-

---

[18] Höfner began producing this acoustic archtop in 1954.

tar of his dreams and calculated the sacrifice. Earning ten shillings a week by chopping railway scrap wood and selling it as firewood, he set his sights on a "chocolate brown, golden sunburst" Höfner Senator. He remembers thinking, "Oh my. I've got to have that. That is for me. That is mine." The cost? "Nine shillings and tuppence a week from my ten shillings," which resulted in "ten whole pence left to get by." However, he "had the guitar, so that's all that mattered."

Höfner's distributor in the United Kingdom, Selmer, had been producing public address systems since at least the forties, but did not produce guitar amplifiers in earnest until 1958. British musicians solved the amplifier problem the way they often solved the guitar problem: they improvised. With rationing still in place during the early fifties and tight restrictions that would remain until June 1959 to address Britain's war debt and balance of payments, guitarists often also had to be electrical engineers. For example, guitarist Dick Denny produced his own amplifier after experimenting with (and destroying) his father's radio. His fifteen-watt amplifier combination (AC15) was the foundation of his company, Vox, which went into production in 1958 (see Foster 2000: 138–141).

With the lifting of import restrictions on American products in 1959, Fender and Gibson guitars and amplifiers suddenly became available, albeit at a price. Cliff Richard purchased a Fender Stratocaster for his guitarist, Hank Marvin, directly from the United States (Foster 2000: 163), but Big Jim Sullivan remembers, "When the imports became legal, everybody and their dog bought U.S. guitars. After that, you never saw a Höfner or Framus or any of the UK guitars on the shelf again. I purchased a Gibson 345 cherry red stereo with a gold plated Bigsby and tuners. It cost about £298. You could have bought a car for that price."

If anything, the challenges that British engineers and musicians faced in the fifties and sixties demanded that they become adept at improvising and experimenting with instruments, amplifiers, and sound recording. Invariably, they worked with technology that was several years behind America, whether it was instruments, amplification, or recording equipment.

Transportation

The British music industry (indeed, British industry as a whole) in the postwar years not only sought to be successful in the United Kingdom and Europe, but it craved a break into the States. By comparison, the American market dwarfed Britain's, and success there could lead to global success. But up until the fifties, a lengthy ship voyage proved the primary means of travel between London and New York. The first transatlantic air service began on 20 May 1939, but the war severely limited its availability; moreover, flying was expensive and its safety questionable. Heathrow Airport opened on the first day of 1946 for commercial traffic and air travel grew over the next decades, despite disasters such as the crash in Sigginston, Wales, that killed eighty. The inauguration of the British Overseas Air Service on 2 May 1952 marks the true beginning of the age when British and American artists could travel quickly between New York and London. Less than a dozen years later, the Beatles would ride one of these flights into music history when they arrived at the recently renamed Kennedy Airport to a crowd of teenagers screaming for something new.

MUSIC AND CHANGE

If we can understand music as culture, then we can expect at least some music to change as culture evolves, and pop music to change perhaps the most. The life of a single in the sixties varied from dead on arrival to weeks. Consequently, musicians and production crews continually scrambled to remain relevant. Various communities of individuals self-identified into social strata within the music and recording industries and, in so doing, have provided illustrations of how class, age, profession, gender, and ethnicity played into the evolution of the London session scene. Selected moments in the lives of these individuals offer data points outlining some of the transformations of British pop. On the production side, producers and engineers managed the recording process. Musicians provided the art. And music directors and songwriters occupied the netherworld between the microphone and the musical instruments. In each category, individuals provide examples of how the system and the music changed.

The sixties recording—a vinyl disk with variegated grooves and a spindle hole—functioned as the currency of pop music. British teens saved whatever income they could from allowances, petty after-school jobs, and babysitting to purchase these statements of fashion and fantasy, and they hoarded them as trolls might guard bridges to their young souls. They played these treasures on a range of machines, starting with small self-contained turntables manufactured by HMV, Philips, and Marconiphone, which included tiny amps and six-inch oval speakers. As adolescent incomes increased, manufacturers marketed larger and more sophisticated component systems with fuller playback spectrums for this emerging society of audio connoisseurs. Often, the very companies that sold the disks (e.g., EMI) also manufactured the disk players, which assured the consumer not only that the playback would be consistent with the product, but also that a continuing supply of new material would be available.

Studios functioned as forges in which producers, engineers, and music directors melded songs and performances into recordings. Moreover, as recording and musical technology evolved between the mid-fifties and the late sixties, each new wave of individuals changed the institution and imagined themselves to be at least as well qualified as their predecessors. In parallel with some songwriters, who feared that knowing more about music might shatter their fragile creative individualities, managers and many musicians began to discount the importance of those who understood the technology and psychology of recording. Instead, these newcomers increasingly saw themselves as empowered to make the recordings themselves. Counterbalancing this group, an increasingly sophisticated cohort of musicians, producers, music directors, and engineers enriched the industry by sometimes reinventing their art.

A healthy ecology resides in a conditional state of continual change. Ecological diversity contributes to both short-term stability and long-term flexibility in the face of environmental fluctuation. In this case, the London recording industry responded successfully to changes in technology, the economy, politics, and other revolutionary forces in the sixties because of the many different kinds of people engaged in solving the problem of creating a hit. Moreover, the recordings they created appealed to diverse consumers: teens and parents, males and females, upper class and working class, a variety of ethnicities, and British and non-British audiences. In the process of change, however, individual parts had to either adapt or face elimination. British studios in this era constituted contested cultural spaces in which dissimilar individuals and groups of individuals competed for dominance and control of the recording process and its product.

Production crews working in clearly differentiated roles brought a wide range of skills and orientations to London's recording sessions. Producers generally dominated, while music directors, engineers, and contractors did their bidding, albeit with varying degrees of resentment and personal enfranchisement. A well-rehearsed production team could ensure the efficacy of a recording session, bringing all of the components together at the same time to ensure that they maximized valuable studio and artist time. A successful production team solved the puzzle *and* created a hit recording.

Nevertheless, the market was littered with failed recordings, even by otherwise talented artists who in other contexts created gems. An uninspired producer, an unsympathetic music director, an uninvolved engineer, and/or a contractor who simply found the most convenient supporting musicians could turn out the perfect flop. However, when a producer could hear potential in a performance (and knew how to create something special), when a music director could elicit great performances from musicians, when an engineer entertained technical challenges, and when a contractor knew the best musicians and got them, they could make pop magic.

EMI had several subsidiary labels, including Columbia and Parlophone, the former managed by senior producer Norrie Paramor and the latter by George Martin. The corporations provided facilities, support staff, a sound library, storage facilities, and some musical instruments. Corporate producers simply signed up for studio time and (unlike independent producers) were not personally responsible for paying the technicians who moved and maintained gear, operated tape decks, and generally ensured that the company ended up with a clean recording and well-maintained equipment.

Perhaps unsurprisingly, the further one moved up the musical food chain, the less likely that musical ability was involved. Sir Joseph Lockwood, the chairman who transformed EMI in the fifties, possessed management skills learned while working with flour mills. And Sir Edward Lewis prognosticated as a stockbroker before purchasing Decca in 1929, bringing old-school financial predictability to a company whose fortunes revolved around public whim. Men such as Lockwood and Lewis were the very definition of the establishment and ironically presided over corporations that provided vehicles for the expression of antiestablishment protests.

Pye Records, on the other hand, had for most of its existence been a manufacturer of electronic components and did not enter the recording business until 1955 by buying Nixa Records, becoming Pye Nixa Records. It enhanced its sales by forming Pye International Records in 1958, prominently distributing American recordings from labels like Chess and King. In 1959, when ATV purchased 50 percent of its stock, Pye Nixa became simply Pye.

One response to the corporate control of recording studios and record releases was the creation of independent or alternative entities in the recording industry, especially as young musicians and producers "sussed out" the laws governing the music business and accumulated enough capital to buy into the game. The areas in which they made inroads fell roughly into three categories: studios, producers, and record companies. Independent studios such as IBC, Olympic, Regent, and Lansdowne provided venues for everything from film soundtracks to radio commercials, but producers could record there free of corporate control. These independents then attempted to lease their recordings to record companies to manufacture and distribute. Songwriters also used these facilities to create demo recordings in order to convince a producer or music director to adopt their songs for their artists and/or recordings.

However, new companies arose that would compete with EMI and Decca while promising creative freedom. Andrew Oldham formed Immediate Records in 1965, focusing on young performers such as the Small Faces and P. P. Arnold and, later, on progressive pop bands such as the Move. Chris Stamp and Kit Lambert formed Track Records in late 1966 to release recordings by Jimi Hendrix and the Who. And perhaps the most notorious independent label arose when the Beatles formed the Apple Corporation in 1968. They promised an alternative to the establishment, just as Tommy Steele and Lionel Bart had with Gimmick Records in 1958 (N.A. 1958b: 1).

Small recording studios associated with publishers were a relatively new idea. Noel Rogers of Dominion Music visited the United States in the spring of 1961 and reported to Hubert David (with some apparent surprise), "Every recognized songwriter has his own private recording unit. He produces his own gimmicks on the trial discs and sells a package deal to a major record company" (David 1961: 4). By early July, James Baring had opened Regent Sound at 4 Denmark Street to serve the numerous publishers in the block, some of which (e.g., Southern) soon set up their own basic studios for house composers.

Promoting records and getting them onto the charts was everyone's business. Brian Epstein has notoriously been accused of buying up copies of "Love Me Do" to bring the disk up in sales (he denied it). Others were open about their manipulation of the charts. The *New Musical Express*'s charts were the oldest in Britain, basing their rankings on sales at selected shops, but the identity of these shops was no secret. More reliable and extensive, the charts compiled by *Record Retailer and Music Industry News* reflected tallies submitted by shop owners. Managers, promoters, producers, and fans knew that, if they spread out and bought enough copies at these shops, they could boost the ranking of their recording. Another approach simply bribed individuals to change the sales figures and/or the ranking. In the end, these tactics could move a modestly successful recording onto the charts, but sustained success still called for a quality product.

2

The Velvet Glove

The Art of Production

Our experiences as listeners shape our expectations of the "authentic" such that the aural environment of a recording constitutes a constructed acoustic space. Producers sculpt this reality. At the height of the beat boom, two broad types of record producers ruled Britannia's wave of recordings. On the one hand, salaried corporate producers labored for Decca, EMI, and Pye. On the other, independent producers licensed recordings to the corporations. The term "producer" was also relatively new in late 1950s London, such that journalist Tony Brown (1958: 3) described them as the "men who manipulate the vocal puppets on the record scene." Moreover, he asserted, "their influence cannot be doubted. The Artists and Repertoire Manager is the most consulted—and the most insulted—man in pop music." Through much of the era, the first wave of professionals tended to use "artists and repertoire manager" to describe what they did, with "producer" coming to predominate by the late sixties. Independents tended to call themselves producers, as distinct from the corporate "managers" who preceded them. Here, we will use "producers" broadly to describe the role in the sixties and "artists and repertoire managers" when referencing their historical origins.

If a producer proved musically adept (i.e., could read music and perform), then he (and in 1960s London, the official producer was always male) worked di-

rectly with the artists in order to help them develop and/or adapt their repertoires. For example, Parlophone's George Martin could score arrangements and
step in to provide some basic musical performances when needed, but he possessed limited technological skills. He relied on engineers to obtain quality
recordings, while he concentrated on the music. Technologically proficient producers commonly engaged music directors or expected the band's management
to prepare their artists. For example, manager Kit Lambert often rehearsed the
Who before they came to a session, allowing producer Shel Talmy to focus on getting a good recording. Producers—corporate and independent—relied on contractors (also known as "bookers" or "fixers") to find musicians for those sessions needing accompaniment or for groups that needed augmentation.

The producer approved songs (repertoire) for recording, determined the resources necessary for performance, and, finally, decided what to release. Of
course, when corporations were involved, others participated in the process as
well; but, in all cases, the producer was responsible for eliciting a convincing (and
salable) performance from the artists and creating a product that would be successful in the marketplace. The only concrete measure of a recording's success lay
in how many copies the company could peddle.

CORPORATE PRODUCERS

Corporate artists and repertoire managers represented the traditional mode of
recording in Britain. With EMI and Decca controlling both the principal recording
studios and record-pressing plants, they developed a system for exploiting musicians and their music. Indeed, following an American model, they often explicitly
described what they did as exploitation, in the sense that they were making valuable resources available for public sale. Artists such as Eddie Calvert relied on producers such as Norrie Paramor to help market their abilities. Indeed, they were
thankful for the assistance, even as they probably resented the power of the corporation. In addition, given Britain's midcentury labor relations, musicians would
rightly have been suspicious of the intentions and long-term support of corporate
managers: an artist's value hinged solely on his or her ability to create salable music.
Corporate managers, however, had similar limits on their value, albeit with a longer
fuse. They could have a few flops, but eventually they too were expendable.

In the early years of the pop era, corporate A&R managers oversaw an industrial process. In 1950, when George Martin began as Oscar Preuss's assistant, EMI
used tape decks only as backup; wax disks that engineers kept at a constant
temperature with heat lamps constituted the primary means of capturing the recording. A lathe cut the live recording while white-coated engineers oversaw the

machine and the vacuum that sucked up the discarded wax. Mechanical clock-work, driven through a weighted pulley, spun the lathe at a constant speed. The engineers and the producer then examined the wax disk visually to see if the lathe had overcut the disk or if imperfections in the wax had otherwise spoiled the recording. (See Martin with Hornsby 1979: 104ff.) Only a corporation could afford to maintain such a facility and consequently would have been reluctant to change the technology of its vested interests. However, as tape recorders became more reliable and widely available, independent studios gained niche advantages.

At the corporations, each label had A&R managers and a production staff. For example, George Martin, Norrie Paramor, and Dick Rowe each had the responsibility of (1) finding singers or musicians from whom they believed they could obtain a convincing performance, and (2) working with publishers and songwriters to find new music that they could match to their performers. In addition, they sought out recordings from abroad, especially the United States, that they felt a British artist could cover successfully. In the 1950s especially, but also in the 1960s, several different versions of the same song commonly shared the charts. For example, in early 1956, both Dick James and Garry Miller had versions of the song "Robin Hood" (associated with the popular television show) competing on the charts. Similarly (but more strangely), in 1965 both Marianne Faithful and the Nashville Teens released competing versions of John Loudermilk's "This Little Bird," each individually produced by partners Andrew Oldham and Tony Calder for their production company, Impact Sound, and leased to Decca.

INDEPENDENT PRODUCERS

Independent producers—as opposed to salaried A&R managers directly employed by EMI, Decca, or Pye—were responsible for their recordings from start to end. A corporate manager like George Martin (before he too became an independent) could concentrate on developing artists and finding good songs for them to record. An independent producer also needed to concern himself with paying for the studio time and, if an orchestra were involved, that expense as well. If a corporate manager's recording tanked, he might be embarrassed, but he did not suffer financially. Independent producers were responsible for funding (or for finding someone to fund) their sessions and for covering any losses they incurred if the recording failed. Of course, they also stood to profit significantly if the song became a hit and, consequently, sought to maintain total control over their product.

Significantly, most early independent producers were outsiders of one kind or another. Joe Meek established the mold, barely concealing his gayness (in an age that legally prohibited homosexuality). That he apparently also exhibited a degree of psychosis illustrates how much freedom an independent producer could have. Shel Talmy, an American recording engineer, forged his credentials. Andrew Oldham functioned best as a public relations manager and drama coach. And "even the most successful British independent, Mickie Most, had to go to South Africa to get his start" (Marsh 1983: 221). More important, they used their outsider status and the emergence of new studios to shake up the British recording industry. Joe Meek, Mickie Most, Andrew Oldham, and Shel Talmy assiduously demanded and obtained jurisdiction over the recording process, albeit to different degrees.

In order to survive, producers needed to be sanguine, crafty, and inventive in order to obtain what they wanted in the allotted time. For example, Meek routinely experimented with the performers who came through his improvised apartment studio on Holloway Road in North London (such as having them march up and down the hall stairway). Their models were Americans like Phil Spector, George "Shadow" Morton, and Don Kirschner, who created soundscapes that were at once identifiable (such as Spector's "wall of sound") and salable. As the British focus shifted from copying American models to creating something unique, change became inevitable.

REPRODUCING AMERICA

By 1968, to be a producer was to be self-evidently important. Those who helped to transform the role in London represented a variety of backgrounds and approaches, beginning with the old guard who had arrived in the forties and fifties. EMI employed Walter Ridley (assisted by Peter Sullivan) for its HMV label; Norman Newell (assisted by John Burgess), Norrie Paramor (assisted by John Schroeder), and Ray Martin operated at Columbia; and George Martin (assisted by Ron Richards) ran Parlophone. Decca's more centralized organization apparently assigned general repertoires to its artists and repertoire managers: Hugh Mendl (jazz, pop, and light classical), Frank Lee (who worked mostly on classical and light classical repertoires), Ray Horricks (theme music and jazz), and Dick Rowe (assisted by Mike Smith in pop). A relative newcomer, Pye Records operated with a much looser production structure: Tony Macaulay and Tony Hatch constituted Pye's production staff in the sixties, but Pye also allowed artists to bring in their own producers. Thus, Donovan had Peter Eden, Geoff Stephens, and Terry Kennedy as his initial producers (before signing with Mickie Most), and the Kinks had Shel Talmy, all of whom recorded at the Pye studios near Marble Arch and released on that label. Later, Johnny Franz and Jack Baverstock would work for Pye's new owners, Philips. As the pop side of the industry grew, assistants became producers in their own right, bringing younger, less experienced, but eagerly inventive minds to the task.

Through all of the fifties and much of the sixties, British studios and producers (and the artists they produced) sought to duplicate recordings they heard coming out of New York, Nashville, Detroit, Chicago, Memphis, and Los Angeles. When they failed, they resorted to a time-honored solution: they sought their own sound. Songwriter and singer John Carter remembers:

> I always used to see American records as being much better than English records, right through the sixties. I thought that we were trying hard to copy, and we never came up to it. We never came anywhere near to it. American records, especially Motown and all that stuff, were so well-produced. And also [the] wonderful harmony groups. They were great productions.

Making a cover version extended beyond simply re-recording the song: London producers attempted to replicate the arrangement and the acoustic quality. Again, Carter comments, "American records were always better. In the early sixties, where we tried to copy American recording artists, we'd get hold of things that had been hits in America and try to do them over. And they were a joke. They were just nowhere near them." Fortunately for British artists, most British listeners had never heard the American originals: "It's only if you knew there had been a recording in America, [and] you could [get] hold of a copy in some back-alley shop that you knew what American really sounded like. They were so much better." As both a songwriter and a musician, Carter worked in every studio in London and with most of the major producers. Consequently, he understood how the system as a whole functioned: "You just took in all the influences and, if you listen, you can see all sorts of American influences." Ultimately, he explains, "What we were trying to do [was] to copy the Americans, to try and get an English kind of equivalent. It means, take their views on production, take what they're doing, but do it in a little more English quirky style."

Hugh Mendl

Early A&R managers of pop material came to their craft sometimes reluctantly and often with little support, since corporations treated the classical and light classical catalog as more important. For example, in July 1954, when Hugh Mendl (dates unknown) asked for permission to record an album of Chris Barber's trad band in Decca's studios, the management told him that he could pursue the project, but not to spend more than £35. Mendl had been visiting jazz clubs, spurred by the popularity of British trad jazz, and hoped he could capture some of this excitement in a recording. Booking back-to-back afternoon and evening recording sessions, Mendl quickly ran the band through their prepared repertoire. Unfortunately, Mendl began to believe that "Chris Barber's Band did not have a very big repertoire" (N.A. 2004). After a break at the local pub and a quickly improvised jam, some of the musicians slipped away, presumably to gigs, leaving the band short of enough numbers for the album. The banjo player suggested that they play some of their skiffle songs. After Lonnie Donegan had tuned up his guitar, they quickly recorded a couple of numbers, including a version of Huddie Ledbetter's "Rock Island Line," which would eventually become one of the biggest sellers in the Decca catalog after the company re-released it in early 1956.

Being associated with a hit had the perquisite of attracting other acts. Less than a year after "Rock Island Line," Lionel Bart, John Kennedy, and Tommy Hicks (soon to be renamed Tommy Steele) brought their "Caveman" act to Mendl. He and music director Roland Shaw put together a backing ensemble made up of some of London's most reliable session men, including tenor saxophonist Ronnie Scott. The recording of "Rock with the Caveman" similarly reached high into the relatively new British record-sales charts, confirming Mendl's reputation. He would continue to produce successful recordings, including some by Adam Faith and notably the Moody Blues, for which he functioned as the executive producer on their groundbreaking album, *Days of Future Passed,* in 1967.

Norrie Paramor

Mendl's best-known counterpart at EMI was Norrie Paramor (1914–1979), who arrived to help rejuvenate its Columbia label in 1952 as "recording director" when Philips lured away his predecessor. Paramor had been a bandleader in London and was probably most comfortable recording Montovani's string orchestrations of a previous generation's favorites. He had numerous successes with Eddie Calvert (e.g., "Oh Mein Papa"), but he also attempted to record rock 'n' roll, notably with various bands put together by drummer and pianist Tony Crombie (which included at one point a young Jet Harris). Paramor had the wits to know that he needed to find a British version of rock 'n' roll and was willing to take chances to find those artists. His breakthrough came in 1958 when he heard a demo by a young coffee-bar singer, Cliff Richard, and his band, the Drifters. In addition to the usual covers of American songs, they were also performing material written by their guitarist, Ian Samwell.

Many describe "Move It" as Britain's first authentic rock recording, in part due to Richard's emotionally convincing performance, to session musician Ernie Shear, who finds just enough guitar crunch to pass as rock, and to a recording quality that has an edge missing in many other releases of the time. Paramor's task in this production was to judge whether the song and the musicians had potential, substituting Shear for the songwriter, Samwell. He also had to capture the sound of an electric guitar, a task in which newcomer Malcolm Addey would assist as engineer. He had been experimenting with bands like Crombie's and other would-be rock artists, but the parts all came together in this recording. His assistant, John Schroeder, would continue the tradition, auditioning Helen Shapiro at a local high school, recording her demo, and convincing Paramor that she would be a success. Like Paramor, Schroeder also contributed songs, writing three hits for Shapiro with his friend Michael Hawker.

Norman Newell

Norman Newell (1919–2004) arrived at EMI's Columbia in 1949 at a time when the label primarily distributed releases from the American company called Columbia;[1] however, Newell wanted to produce music by British artists, a goal he pursued most of his career. In a 1951 memo, Newell decries the lack of support that publishers had been giving British songwriting: they "seem to be of the opinion that the only worthwhile British songs are the type commonly known as the 'corny' variety. Were they to use a little imagination in their choice of British material, we could bring about a great change in the business" (Leigh 2004). Newell had begun as a song plugger and lyricist on Denmark Street and had an affinity for British songwriters. He would continue to provide lyrics to songs, including the English text for the theme song to the film *Mondo Cane* (1962): "More" received an Oscar nomination. George Martin (with Hornsby, 1979: 83) describes him this way: "Norman was a lyric writer as well as a record man. He always wanted to be a Stephen Sondheim. He wrote good enough lyrics, certainly, but his main strength came from his ability to handle big showbiz entertainers. He specialized in making original-cast recordings, especially of English shows."

When the American release arrangement for Columbia collapsed in 1953 (largely because of EMI's lack of promotion and reluctance to update its technology), Philips lured Newell away along with the American Columbia catalog. At Philips, he began working with music director Geoff Love, and the two would cooperate on numerous recordings for the next two decades. Newell returned to

---

[1] The two Columbias had once been part of the same company, but with the formation of EMI, the corporation spun off the American branch of the company to comply with antitrust laws. Nevertheless, the two companies maintained relations sporadically over the subsequent years.

EMI in 1954; the corporation had retained the rights to the name "Columbia" in the United Kingdom, just in time for the emergence of rock 'n' roll. He recorded albums from the television shows *6.5 Special* and *Drumbeat,* but confessed that he had little understanding of the music. Instead, he turned that work over to his assistant, John Burgess, while Newell concentrated on acts like Shirley Bassey, using John Barry as his arranger. Nevertheless, when the beat boom swept Britain, Newell signed up a couple of well-connected schoolboys—Peter Asher and Gordon Waller—to Columbia. Newell produced their recording of Paul Mc-Cartney's "World without Love" using Geoff Love again as the music director, an arrangement they kept for most of their hits. With McCartney continuing to write songs for his girlfriend Jane Asher's brother, Newell became one of the most successful producers of Lennon and McCartney songs other than George Martin.

John Burgess

Some of the most important work at Columbia came from the hands of the assistants, who were younger and generally more sympathetic with the musics listened to by adolescents. Newell gave his assistant John Burgess (dates unknown) early opportunities to try out his production skills, and Burgess succeeded with Adam Faith's 1959 hit, "What Do You Want?" Newell recalled, "I put Adam Faith with the arranger John Barry and, with John Burgess, they made that sensational record 'What Do You Want.' John Burgess would take care of that so I could concentrate on the serious side" (Leigh 2004). Although the song's author, Johnny Worth, influenced British songwriters of the era, the recording itself was a significant part of that package. Burgess would go on to produce a number of very successful 1960s recordings by performers like Freddie and the Dreamers (e.g., "If You Gotta Make a Fool of Somebody," "I'm Telling You Now," and "You Were Made for Me") and top five hits for Manfred Mann ("Do-Wah-Diddy Diddy," "Pretty Flamingo," and "Semi-Detached Suburban Mr. Jones").

Peter Sullivan

Nowhere perhaps were the generational differences among producers and their assistants more evident than in the recording of the 1960 rock classic "Shakin' All Over" by Johnny Kidd and the Pirates. Nominally, Wally Ridley would have produced the session for HMV; however, according to drummer Clem Cattini, the veteran was "a bit of a musical snob and he decided he could let his assistant record us because it wasn't really his scene at all. I presume it wasn't important enough because it was only a rock 'n' roll group and so he just decided to let his assistant do it." Kidd had already released recordings on HMV with modest success, but none of his recordings (before or after) would achieve the triumph of "Shakin' All Over."

According to Kidd biographer Keith Hunt, Peter Sullivan (dates unknown) was the one who heard the rocker perform and who recommended him to Ridley for HMV (Paytress 1996). Nevertheless, Sullivan would have been relatively inexperienced and reliant upon engineer Malcolm Addey to apply as many tricks as he knew. As far as the musicians were concerned, Sullivan was the "boss man." From Cattini's vantage on the studio floor, Sullivan seemed to have "all the ideas for the echoes and various things." Sullivan learned the art of production from experiences like this, especially when the record reached the top of the British charts, and Ridley decided that he (Ridley) should be the producer of the next recording ("Restless").

Subsequently, Sullivan left HMV for Decca and continued his success as a producer with some of the period's most iconic recordings: Lulu's "Shout" and Tom Jones's "It's Not Unusual," as well as numerous other successes. In the mid-sixties, he, George Martin, Ron Richards, and John Burgess formed their own production company, built their own studios, and tied their incomes to royalties instead of corporate salaries.

Dick Rowe

Fans of the Beatles and other would-be critics love to malign corporate artists and repertoire manager Dick Rowe (1925–1986) of Decca. Although he and his assistant Mike Smith had successes with one of Liverpool's original singer-songwriters (Billy Fury), it is their rejection of the Beatles in 1962 that turns up most often in references to him. Earlier in the sixties, Rowe had briefly left Decca to run production at the ill-fated Top Rank Records, which collapsed in the summer of 1960. He returned to Decca, a somewhat chastened and recommitted company man.

Rowe was neither a musician nor much of a technician; however, many believed in his good ear and head for what would be successful. For example, drummer Clem Cattini describes Rowe as "a very clever man because he could tell a hit record," largely because of his status as "a punter which put him in the position of instinctively knowing what the public wanted" (Cunningham 1998: 101). On George Harrison's recommendation, Rowe signed the Rolling Stones to Decca (with Andrew Oldham and Eric Easton producing the sessions), but he also turned down the Yardbirds and Manfred Mann. Mark Cunningham (1998: 101), in his book on music production, puts Rowe in a class of producers who were "unimaginative" and "clueless." In particular, Rowe's lack of musical knowledge is what some musicians remember. Cattini describes a session in which his part during the introduction was marked as "tacit" ("silent"), i.e., that he should not play. Rowe reportedly asked the music director (Ivor Raymonde) if Cattini could play the passage more quietly (Cunningham 1998: 101).

Tony Meehan (who drummed for the Shadows before becoming a producer both for Decca and as an independent) remembers Rowe as having

> a lot of good ideas, but he'd be the first to tell you he knew nothing about music. That was the first thing Dick used to come out with, "Of course, I know nothing about music, but I know what I like." He took gambles and he did try, but Decca was a very old-fashioned company, the way it was run was almost colonial. It was very hard to get things past Sir Edward Lewis and the directors and all these people who really didn't know the first thing about what was happening. (Oldham 2000: 135)

An independent producer, Meehan describes the principal problem that he and others had: they "found it very difficult to get their product placed and very difficult to get into these huge monolithic, colonial kind of organizations that were run like something from the British Empire, from the top down" (Oldham 2000: 136). Ironically, in many ways, Rowe served as a precedent for producers like Andrew Oldham, who similarly did not know much about music, but knew what he liked.

GEORGE MARTIN

His reputation could easily rest on his successful efforts to transform the Beatles from an ambitious bar band into arguably the most influential recording artists of the twentieth century. Martin's productions have routinely won recognition, topped the charts, and had a surprising sustaining power that defies the norms of pop music. More important, his work has almost defined an entire category of the twentieth century's musical canon. George Martin (b. 1926) was perhaps the youngest member of corporate London's old guard, and one of the first corporate men to go independent.

Two factors apparently set him on a musical path from his beginnings in an upwardly aspirant working-class home: a family piano and Martin's facility for remembering musical ideas. His uncle Cyril in the "piano trade" (who entertained at family gatherings) provided the first when Martin was about six, at which point he "fell in love with it straight away, and went and made noises on it" (Martin with Hornsby 1979: 13). Initial piano lessons for the family came from a relative (an "uncle's wife's sister"), suggesting that, although the family was neither wealthy nor professional musicians, it was internally able and willing to nurture musical interest (14). However, he never had more than a few formal piano lessons, and most of his early experiences with the instrument came as a product of his own curiosity. Consequently, he associated the keyboard with exploring and understanding music, obviously with assistance from others in the family (such as his older sister Irene). For example, tonal phenomena such as the circle of fifths (a sequential pattern of harmonic relationships that leads back to the beginning after touching all twelve notes of the octave) eventually helped him to learn some of the basics of Western music theory to a level where he could successfully enter a music school.

Assistance from others notwithstanding, he possessed the determination and perseverance to master these concepts on his own. This personal experience, more than almost any other personal event, might have prepared him for his work with rock musicians who were also largely self-taught. That Martin then went on to study Western classical music positioned him to be an interlocutor between an essentially oral tradition (popular music) and a written tradition (classical music).

In 1943, at age seventeen, Martin joined the Royal Navy's air wing (the Fleet Air Arm) and advanced through the officer training regime, starting as a naval airman second class, and earning promotions through leading naval airman, petty officer, midshipman, and sublieutenant. As part of that training, Martin spent two weeks preparing for his commission by learning how to be an officer and a gentleman, including "how to hold a knife and fork correctly" and how to conduct oneself at a formal dinner. Although it is doubtful that Martin acquired his sense of bearing and comportment in this context alone, the experience would have reinforced behaviors learned in the family context. More important, he would bring this formal attitude to his studio manner.

In the waning days of the war, he saw no more action than training in Trinidad, and in the aftermath the navy relocated him to Scotland, where he helped to reintegrate seamen into civilian life. Eventually, he reintegrated himself into London with a student loan to attend the Guildhall School of Music in London. Two individuals mapped his route to Guildhall: a sympathetic musician who heard Martin stealing time on a piano in an empty hall and an open-minded music professor who gathered the young sublieutenant under his aesthetic wing.

The musician (Eric Harrison) encouraged Martin to send his compositions to Sidney Harrison (no relation to the pianist) of the Society for the Promotion of New Music, who taught at Guildhall. The professor began a correspondence with the young naval airman in which he critiqued Martin's compositions and encouraged him to pursue music as a career, eventually helping him to gain entry to Guildhall. The university experience transformed Martin, broadening his understanding of music both through practical lessons (on piano and oboe) and also in the music theory and history classes he took. He emerged a well-qualified musician with little work, taking jobs playing oboe in pit orchestras and other part-time work. Eventually, he found employment in the BBC's library before Professor Harrison intervened again.

Parlophone

In 1950, when Oscar Preuss at Parlophone Records needed an assistant, Harrison recommended Martin, and when Preuss retired in 1955, Martin at age twenty-nine became the youngest label director at EMI. During Martin's time with Preuss, he apprenticed in the transitional world of an artists and repertoire manager. He seems to have followed Preuss everywhere, encountering the recording industry from the bottom up, beginning with how Parlophone's parent company, EMI, manufactured disks ("[r]eality was a hot and dirty factory, with men stripped to the waist, bathed in sweat and forever grimy with the black carbon dust which hung in the air") to how to promote records (Martin with Hornsby 1979: 107).

EMI may have imagined that a young producer would have affinity with the increasingly important youth market, especially when other young assistants, such as John Burgess and Peter Sullivan, were successful. However, in 1956, when Martin rejected Tommy Steele, he demonstrated that someone who was thirty might not necessarily be familiar with what teens wanted. In fairness, Martin auditioned Tommy Hicks before Larry Parnes transformed him into Tommy Steele, and, in retrospect, we can understand why the skiffle band (the Vipers) was more attractive to Martin than their young comedian singer. The band at least took what they were doing seriously, and Martin would record better comedians.

Early in his Parlophone career, Martin began learning how to work with musicians in a studio environment. On one notable occasion, he remembers asking for more clarity from the bass player in Humphrey Lyttelton's band; consequently, the band stormed out of the session for the way he had made the demand. Martin offers, "Musically I was right. Diplomatically I was wrong." The lesson he learned was that "[t]act is the *sine qua non* of being a record producer. One has to tread a fine line between, on the one hand, submitting to an artist's every whim, and, on the other, throwing one's own weight about." From that point on, Martin realized that he had to be more subtle: "I had to learn how to get my own way without letting the performer realize what was happening. One had to lead rather than drive. I think that now, as then, that is probably the most important quality needed in a record producer" (with Hornsby, 1979: 44). At various points in his career, Martin would test this principle.

Martin had significant success recording comedy (e.g., Peter Ustinov), developing a vocabulary of studio techniques that both endeared him to and prepared him for the Beatles. Recording at different tape speeds, overdubbing recordings, and splicing tape were all techniques that would serve him well with the music that the group would record. Martin even pushed the legal limits of what he did several times, and on at least one occasion Parlophone had to shelve a recording because it could not get clearance to release it. Notably, he once saved a recording by having every utterance of a word carefully edited. After recording a Spike Milligan send-up of the film *The Bridge on the River Kwai*, Parlophone realized that the film studio might sue. Martin's solution was to edit the tape. In the days of analog recording, this meant physically cutting the few milliseconds of consonant by hand. "We got out the scissors[2] and went through all the tapes, cutting out the 'K' whenever the word 'Kwai' appeared. It took ages to do, but at least we were then able to issue the record, and no one could sue us" (with Hornsby, 1979: 93). The result was a skit about the River Wye.

Another recording experience that may have prepared him aesthetically for the musical approaches he would champion in the sixties was his recording of Scottish folk artists, notably the renowned musician Jimmy Shand. Martin's respect for this music (even if for no other reason than it proved an important part of Parlophone's market) illustrates his openness to music other than classical music or the soft jazz pop which was lounging at the core of the recording business in the late fifties. While Shand coaxed raspy trills from his accordion, Martin snared the essence of these performances for others to enjoy. That became his signature approach.

These qualities, combined with his willingness to explore new musical ideas, made him a valuable asset to EMI, which nevertheless paid him a flat salary for his services. In the early stages of his career, around 1953, Martin remembers that his paycheck consisted of a "pauperly £13 9s 3d," which after taxes meant he "took home £12 6s 8d" per pay period (60). In 1954, when Decca's Frank Lee attempted to poach Martin with a promise to almost double his salary to £1200, EMI promised to match the annual salary. Martin stayed (only to receive £1100 when the paychecks arrived). By 1962, Martin was earning £3000 per year, but

---

[2] Martin may have been speaking figuratively of "scissors," as a razor blade and an editing block were the tools for most tape editing. Moreover, Norman Smith remembers that, in EMI's highly differentiated personnel structure, specific technicians were responsible for tape editing: "We had our own editing department at Abbey Road, of which there were probably three editors. They would do the splicing, but would have their orders from the producer." Curiously, Geoff Emerick (with Massey, 2006: 46) remembers Smith doing most of Martin's editing.

beginning to wonder why royalties were out of the question, and soon Martin would go independent. In August 1965, George Martin, Ron Richards, John Burgess, and Peter Sullivan formed AIR, Associated Independent Recordings (London), Limited, and with them went the Beatles, Tom Jones, Manfred Mann, Cilla Black, P. J. Proby, the Hollies, and Adam Faith.

Martin underlines the responsibility of generating appropriate arrangements for the recording session, citing Henry Mancini and Johnny Mercer's "Moon River" (for the film *Breakfast at Tiffany's*) as an example of what could happen if you did not recognize a possible match between artists and repertoire. One of Martin's singers, Eve Boswell, complained that he should have produced a version of "Moon River" with her. Martin, in turn, blames his assistant Ron Richards, who went to the film and reported "some incidental music, but nothing worthwhile" (Martin with Hornsby 1979: 58). Meanwhile, Norman Newell scored a UK number one hit with a rendition of the song by Danny Williams.

Most often, an artists and repertoire manager heard new songs through publishers, from records that individuals brought (usually from America), or by going to films. The power of the publishers in this era, Martin believes, lay in the traditional division of labor between songwriters and performers that underpinned Denmark Street. Notably, in the days of the British music hall, the musical expertise of songwriters—who not only could play piano but could notate what they played—separated them from singers, who were often musically illiterate. The emergence of the tape deck as a medium by which singer-songwriters could record their songs began to change the industry, but not overnight. Publishers still had an important promotional role to play.

In the late fifties and early sixties, once a month, publishers would present their company's new songs to a label. Before the availability of tape recorders, this meant that the publisher's song plugger sat at a piano in the label offices and performed. A good plugger (e.g., Dick James) could sell the song. Indeed, in the days before demo recordings, the song plugger *was* the demo. Not only did the role of the label in selecting music grow more important, but any songwriter with access to a tape recorder could potentially circumvent the publisher. Indeed, a sophisticated demo allowed the songwriter control over the direction of the final product, with music directors and producers often duplicating the demo right down to using the same session musicians.

At EMI, artists and repertoire managers would hold publisher sessions in the morning and, in the afternoon, conduct recording tests in Abbey Road's studio two. Martin (with Hornsby, 1979: 52) remembers, "Every half-hour there would be someone new to test." On 6 June 1962, a band that should have been auditioning in one of these tests arrived for their first recording session, changing Martin's life and the lives of millions.

The Beatles

The story of how Martin came to record the Beatles has been retold so many times (e.g., Davies 1985, Norman 1981, Kozinn 1995, Everett 2001, Spitz 2005, etc.), and yet some details remain vague. Manager Brian Epstein had been attempting to obtain a recording contract for the Beatles, the process including a failed audition with Dick Rowe's assistant Mike Smith at Decca. In a change of strategy, Epstein went to the HMV store[3] on Oxford Street (near Bond Street) to transfer a tape of the Decca audition to a disk, thinking the latter would be more likely to impress an A&R manager. The technician overseeing the transfer (Jim Foy), not recognizing some of the songs, asked Epstein about them. When told that the songs were by two of the musicians on the recording, the technician suggested that Epstein talk to publishing agent Sid Colman[4] from one of EMI's publishers, Ardmore and Beechwood, conveniently located in the same building. Colman, wishing to secure the rights to the songs, called George Martin to demonstrate to Epstein his connections. From Colman's point of view, the songs were no doubt fairly primitive, but the potential of catching songwriters early in their careers would have been attractive. For Martin, the band represented something different, an unusual niche in the recording market.

Despite Dick Rowe's infamous declaration in early 1962 that they were on the way out, guitar-playing groups were not extinct in Britain. A keyboard-dominated recording by the Tornados, "Telstar," became a major international hit that year. And, even though the Shadows had a guitar hit with "Wonderful Land" that spring, Tony Meehan and then Jet Harris had jumped ship. Rowe may have thought he detected a trend. Nevertheless, guitar-playing singing groups were vintage rock phenomena, especially those featuring musicians who wrote and performed their own material. A distinctively guitar-oriented group with a singer, Joe Brown and His Bruvvers, had a self-penned hit ("Picture of You") near the top (or at the top) of most charts in 1962. The question that year seems to have been whether that kind of performing and recording entity could remake itself after the deaths of Buddy Holly and Eddie Cochran.

---

[3] In the forties and fifties, some record companies had their own stores for the specific purposes of promoting and distributing recordings on their labels.

[4] Different spellings of Colman's name appear in various sources. Here, I use the spelling employed by Lewisohn (1992: 56).

The Beatles may have indirectly benefited from Cochran's death in a 1960 car crash and Buddy Holly's airplane death a year before that. In 1962, the year they auditioned for Decca and recorded with Parlophone, record companies released a number of posthumous Buddy Holly and Eddie Cochran disks. And in 1963, Joe Meek would produce a modest hit by former Tornado bass player Heinz Burt, memorializing Cochran ("Just Like Eddie"). Indeed, Cochran was a powerful influence on British musicians, including session musicians like Big Jim Sullivan and Joe Brown, both of whom had accompanied Cochran. Perhaps in this environment, Martin felt the Beatles might have fleeting success in that same market niche.

Martin notes that his weekly routine included a combination of listening to publishers pitch their new songs, fulfilling current recording contracts, and conducting artist's tests. As at Decca, where Mike Smith had auditioned the Beatles for Dick Rowe, the most common protocol was for the producer's assistant to audition the artists. For Parlophone, Ron Richards would customarily have auditioned new artists, but on 6 June 1962 occasional engineer Norman Smith remembers, "George Martin, in fact, was there at the test." He also confirms, "Most of the . . . artist's tests were done by the assistants of the main producer; but George was there for this particular one." Remarkably, documents reveal that the Beatles were not auditioning: they were already under contract. Why Martin had signed them without an audition remains unclear. What had he heard in the Decca audition that Dick Rowe had missed? What had Brian Epstein said? Did Colman offer an advantage? Or perhaps Martin signed the contract thinking that, if the recording attempts proved unsuccessful, no damage would have been done.

Smith recalls that the Beatles "weren't very impressive at all," and that, at the conclusion of the audition in studio two, the production crew brought the band up to the control room, both to review the recordings and to critique the performance and repertoire. Each member of the audition team (Martin, Richards, and Smith) reviewed their concerns with the Beatles. For example, Smith remembers telling the Beatles (which included drummer Pete Best), "if you want to be recording artists, particularly with EMI, you must have some decent equipment. I can only improve your sound if you give me some kind of initial sound in the studio. Then I can embellish; but I can't do it with the equipment you've got at the moment." He also remembers that George Martin "laid into them for, I guess, nearly half-an-hour."

At the conclusion of the audition, Smith remembers Martin asking the team's reaction to the test: "Well, what do you think?" Smith responded, "Well, I know we heard nothing musically, but they're so different. My thought, George, I think we should sign them." Martin said, "Alright, I'll think about it." Whoever else was involved in the decision is unclear, because the next thing Smith knew, "they were going to come back in [to] record their first number." We know that Epstein had already signed a contract, although Martin apparently had special criticism of drummer Pete Best. This recommendation spurred the Beatles to replace Best with the best drummer in Liverpool in their minds: Ringo Starr.

"Love Me Do"

When the Beatles came back to record on 4 September, they had a new drummer and a modified arrangement of "Love Me Do," one of the songs they had auditioned in June, but Martin remained skeptical.[5] Smith confesses that their second attempt at recording the Beatles "wasn't terribly successful," explaining that it "wasn't easy to record them." He may have been referring to their half-hearted attempt at recording "How Do You Do It?" but more likely, Martin, Smith, and Richards may have been unsure how to record the equipment (which included a handmade bass amp). This second session brings McCartney's bass to the fore with a punch, while leaving the drums somewhat distant; nevertheless, it establishes an improvement from the June attempt. Martin emerged unimpressed with the new drummer, and Smith offers that the producer "had a thing about Ringo: he didn't think he could cope on drums." Engineer-in-training Geoff Emerick—who through curious fortune claims to have been in the control booth that evening—similarly asserts that, between takes of "Love Me Do," he overheard Martin expressing concerns in the booth. Notably, "in his private conversations with Norman [Smith], he criticized the unsteady drumming" (Emerick 2006: 46).

For his part, Martin dedicated his time at the session to helping Lennon and McCartney shape their performance of "Love Me Do" after they had audaciously rejected his musical choice, "How Do You Do It?" If he had learned diplomacy with Humphrey Lyttelton, he practiced it with the Beatles. By all accounts, Lennon and McCartney were far more aggressive in their personal assertions

---

[5] Compare Smith's recollection with Lewisohn's (1988: 18) account of this session. Smith remembers that Martin was not there "for the first start. Not when we first started the 'Love Me Do' session. From my memory, Ron Richards would have worked the main part, to start off 'Love Me Do,' but then George came in to finish it, because we were running [into] difficulties. . . . I can't remember the actual detail of the difficulty now, on 'Love Me Do,' but George Martin then came in. But initially, the first session was with Ron Richards. [Lewisohn's notes for 4 September 1962 indicate that Martin was there.] I only said the first start, the first session, but George did come in to finish it. So he would get the kudos for that. Yes." When reminded that Lewisohn has Ron Richards there on 11 September with Andy White, Smith questions that account: "From my memory, no that's the wrong way around."

with Martin than a band rejected by other producers should have been. Subsequently, Martin called for yet another recording session in which he hoped they could get a better recording and performance. This time, Martin (or, more likely, Ron Richards) decided to use session drummer Andy White, with Starr providing tambourine accompaniment. Smith's evaluation of the song was that "it didn't call for a great drummer. Steady, yeah sure, but then the metronome could do that." What they were looking for was a sound (White's Ludwig drums) and musicality (White's instinctive synchronization with McCartney's bass playing).[6]

By industry standards of the time, several things should have happened at this point. First, Sid Colman and Ardmore and Beechwood should have promoted the song to BBC disk jockeys in order to get air play. Second, they should also have attempted to secure radio and television appearances for the band. And third, they should have lobbied EMI to press sufficient quantities of the recording and to push the recording in their stores. Little of this seems to have happened. For example, Epstein complained that his Liverpool store could not get enough copies, and Martin felt that his fellow producers did not take the recording seriously. Because of the comedy records Martin had been pushing, some of his fellow A&R managers even suggested that this was not really a recording by "the Beatles," but might actually be Spike Milligan. Martin sums up the condescension of London toward the provinces: "The people down south simply didn't have confidence in the record, although at least number seventeen was a start" (Martin with Hornsby 1979: 127). Epstein must have been furious with Ardmore and Beechwood. His decision was that "[w]hen the next one comes out I don't want to give the publishing to them" (128). In this light, we might remember Sid Colman as the man who lost the Beatles.

Method

Martin has commented that the "first and most important thing for a producer is to find and work with an artiste whom he likes and believes in" (1983a: 266). However, he also asserts, "the first requirement for a good producer—tact, diplomacy, call it what you will . . . —is the ability to have your will prevail without making it obvious. If you make the artiste believe he has chosen well, that it is his

---

[6] Martin remembers a different sequence in which they arrived for their 4 September session with Starr, only to discover that Martin had hired Andy White. (See Martin with Hornsby 1979: 126.) Lewisohn's examination of the recording logs shows that Andy White was not present until the next recording session on 11 September. Ultimately, Parlophone released the Starr version as its initial UK single, with the Andy White version on the album (*Please, Please Me*) and on the American release over a year later.

idea to do what you want, you have made a big step forward" (ibid.). Elsewhere, Martin (with Hornsby, 1979: 132) remembers, "I would perch myself on a high stool, and John and Paul would stand around me with their acoustic guitars and play and sing" songs they wanted to record.

The symbolic significance of his physical posture, however, betrays a key element of Martin's studio personality: his sense of authority and presumed superior rank. The act of placing himself on a stool to be either at eye level or to look down upon seated musicians suggests someone who demanded respect and who built psychological intimidation into his persona. Emerick (2006: 135) remembers, "he liked being looked up to, so he never sat in a normal chair during routining." Emerick (42) also remembers his first impressions of Martin: "Aristocratic in bearing and elocution—he almost sounded regal to my north London ears." Norman Smith describes Martin as "a very smooth talker. I think that if he were to just lightly suggest something or voice whatever he was thinking," musicians would "readily accept him, whatever he said. Well, it couldn't be wrong." In the class-charged atmosphere of 1960s London, everything from his gestures to his accent conveyed to musicians his opinion of their role in the process. Many interpreted his behavior as arrogance.

Martin's self-presentation as a social superior must have grated on the largely working-class artists whom he recorded, especially the northerners from Merseyside, whose distinctive accents also marked them as provincial. On the one hand, such a demeanor might have been reassuring: aristocratic bearing (even if feigned) implied leadership and authority. One might expect no less from a producer. However, the sixties were a time when British youth challenged such self-proclaimed authority. Martin's control over the Beatles, for example, waned in the second half of the sixties to the point where he began to function as their employee. His enjoyment of the relationship diminished proportionately, in part surely from the increased bickering, but also probably from their questioning of his authority. In the view of others who worked with Martin, especially after his success with the Beatles, they "thought they'd have to go along with it. He could virtually say anything," Smith believes. However, he also posits that Martin always operated in good faith: "He wouldn't just [change music] for the sake of alteration."

If Martin demanded respect in the studio from musicians, he also consulted with his production crew: Ron Richards and Norman Smith (and, later, Geoff Emerick). Indeed, Martin seems to have developed a team approach to many of his musical endeavors, whether in helping Lennon and McCartney hone their musical ideas into recordable art or in trusting the opinions of his colleagues when making production decisions. For his production network, his collegiality and generosity created effective dyadic bonds. To others, however, he could be condescending and patronizing. Nevertheless, even his detractors admit admiration for his accomplishments. He clearly attempted to bring the best musicians in London to the aid of the artists he produced, created compelling arrangements, and applied his knowledge of music and recording to his sessions. For example, Martin often overdubbed piano onto recordings by the Beatles, Billy J. Kramer with the Dakotas ("Bad to Me"), and others, applying his "signature wound-up" piano trick.

After a band had recorded a track and left the studio, he would play the recording back at half-speed so that it was half as fast and an octave lower. He would then develop a piano part at this slower recording speed and record it so that when played back at regular speed with the original recording, the piano's timbre evinced both a shorter envelope (how long the notes lasted) and a shallower harmonic profile. Martin was not the only one to use this technique. Indeed, independent producer Joe Meek had used it prominently in his recording of "Telstar" with the Tornados. Nevertheless, the approach illustrates how Martin was comfortable both participating in the generation of musical ideas and in capturing and transforming the magnetic object.

From Martin's perspective, he simply wanted "to make sure that they made a concise, commercial statement." His aesthetics consisted of a time limit of "approximately two and a half minutes," finding "the right key for their voices," and that the recording "was tidy, with the right proportion and form." Humbly, Martin considered his specialty to be "the introductions and the endings" of songs and "any instrumental passages in the middle" (Martin with Hornsby 1979: 132).

NORMAN SMITH

In February 1966, when EMI promoted Smith (1923–2008) to recording manager, he already had a number of successes as George Martin's preferred engineer. At forty-three, he was also three years senior to his production mentor who, in August of the previous year, had left EMI to form AIR. Smith survived as a corporate artists and repertoire manager in an age when independent producers began to dominate the industry.

Norman Smith's father had been an orchestral percussionist and had taken him "around to the various gigs," where his son "was fascinated just watching him when he was sight reading." In particular, he was amazed by "how many bars he could take in without glancing back, because he had to go round the array of percussion instruments to play his part." His older brothers played coronets, and Smith remembers going to concerts to hear his brothers in competitions. His mother, on the other hand, seems not to have been terribly fond of music. He remembers her being "a band widow." Although not "terribly complimentary" about his son's musical abilities, his father allowed Smith to begin playing on his practice kit when he was about six, and he played on his first gig with a jazz combo when he was twelve.

In 1939, at the age of sixteen, Smith left grammar school infatuated with jazz and believing that he "was born a musician." Perhaps hoping to improve his chances of getting gigs, he broadened his musical abilities, taking up the trumpet, then the valve trombone, and then the vibraphone. At this point, the war intruded on his life, and, in 1943 (the same year that Martin enlisted), he joined the RAF, where he flew for the army's Sixth Airborne unit. In 1947, he and thousands of others went back to civilian life. In Smith's case, this meant forming a jazz quintet in which he played trumpet and vibraphone in and around London. However, by 1959, Smith found that playing jazz was a "very, very difficult [way] to earn a living. My first child was coming along, and I was not earning enough money as a jazz musician. So I had to get myself what is commonly called a 'proper job' and became an engineer for EMI."

Smith at EMI

In 1965, George Martin (with Hornsby, 1979: 183) believed that he had "stripped" EMI "of all its young blood. Only the old remained." Even though Smith initially continued to work on recording projects with Martin at Abbey Road, his mentor's defection clearly left the engineer stranded. AIR served as a producers' venture; they brought their secretaries, but no one else. The engineers remained employees of the studios where Martin and his colleagues still did their recording. Not surprisingly, engineers and the remaining producers' assistants competed to see whom the corporation would appoint to replace Martin and the others. When the dust settled, Norman Smith—the musician-engineer who had proved to be so important in the recording of EMI's most lucrative franchise, the Beatles—became the director and principal producer for Parlophone Records.

This success came with its benefits and drawbacks. First, one of the primary reasons that Martin had left EMI—the company's self-interested economic meanness—ensured the corporation significant income and everyone else a relative pittance. Smith occupied the top of the engineering personnel hierarchy, leaving him only two options for significant additional income: (a) taking outside work (which he was already doing), and (b) leaping to the next level. EMI frowned upon the former, while the latter had proved almost impossible. Moving from engineer to producer at EMI paralleled the problem of moving from one class to another. EMI would rather that you knew your place and stayed there.

With the coveted promotion to producer, Smith accomplished two personal goals: he increased his income and raised his social rank at the studio. However, with these career advancements came a concession: he would no longer be George Martin's go-to engineer at Abbey Road. At first, he thought he could do both. Geoff Emerick, who succeeded Smith as the Abbey Road engineer to the Beatles, summarizes the situation:

> There was no way George wanted another producer in the room with him when he was working with "the boys"—that would undermine his authority and place him, and everyone else, for that matter, in an extremely awkward position. George always wanted the limelight to shine on him alone. Having a peer in the control room was completely unacceptable. (with Massey, 2006: 109)

Smith would engineer *Rubber Soul,* but not *Revolver.*

Moving from balance engineer to artists and repertoire manager also meant a more extensive introduction to corporate bureaucracy. When recording a group, Smith remembers, EMI was very generous with studio time: "There was never any question. You could go in [the studio] as many times as you wished." Hiring orchestral musicians meant filling out forms for EMI to approve. The "Red Form" he submitted "wouldn't have to be exactly to the last penny"; however, "they would have a yea or nay on it," even though Smith "never did get a nay." His most risky investments were solo singers who "would involve a large orchestra" and whose records sometimes "barely broke even." Smith recalls, "I had a few of those, but I wouldn't be called up about it or anything like that, so long as your budget was balanced with credits and debits and pretty even, then they didn't mind."

To arrange studio time, Smith's secretary would call her counterpart at Abbey Road "to see what available time there was at the studios on any particular day." The process equally applied "whether it would be a morning, afternoon, or an evening session." Once EMI had approved the fees for an orchestral session, "they didn't really interfere with whatever you wished to take into the studio," with the inevitable caveat that "you would not get away with too many failures before things were tightened up." The producer then had to demonstrate that the expense of hiring music directors and especially an orchestra was worthwhile:

> If they could really see the point in your finished record—the reason why you thought it was going to sell and be commercial—and if they agreed, well then they would not blame you at all. It's just one of those things that nobody, obviously, can foretell exactly just how commercially successful it might be.

In Smith's productions for EMI, he always understood that "[y]our end product had to be justifiable to the office." However, justification did not necessarily equate with record sales. For example, some recordings were "turntable hits," that is, disk jockeys liked the recordings and played them often, even if consumers did not rush out to make a purchase. Demonstrating that a recording had attracted media attention (through receipts from the Phonographic Performance Limited [PPL], acknowledging broadcasts) would be enough to bring performers back into the studio with the idea that the next recording could sell records.

Unlike Martin, Smith had no Guildhall education in arranging and composition; however, he understood how jazz combos functioned and how arrangements mixed composed heads with improvisational space. For orchestral scoring, he used Johnny Spence, arranging parts for smaller ensembles himself. Emerick (with Massey, 2006: 98) believes that George Martin relied deeply upon Smith:

> George and Norman made for a very good working team because George had sophistication and formal training ... , while Norman had the musical vocabulary to relate to modern bands. George simply didn't know the vernacular of popular music. Norman might suggest to George, "Tell them to accent the backbeat," and George would dutifully relate [sic] the message. He relied on Norman for that kind of input.

One thing Smith did not have to do when he became a producer was promote his records: "We had our own 'pluggers' at EMI." That much seems to have changed from Martin's first days. Indeed, in Smith's opinion, plugging records constituted "dirty work" that distracted him from making records, an opinion that also references how deeply ingrained hierarchy and status were in the system. His principal promoter, John Reid,[7] would report regularly on how he had pushed records and to whom he had pushed them. Reid would also find out "what may be coming up from me as a producer."

However, as a new producer, he needed to find performers to record. One of his first ideas included sending "a letter to all relevant agents, to potential recording groups, and anybody that could manage or be agents of artists" in search of artists who might be suitable for recording. The letters generated considerable interest, but one of the letters mistakenly went "to a record manager of another company. And he, in a sort of nasty way, reported me back to the chairman of EMI, Sir Joseph Lockwood." In the sixties, even though people were lobbying each other aggressively in private, a formal letter looking to lure a performer to a company appeared impolitic. For his efforts, Smith "got hauled over the coals about that. I had only been a producer something like a month and I very nearly lost my job. My job was very nearly terminated because of that." He would learn and survive.

Smith insists that a producer "had to really believe in whatever he was recording. He had to really believe that this should sell records. In other words, to appreciate what his artist offered." Smith's position was that "I wouldn't sign them

[7] Reid would become a manager for both Elton John and the group Queen.

unless I had that kind of belief." Nevertheless, he did make exceptions, including a band that helped to define the end of one era and the beginning of the next.

Pink Floyd

When the man whom John Lennon often called "Normal" entered the UFO club on Tottenham Court Road in early 1967 (or possibly its predecessor, the Daytripper, in late 1966), he felt dismayed. The band's managers had promised Smith that no other group in London could compare. Smith had heard about Pink Floyd, but what he heard and saw left him dumbfounded: "I didn't really understand what the hell they were getting at with this psychedelia. That was not my bag at all." In addition to the rambling guitar and keyboard solos, "we didn't have an awful lot in common in terms of their songs and lyrics. To be honest, I didn't know what the hell they were talking about very often." Nevertheless, London buzzed about Pink Floyd, their *son et lumière* presentations (in imitation of San Francisco light shows), and their unorthodox stage presentations, which attracted a devoted (if chemically altered) audience. Smith decided, "Well, this could be the start of something big, I suppose." Smith and EMI would have known that other labels were interested in Pink Floyd: they couldn't afford to pass them up. Manager Peter Jenner and Pink Floyd wanted the financial support of EMI. EMI wanted a reliable hand in control of the recording process. They pushed Smith, although "I couldn't have any musical belief in them because I didn't really understand their kind of music. In fact, to me, it wasn't really music." Nevertheless, the uniqueness of the band did interest him.

Difference mattered, particularly for singers. A unique voice could sell an initial hit single, but subsequent hits depended upon the marketability of an identifiable voice. Smith looked for "the sound of their voice, because you were looking for something different: you didn't want to sign somebody that was trying to sound like Tom Jones, because that had already been done." When working with musicians, Smith looked "for an individual identification. You would think you could sell some records on that, and it often proved exactly right. Aesthetically, it shouldn't really be there, but there it [was] at the top of the charts."

Appropriately, both Smith and the members of Pink Floyd wanted to explore new sonic realms: "I was very interested in sounds and, of course, this is something that I did share with Pink Floyd. They were very much interested in sounds, and perhaps sounds I had not even heard before. So we did spend a lot of time in trying to develop those kind of sounds." Together, they established a recognizable sonic identity and, in the process, helped to set the stage for a wave of musical and aural innovation.

When Pink Floyd signed with EMI, they released a recording they had already made with engineer Joe Boyd, "Arnold Layne." However, the corporation insisted that Smith produce new sessions. Drummer Nick Mason summarized the new approach, saying, "Norman was more interested in making us sound like a classical rock band. It was a bit like the George Martin thing, a useful influence to have. But I think Joe would have given Syd [Barrett] his head, let him run in a freer way" (Palachios 1998: 121). However, Peter Jenner believes that Smith's experience and familiarity with Abbey Road made for good recordings:

> I suspect that Norman was rather better for them [than Boyd]. He had been the Beatles' engineer up to that time and had graduated to become a producer and he tapped them into that Beatles tradition. He helped them make good records. . . . There was enough madness flying around and the sanity and the boringness of Norman helped ensure that the Floyd made hits. (Palachios 1998: 121)

The challenge for Smith and the members of Pink Floyd resided in the former's association with EMI and the latter's identification with the counterculture.

In Smith's first Pink Floyd production, "See Emily Play," guitarist-songwriter Syd Barrett referenced the Games for May festival at Queen Elizabeth Hall on 12 May 1967. The recording (released the next month) was a top-ten hit and introduced the band's unusual sound palette of electric organ, sliding guitars, and droning ostinatos. The song's core musical materials exude normality: a verse with a refrain stated three times. But between each of these verses, the production inserts material. Between the second and third verses, the band engages in parallel guitar and organ solos over a drum and bass drone that, in a live performance, would have been an opportunity for an extended improvisation. In the recording, Smith apparently has edited the improvisation to bring the disk under the common three-minute time limit. Immediately after the first verse, Smith inserts the "wound-up piano" effect (with guitar) that he and Martin had used with the Beatles, playing a musical interlude that contrasts dramatically with the rest of the song. Although he uses the sped-up piano feature throughout most of the recording, in this break he seeks to imitate the sound of a toy piano and to evoke childlike play (implying the song's title character).

In his subsequent productions with Pink Floyd, Smith would help them to define their sound such that eventually, the value of his expertise would diminish. He had enabled them to pursue their own path.

Smith on Producing

In coaching musicians, Smith insists that a producer "has got to tread lightly. Obviously, you do not want to upset anybody, so you [have] to be careful." A producer might "suggest a different way of phrasing a line, or, whatever, and if they agreed, then they would go ahead and do it. If they didn't then, well, I wouldn't exactly say that they would argue with you." Indeed, EMI producers had an advantage others often did not: they had EMI's recording studios in Abbey Road. In general, Smith found that, when new artists came into the studio, "they would be so struck by the fact that they were coming into Abbey Road" that, even though he was "an unknown producer and a newcomer, they would naturally accept" his recommendations. Essentially, "they were overwhelmed by the fact they'd been signed by EMI and were coming in to Abbey Road to record."

Smith has an unusual place in the music-studio culture of 1960s London: he moved from the engineer's chair to the producer's without having to leave the country. Glyn Johns (who engineered for the Who and the Rolling Stones) qualifies as the only other well-known recording professional to start as a musician, become an engineer, and eventually produce. Smith believes that his personal history significantly shaped his approach to being a producer:

> When I first applied to the production department at the BBC, they told me, "You've got to come up through the rank[s]." And then, it made me think, when I became [a] producer, after being an engineer, really and truly in my book, that was the right way to become a producer: to go through the engineering side first of all. If possible, of course, also be a musician, and that would be my ideal producer.

Smith certainly had his successes in the late sixties. Despite his reputation as a straitlaced and sober technician, Smith oversaw the creation of two of the era's most important psychedelic albums: Pink Floyd's *Piper at the Gates of Dawn* and the Pretty Things' *S. F. Sorrow*.

Competition between producers was real. Limited socializing with other producers and a subsequent sense of isolation could pervade their professional lives. The number of hours devoted to recording in the studio also placed a strain on Smith's personal life. In his early years at Abbey Road, extended late-night sessions were rare because of the studio's location in a residential neighborhood. The reason was not so much sound leakage from the studios, but rather people "getting into cars, making any noise, and shouts that the groups would do." In well-heeled St. John's Wood, "that's the kind of thing that restricted the hours at Abbey Road." Smith remembers "many all-night sessions," after which he found himself coming "home for a shower and maybe a little bite to eat for breakfast, with just two hours" before having "to be back in the studio again." He adds that such a situation "happened quite a few times."

JOE MEEK

Where Norman Smith was a musician who became an engineer, Joe Meek (1929–1967) was an engineer who was never much of a musician. And, where Smith surprised people when the mild-mannered, sober, bespectacled technocrat with a Windsor-knot tie produced some of the landmark psychedelic works of the era, they expected weird things from Meek. More significantly, where Smith always seemed to be most happy in the corporate environment, advancing from tape operator to producer, Meek jumped from the corporate ship early in his career. Working for someone else never constituted a happy situation for him—and thus emerged one of Britain's first independent producers in the age of rock 'n' roll.

Robert George Meek's birth in the rural town of Newent in northwest Gloucestershire on the eve of the Great Depression came in a context from which escape would become a necessity. John Repsch (2000), whose biography constitutes the most extensive work on this British icon, describes Meek's father, George, as an ex-farmer who shifted through a variety of occupations and his mother (Biddy Birt) as a primary school teacher who played the piano. George's mother (with whom they lived) called their second son "Joe" (rather than Robert) in memory of a son she had lost in the First World War. By the time he was five, Joe had become fascinated with gramophones and begged for one for Christmas, thus beginning a long relationship with recording technology. A life-changing event came while he was playing with a mechanical player driven by a spring-wound mechanism; the young Meek discovered he could record on the inner grooves of a disk by shouting into the amplifying cone (Repsch 2000: 7).

Meek both inherited his father's mercurial character and bridled at his rural farm town's conservative expectations. Routinely wearing dresses in his self-produced plays seems only to have won him ridicule and worse from his schoolmates, brothers, and father, such that music and electronics became his refuges. Fate intervened when, after an artillery demonstration in the town square, an explosion severely burned his hands. During the six months of his recovery, he began his habit of collecting and rebuilding bits of electronic equipment. At thirteen, Meek began experimenting with a magnetic pickup and building his "first one-valve radio" and "one-valve amplifier" (Repsch 2000: 15). In 1948, at nineteen, Meek entered the RAF's radar program for his national service, servicing outposts in the West Country, and then returning to Newent ostensibly to become a radio and television repairman. However, he never gave up his interest in writing and recording dramas, and he used the shops where he worked to build tape recorders and disk cutters and to continue to play with recording techniques.

Meek in London

Moving to London in 1954 (again ostensibly to repair radios and televisions), he answered a newspaper ad for IBC (Independent Broadcasting Corporation) and soon transferred within the company to a position recording a weekly program for Radio Luxembourg. "I went as the junior engineer and had to rig the microphones and run cables, but I really enjoyed every minute of it" (Repsch 2000: 28). In addition, his responsibilities included editing out mistakes and ensuring that the program fit a thirty-minute broadcast. Very quickly, promotions led to occasional recording sessions for Pye and, over the next year, to balance engineer when he began recording music on a regular basis.

As the smallest of the major corporations, Pye had limited studio space in the fifties and employed a combination of its in-house and independent artists and repertoire managers to provide the content the company released. In April 1956, as an engineer, Meek recorded one of the few trad jazz records to enter the pop charts: Humphrey Lyttelton's "Bad Penny Blues." The producer, Denis Preston, places the success of the session on Meek's ability to capture the sound of the band: "He had a drum sound—that forward drum sound which no other engineer at that time would have conceived of doing, with that echo. And it was the sound that Joe Meek created that made that record for Humphrey Lyttelton" (Repsch 2000: 31). Part of his success derived from his employment at IBC, where film soundtracks and sound effects were often more common than pop music recordings. With willing artists and repertoire managers, he eagerly applied to recordings the latest technologies for compression, limiting, and echo to invent sound environments that other studios religiously avoided. And what the existing system could not provide, he would alter, which put him at odds with others using the facilities.

His father's son, Meek could often be less than meek when it came to working with others. IBC studio manager Allen Stagg remembers, "The guiding force in Joe's life was selfishness; he was ruthless in his selfishness." Although the prevailing approach in British studios was a reliance on diversification and the stratification of tasks, Stagg notes that Meek "could never ever work as a team man." Moreover, at IBC, "people were very team-minded because it was necessary for everybody's success to be able to rely on somebody else" (Repsch 2000: 38). Given the success of other London studio teams, Stagg's complaints about Meek express the heart of the British recording industry in this era: cooperation paid off while individuality exposed the entire studio to danger. Repsch's well-researched biography puts Stagg's criticisms down to envy and homophobia; however, the evidence allows for a more textured interpretation.

Meek certainly exhibited an instinctive facility with electronics and a well-nourished proclivity for recording. His experiments had begun with the sound-scapes of childhood plays; however, his musical and technological ideas were hardly autochthonous, as they built on the innovations of others. Meek not only wanted to control his environment, he was absolutely sure that his way was the only way to make recordings. As his brother Eric described the family penchant, "All the Meeks thinks they'm pretty clever at theirselves" (Repsch 2000: 12).

As for homophobia, Repsch accurately describes the British legal stance and the broad public attitude toward homosexuality in the sixties. Even in the theatrical and musical arts, where gays were hardly an unknown, many found Meek's overt sexual identity disconcerting, exacerbated no doubt by his apparent general contempt for the work of others. Nevertheless, however inhospitable Britain may have been to homosexuals in the fifties and sixties, gays certainly had their niches, as managers Larry Parnes and Brian Epstein demonstrated. A studio like IBC, which dealt extensively with film and television, would probably have been even more accommodating for these individuals.

Repsch argues that the hostility of IBC engineers to Meek derived from his homosexuality, compounded by jealousy of his successes. Perhaps even more important was Meek's delicate mental state. His assistant Jimmy Lock described his employer's situation: "There's no doubt about it that there was a certain madness always within Joe—there's no question. This delicate balance between Joe in a happy mood and Joe just becoming impossible was a thin thread" (Repsch 2000: 41). Meek's principal problem involved his insistence on control, and when someone challenged his power, he could fly into uncontrollable rages. Indeed, perhaps his search for control over his recording environment related to his problematic control of himself.

By 1957, rather than helping producers to capture the sound they wanted, Meek began telling artists and repertoire managers what he thought they should do. One of them, Arthur Frewin, described a particular session where Meek told a producer, "If you can't bloody well do the job right, don't do it" (Repsch 2000: 45). He could also ruthlessly berate musicians if their performances did not match his expectations, despite his own very modest musical abilities. Ironically (and perhaps frustratingly), Meek would come to rely upon musicians to translate and realize his ideas, despite how vague they might be.

Meek Produces

Typical of Meek's desire to control his surroundings, his first solo experience found him writing, engineering, and producing a recording, which included rehearsing the skiffle group and renaming it Jimmy Miller and His Barbecues. For his song "Sizzling Hot," he enlisted the help of a piano-playing office assistant from Essex Music.[8] Charles Blackwell became Meek's musical interpreter, taking basic musical ideas and making them into songs. Leaving IBC, Meek found financial support to become an independent producer when Denis Preston decided to set up his own studio. In December 1957, Meek discovered a studio that Preston could purchase and that Meek could convert into a state-of-the-art recording facility. Just a few hundred feet down Lansdowne Road from the Holland Park underground station, the two basement rooms were small but suitable, and Meek commenced spending Preston's money. He installed EMI BTR stereo decks and designed a mixing board that would become the core of the Lansdowne Recording Studios.[9] In August, Meek became its manager and principal recording engineer at a salary of £1000 per year plus 5 percent of the studio's profits (Repsch 2000: 63). The studio functioned much the way that IBC had, except that Meek and Preston focused on music, the former concentrating on pop and the latter on jazz.

At Lansdowne, Meek continued to hone his skills as a producer, pushing his own songs and experimenting with recording techniques. Then, in November 1959, recordings that Meek had produced and engineered scored on the British charts. On 30 October, Emile Ford and the Checkmates' "What Do You Want to Make Those Eyes at Me For" (co-produced with Ford) and Mike Preston's "Mr. Blue" both entered the British charts. Both would sell well, with Ford's disk topping most British charts. Success emboldened Meek and brought him into conflict with Denis Preston as he attempted to assert his opinions on his employer's productions. In early November 1959, their differences came to a head when Meek walked out in the middle of one of Preston's recording sessions. Preston fired him.

His eviction from Lansdowne merely served as a setback in Meek's ambitious plans. He had long been fascinated with disk cutters and now sought to set up his own record company, a significant challenge at the end of the fifties when Decca and EMI ruled the industry and even Pye had to scramble for a share of the market. Finding a like-minded promoter in William Barrington-Coupe, they established Triumph Records in a toy warehouse in Empire Yard, 538 Holloway Road, North London, on 25 February 1960. Meek now brought Charles Blackwell to Triumph as its music director; however, neither Barrington-Coupe nor Meek knew how to get their products into stores, dooming their disks and ultimately the company.

[8] Essex Music published a number of skiffle hits in the fifties, including "Rock Island Line." Meek would have run into Blackwell in the Essex offices in 4 Denmark Street.
[9] The Holland Park Lansdowne Recording Studios closed on 13 October 2006, and its main facilities moved to more spacious accommodations in Watford.

304 Holloway Road

Six months later, Meek found another backer in Major Wilfred Alonzo Banks and surrendered the idea of being a record company mogul, returning instead to the niche he had developed at IBC and Lansdowne as an independent producer. His first task was to sell recordings he had made for Triumph to Dick Rowe, who had taken the position of recording manager at Top Rank Records. However, Top Rank closed its doors almost immediately when Decca purchased it, bringing Rowe back to West Hampstead and leaving Meek with one less independent outlet to distribute his productions. Independent producers routinely encountered this kind of challenge.

Meek perennially had problems using other people's studios, especially in the matter of equipment. In September 1960, he began setting up a studio in his flat at 304 Holloway Road, on a busy North London traffic route used by truckers and merchants. The studio sat above a leather goods store and consisted of the main performance area on the second floor (the "bedroom" as some described it) with other rooms serving multiple functions (Repsch 2000: 95). According to one of Meek's assistants, Ted Fletcher, "The main studio itself was on the third floor" with the attic serving as a reverberation chamber. "The control room was a very small room of about eight feet square" (Cunningham 1998: 90). Everyone who visited or worked at the studio remembers the floor as covered with tape and cables.

Fletcher describes Meek's recording technique as beginning with a full-track recording on the EMI BTR/2, in part because that machine "had a tremendous overload margin" (Cunningham 1998: 90). He would then transfer the tape to the Lyric stereo deck where he would erase one track (leaving the accompaniment on one half the tape width). Having cleared a track, he would then add the vocal parts, both the solo and backing vocals, before sending the recording back to the BTR/2 and adding an additional track in the process. "He was pretty sensible because the backing track had only gone through one generation and yet he had two overlays and an original—three separate recordings" (Cunningham 1998: 90–91). He often then recopied the recording, added additional compression, and sometimes sped up the recording slightly. Both guitarist Joe Brown and bassist Chas Hodges remember another unusual method to Meek's recording techniques: rather than record their guitars with microphones, he took a lead directly from the amp or guitar (Cunningham 1998: 93).

With the collapse of Triumph, Meek needed a better way to get his songs and recordings promoted and began looking for a new publisher. Although Southern Music had one of the best promotional departments in the business (and he continued to work with them), Meek wanted assured airtime. Publishers Campbell Connelly had a unique arrangement. In the fifties, producers like George Martin scrambled to get their disks on programs like the BBC's *Housewives' Choice*. However, given the BBC's grip on British broadcasting, recording companies commonly bought time on Radio Luxembourg to promote their disks. Signal reception from Luxembourg in the United Kingdom varied with the weather, but the largely English-language station demonstrated few qualms about being commercial. Someone at Campbell Connelly hit upon the idea of forming a joint-venture publishing company with Radio Luxembourg: Ivy Music ensured that songs received airplay. As a composer with Campbell Connelly, Meek could get fifteen minutes five times a week on *Topical Tunes* (Repsch 2000: 98–99).

"Johnny Remember Me"

Meek, however, could not rely solely on his own compositions for the recordings he would produce. Nor could he count on always finding new artists. He needed to form alliances with songwriters, agents, managers, and promoters in order to ensure a supply of hit songs and artists. Consequently, he began working with a young songwriter from Southern Music, Geoff Goddard, and the Australian promoter Robert Stigwood. Goddard had been a student at the Royal Academy of Music with aspirations of becoming a singer, but found writing songs more exciting, while Stigwood demonstrated early his ability to secure contracts. Stigwood aggressively sought work for his clients, including the aspiring actor John Leyton, who attracted Meek's attention as a good-looking potential star with a modest voice. All he needed was the right song.

Stigwood managed to book Leyton onto an episode of the weekly television drama *Harpers West One*[10] in which his character would sing his latest recording. Opportunely for Meek and Goddard, neither the recording nor the song yet existed. Goddard—believing that Buddy Holly had dictated the solution to him in his sleep—brought Southern Music "Johnny Remember Me." "I had just opened my eyes. I always keep a tape recorder by my bed, and I sang that song into it without working on it at all" (Repsch 2000: 117). Following both supposed supernatural guidance and common sense, he "did the rounds of Denmark Street publishers," and Southern Music put Goddard and Stigwood together.

Joe Meek had something that major studios did not: the flexibility not only to record Leyton on short notice, but a willingness to work with him extensively. Moreover, Meek saw Leyton's untrained and untested voice as a blank canvas ready for electronic elaboration with an array of largely homemade equipment.

[10] The sixty-minute ITV1 drama series first aired on 26 June 1961 and ran until 1 January 1963.

He hired a local rock group, the Outlaws, as a house band to accompany his singers and to interpret the musical ideas for "Johnny Remember Me." Facilitating the creation of music, Charles Blackwell worked with Leyton to find a good key and to coach him with his singing (especially the singer's pitch intonation problems). Blackwell and the Outlaws then translated Meek's and Goddard's ideas into a performance.

In the recording process, Meek applied his homemade electronic reverberation to Leyton's voice and dubbed and redubbed, adding material every time he bounced the recording from one machine to the next. Leyton remembers that, during the session, "We did it over and over. Joe wanted plenty of exciting atmosphere in it, and it was a really exhilarating sound with the galloping, driving beat. He was getting all excited, slapping his leg and combing his quaff. I was singing along but my voice was dubbed on afterwards with those of the session singers" (Repsch 2000: 108). Meek created a noisy but distinctive montage of voices treated with layers of reverberation over a proto-disco rhythm. The voice in particular received considerable attention in the press when critics complained about the electronic treatment. Leyton responded in *Melody Maker* by saying, "My critics say all my records are just electronic—that I wouldn't succeed without echoes. But no record succeeds through technique alone. Even Frank Sinatra has echo effects. Pop records today must be as exciting as possible" (Repsch 2000: 130). Meek, naturally, supported Leyton, saying, "I try to inject punch and drive into my productions with John. But he is basically talented. He would have made headway with whoever put him on record" (ibid.).

The battle between Meek and the musical establishment (represented this time by musical director Martin Slavin in *Melody Maker*) consisted of one part clash of aesthetics and two parts advertising spin. Repsch interprets the series of exchanges in *Melody Maker*, *Disc*, and *Record Mirror* as an attack by threatened corporate producers on the brave outsider. However, the exchanges also drew considerable attention (and free advertising) to Meek's RGM studios, to his unique recording approach, and to Meek himself. With "Johnny Remember Me" on its way to the top of the British charts and lots of free advertising (including the premiere on the television series, where thousands saw Leyton perform), Meek felt in the driver's seat.

"Telstar"

The recording which received the most international attention, "Telstar" featured the Tornados and followed a year after "Johnny Remember Me." The launch of the first telecommunications satellite and the subsequent broadcast of President Dwight Eisenhower's greetings deeply inspired Meek, who had already produced a disk imagining a futuristic soundscape. As was his practice, he framed his songs more as impressions and left his musicians the task of deciphering the possibilities. "Telstar" was no different. The recording process involved Meek's usual practice of recording and re-recording material. Tornados drummer Clem Cattini describes Meek's method as "from one tape machine to another. It was one generation onto another. We basically recorded one track, played it back, and recorded another track, and bounced it from one tape recorder to another." In addition, Meek would "sometimes play tricks like, slow the tape down and we'd play on it, or speed the tape up and we'd play on it, so you got unnatural highs and lows."

"Telstar" possessed all of the characteristics of an early 1960s Meek production, with a tightly compressed sound that brought melody and accompaniment into the foreground. Sold to Decca, the recording steadily climbed the UK charts and then took hold in the United States, where it also climbed to the number one spot. An elated Meek felt vindicated, despite the almost obligatory challenge to the song's authorship and months of legal negotiations. As "Telstar" continued to dominate British charts at the end of 1962 and into the beginning of 1963, a sudden invasion of northerners disrupted his reign. The Beatles, Gerry and the Pacemakers, and other Liverpool and Manchester groups came bounding into London, leading a revolution that would change the British recording industry. Almost as soon as his recordings had established a unique and highly commercial sound quality, Meek's products were passé. He modified his approach and bought new equipment (an Ampex tape deck) so that he could create cleaner-sounding recordings.

A North London group founded by a hairdresser recorded Meek's most significant hit in the wake of the beat invasion of London's studios. Ken Howard and Alan Blaikley, having written "Have I the Right," sought a band both to record the song and to manage. After cruising dances and pubs in search of performers, they heard the Sheritons playing at the Mildmay Tavern[11] and began rehearsing "Have I the Right" with them. When Meek went to record them, he sought both to exploit the heavy four-four feel that pervaded that year's British charts in tunes as disparate as the Dave Clark Five's "Bits and Pieces" and the Beatles' "A Hard Day's Night." Where the Dave Clark Five stomped on the studio's floor, singer Denis D'ell remembers that Meek "lined us up on the stairs; Anne [sic] stayed on the bass drum. We had about four mikes to cover the length of the staircase, with bicycle pump clips under the stairs and he just clipped the mikes into them. For about an hour we all stood stomping in time with the music"

---

[11] This was located at 130 Balls Pond Road, Islington, not far from Holloway Road.

(Repsch 2000: 232). Before Pye would release "Have I the Right" in mid-June, it renamed the group the Honeycombs (to reflect their unique use of a female drummer, Ann "Honey" Lantree, and her occupation as a hairdresser). It took until the third week of July before the recording entered the British charts; however, the recording eventually climbed in sales to the top.

Unfortunately, as the mid-sixties gave way to the era of psychedelia, Meek's mental state deteriorated, and he became increasingly paranoid and aggressive. On one occasion, he threw a new Ampex tape deck down the stairs after Clem Cattini. Moreover, musicians in this era increasingly felt empowered to interpret what they heard. In one such instance, while recording with a new incarnation of the Tornados, Meek threatened drummer Mitch Mitchell. Mitchell insisted on putting in fills where Meek demanded a simple beat. The organist, Dave Watts, recalls, "The next thing, he [Meek] come in with a shotgun with the pin pulled back. He came straight across the floor, no smile at all on his face—an absolute mad look on his face—and poked it right at him. He said, 'If you don't do it properly, I'll blow your f—— head off!'" (Repsch 2000: 249). Mitchell simplified his pattern. However, Meek's condition worsened. In February 1967, he no longer felt able to tolerate his landlady's complaints about the noise and the rent. After murdering her with the shotgun, he put the gun to his own head and pulled the trigger.

MICKIE MOST

One of the most musical of the independent producers, Mickie Most (b. Michael Peter Hayes, 1938–2003) adopted an eloquently adaptive and consistently successful approach to recording. The artists he brought into the studio routinely found their popular voice, prompting other would-be stars to seek him for their shot at fame such that, by the mid-sixties, disk jockeys and reviewers alike would automatically give every "Mickie Most production" listening preference. In the summer of 1964 alone, Most had hit recordings by the Animals ("House of the Rising Sun"), the Nashville Teens ("Tobacco Road"), and Herman's Hermits ("I'm into Something Good") on British and American charts.

A military family, the Hayes household in Harrow (northwest of metropolitan London) could pick up the American Forces Network from which the young Mickie soon developed a taste for American rhythm-and-blues and, subsequently, rock 'n' roll. A foot injury in a sheet metal factory preempted his military service, and he employed his recuperation time to develop his guitar technique. As rock and skiffle grew in popularity, a guitar-playing and singing Hayes found work at the 2i's in Old Compton Street, waiting on tables and occasionally performing (see Buskin 2003; Tobler and Grundy 1982). He and school friend

Alex Wharton formed a rock duo, calling themselves the Most Brothers, which he describes as "a very good band for that time" (Oldham 2000: 54). Membership variously included Hank Marvin, Bruce Welch (who had recently arrived from Newcastle), and Jet Harris, all of whom would soon be lured away to accompany Cliff Richard. Mickie Hayes also became "Mickie Most."

His first experience with the recording industry came when Decca signed the band in an attempt to cash in on what it saw as the fleeting popularity of rock 'n' roll. He remembers, "The British record companies at that time took tremendous advantage of artists," such that he "never knew what the royalty was on my contract"; moreover, he "didn't care. The royalties meant nothing. I made records" (Oldham 2000: 54). Most remembers (Leigh and Firminger 1996), "They would tell you that you were in the studio next week. The A&R man would say, 'this is the song you'll sing' and you would work out the key with an arranger." The singer typically had no choice in repertoire or style and functioned merely as a vehicle for the creation of the music. Once at the recording studio, he remembers, "you sing in a booth with the band they've booked outside"; the singer's usual band was often excluded. Nevertheless, the system worked, and Mickie Most would adopt this approach in his own productions, often replacing band members with reliable sessioneers.

Finally, of his years as a recording artist he notes, "You never go upstairs to hear the tape. Suddenly a voice comes over the PA, 'That's a good take, see you in the pub.' You don't hear the record until it is pressed. If you don't like it, there's nothing you can do about it. Artists were not in a position to say, 'I don't like it.'" Succinctly and in a very class-conscious way, Most describes the rule as "[w]here the carpet begins, you end" (Leigh with Firminger 1996: n.p.).

In 1959, the Most Brothers disbanded, and the twenty-one-year-old singer followed his heart and family instincts: "Christine was from South Africa, and when she returned there her family said I would have to follow her if I wanted something more permanent" (Buskin 2003). Her family might have presumed that their move back to Africa would thwart the aspiring rock star's intentions to marry their daughter: they were wrong. So, they placed one more impediment between the lovers: "they then made it clear that I would have to spend four years there as they didn't know me" (ibid.). He did, and they would.

While establishing these familial connections, he continued to pursue his performing career, scoring a string of South African hits with covers of American rock 'n' roll records, developing an ear for hit songs, and gaining invaluable experience at how to get good sounds in a studio. "I was doing it all myself, engineering and producing" (Tobler and Grundy 1982: 126). Meanwhile, his former school and band mate Alex Wharton had rechristened himself "Alex Murray" and had become one of the youngest artists and repertoire managers at Decca.[12] During a hiatus from production in 1963, Murray visited Most in South Africa and encouraged him to return to his career in Britain.

When Most reencountered Britain, music had seriously changed: rock groups had displaced crooners, and soon Most found himself as the opening act for the Everly Brothers and the Rolling Stones. "When I returned from South Africa the 2Is thing had disappeared. There were a few more chords around than the three I left behind: there were five or six now, it was a bit more musical. Also there was a great interest in Chicago blues" (Oldham 2000: 204). Most immediately recognized that "this was what I'd been looking for since I'd arrived back in England." When he had left the United Kingdom, "the music scene was really bland, with people like Eden Kane and John Leyton," but now the Beatles and similar groups were scoring hits, and he found himself "fortunate to be in the right place at the right time" (Buskin 2003). London had also changed culturally: "It was very difficult to tune people in to this new way of thinking. You had the fashion, Mary Quant, Carnaby Street, the sexual revolution, the pill . . . , a whole different thing. It was actually very hard to try and tune people in who were ten years older" (Oldham 2000: 191).

In 1963, independent producers like Joe Meek and Shel Talmy were producing hits. "When I came back from South Africa the main reason was to produce records. I produced all my own records in South Africa; I felt I had more to offer as a producer than anybody else" (Oldham 2003: 206). The industry had begun to accept the idea that young independents had a flexibility and cultural sympathy that older A&R managers might not. Of course, independent producers also took many of the fiscal risks up front, saving the corporation valuable development funds. Nevertheless, Most believed that the changes unnerved corporations: "The record companies didn't like the idea of you doing things that were outside the norm." As an independent, Most "just signed the groups to myself and I financed them, offering them a royalty and a deal, and then it was up to me to make this deal work" (Buskin 2003).

Animals in Kingsway

His South African experience had taught him that he needed good material and that the best material came from across the Atlantic, so in 1963 he headed to America, where he heard "Baby Let Me Take You Home," which Bob Dylan[13] had

---

[12] Alex Murray would produce the first Moody Blues hit, "Go Now."

[13] Dylan calls his version "Baby Let Me Follow You Down," which he credits to Eric von Schmidt, from whom Dylan had learned the song. However, von Schmidt would have learned the song from another source.

recorded. Most claims not to have heard the Dylan version, but "a single I picked up at Chess Records in Chicago."[14] In addition to the convenience of the song being "traditional" (i.e., uncopyrighted), Most liked "the feel of it, the [backing] track more than the melody" (Tobler and Grundy 1982: 127a). One of his stops while touring with the Stones had been Newcastle in the far north of England, where a local band, the Animals, impressed him enough to invite them to London to record. Most's enthusiasm convinced them to make the trip and to record "Baby Let Me Take You Home." He promised to bring them to London, where Most would pay for the recording session, and "if you don't like it, then that's it—you've got nothing to lose" (Tobler and Grundy 1982: 126b). The recording fared well, but not nearly as well as their second release.

From that same first Bob Dylan album, another tune, "House of the Rising Sun," apparently impressed Most as an even better vehicle for them.[15] Eager to record while the buzz on the first release still resounded, he booked them on a "sleeper train" and "picked them up early in the morning" along with their equipment. He recorded them in Kingsway Studios during a three-hour session beginning at 8:00 a.m.; however, "by 8:15, take two," he told them, 'That's the one'" (Buskin 2003). The Animals-Most recording of "House of the Rising Sun" illustrates both Most's attitude at that point toward recording and some of the pitfalls of the era. The band arrived with the song well rehearsed: "I didn't dictate the arrangement, I'd just give them the song, which would usually be very different from the way the Animals would eventually do it, but I'd tell them to listen to the words and the melody, because that's the key to it. Then if they could roughen it up a bit with their sound, it would self-produce" (Tobler and Grundy 1982: 128).

The band's arrangement of the song builds, adding instruments and modifying playing patterns to create tension. Singer Eric Burdon and the band deliver a convincing performance; he drops his voice at the beginning of sections and wails toward the end, a feat no less impressive given the time of day they made the recording. Unfortunately, organist Alan Price's claim to royalties for the arrangement of this traditional tune increased the ill will of a band in which tension between the singer (Burdon) and the founder (Price) festered. Perhaps one of the

---

[14] It is unclear to which recording Most refers. A number of East Coast folk singers had this song (also known as "Baby Let Me Lay It on You" and "Momma Don't You Tear My Clothes") in their repertoires in the early sixties, and the song had been around as early as the thirties.

[15] Richard Green (1964a: 5), in an interview with the Animals, observes, "Certainly every time I have visited the Animals in the past few months, out has come a Bob Dylan LP and 'House of the Rising Sun' has been played."

most remarkable aspects of this recording is its length: approximately four and a half minutes (utilizing most of the available space on a microgroove disk) in an age when the two and a half minute single was the norm. The U.S. distributor (MGM) divided the recording in two, but Columbia issued it in the United Kingdom without edits. Most argued that the length of the recording was immaterial, "if it's boring then it's too long, and if it's not boring, it's got to be right" (Tobler and Grundy 1982: 127b).

The combination of a carefully crafted and convincing performance and the extended use of the medium meant a compelling product that was at once acceptable as a pop recording and effective as a blues recording. Indeed, the length probably contributed to a sense of authenticity for listeners in 1964. Most's production places the instruments prominently in the recording mix, with Burdon's voice slightly distanced through reverberation, while the various doublings of guitar, organ, and bass enrich the instrumental timbres. With this recording, Most knew instinctively that the performance worked:

> There has to be that bit of magic. The song, the recording; the whole thing has to add up in my mind to a hundred, and when I hear it I go, "That's it!" At other times, I might hear a great song, but the arrangement isn't doing it for me, so I'll rework it and often that'll turn out to be what is needed. I just seem to have the ability to do that, I don't know why. (Buskin 2003)

"Tobacco Road"

When Most had first returned to Britain as a singer, agent Don Arden had booked him on programs and, through these gigs, Most had first heard the Animals, whom Arden was also booking. Now that Most had triumphed with the Animals, Arden proposed another band, hoping Most would duplicate the magic. The Nashville Teens were from the London suburbs and, like many other British bands, had done their time in Hamburg. On the strength of his Animals success, Most convinced Decca that the Nashville Teens performing another gritty tune could be just as successful. For the producer, the session was "simple": "They were doing this song 'Tobacco Road' on stage, and I thought it would be a hit" (Tobler and Grundy 1982: 128). The recording they made at IBC features a prominent bass line, a musical characteristic that would also become a trademark of Animals recordings (e.g., "We Gotta Get Out of This Place"). The recording is also noisier than his Animals recording in that the instruments are more distorted, possibly because of the volume at which they were playing in the studio. "Tobacco Road" too reached into the upper parts of the British and American charts.

The song's theme of the poor making it rich and returning to clean up the neighborhood would have been a stretch for a suburban middle-class Weybridge band, but the idea of a working-class protagonist making it good and returning to fix the neighborhood suited contemporary romantic notions about British class struggle. Nevertheless, the contract terms gave the group a jolt of fiscal reality. The arrangement that Most and Arden made for the Nashville Teens as recording artists, while typical of the time, made them far from wealthy. Their contract rewarded the band with seven-eighths of a penny for each disk. Selling approximately 200,000 copies in the United Kingdom and 600,000 in the United States, their net take for "Tobacco Road" was 2,912 pounds, 11 shillings, and 5 pence, which, when divided, meant that each member of the six-piece band received about £486 (see Rogan 1988: 91).

"I'm into Something Good"?

Thus far, Most's hits had been with gritty tunes performed by bands with a bluesy edge. But he understood that to tap into a softer and potentially more lucrative portion of the teen market, he needed something different. The song he had in mind, "I'm into Something Good," struck him as "really catchy." All he needed was "somebody youthful-looking" to perform and sell the recording (Buskin 2003). Given his success that summer, managers lobbied him to make their charges the next British pop stars. One photo caught his eye: "Herman's Hermits' management had called me many times and asked me to take a look at them, so I said, 'Send me a photograph,' and as soon as I saw the photo I envisaged Peter Noone as a young [President] Kennedy" (ibid.). Sending them a disk of the song, he "told them to learn the song by Sunday," at which point he brought them into the studio (ibid.).

Most was sure the song would work: "I was always responsible for choosing the material." Nevertheless, in a tight spot, he would go with what they already knew. By working with groups that had been working "ballrooms and clubs where they were maybe playing for two hours a night," he knew that they often had "quite a lot of repertoire." Thus, when pressed to create recordings quickly, he turned to their song list, just as George Martin had done with the Beatles in February 1963. In this case, Most received "a phone call from MGM in America saying they needed an album by Thursday." Bringing Herman's Hermits back to the studio, he drew on their stage routine, which included "something about 'Mrs. Brown.'" When MGM released the song "Mrs. Brown You've Got a Lovely Daughter" as a single, "it sold well, over three quarters of a million in one day" (Tobler and Grundy 1982: 129).

A pattern emerges in these recordings: Most needed studio efficiency and, with his success, could afford the resources that allowed him to take some of the chance out of the process. Despite his recollection that the band learned the song and then returned a few days later to record "I'm into Something Good," session musicians clearly remember participating in this recording. More specifically, in the case of "I'm into Something Good," Herman's Hermits had no pianist (who has a modest solo in the recording), and the backup vocals are clearly the work of professional singers, not guitarists who sang occasionally. Thus, perhaps a more complete story is that the band learned the song, but Most augmented them for the recording session. In another context, he comments that he relied on session musicians for his recordings of this band and others: "I always used to use the people who I'd used on the Herman's Hermits records, the session guys" (Tobler and Grundy 1982: 131). Guitarist Vic Flick remembers that, in the sixties, "there was a whole big thing in the press about this, 'Is it them or is it the ghosts we're listening to,'" and he specifically remembers recording at Kingsway Studios, particularly the subsequent Herman's Hermits tune, "Silhouettes."

For reasons both economic and aesthetic, Most seldom pushed for complicated music, even if he recognized that trend with other producers and artists: "I thought that [George Martin] did the right thing with the Beatles, but if I'd tried to make Herman's Hermits more musical, I'd have lost the little charm they had." Consequently, his recordings were seldom protracted affairs: "we'd still start sessions at seven in the evening, and I'd have a table booked at the Italian restaurant in Romilly Street for ten-thirty. I'd meet my wife there for dinner, I'd never be late, and by that time, the record would be finished, mixed, boxed-up, labeled and probably on its way to America" (Tobler and Grundy 1982: 129).

Making the Most of Donovan

In the wake of his 1964 successes, Most continued working with the Animals and Herman's Hermits, as well as with performers like the Seekers, Lulu, and even American Brenda Lee; but some of his best-known recordings were with the Scottish folksinger Donovan Leitch. When Donovan first emerged on the British scene, he was a protégé of songwriter Geoff Stephens, who rightly saw potential in the young bohemian. He, Peter Eden, and Terry Kennedy helped to promote the singer and produced early recordings like "Catch the Wind," which drew both comparisons with Bob Dylan and the recognition that Donovan was a gifted artist. Stephens remembers, "I happened upon Donovan through a friend of mine, because I lived in South End and Donovan was playing down there in a café, which I knew very well. We got him twelve slots on a major television show, *Ready Steady Go!* without any record contract." However, as the sixties became psychedelic and Donovan's involvement with drugs increased, Stephens and Eden separated from Donovan. His booking agent, Ashley Kozak, replaced them as manager, which led to American Allen Klein renegotiating the recording contracts and, consequently, Mickie Most taking over as producer.

Thus far, the performers whom Most had produced seldom wrote their own material. Songwriter Donovan had a different problem: an apparent slump in his career. Not surprising, given Bob Dylan's mid-sixties rock transformation, the obvious strategy emerged to electrify Donovan. Their vehicle would be "Sunshine Superman." The catalyst would be musicians John Cameron and Spike Heatley, who "worked hard on an arrangement," so that when they "went into the studio at two o'clock on a Sunday afternoon," they had it finished "by five o'clock" (Tobler and Grundy 1982: 131). Donovan indicates that the recording session was a bit more complicated, describing the song as "a three-chord Latin rocker" with harpsichord: "Baroque & Roll!" Leitch recalls that, "as soon as the unusual array of sounds leapt out of the speakers in the control room, Mickie's face lit up with delight. He knew this was a hit single. He just knew" (Leitch 2005: 124–125).

Over a year later, after renouncing hallucinogenic drugs and deeply impressed by Jimi Hendrix, Donovan returned from a Maharishi Mahesh Yogi meditation retreat in India with a song ostensibly about bards. Although he initially wanted to give the song "Hurdy Gurdy Man" to Hendrix, Most insisted that this constituted the next single and tried to get Hendrix to play on the recording. (Hendrix was on tour and unavailable.) Again, they relied on session musicians, one of whom also served as music director: John Paul Jones. The performance begins with Donovan humming, his voice modulated with a tremolo unit. When he begins singing the first verse, he accompanies himself on an acoustic guitar. The arrival of the first part of the chorus introduces the electric guitar, drums, and bass into the mix and, with the second half of the chorus, Most adds the tambura (an Indian string instrument used for buzzing drones) and double-tracks Donovan's voice. The second verse drops back in intensity, but the double-track now shows noticeable reverberation. The second statement of the chorus starts out the same as the first, but the second half drops some of the reverberation, bringing the voice closer psychologically to the listener. After a suitably intimidating guitar solo, Most closes the performance with the second half of the chorus and Donovan doubling his voice at the octave. Thus, the performance continually builds and evolves, seldom repeating itself exactly, and always leaving the listener with something new.

Most Producing

Mickie Most maintains that he was not attempting to impose a particular imprint on any of the artists with whom he worked: "I never went for a sound, not like Shel Talmy. I tried to make the artist and the sound work" (Oldham 2003: 191). And so, we see him matching material with artists and seeking the best ways to present those ideas. However, his methods were far from entirely intuitive and involved experimentation to find the right combination of music, arrangement, performance, and sonic atmosphere. He rationalizes that sometimes, no matter how good the recording is, if "it was the wrong timing for the record; it came out too early or too late, we didn't pick up the airplay, whatever—but if it doesn't succeed, it doesn't succeed, and making excuses is a negative. You just have to say, 'OK, I goofed, I've got to try harder next time'" (Buskin 2003).

Donovan recalls that Most did have a strategy and philosophy for putting together arrangements: "Mickie related the pop form to three gears on the car: pull away in first, go down to second for the first chorus, go into third for the second verse and go back to the chorus again" (Oldham 2003: 234). On recordings like "House of the Rising Sun" and "Hurdy Gurdy Man," the arrangements build in musical intensity in predictable ways, starting quietly, ratcheting up in intensity, and dropping back before taking off again.

However, Most also understood the inherent tension that advances in recording equipment were bringing to the industry: "As we moved towards the late '60s things were changing technically. We went from mono to stereo, four-track to eight-track to 16-track, and things obviously began to take longer, but I personally like to be in and out of the studio. I just can't keep things up for that amount of time; it's too long" (Buskin 2003). Like others commenting on changes in the recording process in the sixties, Most appreciated the efficiency and the spontaneity of the old recording sessions. He notes that he made "House of the Rising Sun" with the Animals in fifteen minutes and that no number of retakes and editing would have made it a more successful recording. Indeed, such work might have made it worse. "As you get older you don't want to waste so much time doing something that you used to do in three hours. We used to do a whole single and maybe a spare 'B' side in a three-hour session—certainly we'd get the master done—and even all of those Donovan records, some of which were quite complicated, were done in three hours" (ibid.).

Record executive Peter Knight, Jr., describes Most's uncanny ability: "He had the most successful track record ever of any producer, because he had the extraordinary ability of finishing a record, standing back, and saying 'Nah. It didn't work.' Whereas we would say, 'Hah. It's great! Let's get it out to promotion.' He was very objective about his own work."

SHEL TALMY

If Joe Meek felt like an outsider, then Shel Talmy (b. 1940) arrived celebrating that status. Talmy would produce some of the best-known performers of the era, and, interestingly, this American would help to shape seminal works by two of the most identifiably British songwriters of the era: Ray Davies and Pete Townshend.

Indeed, if the British recording industry sought at first to imitate American models, this American helped some artists to find an identifiably British voice. He also produced some of the most important recordings to come out of London in the sixties, including Kinks hits like "You Really Got Me," early Who recordings like "My Generation," and other gems, including the Easybeats' "Friday on My Mind" and Creation's "Making Time." Moreover, his recording sound both marked a departure from British production aesthetics and established a much-imitated model.

Shel Talmy grew up on the north side of Chicago, demonstrating his characteristic self-confidence as a child by appearing on a local television program, *Quiz Kids*. When his family moved to Los Angeles, he found himself in the same grade at Fairfax High School as Phil Spector.[16] He also developed an adolescent interest in rhythm-and-blues, which inspired him musically:

> I liked all kinds of music and spent a lot of time listening to the radio. I was very into what was being played as top 40, but I also did a lot of station flipping looking for new things. I still remember the first time I heard "Gee" by the Crows as something completely different that blew me away and made me a lifelong fan of R&B.[17]

After majoring in psychology at UCLA, he began pursuing what he thought would be a career in film by finding work at ABC, making contacts, and learning the basics of recording. One of those contacts was a British recording engineer, Phil Yeend, who mentored Talmy in his studio: "I told him I was interested in engineering and he very kindly volunteered to teach me." Yeend established his own recording facilities, Conway Studios, and Talmy went to work, learning what he could. "Engineering at that point wasn't like it is today, going to school for months. Two days later, I was doing my first session! Of course it was only a rotary pot board with 16 inputs, three-track and mono tape machines, and by today's standards, primitive outboard gear."

Talmy in London

On Yeend's recommendation, Talmy headed to London where, arriving in July 1962, he passed himself off as a burgeoning pop producer. Yeend had sensed that London studios would be hungry for American producers, even if the British wanted their own products. Talmy provided the opportunity to have an Ameri-

---

[16] Producers Herb Alpert and Jerry Lieber, both born in 1935, also attended Fairfax High School.

[17] "Gee" was a local hit in Los Angeles in December 1953.

can producing a British product. A Los Angeles friend at Capitol, Nik Venet, provided Talmy with credentials in the form of recordings, which Talmy passed off as his own to Dick Rowe at Decca. Talmy told Ritchie Unterberger in 1985:

> The two things I selected to play for Dick Rowe were the Beach Boys' "Surfin' Safari" and Lou Rawls' "Music in the Air." I played that, and Dick Rowe said, "Thank God you arrived, you start next week!" So I did. By the time they found out it was all bullshit, I'd already had my first hit, and they were very gentlemanly, never mentioned that they knew that I knew that they knew.

Talmy brought something very American to the British scene: independence. Although American corporations certainly had artists and repertoire managers, independent producers played an important role in the evolution of American popular music. If not for Sam Philips, the Chess Brothers, and numerous other independent producers, some of the most remarkable music of the fifties might never have been heard. Talmy knew from the beginning that, rather than a predictable but modest salary as a corporate producer, he wanted to own recordings and earn royalties: "When I walked into Decca and lied about all the records I'd produced, I also said I was an independent producer." His chutzpah relied on the knowledge that he "had nothing to lose." Moreover, he reasoned that the "worst they could say is 'goodbye,' and I had a deal waiting for me back in LA. So I said, 'I want royalties,' and fortunately for me Dick Rowe was very plugged into what was going on in America, and agreed."

Talmy saw the derivative British popular music industry as ripe for innovation. Unlike other British accounts of the equipment in London studios, Talmy remembers that the technology he encountered was "equivalent to America. What constituted 'state of the art' was pretty much the same [on] both sides of the Atlantic." However, elsewhere he has qualified that statement by saying, "The equipment, although basically the same, was still not up to what I'd worked with [in the United States]. It was more primitive" (Unterberger 1985). Initially, he recorded at Decca's West Hampstead studios, but soon came to prefer the facilities at IBC and Olympic,[18] where they were amenable to his distinctly un-British studio techniques. In particular, he found independent studios willing to allow musicians to play at club volume levels and recalls of the musicians with whom he worked, "that's where they 'loved me.' I used to crank up the volume!" His preference for IBC also came through Yeend, who had worked in that studio (Barnes 2006). As such, Talmy describes IBC as "the font of all engineers" and "the studio

---

[18] Talmy disliked EMI's facilities, finding "both acoustics and equipment inferior to many other studios." Moreover, EMI would certainly have restricted his access.

from which damn near every engineer who went anywhere started." Moreover, of the different London studios, IBC constituted "the state of the art." In particular, the people who worked there included a "very good maintenance staff and very good technical people. They were building their own boards and were innovative."

In 1962, Talmy had arrived to find British music to be "very polite." By contrast, Talmy describes himself as "not polite," by which he means "using distortion at the very beginning." In particular, he points to the Who recording of "Anyway, Anyhow, Anywhere" as one of the first to feature distortion. However, with this volume came other issues, notably the ability to control balances within the studio: "I spent a lot of time experimenting with sounds, especially with isolation of instruments so they wouldn't leak onto each other." Of course, with louder volumes, that separation became more difficult, so that he worked "within the technical abilities of the time to try to extend the envelopes." Like Joe Meek, Talmy tried to produce recordings that were loud so that when they were played in comparison to other releases, his would stand out. "I could cut hotter records than anybody did and I think for the most part I did" (Barnes 2006).

In recordings by the Kinks, the Who, and (later) the Creation, Talmy obtained a distinctive sound from the musicians with whom he worked, applying techniques he had learned at Conway back in Los Angeles. For example, he remembers, "I would pull up an instrument on two channels and ratchet up the distortion on one with a limiter, and keep the level down under the non-distorted channel. The 'apparent' level would sound much louder, and to this day I don't know if it was really louder or just sounded that way." Another distinctive aspect of his recordings was the sound of the drums: "I started miking drums with 12 mikes, another result of many hours of experimentation at Conway, and was told it couldn't be done, as phasing would make it impossible." That is, with different microphones on the same musical source, their placement could result in uneven levels as waves canceled each other. However, Talmy had already learned how to record this way. He recalls, "I just smiled and did it anyhow and a few months later, everybody was doing it." As an independent, if he failed, he suffered directly: "I was given latitude because I'd arrived with different techniques and was probably given enough rope to 'hang myself' if they didn't work."

Talmy Producing

As someone whose background was largely in the technical areas of recording, Talmy began by both coaching musicians and setting the recording parameters. His first major success came with the Irish trio the Bachelors, whom at first, he recalls, "played harmonica and did not sing" (Unterberger 1985a). He acted as his own music director, rehearsing them in his apartment "for six weeks, teaching them how to sing harmonies," and "almost got tossed out of the apartment" (ibid.). Like many British acts of the time, they imitated American models and their first hit, "Charmaine," was no different. Talmy told Ritchie Unterberger (1985a) that the recording took "15 minutes to do" and that he "hated it because it was pseudo-country and western, simply because they couldn't do authentic country and western." Nevertheless, the recording was a hit around the same time as the Beatles were having their first major success with "Please Please Me."

This success led to two things. First, he gained the attention of managers just as the British beat boom began to explode and every label sought to sign potential competitors to the Beatles. Second (and a corollary of the first), he grew frustrated with British agents, managers, and corporations, which became a theme during his British career. Indeed, his outsider status perhaps led some to believe that British individuals and institutions had privilege over his rights. As an outsider, he simply did not accept the idea that he had fewer rights than a Brit. In either case, Talmy proved himself a worthy foe (perhaps setting a precedent for Allen Klein). Talmy's first contest came when the Bachelors' manager, Phil Solomon, withheld royalties from "Charmaine," forcing Talmy to bring a lawsuit. He also learned that he had few allies within the corporations. In particular, Dick Rowe demonstrated Decca's unwillingness to support Talmy in the Solomon case and was at least complicit in the scheme. In short, an independent producer in London swam with the sharks.

Although the American soon found others interested in his abilities, all situations seemed fraught with problems. At Pye records, the chairman, Louis Benjamin, withheld funds (a common theme), and recording in Pye's Marble Arch studios presented a challenge in that they "were the smallest [and] certainly the most backward" of the corporate studios in London. However, the economic advantage of working with Pye artists (such as the Kinks) included easy access to their studios. "Their sessions didn't cost a whole lot, they had their own studios, so it wasn't a bad deal for Benjamin to give me a sort of deal. I brought in an artist, recorded, and nobody was going to spend a lot of money." However, dealing with the Pye management meant difficult negotiations over the ownership of recordings: "It was a trying time—Benjamin was not a wonderful person, but we marched on" (Unterberger 1985b).

Approach

With increased creative independence came the need to develop support mechanisms. With success, he hired assistants. The "techs were always good [and the] second engineers were usually very good." Indeed, some he found to be "outstanding." Initially, he remembers doing "a lot of my own recording until I decided to concentrate on producing and then found an engineer [Glyn Johns] who was compatible." Perhaps most important to Talmy in this era was having an engineer upon whom he could rely. He describes Glyn Johns to Unterberger as "an asset for me because he was such a super-duper engineer. He certainly helped with the sound, and one of the best things was, we had enormous rapport in that I didn't have to explain to him in any kind of detail what I wanted. By the time we'd worked together for a short time, he knew what I wanted and gave it to me" (1985b). However, John Entwistle failed to see the cooperation: "Glyn Johns was doing most of the work on the sessions and Shel was getting that for doing sweet FA, so we got out of that as quickly as we could" (Cunningham 1998: 106–107). From Talmy's perspective, having an engineer who knew what he wanted "freed me up to concentrate on producing a record and not have to worry about the sound" (Unterberger 1985b).

Perhaps as important, he needed to find ways to pay for the recording process, from renting studio time to paying session musicians. For session musicians, he would work "generally through a fixer," especially when "working for a label or if I needed strings and horns on my own productions. [I'd] tell him who I wanted, when I wanted them." Sometimes, the artist's management paid for these expenses; however, Talmy recalls, "I certainly did that on occasion. Most often as an indy producer, I financed my own production, which is what I did with the Who."

To a working-class musician barely out of his teens from West London, Talmy must have seemed a mystery. Brash and American, he represented how an outsider to the system could succeed. However, Talmy also wanted control over the music, including elements into which Entwistle had probably invested no little time and personal commitment. Talmy describes himself as a "hands-on producer. After I start working with an artist, I choose the material, I work out the arrangements with them, [and] I hire the musicians, if there were session people." As producer, he had the primary say in whether the arrangements were ready, so that he produced "the entire session starting with the sound all the way through to vocals and mixes and following it through to mastering." Like Most, musicians arrived with material already rehearsed; however, Talmy apparently pushed to put his own stamp on the process. Ray Davies, for example, suggests that some of the Kinks' material evolved this way in the studio.

Talmy steadfastly avoided getting involved with the professional lives of musicians outside of the studio and "had nothing to do with the management or the PR." His primary career revolved around "doing the music" and avoided how management "presented the artist. My only concern was getting the record right." Allowing artists control might have made them feel good about themselves, but his responsibility was producing a recording that a label could sell. Consequently, he remembers, "I went with anybody who could help make it better." A case in point would be the Who's first hit single, "I Can't Explain," about which Talmy remembers, "I used the Ivy League to do the backing vocals because the Who were incapable at that point in time." Both Townshend and bassist John Entwistle have expressed resentment at the use of session singers John Carter and Ken Lewis on this recording. However, Talmy believes his decision "spurred them into action because they went out and learned after that." Indeed, many Who recordings in the future would employ the same kinds of falsetto responsorial singing as featured on the Ivy League's recordings.

The production problems for the Who began when their manager, Kit Lambert, decided that he could produce. In the process of fighting with Talmy, he also secured the lasting resentment of engineer Glyn Johns, leaving many of their subsequent recordings shallow and noisy. Moreover, not everyone resented Talmy's substitutions. Dave and Ray Davies both immediately recognized the value of having session drummer Bobby Graham in the studio to provide a punch and consistency that their drummer, Mick Avory, simply could not provide, at least on such short notice.

An Ear for Success

Like other producers at the time, Talmy was dependent on Denmark Street's music publishers to find new material and would visit their offices to hear new material. In late 1963, Talmy was visiting Mills Music[19] when one of the managers of the Kinks, Robert Wace, arrived with a demo that they had recorded down the street at Regent Sound. Talmy recalls telling him, "Sure, I'd love to listen" and, consequently, "made a deal and brought them into Pye" (Unterberger 1985b). He came by the Who differently, when he listened to a demo played over the telephone. Talmy has maintained that success depends on the song. Perhaps this attitude toward songwriters positioned him to attract some of the most prolific and original pop composers of the era in Ray Davies and Pete Townshend. In evaluating how much of the success of a recording is due to a good composition, he remembers, "I think I said 75%, but it's probably closer to 90%. It's certainly a truism, which I'm sure I've said somewhere or the other, is that 'a bad band can have a hit record with a good song, but the reverse isn't true.'" His recognition of these songwriters contributed to the flourishing of British music in the mid-sixties. He believes that what happened was "a renaissance. All of a sudden there were a slew of people who could write great songs in the 60s." His work with two of the most

---

[19] 20 Denmark Street.

prolific singer-songwriters of the era at a time when the concept was still novel hardly seems a coincidence.

Talmy describes producing as "an extremely individual thing. If you have the same band with the same song and six producers, you're going to get six different records." However, when describing the process by which one makes records, Talmy seems to be of two minds. First, he believes that producing has "no secrets. . . . If [artists] want to learn techniques, fine, I'll teach them techniques." Moreover, he maintains that, if performers "wanted to go out and produce their own stuff afterwards, it was fine with me. I used to encourage it." Indeed, he claims, "I preferred to do the records with them." His reason? "Producing a record should be very much a symbiosis, a partnership between the producer and the band. And if it isn't, then it's not worth doing." However, he has also stipulated that he does not co-produce: "Somebody's got to steer the damn ship, and I don't think you can have two captains trying to steer in two different directions. That's certainly the way I always worked" (Unterberger 1985b).

Perhaps the most exiting aspect of pop recording in London in the sixties for Talmy came with the experience of

> breaking new ground. What we were doing was exhilarating because everything that we were doing was brand new. There were no rules to follow, and that's what was constantly uppermost in my mind. I felt, hell, I could do whatever I feel like because I'm not copying anybody, we're blazing trails, new sounds, methods of recording, and unusual instruments.

Talmy considers producing to be a combination of a highly developed personal musical insight and well-honed recording skills, the product of nature and nurture. His primary interest (creating a hit recording) was often at odds with the management, as illustrated by the Who, the Kinks, and the Easybeats. However, they were not the only ones seeking to meddle in the studio. He recalls, "With a couple of exceptions, I don't think I've ever run into sales and promotion [people] in a record company who didn't think they were A&R people." His response to them: "Why don't you go out and do your own records? Why tell me how to do mine?" (Unterberger 1985b). In one remarkable case, a publicity agent did just that and with startling results.

ANDREW LOOG OLDHAM

Of all those who claimed the title "producer" in 1960s London, few achieved the notoriety of the man who would both manage and produce the Rolling Stones. Where musician George Martin apprenticed in the role of artists and repertoire manager, and engineer Shel Talmy bluffed his way to opportunity, Oldham's strengths resided in sheer ambition and audacity. As neither musician nor engineer, he nevertheless proved to be a formidable force, blurring the lines among management, public relations, and record production, redefining each as he went.

Born during the war (1944) to an Australian Jewish mother from a liaison with an American airman, Andrew Loog, Oldham grew up mostly in the Marylebone and Swiss Cottage areas of London. He came to prefer the exclusive schools in which his mother was able to enroll him, a consequence of the patronage of a wealthy furniture manufacturer and lover. From an early age, Oldham came to expect privilege, choosing clothing and transportation to communicate his status and rank. He also took an early interest in television, film, and jazz and in their personalities; however, Johnny Ray's "Cry" awakened him to the idea that music could be about sex.

Oldham provides us with an interesting example of someone who sought to confront and overturn the establishment, while at the same time seeking many of its privileges. He cannot be understood as an advocate of the working class. Nevertheless, he sought to be part of a youth culture that was coming into positions of power, especially if he profited in the process. One of his earliest occupations was working for the clothing designer Mary Quant in her Chelsea store, Bazaar, where he gained a deeper appreciation of not only how clothing functioned as a social marker, but how that social marking could be marketed. He describes the lesson: "At first, fashion was *the* fashion, then fashion became music" (2000: 94). Like Malcolm McLaren a decade later, Oldham paid close attention to clothing as a path of rebellion against the establishment, both setting trends and paying close attention to them. In such light, Mick Jagger—as Oldham's theatrical and musical alter ego—existed in equal parts model, musician, and anarchist.

Oldham's music experience came at clubs in Soho. "I worked at Ronnie Scott's from seven till midnight throughout the week and till 1 a.m. on Saturdays. I checked the coats on the cloakroom, showed people to their seats and brought in food for the patrons from the Indian restaurant over the road. The music I got to hear live at Ronnie Scott's was world-class." But two jobs were apparently not enough: "Down the block from Ronnie Scott's on Lower Wardour Street, Rik and John Gunnell hosted late nights at the Flamingo. I signed on for the after-midnight shift" (2000: 106–107). However, the strain eventually pushed him to drop all three and to take up hustling British tourists in the south of France for a summer. He was seventeen.

Returning to London in the fall of 1961 as a gofer in a public relations firm, he tried freelance promotion, eventually finding menial work at the Leslie Frewin Organization, an old-school PR firm. There, he continued to do freelance promotion after hours, including briefly for Joe Meek (who frightened him). By the fall of 1962, he left Leslie Frewin to work for manager Ray Mackender promoting Mark Wynter and his hit, "Venus in Blue Jeans." Working in this context, he developed both knowledge of how to get a client into the press and an appreciation of the relationship between managers and artists.

In 1963, Oldham set his sights on becoming a manager after the models of Larry Parnes and Brian Epstein (who had also briefly employed him). Seeing the Rolling Stones perform at the Crawdaddy Club, he deftly severed their unofficial relationship with then-manager Georgio Gomelsky; however, as a minor, he was unable to book performances. Oldham needed someone with a license to act as an agent. So, he went to the old timer from whom he was renting office space: "Eric Easton was an agent, he could get the band work, and he could finance the recording operation I had in mind as a must" (Oldham 2000: 195). His mistake was making Easton a co-manager, who overlooked the conflict of interest to his advantage.

Oldham Producing

Oldham's inexperience as a producer, with no expertise in either music or engineering, put him into an unusual spot: what was his role? Like Dick Rowe, Oldham had little to go on except his self-confidence. He had an idea in his head of what kinds of recordings he wanted to make, but he did not know how to make them. This left him subject to the abilities of his music directors (Arthur Greenslade and John Paul Jones) and his engineers (Roger Savage, Bill Farley, Glyn Johns, and Dave Hassinger). Instead, he concentrated on obtaining compelling performances from artists. Consequently, while his recordings lack consistency, they have energy.

Indeed, his role proved more akin to that of a film director. In his pastiche autobiography, he often cites the character Johnny Jackson from the film *Expresso Bongo* as a model. Marianne Faithful (with Dalton, 2000: 22) describes him as "a great fabricator of selves, and once in the studio he transformed utterly"; he became an "agitated and distracted Maestro Loog Oldham" who "strode up and down like a manic Ludwig Van on a handful of leapers" (ibid.). She describes this as his "Phil Spector imitation: dark glasses, Wagnerian intensity, melodramatic moodiness. It was all a game" (ibid.). Arthur Greenslade confirms that Oldham held the American as his model: "Now Andrew Oldham wasn't a musician, but he could more or less tell you what he wanted. Andrew was more or less like an English Phil Spector." Faithful recalls that Oldham's "only bit of direction to me was to sing very close to the mike" in order to change the "spatial dimension. You project yourself into the song" (24). She describes her version of "As Tears Go By" as "electric and subjective" and a consequence of Oldham's focus on the performance. "Pop According to Andrew is more like Method acting. There's no distance. It becomes breathy and intimate, as if you're inside my head and you're hearing the song from in there" (ibid.).

Like Meek, Most, and Talmy, Oldham saw the advantage of owning recordings and leasing them. Oldham formed his own record company (Immediate Records) as a way to leapfrog to the top of the corporate food chain. Few independent producers could have survived in a corporate environment, both because their ambition outstripped their patience and because of their outsider status. After all, corporate presidents had little if any intrinsic interest or experience in music; for them, the music business was just that: business.

Oldham's path to becoming a producer began rather inauspiciously when the Stones recorded a cover of Chuck Berry's song "Come On." Oldham and Easton had very little money with which to do anything, let alone mount a major recording, so Oldham talked engineer Roger Savage and Olympic Studios into letting them record after hours at a discount. Savage believes, "It was sorta an illicit session, really just a favour to Andrew without any strings attached. It was one of my first real recordings" (Oldham 2000: 208–209). Oldham recalls that the three-hour session cost them £40 and describes the recording space (a former church and synagogue) as inhospitable: "The control room was upstairs, and I didn't like that because it's like a machine-gun turret—one is literally talking down at the act. The session was cold" (Oldham 2000: 209). From the perspective of a manager who saw himself as an integral member of the band and who saw his role as the one who inspired performance, the distance was an impediment. Marianne Faithful (with Dalton, 2000: 22), whom Oldham produced a year later, has similar memories of the space, describing the layout as "exceedingly odd. The control room was far above the studio," and Oldham and others "all sat up there like gods looking down on us. We were like the workers toiling in the factory while the fat cats directed operations from on high. There wasn't even that much to do in a control booth in those days."

In 1963, Oldham had little understanding of recording technology: "I thought the electric guitars would be plugged straight into the studio walls, so that nobody would ask me to pay for an amp" (Oldham 2000: 210). On the cheap, they gained access to quality equipment. Engineer Roger Savage remembers that, in 1963, "four-track was pretty unusual" and that Olympic had "a big Ampex machine that stood as tall as a person" (ibid.). As both manager and chief image architect of the band, Oldham began implementing his vision, which included the notion that six Rolling Stones were one too many: pianist Ian Stewart posed an inconsistency. As the tapes rolled, he put his decision into effect by dropping Stewart from the mix. Savage remembers the awkward moment when "Andrew told me to turn Ian Stewart's piano microphone off." As the engineer on the session, he followed Oldham's instructions, but "was a bit embarrassed about doing it," especially when "they came up the stairs to the control room to play back [and] there was no piano! Nobody said anything" (Oldham 2000: 209).

Savage's other memories of the recording session confirm those of Oldham and others who were there: Oldham "couldn't really get his head round the mixing, from four tracks down to one track, he didn't really understand how that was gonna occur. None of them had any experience of recording, so basically they sort of left it up to me" (Oldham 2000: 209). Oldham confirms, "He explained that the basic recording had been made on four channels and we now had to reduce them to stereo and mono for public consumption. I said, 'Oh, you do that. I'll come back in the morning for it.' Because I figured if I wasn't there I wouldn't have to pay for it" (Oldham 2000: 210). He also clearly did not understand the importance of this process. Nevertheless, ever self-confident, he declares that, a "year later I was an expert and nobody was going to stop me divining exactly how four channels would be pared down for public consumption" (ibid.). The recording of "Come On" features a prominent bass part, its upper partials emphasized by a pick. The other instrumental parts (with the exception of the piano) are distinct and Jagger has double-tracked his voice. That is, after recording the voice (probably at the same time as the instruments), he has gone back and tried to duplicate the interpretation, which in Jagger's case is challenging, given how much he varies each performance.

Rather than Oldham managing the sound of the recording, Savage says, "I would be controlling the mix, telling them what was going on or what was happening with the process" (Oldham 2000: 210). Interestingly, Savage separates the sound he captured on the recording from the band's inherent sound, which he describes as "more of a mess, looser, with less separation between the instruments" (ibid.). How he went about separating the sounds, he does not explain, and he may be confusing their playing style with his ability to allow us to hear all of the instruments (with the exception of the piano). Other recordings by the Stones evince a ragged rhythmic expression, particularly between Charlie Watts and Keith Richards, although in a number of instances tambourine strikes conflict with the drums too.

Regent Sound

Oldham moved the band to Kingsway for their second single, "I Wanna Be Your Man," but, when they tried the tiny Regent Sound Studios in Denmark Street, he believed he had found a home. Perhaps what convinced him was the appearance of one of his music idols, Phil Spector, at one of these sessions. The owner and manager of the studios, James Baring, describes the studio as a "very small player." The niche they filled enabled "a lot of people to have a go at a low price while we were learning about things." The cost of recording at Regent Sound was "£5 an hour, tape at cost." You could also have Regent press an acetate disk of your tape recording; "the 7-inch ones were a fraction of a pound." That part of the business kept the "disk cutter running all day," with "a Lyrec direct drive motor after 1963, driving a Neumann table and the cutting head, maybe Neumann or Telefunken." He soon moved that part of the business to a room on Denmark Place (an alley just to the north of Denmark Street). Baring remembers:

> When I took over there was a Berlant. I moved the Berlant to the new cutting room in Denmark Place and installed a twin-track Ampex. The weak spot was the Vortexion mixer, mismatched into the system. It took me some time to re-place it with London's first transistorized studio mixer, designed by Eddie Baldwin. That's why some of the early Stones stuff is pretty dodgy. But Andrew Oldham liked it. "Sounds nutty, James. That's what I want!"

With the growing success of the Stones recordings, the cost for the studio went to "£7.50/hr some time mid sixties" and, when Baring opened a facility just off of Tottenham Road on University Street, it charged £15 per hour and converted the Denmark Street address to the company office. Recording at Regent Sound was almost always done "on account," because it almost always knew the people who were recording:

> Usually there was a publisher or an arranger or an A&R man or manager that we had heard of making the booking on behalf of the performer, or we knew the performer. So we could take cash, but most people just went away with the stuff and an invoice, and if they hadn't paid by the end of the month we sent them a statement.[20]

Oldham (2000: 252) describes Regent Sound as "magnificent. You'd pass a small reception and be straight into the studio, which was no larger than an av-erage good-sized hotel room. The control room was the size of a hotel bathroom, but for us it was magic." Unlike other studios, where the facilities allowed you to discretely separate one instrument from another, at Regent, the "sound leaked, instrument to instrument, the right way. You'd hear the bottom end of Charlie's drums bleeding through Keith's acoustic, and vice versa, Keith's guitar delay bleeding through the drum track. Put them both together and you had our wall of noise" (ibid.).

---

[20] Baring remembers that "Robert Stigwood had to be chased, but he always paid."

Bill Farley engineered this sound, and Oldham (2000: 252) believes that he "gave a little more, because for the first time he was making master recordings." For the Stones and Oldham, "Farley did everything he could to get the right sound," meaning that he was willing to work with Oldham's inexperience. Rather than tell the engineer to compress particular sounds, to use limiters, or reverberation, Oldham asked Farley to imitate the sound of other recordings. Their first major hit at Regent Sound, "Not Fade Away" (unlike the electric sounds emphasized on their first two releases) features Keith Richards strumming both electric and acoustic guitars, the latter residing prominently in the recording mix. Unlike both "Come On" and "I Wanna Be Your Man," Jagger does not double-track his voice, allowing more freedom to inflect the vocal dramatically. That decision would prove to be invaluable as the Stones sought unique performances rather than consistent and reproducible renditions.

Oldham (2000: 253) recalls that because Regent Sound

> was relatively cheap and they were glad to have us, we could stretch out a bit, experiment and learn from our mistakes. I have no doubt the feel of those early Stones records was due in no small part to avoiding the major studios, and the lessons we learnt would be unconsciously applied over and over by anyone trying to build a recording track from the ground up.

Stretching out constitutes exactly what Oldham did with the Stones' recording studios in 1964 and 1965. When they began touring the United States, he chose to record them in American studios, first in the hallowed if humble premises of Chess Records in Chicago ("It's All Over Now") and then at RCA in Hollywood ("The Last Time," "Satisfaction," etc.). In his early stages as a producer, Oldham sought to balance obtaining comfortable recording contexts for himself and his artists with the cost of the recording studio. Regent was an ideal place to begin his production career because he did not have members of the recording establishment looking over his shoulder. He could make mistakes without continually fearing ridicule. In the United States, the homey surroundings of Chess and the laid-back attitude of RCA allowed him to grow into being a successful producer.

By 1966, his relationship with the Rolling Stones was beginning to disintegrate as they discovered that they could function as their own producers. The recordings at Olympic's new studios in Barnes increasingly resembled a rudderless ship, Oldham sometimes entirely absent from the recording sessions. Sometimes, recordings worked (e.g., "Ruby Tuesday"), but increasingly everyone grew frustrated. The situation deteriorated further upon the arrest and prosecution of Mick Jagger and Keith Richards in 1967 for drug possession, at which time Oldham essentially disappeared, fearing he would be next. He never regained their confidence. When the Stones reconvened to record in 1968, they engaged an American, Jimmy Miller, to find ways to reenergize them with "Jumpin' Jack Flash" and "Street Fighting Man." Unlike Oldham, who sought to mold the Rolling Stones into an identity he had created, Miller recognized and realized the inherent potential in the rock 'n' roll band.

PRODUCING CHANGE

The sixties saw the beginning of the eclipse of corporate artists and repertoire managers by independent producers, an increase in the number of studios, and the introduction of multitrack recorders. George Martin represents both how class-conscious corporate artists and repertoire managers functioned within a system dominated by a few big studios and how one could emerge with an independent but symbiotic relationship with those same studios. Norman Smith and Joe Meek both began as engineers within studios and moved up to become producers. Smith accomplished this promotion by staying within the corporation, attempting to be independent within EMI's own studios. Meek sought total independence, although he relied on corporations such as Decca (the Tornados and "Telstar") and Pye (the Honeycombs and "Have I the Right") to release his recordings. Mickie Most and Shel Talmy discovered how to be independent and successful (something Joe Meek never quite accomplished), establishing themselves immediately as the best way to bypass the corporate filters at EMI and Decca, even if they too released on corporate labels. Finally, Andrew Oldham demonstrated that image matters. The Rolling Stones succeeded in no small part because of Oldham's sense of style and timing and his emphasis on interpretation. Indeed, his ignorance of production technology may have contributed to the innovations they chanced upon in the various studios they rented.

The art of production in the sixties meant getting results, whether you knew exactly how you had accomplished this or not. Experimentation with the ever-changing equipment and the expectation that the equipment would change created a culture of anticipation that seemed always in pursuit of musical and technological innovation. That recordings as different sounding as Joe Meek's compressed montages, George Martin's and Norman Smith's transparent montages, Shel Talmy's overloaded riots, Mickie Most's dry still-life renderings, and Andrew Oldham's noisy accidents could occupy the same airwaves testifies to the tolerance and diversity of the sixties. Each producer coped with a different set of social restraints and opportunities that underlay sixties life.

Class, generation, professionalism, sexual orientation, and ethnicity shaped how each of them operated within London's recording industry. Mickie Most succeeded in 1960s London in part because his class assured him that he could not fail. However, Martin's penchant for authoritarianism and class condescension both tamed the Beatles and alienated them, even as Smith brought a workmanlike focus to recording. Oldham's revolt was generated as much from his rejection of a previous generation's gentility as from his reaction against an industry designed to take advantage of the young and to block outsiders. Shel Talmy constituted the inside outsider: the British recording scene accepted him because of the results he obtained, even as individuals disdained his abilities and rights. And Joe Meek's productions created worlds where, perhaps, he hoped his identity would find acceptance and his demons would be silent. Some formed bonds with the engineers (Martin, Talmy, and Oldham) and with musical directors (Meek and Oldham), while some attempted to be engineer-producers (Meek and Talmy) or musician-producers (Martin, Smith, and Most). Each brought a different mix of capabilities to the tasks.

They all have at least one thing in common: each of them produced recordings whose shelf lives have far exceeded their initial expiration dates. Each adapted to changes in musical tastes and recording technology and, in the process, changed musical history.

3

A Question of Balance

Engineering Art

In the Beatles' improbable rise to musical and cultural triumph, an HMV technician changed the course of history when he offered the opinion that some of the material on Brian Epstein's tape might be publishable. Jim Foy inadvertently set in motion more than his disk cutter; he facilitated a revolution in popular music. As with many of the best-known recordings of the era, our historical and ethnographic sense generally ignores the roles of technologists. However, if technology helped to define the era and fuel upheaval in the recording industry, then the varied individuals who bore the title "engineer" facilitated the insurrection.

An "engineer" constituted anyone whose primary studio role lay in his technological abilities, e.g., overseeing recording levels, running and maintaining tape decks, and setting up and positioning microphones. Some, such as Malcolm Addey, consider the term "engineer" to be a misnomer:[1] "None of us were really 'engineers.' We were sound mixers." Like others bearing the same title, he recognizes that the occupational term has "come into the lexicon of the industry." He

---

[1] The individuals whom I interviewed interchanged the terms "balance mixer," "music mixer," and "balance engineer."

complains that the title has become "such a put down for what we do. It's easy to say, 'Oh he's *only* an engineer,' but you know [feigns condescending accent] if it was 'producer.' And I think that's why a lot of engineers like to call themselves 'engineer-producers.'"

Whether engineers or not, a variety of technologists expertly transformed musical performances from studio sound to consumable product. Before the instant of performance, these individuals aligned microphones and tape heads, established recording levels, and set tape in motion. When the producer and/or performers imagined possibilities, willing engineers imagined solutions, invented devices to alter the sound, and sometimes created new uses for existing equipment. They also edited the magnetic tape or "dropped in"[2] music to combine the best parts of several recordings into a single virtual performance. But the process did not end there. By extension, the individuals involved in the mastering, cutting, and pressing of vinyl disks were members of this technology chain too, helping the production crew to create a product that consumers would love.

At one end of the British music industrial complex, EMI created and marketed its own tape decks, employing an extensive staff to record music, to maintain its studios, and to manufacture disks. Smaller companies had to find someone else to press their material, and independent studios could only provide facilities for taping and mixing. Joe Meek (perhaps the most eccentric individual of the milieu) often designed and built his own peripherals, including an electronic reverberation unit constructed around a garden-gate spring! For a while, he even pressed his own disks, but he lacked the distribution network to place his product in enough stores to make a significant difference.

No one knew better than studio technicians the limitations and possibilities of a studio's equipment and physical space. Not only did they record every day, but they routinely tested the limits of their environment. More important, they functioned as the linchpins between the music performance and the product that appeared on store shelves. Some engineers could have equipment up and ready for a session in the seeming blink of an eye, a critical skill considering the preciousness of London studio time in the sixties. Most often as employees of the studio, they ensured that those who came to record treated the equipment with care. After all, although one producer might want to push the envelope of what a microphone could survive, the production crew using the studio two hours later expected to be able to use the same equipment and obtain predictable results. Even more prob-

---

[2] Americans are more likely to say "punch in" for the act of cueing tape and recording from a specific spot.

lematically, some independent engineers (e.g., Joe Meek) wanted to rewire mixing boards when they came to a studio; however, in a communal industrial environment, house engineers did not want to waste time discovering that microphone inputs no longer went to the same channels that they did the previous day.

Interestingly, in this era, someone carrying the title of engineer might have little or no training in the electronics and/or the mechanics of recording (the core of Addey's complaint). One of the most notable engineers of the era, Norman Smith—who worked on almost all of the Beatles' historic recordings up to 1966—worked odd jobs and played music to support himself before arriving at EMI. Others, like Meek, had learned about recording and audio equipment in the armed services and from their own tinkering with radios and televisions. Many had been amateur electricians as teenagers, building mixers, record cutters, and, sometimes, small illegal broadcast facilities. Consequently, the competition between engineers could be intense, and some only moved up in the studio hierarchy when someone else slipped up.

The staff at EMI Recording Studios[3] included a variety of people whose combined purpose was to create successful recordings. Kevin Ryan and Brian Kehew note in their exhaustive book on the recordings of the Beatles, "there was also a clearly defined hierarchy within Abbey Road, and the studio had a well-established path that employees must take to progress through the ranks" (2006: 42). The beginning position at EMI was commonly that of the "tape operator," with the position of "balance engineer" the goal of many engineers. Assisting them were the "technical engineers," who set up microphones, compressors, etc.; plugged or unplugged them; and maintained all of the equipment. The principal engineering roles in the studio involved (a) the balancing of instruments in the recording, (b) the operation of the tape decks, (c) the installation of microphones on the studio floor, (d) the maintenance of equipment, and (e) the mastering and cutting of disks.

Sometimes, a single individual might assist a producer. For example, Glyn Johns operated tape decks for Shel Talmy (who did his own balancing), and Bill Farley commonly ran the tape and balanced the mikes for Andrew Oldham at Regent Sound. More unusually, Joe Meek attempted to do it all. However, in large studios like EMI, several individuals worked together in coordinated roles (e.g., Richard Lush assisted Geoff Emerick who served George Martin). In the early sixties, you often had only three hours in which to complete several finished recordings and, consequently, a team of skilled hands and minds could make all the difference. Unsurprisingly, London experienced no shortage of individuals

---

[3] EMI renamed its facilities Abbey Road Studios in the 1970s.

who thought themselves potential engineers; however, gaining admittance to the industry and climbing the studio hierarchy could take years at a tape deck or lathe. And sometimes, promotion could come over a lunch break, or a lucky break.

John Leckie (who started at EMI in 1970) describes the tape operator's specific role as "to start, stop, rewind, and fast-forward the tape. That was the tape op's first priority" (Cunningham 1998: 158). At any moment, a producer could demand, "Run the tape" or "Go back to the second verse," and for the tape operator, "the whole focus had to be on being able to act on his instruction as quickly as possible" (ibid.). In pop recordings, where producers often wanted to add touches by inserting musical lines at particular places, the tape operator had the responsibility of cueing the tape to exactly the right spot as fast as possible. Ryan and Kehew (2006: 43) note that being the tape operator "could be sheer terror, as intense classical sessions required quick handling of tapes while an impatient and expensive orchestra and conductor waited." "It was down to you to record the tracks, do all the drop-ins, and take care of the headphone sync mix," Leckie remembers. "Invariably you had to be one step ahead of what everyone else on the session was thinking, but also be ready to go one step back" (Cunningham 1998: 159). Ryan and Kehew also observe that the tape operator's duties included annotating the session, indicating which takes and edited pieces a reel contained. EMI engineer Richard Langham, echoing comments by other 1960s contributors, muses, "If I'd known the notes were going to be so historical, I'd have used better penmanship" (43).

Gus Dudgeon, who started at Decca in 1962 and worked his way up to becoming an independent producer, remembers how he received a sudden promotion to balance engineer at the Zombies recording session for "She's Not There":

> This other engineer, Terry Johnson started the session. He was my boss, and I was just the tape operator, the tape jockey. But Terry had a bit of a problem with booze and at lunch he'd got paralytically drunk. He came back and he was so drunk that they threw him in a taxi and sent him home, and [producer] Ken Jones looked at me and said, "Well, I guess it's down to you." So I moved to the engineer's chair for the first time, and had a ball doing it. (Palao 1997: 17)

The success of the record guaranteed Dudgeon's career, even though Decca let a sobered-up Johnson back into the studios.

Geoff Emerick (1983: 256) floridly describes the balance engineer's primary role as "painting with sound" and the audio equivalent of photography:

> The sounds produced in the studio must be captured and faithfully reproduced, and this is where the recording engineer comes in. To make sure that the sounds are being recorded at the correct levels and that things are in phase

with each other, he will be constantly alert to any distortion and break-up in the incoming audio signals, and must be able to quickly diagnose any faults that may be occurring.

However, the engineer also has a social role:

> The two most important things any good recording engineer must bear in mind are: first, not to create a panic which might unnerve the artist and/or producer; and, secondly, to use his discretion if he does discover a fault. He may even have to take preventive measures during the recording session itself. (ibid.)

As the technology of the fifties and sixties changed, the responsibilities of the engineers—particularly those in the recording booth—grew more complicated. Classical, jazz, and especially folk sessions were grounded in the conceit that the recording had captured a real event, even if ultimately they might be made from numerous separate performances spliced together. However, pop music embraced the opportunities that multitrack recording afforded and especially the notion that one could construct a recorded performance from asynchronous events. That is, the recording represented an imaginary performance to which musicians could return and add ideas after the original session. As the sixties unfolded, production teams and musicians attempted to create fictional sonic worlds that could only exist on tape.

Pop recordings usually started with a basic "rhythm track" to which the production team could add instrumental solos and singing, the sound of a speaker in an empty room for echo and reverberation, and anything else until the gradual degradation of the magnetic signal became unacceptable. The quarter-inch-wide tape that the Germans had developed before the Second World War first allowed engineers in the sixties to record two tracks. However, by the beginning of 1968 in London, quarter-inch stock had given way to inch-wide magnetic tape, allowing eight parallel tracks onto which a production crew could record and re-record instruments, voices, and other audio signals to build complex aural structures.[4]

Each of the important studios—EMI, Decca, Pye, IBC, Kingsway, Olympic, Lansdowne, and even little Regent Sound—employed engineers to guard and to operate the precious equipment they had obtained either from the few domestic suppliers or from manufacturers in the United States, Switzerland, and Germany. For example, Decca's prized team of technicians included Mike Vernon, Gus Dudgeon, Jack Clegg, Arthur Bannister, and Derek Varnals. In contrast, Regent

---

[4] Those who could not wait, such as the Rolling Stones and the Who, went to the United States, where eight-track recording decks were already in some studios.

Sound in its heyday had only Bill Farley, and Glyn Johns remained an independent engineer, relying upon the growing power of independent producers to gain him access to London's studios.

Of all the studios in London, EMI's facilities in Abbey Road often set the standard. Other studios could sometimes boast newer equipment and certainly had great staff, but EMI was quick to match the competition. Comparing the work of three different and notable EMI engineers—Malcolm Addey, Norman Smith, and Geoff Emerick—illustrates how the engineer's role changed in this era. In 1958, Addey quickly established himself as the studio's wunderkind, capturing some of the most significant performances of the era and participating in the transformation of EMI's attitudes toward rock and pop. A few years later, Norman Smith, although no adolescent and learning from Addey's example, created a sound for the Beatles that would set a world standard. And Geoff Emerick, treading in Smith's footsteps, proved to be a catalyst in the transformation of the Beatles from a touring band to a studio entity. Each came with a different set of skills and aptitudes that molded the music they recorded.

MALCOLM ADDEY

At twenty-four, Malcolm Addey (b. 1933) had fulfilled his national service responsibilities and had already worked at audio-related jobs when his wife convinced him to apply at EMI. Within a year, he had recorded what is perhaps Britain's first authentic example of rock 'n' roll, "Move It," and EMI had begun a cultural transformation. In the following decade, he would engineer a string of hits not only by Cliff Richard and the Shadows, but also by other artists, such as Johnny Kidd's landmark, "Shakin' All Over." In the late fifties and early sixties, EMI producers routinely requested Addey for important pop recording sessions.

Addey grew up in the home of an older couple after his mother (a pianist with a music degree) died. These friends of his mother's arranged for piano lessons for him when he was five, providing music study (and conservatory exams) until he was fifteen. Having succeeded on his eleven-plus exams, he earned enrollment in a grammar school, where he and his friends entertained their dreams of becoming broadcasters through an amateur closed-circuit radio station they had cobbled together. He got his first taste of national exposure when the BBC broadcast them twice. Addey learned to supplement their meager studio by "building my own little mixers and an amplifier. It was fun, I enjoyed that. And that was the background of my technical side. I was totally self-taught, of course."

Addey's family background had a significant impact on him. He describes his father as upwardly mobile working class and the couple who raised him, in contrast, as "veering on upper middle-class Victorians. I was brought up in the Victorian manner, and that includes manners. It includes speaking well and all the things that have, of course, become so damned old-fashioned today." By 1949, at sixteen, his "aunt and uncle" had passed away and, after a brief stint in the home of his stepmother, Addey left school to make his own way. Two years later, his national service allowed him to pursue his interest in broadcasting, albeit in a very curtailed way, when he became a wireless operator, "which was the obvious thing to do: Typewriting, teleprinting, Morse code, the whole damn lot." After demobilization in 1953, he spent the next few years working for the Civil Aviation Authority, in a hi-fi shop, and at a company that provided a British form of Muzak—in addition to getting married. But no matter how much he enjoyed tinkering with audio, the work left him unfulfilled.

By 1957, his wife complained, saying, "I'm sick of hearing you talk about getting into doing recording and all that kind of stuff. Why don't you just do it?" Two weeks later, he had an interview with Chick Fowler (manager of Abbey Road Studios) and Barry Waite (the assistant manager). They offered him an assistant position at the princely wage of £11 a week: the door opened and Addey entered. "Chick Fowler seemed to see something in me and took me on. I didn't let him down." The two pop engineers (classical and other musics had their own engineers) at EMI were Stuart Eltham and Peter Bown. Addey remembers the former as "very, very conservative. I think you'd probably say he was more like a BBC engineer than anything. Everything was very, very workman-like; but there was no inspiration, nothing unusual, nothing that would make you sit up." Bown, however, "was very devoted to it. He was more my mentor than anybody. [His] life was totally recording." And from Bown, Addey adopted the habit of "trying new things. If a microphone came along that he wanted to experiment with, he would do so. He would get the interesting gigs, the jazz and whatever rock we had."

Addey's career at EMI began as a tape operator:

> We were more like clerks: we took notes, we didn't even set up or touch any microphones, that was all done in those days by the electronic maintenance department. They used to set up floors according to our layouts. That's why they produced so many sessions in a day so easily; somebody else was doing that work for us.

The balance engineer, however, "could just walk in, and adjust the microphones in their final positions and did the mixers of course." The tape operator's note taking consisted of a "big ledger, with about four or five carbon copies, which gave you the artist, the studio, the time of starting, the time of booking, the time of starting and finishing each title, take numbers, accurately recorded with the publishers and songwriters if known. Every single thing about that session was on there." He did not see this as a particularly rewarding position to occupy, his principal responsibilities being operating tape decks at the command of the balance engineer and walking tapes for storage, duplication, or editing. The benefit of the position was the ability to sit in the control room, where he could observe and learn so that someday he could take over the engineer's chair.

Addey's upbringing and schooling made him particularly observant of the dress code, and he bristles at the depiction of EMI engineers as "white coats." "I'm sick of the white coat routine. Everybody in those days wore suits. There was no such thing as a pair of jeans. There were no such things as long hair and scruffiness. Everybody arrived at the studio very presentable, polished shoes and everything." The only deviance came when they worked the Saturday shift every other week: "we still worked five-and-a-half-day weeks. So it was commuted eventually to alternate Saturdays, which meant you didn't [work] every Saturday, [but rather] alternate Saturdays. And, on that day, you were allowed to wear a sport jacket and flannels." The only people to don lab coats were the maintenance engineers, who could be seen "pushing dirty tape machines around and working the equipment and stuff. It was a white lab coat that they would wear just to protect their clothing."

One of the things that attracted Addey to EMI was the technology. As an amateur, he had practiced recording on available equipment, but as a professional, he got to thread and operate the best machines Britain could manufacture. As a way to counter Britain's postwar balance of payments problems, the Board of Trade made the purchase of American equipment very difficult until the end of the fifties:

> And that's why EMI had to make everything they made. They'd already made a machine to the BBC's specifications, it was called BTR/1, and that was just going out of use when I arrived in '58. We started using the BTR/2, the mono version. Stereo was really very much still in its infancy. But there was a stereo version of the BTR/2, which we were using too.

However, the BTR decks could not compare with American equipment: "They were just nothing like the Ampex, which was the most beautiful piece of minimalist engineering I've ever come across in my life."

"Move It"

Although EMI had begun to allow him to do routine recording, the professional emancipation of Malcolm Addey took place on 24 July 1958. In the few months he had been at EMI, he had established a reputation as an ambitious, bright, and talented studio acolyte, such that engineer Peter Bown felt comfortable leaving him in charge of what he probably felt would be a nondescript session. Norrie

Paramor, still on the hunt for a convincing rock 'n' roll artist, had scheduled a group of promising young musicians for a test recording. Cliff Richard and the Drifters arrived with a song written by their guitarist, Ian Samwell, "Move It," and settled into teaching the parts to session guitarist Ernie Shear and bassist Frank Clarke. Bown found his commitments to be divided: record a bunch of teenagers or go to the opera.[5] Addey had the occasional artist's test and other sessions to record, even though the assistant had only been at EMI for about three months, "because they really needed somebody badly. They didn't have anybody who had the gumption." Bown asked Paramor, "Why can't Malcolm do it?" The producer reluctantly agreed, on the condition that the senior engineer would "[get] him started." Addey and Bown took some time in advance to plan the session, and that evening, Bown "just stood around for about fifteen minutes" before saying, "Well, you're doing OK, Malcolm. I'm off."

Ian Samwell's memories of the session include spending "most of the session recording 'Schoolboy Crush.'" He particularly remembers that "assistant engineer Malcolm Addey stepped in and, being our age, he cracked it. He's as responsible for 'Move It' as anybody else. The unsung hero. What a mix!" (Foster 2000: 158). For Addey, things would never be the same: "once you have a hit, I mean, you don't go back to sweeping the floors after that. You never did." His sudden ascension to balance engineer status ruffled more than a few feathers around the studio in Abbey Road, as did the team that participated in the recording. In the coming years, potential engineers would often be asked their opinion of Cliff Richard's recordings during their interviews, making Addey a kind of professional touchstone.

In his brief apprenticeship under Bown, Addey had come to recognize that the selection and placement of microphones was the key to getting a good recording. He and Bown would draw rough sketches of the studio "using some kind of signs we'd been all using for years for booms and stands, and have a little circle for the microphone, the type it is, what input we want it in, and that's it. And then of course, when the guys come, we do all our adjustments. We could change our mind about the whole thing, of course, when we got there." He compares his placement of microphones to the "way a cameraman focuses his lenses." His approach also meant helping musicians to get good sounds, which included letting the ensemble set the volume level: "I don't ever remember restricting anybody to play any way

[5] In June 1958, Covent Garden celebrated the centenary of the building with productions of "The Bohemian Girl, The Trojans, Peter Grimes, Aida, I Puritani (Maria Callas singing), plus the Royal Ballet's Birthday Offering" (N.A. 1958a).

other than naturally. That's the way I work anyway, always have done. I don't re-member anybody being made to play quietly." Nevertheless, even with the careful placement of microphones, a judicious eye on the balance meters, and allowing musicians to define their sound, the studio itself provided an acoustic signature.

Of course, EMI did have rules, which Addey insists production crews broke "left, right, and center when nobody was looking." For example, EMI had always mandated six seconds between bands on a disk, because "that's what we've always used between movements in the symphony." However, listening to American disks (which he did often), he heard "hardly a pause between one song [and] the next. Like two to three seconds at the most." He recommended to Norrie Paramor, "Let's just do it and see what happens." When they reduced the silence between the bands on a Cliff Richard record, "nobody would've known. They didn't even notice."

Technology Changes

The technological literacy of recording engineers evolved in fundamental ways during the sixties, and no less so than in the relationship between tape and vinyl. Many at EMI spent time in the mastering and cutting rooms upstairs, where they learned how to bring out the nuances of a tape recording on a disk. Addey be-lieves that his arrival at the studio marked "the beginning of the time when most engineers had not really done any cutting at all. And, although I had an amateur basis of course, I'd never done it professionally." With the increasing importance of stereo recordings, the challenges of cutting a disk were such that "you could get some phasing problems and the poor cutter would try to turn itself inside out, and then the needle would go flying off the record."

Similarly, in the position-segregated world of EMI, a balance engineer seldom edited the tapes he recorded, leaving that task to a "three-member fulltime staff of editors," who were "constantly very busy because half of Abbey Road's work was classical." These editors were necessarily all "part-time musicians. The head editor for example was a conductor, organist, and choirmaster and the other two were also involved in similar things, and so they all were able to read and write music extremely well." The producers (sometimes with assistance from conduc-tors) would "just mark the scores and they would do the cutting in their own rooms." Addey does not recall much tape editing with the pop music he recorded: "most of the songs are three minutes and most of the stuff was done in a com-plete take," although if they had something they needed quickly, they might do the editing themselves. However, Addey remembers that artists often underap-preciated the labor and artistry involved in editing. At a late-night session early in his EMI career, he volunteered to edit takes by a group of singers while they went to dinner. They promised, "Oh, we'll bring you something to eat, Malcolm, when we come back." When they returned without any food for him, he "knew exactly what position in the hierarchy was due the recording engineer."

The central relationship in the control booth—the engineer's rapport with the producer—created an environment that could make or break a recording project: "I can tell you that that is probably the most important component to making a hit record. The relationship is extremely important. In fact, it is really a personality thing, a very important personality thing." Addey, as an EMI engineer, worked with different producers at Abbey Road and learned how to complement their strengths and proclivities:

> Different producers have different ways of working with engineers. Norrie Paramor and Norman Newell were particularly dependent on the engineer. They would just listen and say, "I like it," "I don't like it," or "This is what we're gonna do; can you do this for me?" But they would never, ever tell you how to do it because both of them didn't really know. They didn't want to know.

More problematically, producer Wally Ridley sometimes tried to involve himself in the mixing and "had a habit of grabbing a fader from you and pushing it up, and of course it would throw everything off and you'd have to do the take all over again anyway."[6]

In particular, Addey and Parlophone's director-producer George Martin had such contrasting styles that the two seldom worked together. The engineer's principal contention involved Martin's tendency to "inject himself into everything." As with others who worked in the studio, the issue of class and bearing, including Martin's accent, affected their relationship. Recognizing the importance of personal reinvention in which people "go to London" and become "something quite different," the two clearly avoided working together. Ultimately, his perception that Martin felt he was socially "superior to everybody" seems to have most bothered Addey. In an environment of shared responsibilities and cooperation, Addey's self-confidence and Martin's sense of authority clearly conflicted.

Addey's most noteworthy work was with Paramor, whom he describes as "a very, very quiet guy. Very unassuming. And knew his music of course [as] a bandleader and piano player in a British band, [although] he was rather corny." With the success of "Move It" and other recordings—both with Cliff Richard and with

---

[6] Addey's location in the studio also offered the chance at one of the hallowed traditions of the recording industry: the B-side, or getting your song on the flip side of a record you know will be a hit, knowing you will reap royalties. Addey and Norman Smith collaborated on a song and convinced both the Shadows to record it and Norrie Paramor to place it on the B-side of the Shadows hit "The Rise and Fall of Flingel Bunt." "It's a Man's World" has the clever internal acronym MANS (*M*alcolm *A*ddey *N*orman *S*mith).

his backing band, the Shadows—Paramor and Addey came to know each other outside the studio, although clearly still in a hierarchical context. The Paramors would sometimes invite the Addeys, who lived in Muswell Hill, to "their big house in Hampstead Gardens Suburb." Moreover, Paramor gave the Addeys the use of a flat "on the coast of Spain one summer for a couple of weeks." In return, Addey is confident that "[h]e always knew that I would come up with something that would make him smile. That's exactly what I would do, and he would say, 'Ooo, I like that.' And therefore, I got most of his work."

With his success, Addey occasionally found musicians asking him to help them to reproduce a sound despite the differences between the physical and acoustic spaces of studios. Engineers would rather, he believes, help performers to establish their own sounds. In particular, he notes that "frankly you can't duplicate the sound of the Shadows; it's a sound of Hank [Marvin]'s particular guitar and the sound that he's making through his amplifier, and all the other things that go with it." The engineer can only capture sounds that are in the studio. Besides, producers at EMI, in his experience, wanted their own sound.

Ryan and Kehew (2006: 49) note that Addey was the one "who first dared to place the Neumann microphones inches from a loud guitar amplifier; a practice which would be standard by the time of the Beatles." Addey conditions that description by saying that he simply placed the microphones closer, largely out of concern for separation, and EMI seldom challenged him when he tried something new. Junior engineers at EMI clearly wanted to emulate Addey's abilities. EMI engineer Brian Gibson (ibid.) remembers that Addey would adjust the mikes and "adjourn to the Control Room where he would pre-set the mic attenuators and any EQ on the desk. Next, he would set the mic faders. Finally, as the musicians were doing the first run through of the song, he would push up the four main faders to reveal an almost perfect balance." Gibson describes this as Addey's "party trick." Other junior engineers imitated his approach, declaring, "I'm gonna do an Addey!" without much success. Addey explains that he recorded so much in EMI's three studios that he knew exactly how to set the equipment and that his party trick emerged from his boredom. A constellation of issues emerged (not the least of which was control over the recording process) such that he made the leap to New York in 1968, leaving EMI for greener pastures and higher paychecks.

NORMAN SMITH

In 1959, with children at home and supplementing his vocation as a jazz musician through odd jobs, Norman Smith (1923–2008) saw an advertisement in the *Times* of London "for a recording assistant at Abbey Road." Problematically, EMI indicated that it desired someone no older than twenty-eight. Lying about his age to get an interview, he pitched himself to EMI as having valuable experience and baited the company with the tag that he "hoped this would not disqualify me from an interview." In part, his confidence and maturity probably convinced EMI's studio management that someone with little electronic familiarity, but musical knowledge, could be a good studio assistant.

When he met with Barry Waite and Chick Fowler, Smith remembers the interview going well until Waite asked him what he thought of Cliff Richard. The jazz musician responded unflinchingly, "Nauseating, I'm afraid." Waite laughed and proffered, "Well, I'm going to tell you something Mr. Smith. He does me as well." However, Waite continued: "If you are lucky enough to get this job, you would have to record people like that in pop." Smith recovered with, "Ah, well excuse me sir. You asked me what my opinion was. Now that doesn't mean to say that I couldn't work with [him]. So, I hope you'll bear that in mind that you did ask me my personal opinion." Smith later learned that "about 200 of us actually applied for the job: they took on three and I was one of them." Consequently, between 1959 and 1966, Smith worked as an engineer with various artists ranging from Shane Fenton to Manfred Mann; however, undoubtedly his most important work came with George Martin and the Beatles.

Arriving at EMI with little experience in audio engineering, Smith began near the bottom of the hierarchy, gradually gaining more responsibilities as he waited for opportunities. He began as a tape operator or "button pusher on Cliff Richard's sessions," where he worked "mainly with Malcolm Addey, but also Pete Bown and Stuart Eltham" (Ryan and Kehew 2006: 43). All the while, he "watched how they performed, what mics they were using, and how they were placing them" (ibid.). Newcomers like Smith also had more menial tasks, such as keeping

> the control room clean. You'd be a gopher [*sic*] as well. And you'd make any tea or coffee or whatever might be needed. If the guys wanted cigarettes, you'd have to go out and get them. So I was starting as a boy at the ripe old age of thirty-six. However, it was something that I had ambitions to make the best of and I thought that it would lead to better things. And, well, so it did.

From his vantage in the control room:

> one did get information as a tape operator. One got to know the capabilities of the microphones simply by watching the sound engineer you were working with and, whether it would be a choice of a ribbon microphone, or a condenser, or whatever. One got to know all the different microphones as a tape operator.

Occasionally, the sound engineer "might allow you to put a microphone out so long as you put it exactly where he wanted it. So, that's how it was. Extremely strict at EMI for that." By 1962, he had covered most of the studio tasks; however, promotion remained elusive: "In my time at EMI, there was only one I think that did become a sound engineer. There weren't that many opportunities for tape ops to progress to sound engineer. Not in my time anyway." His work as a tape operator and sound engineer included recording performers like Paul Raven,[7] "but no hits came along," which meant no promotion. Smith considered this to be "a terribly unfair situation at Abbey Road: one was never considered for an increase in salary until such time as you managed to record a hit."

Putting in his time as a tape operator, he craved a chance to become a balance engineer, because "in those days, there were only three main pop engineers: Malcolm Addey, Stuart Eltham, and Peter Bown." The only opportunities that EMI provided junior engineers to have a "chance to at least sit at the mixer" were through safe sessions, such as artists' tests. Such sessions brought aspiring musicians into the studio where junior engineers and assistant producers made test recordings. The producer who had approved the session would listen to the test recordings to gauge how well they might sound if he produced them. For example, the Beatles underwent (and failed) an artist's test at Decca on 1 January 1962. Such tests provided a context in which musicians, engineers, and would-be producers could learn the art of recording, while at the same time allowing producers time to work on other projects. In the end, the producer had the responsibility of deciding whether any of them were ready to move to the next level. In the case of the Beatles at Decca, Dick Rowe let his assistant producer Mike Smith decide, perhaps as a way to give him experience in making difficult decisions.

The turning point for Norman Smith appears not to have been with George Martin or the Beatles, but with producer Norrie Paramor and a fading artist. Frank Ifield's string of modest hits had ended in 1960 and, by the spring of 1962, EMI contemplated cutting him from its roster. Paramor agreed to give him a commercial test of a song that Jimmy Dorsey had recorded in 1942: "I Remember You." A "commercial test" constituted the equivalent of an exit interview for artists who had produced hits in the past, but who had apparently lost their potential to sell records. EMI had sent engineer Stuart Eltham (who would normally have served as the balance engineer with Ifield and Paramor) to Ireland on a project, so the producer asked Smith if he would act as the balance engineer. "It was a weekend session [and] Ifield's last 'test,' as it were, to prove any commercial future for him as far as EMI was concerned." Paramor and EMI decided to release the recording, and it went to the top of British charts. "That rescued Frank's ca-

---

[7] Paul Francis Gadd, who later went by the name Gary Glitter.

reer with EMI and, of course, gave me a number one as a sound engineer." With this success, other producers asked Smith to work on their recordings, which also rose in the charts. "It happened in that way a few times. It was all crazy, really, to suggest that I could turn what would otherwise be a miss into a hit. That's the reputation one got in those days, and all kinds of funny reputations were floating about. That was one of them: I was the Midas touch."

Smith indeed brought a musical instinct and a developed tape prowess to the position and worked with several of EMI's producers, especially George Martin. When Geoff Emerick (2006: 46) first encountered Smith at the Beatles' second session, he remembers being amazed at his dexterity, as he cued tape with the virtuosity of a concert artist:

> Norman sat down at the tape machine, displacing Richard [Langham, the tape operator]. With bewildering speed and precision, he began editing together the best bits of the two most satisfactory takes, then moved back to the console to do a quick mix. Moments later, he dispatched Richard and me to take the mono mix upstairs to the lacquer cutting room so that the acetate listening copies could be run off the next morning.

Smith and the Beatles

Smith continued to do artists' tests for Martin, as well as Martin's occasionally unorthodox sessions, which called for creative engineering solutions: "You had an awful lot of ambitious groups that were coming in trying to get recording contracts and that's how one started, recording those kind of things. My artist tests continued until such time as one day in came four guys, four lads looking most ridiculous as I thought with these haircuts." The Beatles arrived for their recording session[8] in June 1962 with Pete Best as their drummer and the sting of Decca's rejection fresh on their minds. Smith remembers:

> [T]hey did not really show any great potential, certainly not in songwriting. They had only recently come back from the Hamburg gigs and, so, all they were doing at the artist's test was virtually performing the stage act they would do in the clubs in Hamburg. So we saw no potential of their songwriting abilities that were to come.

From the acoustic perspective, Smith first encountered the problem of their equipment: "They had tiny little Vox amplifiers. I had their little amps stuck on chairs for the test, and the microphone over in front of that. And when I opened

---

[8] Smith seems to have been unaware that Martin had already completed a recording contract through Brian Epstein for the Beatles.

up the microphone, all I got was just extraneous noises; they were that bad." The solution involved both making repairs and finding substitute equipment: "In those days, we had a separate echo chamber, and in the chamber were speakers and microphones. I had to raid the number-two echo chamber in order to fix Paul McCartney up with some kind of a sound on his bass. I think I did a bit of soldering as well. All you have to do was try and fix some of the amps." Smith, believing this to be an artist's test, also recalls that this session appeared to be different from others in that the producer came to listen for part of the session.

Smith's account of their review provides nuance to a well-known story:

> Number-two control room was above the actual studio; you look down into the studio. And so we brought the four boys up and laid into them a little bit about, "Well, if you want to be recording artists, particularly with EMI, you must have some decent equipment." And I said to them, "I can only improve your sound, embellish, if you give me some kind of initial sound in the studio, then I can embellish, and whatever. But I can't do it with the equipment you've got at the moment." And things like that.

Smith remembers the Beatles remaining silent for the duration, until George Martin asked, "Well, now look, we've been laying down the law. Is there anything you want to say to us?" After a moment of silence, George Harrison remarked to George Martin, "Yeah, I don't like your tie." Smith remembers, "I nearly fell off my chair. That was the start of the Liverpudlian humor, and they didn't stop, to be honest with you. We had almost half an hour cabaret from them, at least I thought it was. I always thought the Liverpudlian accent was funny anyway."

Of course, the Beatles would be back to attempt recordings of Mitch Murray's "How Do You Do It?" Lennon and McCartney's "Love Me Do," and other songs. Soon, Martin and Smith "became extremely popular as a team because of the success of the Beatles," and Smith's reputation as a balance engineer grew with hit recordings by Billy J. Kramer, Freddie and the Dreamers, and Manfred Mann.

Smith's Approach

Smith benefited from being a performer in his ability to hear a good musical blend from the sound stage. "Being an ex-musician, I would get the balance that I thought there should be, and then it would be up to the producer to say, 'Well can I have a little more of this or a little less of that.' And that's how it worked. Your contribution was not just a question of microphone placement." Notably, Smith believes that his approach to recording helped to establish the "Mersey sound":

> I used microphones not right up close to things. And I relied quite a bit, to get in the right sort of balance and the right proportion, on splash-back off the

walls, so one had kind of a natural reverberation. And that's how, in my view at any rate, the Mersey sound was born: placing the microphones further away or equidistant, shall we say, from their instrument and the wall, or the splash-back. In other words not that great separation on each microphone.

Smith does not explain how this recording technique developed. By his own account of the artists' tests, he placed the microphones immediately in front of the amplifiers, and photos of early sessions[9] support this statement. In an attempt to separate instruments in the recording mix, placing a microphone immediately in front of a speaker would give one some control over the loudness of each instrument in the recording. However, if the amplifiers were noisy, then perhaps some distance would minimize the hum of the amplifiers. By 1963 and the era of "Mersey beat," the Beatles had replaced their amps and the hum should have disappeared.

Smith's experience as a sound engineer and his continued employment with EMI put him in the position of compromising studio precedent with musical priorities: "I had to adhere to what the senior engineers had been doing, and that was the use of . . . screens and things like that, which I didn't like." His principal complaint about this approach was that it separated the musicians from each other. His own experience as a performer (which he continued while working at EMI to supplement his income) led him to believe that musicians played better when they were in close proximity to one another. With the Beatles, he felt that "with this sound the boys were producing—their songs—that they wanted to be close together. And so I set them up virtually as they would be set up on stage." Consequently, he remembers, studio managers sometimes reprimanded him; nevertheless, they allowed him to record this way, telling him that the approach had "better be successful . . . and it was." Besides, he reasons, the set up was "more comfortable for [the Beatles]."

Of course, this placement led to problems with the sounds of one instrument leaking into the microphone of another. The sound engineers at EMI

> wanted 100 percent separation recording between each microphone and no spillover. If you opened up the bass mike, you didn't want to hear any drums on it. I never could understand that. I used the position whereby I could get

---

[9] For example, photos in Lewisohn (1988: 29) purportedly show the band on 5 March 1963 with Neumann microphones slung immediately in front of Harrison's and Lennon's two Vox AC30 amps. McCartney's bass amp also has a microphone slung in front of it, plus a baffle to block sounds from the other amps (or perhaps to block the bass from projecting into the Neumanns). The band's physical situation resembles how they would have stood on stage.

the right kind of spillover to get this kind of reverb. That made it sound more natural, like a live performance.[10]

Moreover, most of the early recordings were destined for mono, with stereo mixes an afterthought, and in those mono mixes, Smith combined the instrumental parts into a single backing track over which he then dubbed vocal tracks. As stereo grew in importance toward the end of Smith's time with the Beatles, separation became a priority.

Smith's work with Martin and the Beatles drew considerable attention from artists looking to capture some of the magic. He insists that, as "a team, we could only embellish whatever we were presented with originally." Nevertheless, "the Beatles era" was one of "innovation," particularly in regard to "English recording success," which he would continue with Pink Floyd.

GEOFF EMERICK

Arriving at EMI fresh out of secondary modern school at fifteen—unlike both Malcolm Addey (who had been in his twenties when he started) and Norman Smith (who had been in his thirties)—Geoff Emerick (b. 1946) clearly lacked the technical and musical experience of his predecessors, but he also lived in a different world. Addey (only thirteen years older) had grown up with disk cutting as an important primary way of recording sound (and, like Meek, had even used a lathe as a teen). Emerick embraced magnetic tape as his first medium. And, where Smith (twenty-three years older) understood musicianship, Emerick had the naïve enthusiasm of a teenager who would not need to fear national service.

When Emerick interviewed at EMI, they asked him, "Do you like Cliff Richard and the Shadows?" However, unlike Smith, his response was in the affirmative: "Yes, sir." He also recalls thinking: "Why the hell is he asking me such a dumb question?? Every teenager in Britain likes them; doesn't he know that?" (Emerick with Massey 2006: 33). Recounting the conversation to fellow assistant engineer Richard Langham, they reached the conclusion that the question's purpose amounted to a test of the individual's composure; however, the query also reflected an ideological divide established by Malcolm Addey's recordings. Emerick's view of EMI saw cultural divisions, both between classical and pop and

---

[10] By necessity, most other production teams took this approach too, such as producer Chris Blackwell and engineer Adrian Kerridge, who recorded the Spencer Davis Group so that the sounds of the organ, guitar, and percussion bled from one mike to another, producing the unique quality of recordings such as "Gimme Some Lovin'" (see Cunningham 1998: 113).

between different producer-engineer alliances, such that engineers Addey and Bown tended to work one set of recording projects, while Smith and Eltham worked on others. In Emerick's opinion, EMI was rife with factions (if not vitriol) in the sixties. Neither Addey nor Smith mention anything but cooperation among the production staffs, albeit tinged with competition and a degree of professional secrecy.

Emerick's North London, middle-class background (his father was a butcher) included picking out melodies and chords on his uncle's piano in an environment worthy of a gothic novel. "His house was dark and forbidding, with heavy curtains to keep the draft out, but I was always happy to visit, because it gave me an opportunity to tinker on that piano" (Emerick with Massey 2006: 16). His parents complemented his musical interests with a record player, and he discovered his grandmother's collection of classical and jazz recordings. Last—and perhaps just as influentially—the gift of a crystal radio set, a "Cat's Whisker," led him to discover Radio Luxembourg: "Their disk jockeys played exciting skiffle and rock 'n' roll records instead of the bland music of my parents' generation, and, like so many other British youths of my generation, that was how I discovered pop music" (18).

His interest in music and broadcasting took him to the annual Television and Radio Show in Earl's Court, where he witnessed a live broadcast monitored by a "sound engineer." Even more important, tape recorders so captured his imagination that he sold his train set and bought a "[s]hiny new Brenell two-track model, complete with a microphone and an instruction book that explained the procedure for using a razor blade to cut and splice sections of tape together" (25). He proceeded to tape music from the radio, editing out the announcer's comments and splicing together the songs in the order he wanted to hear them. The experience would prove to be invaluable when he arrived at his EMI interview.

In his senior year of secondary modern school, he concluded that becoming a recording engineer would be his goal. After a brief conversation with a local record-store owner, he sent off letters to EMI, Decca, Philips, and Pye, asking about a position as a recording engineer. Their rejections (or lack of response) disappointed but did not deter him. And then he got lucky. His guidance counselor managed to arrange an interview at EMI with Waite and Bob Beckett. After the first question about Cliff Richard, the interrogation slid into the practical: "Have you ever operated a tape recorder? Do you know how to thread up a reel of tape? Do you know how to edit tape?" (33). Emerick's hobby paid off in this regard: he knew how to do all of this, at least with his Brenell and with quarter-inch tape. However, Waite's final question reflected how, in many ways, EMI had not changed: "Pretend this is a plan of a pulley wheel. . . . Can you do the side elevation of this for me?" (ibid.). The request came from the days when weights, pulleys, and lathes were the primary method of cutting a disk. Emerick—for whom tape had defined the notion of capturing sound—completed the task, but "didn't have the vaguest idea what this had to do with recording" (ibid.). Nevertheless, he got the position and, although he could have made "more sweeping floors in a factory," he was happy with "the magnificent starting salary of four pounds two shillings and sixpence" (35).[11]

Emerick began work at EMI's Abbey Road facilities on Monday 3 September 1962, shadowing fellow assistant engineer Richard Langham. During his second day on the job, he attended a Beatles' recording session where Langham assisted Norman Smith. Over the coming weeks, Emerick (58) would learn the protocol of Martin's sessions: "the balance engineer—and, of course, the assistant—[kept] his mouth shut unless spoken to. Any unsolicited opinions were perceived as undermining the role of the producer. Whether the producer was right or wrong, the engineer wasn't allowed to say anything." Moreover, "that's the way George Martin liked things."

The studio education of Geoffrey Emerick seems to have come primarily from observation:

> Naturally, whenever I was assisting on a session, I'd be watching the engineer closely. They wouldn't actively instruct us, but if you asked why they were doing something, they'd tell you. Both Stuart [Eltham] and Norman [Smith] were great that way. Stuart taught me a lot, especially about mic positioning, and Norman was a brilliant engineer with a keen mind. (Ibid.)

In this context, Emerick learned not only about the technical art of recording, but also about the protocols and priorities of a production crew. Working with Smith, he absorbed his recording philosophy: "As he sat behind the mixing desk, he would often say to me, 'The hit's down there, not up here.' His point was that no engineer could create a hit alone: the equipment we used and the skills we developed simply provided the means for recording and enhancing a performance" (58). Through the next few years, he would learn the art of engineering from Smith: "I was constantly asking Norman questions about what he was doing and why he was doing it, and he was very good about answering them and being patient with me" (69–70).

---

[11] By comparison, Addey remembers that his starting salary at the end of 1957 was £11 per week. Norman Smith's contract letter states that he was to be paid £12 per week. However, Addey had been in his twenties and Smith, his thirties. Emerick (a teen) probably received less than half of their rate because of his age.

The hierarchy of the studio also implied a chain of exploitation in which those at the top drew upon whatever skills those below them could offer. Producers requested engineers based on their particular skills. For example, "Stuart [Eltham] excelled at editing and creating sound effects," a proficiency that Martin found particularly useful on his comedy records. However, Norman Smith was Martin's choice when it came to recording rock and pop, and Emerick believes that Martin "realized that he himself was a bit out of his depth; he simply didn't know all that much about rock 'n' roll music" (2006: 58). Emerick reasons that Smith "seemed to relate well to pop musicians because he was one himself. So George relied on Norman for musical, not just technical, input" (ibid.). As evidence of this reliance on Smith, Emerick remembers, "George would relay Norman's thoughts to the band as if they were his ideas. Norman tolerated that well; he knew it wasn't his place to speak up. In those days, the producer was still very much in charge, and his methods were not to be questioned" (ibid.).

Emerick's Promotion

Emerick's first promotion introduced him to the mastering process, copying recordings to disks. "I was now stuck in a small room upstairs, making one-off acetates so that people could listen to their day's work at home" (87). When EMI promoted Malcolm Davies to balance engineer, not only did Emerick develop his ability to create master mixes of recordings ("putting the final touches on a mix as it was transferred from tape to vinyl for replication"), but the move also prepared him to create better vinyl pressings of Beatles recordings (105). In EMI's studio ecology, a domino sequence moved Davies downstairs to become an engineer, Emerick to the next chair to master, and Ken Scott to become his assistant.[12]

Although both Addey and Smith had become balance engineers through their involvement with hit recordings and artists, Emerick received his break as the system began to break down. When Martin formed AIR in 1965 and left EMI, the corporation selected Smith to replace him as the head of Parlophone Records. At first, Smith wanted to be both a producer and an engineer, but the reality of corporate hierarchy won out: Smith produced and Emerick became the new balance engineer in the house. He first established a reputation by assisting John Burgess on Manfred Mann's "Pretty Flamingo," but on 6 April 1966, he went back to work for Martin and the Beatles, beginning with "Tomorrow Never Knows." His selec-

---

[12] Scott and Emerick would engage in an interesting exchange of public letters about the accuracy of Emerick's biography, Scott in particular decrying slights against George Harrison. See Scott (2006a, 2006b) and Emerick (2006).

tion seems to have been as much a consequence of Martin wanting continuity, as it was his abilities and personality.

Martin chose Emerick over other candidates (for example, Ken Scott, who had assisted Norman Smith on the Beatles' *Help!* and *Rubber Soul* sessions) probably because of how they related personally. Emerick describes the Beatles' producer as a man with "a dry wit and a great sense of humor. Always well dressed and well mannered, he clearly enjoyed being an authoritarian figure" (98). Nevertheless, the new balance engineer believed that, for "all our differences in upbringing, training, and aptitude, he and I always seemed to relate well, from the earliest days" (ibid.). Emerick credits the success of their relationship to his willingness to keep his thoughts to himself: "I knew that from his point of view, there was nothing worse than having someone in the control room who was talkative and opinionated" (ibid.). Moreover, even with the promotion, "there wasn't ever a whole lot of conversation between George and me" (ibid.).

Another way to imagine the relationship might be to say that Emerick knew and felt content with his place. He could not provide the kinds of musical advice that Smith had, but by this time the Beatles had begun challenging Martin's authority in the studio. As Emerick describes his position, "Simply put, I presented no threat to him" (110). Ryan and Kehew (2006) have an additional explanation: by this time, no one else wanted to work with the Beatles, given their unconventional hours (they had taken to recording through the night) and increasingly unrealistic (and vague) demands. Who else but an optimistic, unmarried youth would be willing to spend most of his waking hours recording his favorite band?

As a balance engineer working on pop sessions, Emerick encountered the same resistance to change as Addey and Smith had before him. In part, the tension emerged between (a) an electronic musical medium that embraced and hinged on the recording arts to create a virtual performance on vinyl, and (b) an acoustic medium that sought a representation as close to acoustic as possible. For many classical audiophiles, vinyl representation constituted an inconvenience, which they would attempt to abolish with the illusion that the recording did not exist: the orchestra was there in the room with them. Pop music, by contrast, commonly created performances that could only exist in an electronic world. Where engineers like Meek had helped to invent this kind of recording, Emerick knew almost nothing else. Recordings made by engineers like Meek and Addey had defined Emerick's aesthetic sense such that he was entirely ready to experiment with techniques to create unique audio environments that performers could often never adequately recreate in concert. He also arrived at EMI at precisely the moment when the Beatles were ready to abandon live performance. Notably, McCartney (with whom Emerick seems to have built a relationship) had been immersing himself in the music of the avant-garde and the idea that recorded music amounted to a sonic art form unto itself.

EMI's segmented engineering hierarchy—designed with the idea of developing new technology—could also hinder change, or at least cautiously weigh its possibilities. A balance engineer pushing the limits of equipment specs could incur the wrath of some studio managers, even if the results were successful. Emerick occasionally received rebukes from EMI for his work with the Beatles, such as in 1966, when he and Paul McCartney (with the assistance of Ken Townsend) searched for a better bass sound and hit upon the idea of using a speaker as a microphone to capture low frequencies. This bass sound distinguished recordings like "Paperback Writer" and "Rain"; nevertheless, EMI criticized them over mismatched impedances (Lewisohn 1988: 74).[13]

The changes manifested in "Tomorrow Never Knows" were as much products of the milieu of swinging London and the Beatles playing with their own tape equipment as of novel engineering. Each of the Beatles contributed material for tape loops, and Emerick's first problem involved linking up tape decks in order to fade the different sounds into the mix. He came to rely upon EMI's infrastructure: "there were plenty of other machines in the Abbey Road complex, all interconnected via wiring in the walls, and all the other studios just happened to be empty that afternoon" (Emerick with Massey 2006: 112). The other problem came with Lennon's demand that his voice "sound like the Dalai Lama chanting from a mountaintop," for which Emerick arrived at the solution of having Ken Townsend rewire the Leslie organ speaker so that one could plug a microphone through it (8–9).

Of the challenges that Emerick and other engineers encountered as the sixties wore on, the increasing and conflicting demands for audio clarity and musical overdubs challenged their equipment the most. In 1967, although American studios were using recorders that could capture eight parallel tracks, EMI and other London studios were still using four tracks. In the recording sessions for John Lennon's "A Day in the Life," they had already filled four tracks with the basic recording before the Beatles (with Martin's acquiescence) planned orchestral overdubs. Emerick proposed using two four-track recorders, again relying on Ken Townsend to regulate the speeds of the two recorders so that they would stay in sync. Tape operator Richard Lush had the challenging task of manually lining up the machines and getting them to stay together as they made a number of attempts at keeping the two decks linked. A year later, the Beatles would be exper-

---

[13] Emerick (with Massey, 2006) would abandon the technique used on the recordings "Paperback Writer" and "Rain" because he perceived the sound to be muddy.

imenting with other studios, particularly Trident, which had imported an eight-track recorder from the United States (albeit one that ran at a different speed than British machines).

Emerick's Models

Like Addey and other successful engineers, Emerick declined invitations to reproduce the sound he obtained for Beatles recordings for other artists. Although his role was to serve the producer and the artists, he adopted Norman Smith's axiom that the sound began with the artist and that the engineer captured and manipulated that material. Perhaps what changed dramatically between the time of Smith's work with the Beatles and Emerick's was George Martin's role. Where Martin had been the early master, the Beatles now demanded their own say, including participating in the mixing of recordings, something very unusual until then. Technology advances were enabling musicians to do new things, including understanding and participating in the act of recording. Musicians now asserted themselves in ways that EMI had never anticipated.

Of the many factors at play in British recording studios in the sixties, class differences and expectations predictably came to bear upon the work of engineers and others in the studio. Emerick, in his biography, unleashes several blunt criticisms of Malcolm Addey, in terms of both his recording techniques and his personality. Addey's limited participation on Beatles sessions resulted in part from his own busy recording schedule and his refusal to work irregular hours. However, perhaps Addey's privileged grammar school education and bearing wore on Emerick's secondary modern sensibilities. Where Addey had learned self-confidence and how to feel comfortable expressing himself, Emerick had adopted the working-class ethic of keeping his mouth shut.

The only individual in the sixties at EMI who had mastered the ability to "pull an Addey" and to know precisely how to set up equipment in anticipation of a recording session would naturally need to define himself as different. If cultural change in Britain in this milieu grew partially out of competition between classes and generations, then Addey and Emerick were bound to have their differences.

And if Martin projected an air of royal authority and Emerick dutiful obedience, then the northern working-class accents that demanded change must have rattled everyone at Edward Elgar's prized recording facility and shrine to privilege. Emerick observes, "[T]here was an almost mystical bond between the four of them [i.e., the Beatles], which extended to Neil [Aspinal] and Mal [Evans] most of the time. It was a bond that created a wall impenetrable by any of us at

EMI, even George Martin" (Emerick with Massey 2006: 104). Moreover, the musicians who became synonymous with much of the musical change in Britain "always had a kind of 'us versus them' attitude that went beyond the fact that they were Liverpudlians and we were Londoners. They were very into being antiestablishment, and they saw us as being the establishment because we worked a proper job and had to wear suits and ties" (ibid.). In many ways, the success of the Beatles enabled musicians in Britain to have more of a say in the music they were recording and how studios treated them.

ENGINEERING CHANGE

Within the hallowed halls of EMI's Abbey Road facilities, Addey, Smith, and Emerick rode a juggernaut of technological change that careened through the recording industry during the sixties and highlighted the tensions of class and generation in their work. They arrived at the end of an era when mechanical lathes cut disks and studios were beginning to discover the possibilities of magnetic tape. By 1968 and the beginning of eight-track recording facilities in London, these engineers had helped to shape the sonic profile of popular music. Indeed, one can almost trace the history of 1960s British rock and pop through their recordings: "Move It" (1958), "Shakin' All Over" (1960), "Apache" (1960), "Love Me Do" (1962), "Please Please Me" (1963), "I Want to Hold Your Hand" (1963), "A Hard Day's Night" (1964), "Tomorrow Never Knows" (1966), Sgt. Pepper's Lonely Hearts Club Band (1967), and Piper at the Gates of Dawn (1967) represent just some of their "soundmarks." However, technological innovation alone cannot explain where the recording industry arrived at the end of the sixties.

The nature of the role of the recording technician and his (they were all men) relationship with producers and musicians shifted from that of servant to that of enabler. Although social hierarchy (often interpreted as "class" in this environment) remained an unpleasant fact in British studios, the respect accorded to engineers by the recording and music industries grew during this time. Everyone came to recognize that an experienced engineer could package a good performance into a great-sounding recording; meanwhile, the performers' and producers' expectations for magic increased exponentially. However, who became an engineer also shifted.

Smith served during the war, Addey in the postwar years, and Emerick not at all. Consequently, their relationships with the establishment reflected different levels of investment in the cultural system and different expectations for rewards. With a pre–Butler Act grammar school education,[14] Smith remained a company man through the sixties, demonstrating his dedication to an institution that gave a musician a chance to become a tape operator. Addey—the product of a postwar Butler Act grammar school education—brought a combination of technical and musical knowledge (not to mention inestimable self-confidence) to EMI, where he proceeded to define how pop records should sound. And Emerick, who managed to evade the career choices dictated by his secondary modern education, evolved into a studio risk taker. Notably of the three, Emerick possessed the fewest musical skills, perhaps signaling the arrival of the audio technologist and the disappearance of the aesthetician. Smith and Addey began with musical performances and found technical solutions to present those performances. For Emerick, technical solutions often constituted part of the musical performance.

All had in common the willingness to take risks. Indeed, they arrived at EMI in part because they were willing to take a chance on the future. Smith applied with little knowledge of recording equipment. Addey had built his own equipment. And Emerick had played with his recording equipment and tapes as a teen. Each provides us with a snapshot of a system in transition.

---

[14] The Education Act of 1944 (also known as the "Butler Act" after R. A. Butler, who drafted the legislation) mandated universal public education for students between the ages of five and fifteen. The act also instituted an exam to be taken by eleven-year-olds that would direct them into one of three hierarchical ranks of schools: technical, secondary modern, or grammar.

Bryan Daly, ca. 1950. Photo
courtesy of Robert Daly.

Allan Weighell, ca. 1960. Photo courtesy of Michael Weighell.

Les Reed, 1960s. Photo courtesy of Les Reed.

Clem Cattini with John Carter and his bride, Jill, in May 1966. Photo courtesy of John Carter.

The Ivy League's vocalists (*left to right*): Ken Lewis, Perry Ford, and John Carter. Photo courtesy of John Carter.

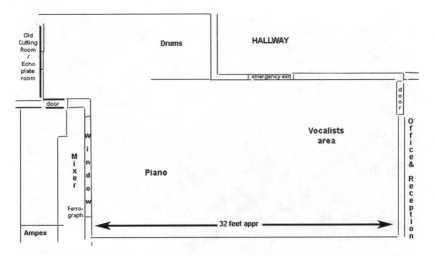

Old Cutting Room / Echo plate room

Drums

HALLWAY

door

emergency exit

door

Mixer

Window

Ferrograph

Piano

Vocalists area

Office & Reception

Ampex

32 feet appr

Regent Sound floor plan. Drawing courtesy of James Baring.

Joe Moretti, ca. 1958. Photo courtesy of Joe Moretti.

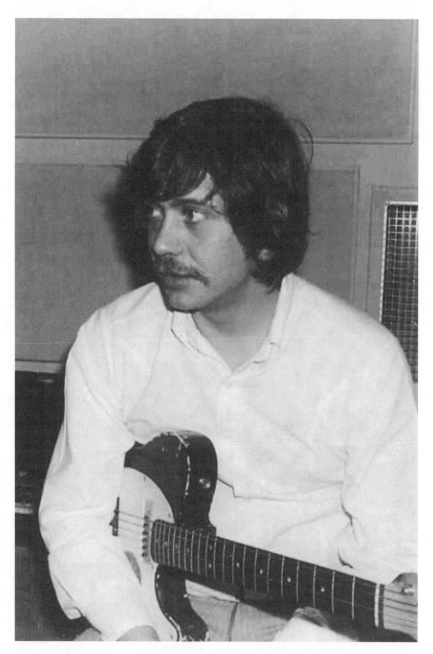

Joe Moretti at IBC Studios, ca. 1966. Photo courtesy of Joe Moretti.

Johnny Kidd listening to a playback in studio two at EMI (*left to right*): Guy Robinson (Kidd's manager), Peter Sullivan (producer), Kidd (with eye patch), Harry Moss (disk mastering engineer, *back*), Malcolm Addey (balance engineer, *at desk*), and Malcolm Davies (tape operator, *back*). Photo courtesy of Malcolm Addey.

The Breakaways recording in Decca's studio two in February 1964. *Left to right*: Margot Quantrell, Vicki Brown, and Jean Hawker. Photo courtesy of Margot Quantrell.

Andy White on stage at the London Palladium, ca. 1958, with his diamond black-pearl Ludwig drum kit. Photo courtesy of Andy White.

Freddie and the Dreamers with Mitch Murray: Roy Crewdson (rhythm guitar), Pete Birrell (bass), Freddie Garrity (vocal), Derek Quinn (lead guitar), Mitch Murray (songwriter), and Bernie Dwyer (drums). Photo by Bruce Fleming and courtesy of Bruce Fleming and Mitch Murray.

Dave Berry recording for television in the Carre Theater, Amsterdam, ca. 1965.
Photo courtesy of Dave Berry.

4

Mediating Change

Setting Musical Directions

Even the most musically adept producers relied upon a group of music professionals to help prepare arrangements, coach musicians, and conduct ensembles. The music directors,[1] arrangers, and conductors who acted as interpreters for producers had often prepared for their roles as musicians in sessions or as music copyists, playing, reading, and learning from others. The quickly changing tastes of pop music audiences in the early sixties challenged many producers whose musical predilections frequently resided in the big bands of the forties. Producers needed musicians who understood the new musical styles, who could translate the producers' ideas, and who could communicate effectively with other musicians. A good music director needed the abilities (a) to think through the formal structure of a performance, (b) to recommend possible instrumentations, (c) to write for those instruments, and (d) to lead the musicians in convincing performances. A successful music director exhibited all of these characteristics and creatively combined the musical material (the melody and harmony) with grooves that perhaps the songwriter had not imagined.

---

[1] Also known as "musical directors."

As the interlocutors, music directors, arrangers, and conductors often had to contend with several different kinds of skill variables. First, some producers were musicians who could have played (with the right technology and sufficient time) most of the music themselves. Others were better at keeping accounts balanced and keeping corporate executives happy than at knowing an English from a French horn. Producers thus defined the tasks of the MD (as practitioners often abbreviated the role); however, they too were a diverse lot in terms of skills and confidences. Dick Rowe and Andrew Oldham knew what they liked, but lacked the musical skills to be able to manage the music in a session. Consequently, they relied on music directors for the control of a musical event from the preparation of arrangements to the coaching of musicians. In other instances, the MD functioned as insurance that the session would go well, coaching both the musicians and the producers.

American Tony Visconti recalls his first project with Denny Cordell when the British producer arrived in New York to record Georgie Fame. When Visconti asked to see the music, Cordell replied that he had no music, but that his strategy was to "just roll a joint, play them the demo and they'll figure out their parts that way" (Cunningham 1998: 120). Seeing an expensive disaster with some of New York's best musicians in the works, Visconti quickly listened to the demo and wrote out parts for most of the musicians. After the session, Cordell told him, "I need a guy like you. I can't read music, I can't play an instrument and I often find myself at a loss for words when I'm trying to explain things to musicians. But you translated my ideas immediately on to notepaper and really helped me out of a potentially embarrassing situation" (ibid.).

Similarly, two differently skilled groups of musicians played in London's studios in the sixties. While most rock musicians memorized basic patterns and could play convincing variations on what they knew with minimal preparation, their restricted knowledge could severely limit what they could accomplish in the studio under time limits. In contrast, wind and especially string players could play almost anything, but required musical notations. Where one group specialized in the feel of a pop performance (something many classically trained and even some jazz musicians did not usually understand), the other had a consistency, rigor, and virtuosity that many pop musicians lacked. Someone who knew how to obtain the best from both worlds proved invaluable in the studio.

Artists on tour (where many often earned the majority of their income) seldom had the time or the energy (or, sometimes, the ability) to develop new material for recording. The responsibility for selecting and imagining the presentation of new repertoires ultimately fell on the producers, but they commonly relied on others to help them make those decisions. What would the predominant rhythmic groove be? What musical lines would accompany the main melody? Which instruments would be playing these lines? Sometimes, members of the group developed the arrangement (as the Animals did for "House of the Rising Sun"). However, music directors could help producers and performers to imagine something new, especially if they had a little time to think about the possibilities themselves. Almost as important, a good music director knew how to tailor arrangements to specific performers, taking advantage of their specific strengths and highlighting their marketable individualities.

The music professionals who filled the various niches in this environment learned their art in the trenches. For the first wave, successful jazz bands depended upon the services of clever arrangers who, if not the bandleaders, played in the band or, even rarer, provided services independently. (Consider Billy Strayhorn's musical relationship with Duke Ellington.) London attracted numerous talented and adaptable musical arrangers and musicians, many of whom learned convincingly how to copy American musical styles and to follow the originals as closely as possible, albeit sometimes with relatively stiff results. However, complicated orchestral and brass-reed arrangements required professional attention.

In the late fifties and early sixties, pianists routinely served as arrangers through the musical capacities of their instrument, which allowed them to identify individual parts and to provide harmonic accompaniment. Among the most notable of these piano-playing music directors were Les Reed, Arthur Greenslade, and Reg Guest. In an era when the British pop music industry was fixated on aping America, the ability of these men to recreate those foreign sounds with local artists added to their value. If you wanted to clone Steve Lawrence's "Go Away Little Girl," then you looked for someone who could quickly imitate the sound of his hit record. Naturally, not all jazz-based music directors and arrangers had an ear for or sympathy with pop music, leaving these recording sessions to a relatively small cohort who combined ability and affinity.

Many of the most interesting covers in 1960s British pop took music from one style and reimagined it in another. When the Beatles performed songs originally recorded by the Shirelles (a female singing quartet usually accompanied by saxophone, piano, bass, and drums), they did so by reinterpreting the music for what was essentially a rockabilly band (a singing trio with guitars, bass, and drums). Their conversions were usually quite homologous with the originals, even when George Martin substituted celesta for the organ solo in "Baby It's You." More dramatically, when the Spencer Davis Group took on Jackie Edwards's "Keep on Runnin'," they reimagined Jamaican ska as rock. For original music, an arranger could help the songwriter and producer to create a new sonic reality for their song. When Paul McCartney wanted strings and harp accompaniment for his

"She's Leaving Home" (and to bypass George Martin), he turned to Mike Leander to imagine and score the accompanying melodies and rhythms.

MDs such as Harry Robinson (*Oh Boy!*) and John Barry (*Drumbeat* and *6.5 Special*) were most in the public eye, often appearing weekly on television, where they provided the musical backbone of shows. In these cases, the music director worked with an in-house band to provide backup for featured artists, musical punctuations at the beginning and end of the show, or even dance music. The skills learned in putting on a thirty-minute weekly program paralleled those needed in recording sessions, where precious studio time demanded efficient and effective music making. However, the studios into which these television music directors often moved as composers were associated with the relatively more lucrative and glamorous film business. Harry Robinson, for example, scored for Hammer horror films, while Barry went on to fame with Bond films.

Much of an MD's work happened in anticipation of performance events, and his success lay in the groundwork that assured producers that they could obtain the best possible musical results with the performers and materials available to them. Sometimes, preparation meant finding an appropriate key for the singer, arranging parts, and rehearsing the musicians for a recording (also known as to "routine" a session). For example, Peter Knight, Jr., remembers his father, Peter Knight, Sr., rehearsing singers in their home, finding the right key for their voices, and working on arrangements: "Dad was at home, and the singers and the A&R men would come to the house to routine the next recording session. So, Pet Clark and anybody would come to the house and they'd work out the keys, the tempo, the duration, the instrumentation." Knight Sr. also applied his skills to one of the landmarks of 1960s British pop when he sewed the various pieces of the Moody Blues' *Days of Future Passed* together into a coherent musical whole, composing the transitional symphonic music and conducting the orchestra.

After establishing the best key (both for singers and instruments), their next task involved the recording's duration. Given that standard radio airtime for a recording was two to three minutes (a historical consequence of the 78-rpm disk), putting order to verses, choruses, and solos and bringing musical cohesion to a song often meant being creative with the materials at hand. George Martin (1983b: 78) suggests that his early Beatles records "show arranging at its most basic." For example, "Can't Buy Me Love" at first had no introduction, "so I took the first line of the chorus, repeated the last word twice and changed the harmonies, and started with that, before letting rip on the verse" (ibid.). Martin's only other duties included working out the guitar solo with George Harrison.

Martin emphasizes that, for him, the melody and lyric represent the core of a song, and an arrangement should never compromise that prominence. Moreover, he suggests that simple countermelodies can highlight the musical identity of a song. Beatles recordings in the mid-sixties feature a number of complementary and countermelodies, as in "Help!" and "Eleanor Rigby." Notably, Martin cites the guitar solo in "Nowhere Man" as an example of a countermelody derived by turning the main melody roughly upside down (1983b: 78). And examples of Martin's use of countermelodies (albeit sometimes on a very simple level) can be found in many of his non-Beatles productions of the era for artists such as Gerry and the Pacemakers and Cilla Black.

Another important method of highlighting the melody and lyric lies in the instrumentation and the articulation of the accompaniment. Even in the core of a pop group, a difference in emphasis on either guitar or keyboard can have a significant effect on the arrangement. Consider the differences in the sound of the Spencer Davis Group with Steve Winwood playing guitar ("Keep on Runnin'") or organ ("Gimme Some Lovin'"). More complicated and extended accompaniments demand an MD who understands a variety of instruments and how musicians play. Although some arrangers claim they got their start by simply looking at a chart to determine an instrument's range and whether they needed to transpose, they invariably knew how the instrument sounded from firsthand experience.

After the music director/arranger identifies the available resources, appropriateness remains the question. A new artist could hardly expect a complicated arrangement for a large orchestra, whereas an established artist, like Dusty Springfield, could (and did) demand the limit. Sometimes, instruments became popular and arrangements imitated, as when Mike Leander included an English horn in the accompaniment for Marianne Faithful's "As Tears Go By" a few months after George Martin had featured the instrument prominently in Gerry and the Pacemakers' "Don't Let the Sun Catch You Crying."

Musical directors often specialized in (or found themselves pigeonholed into rendering) particular kinds of arrangements. For example, Peter Knight, Jr., remembers a recording session at Pye for Sammy Davis, Jr., where his father arranged one side of the disk—"all strings and choirs"—and John Keating, whose specialty was "brass and raspy stuff," the other side. In this regard, the pop groups who invaded studios in the mid-sixties could be quite cost efficient if they were proficient enough to be able to record their own material.

Besides putting a singer through a "routine" (finding the right key and delivery style), the MD considered which instruments to include and then drafted explicit musical directions. In some cases, especially first attempts, the arrangers would copy out the parts themselves; however, the more established they became and the more elaborate the productions, the more likely they would hire a copyist to prepare the parts. The copyists, in the meanwhile, learned something of the arranger's art, often graduating to become arrangers themselves.

Over the course of the sixties, the nature of arranging and music direction changed. At the beginning of the decade, arrangers often notated every part precisely and expected musicians to render their instructions exactly. By the mid-sixties, a more flexible approach emerged for a growing number of sessions. Scores remained important and the music director and producer still expected many musicians to play parts exactly, but MDs with rock and pop backgrounds emphasized the spontaneity of rock and pop, leaving room for musicians to improvise. Arrangers such as Geoff Love continued to write fixed arrangements for some instruments, but not others. Guitarist Vic Flick remembers that, at the session for Peter and Gordon's "World without Love" (which Love arranged), "I was presented with a chord chart with a couple of lines indicated, the rest of it was up to me. The organ player [Harold Smart] was a very straight player and had to have his part notated, but apart from that, it was pretty loose." In this era, "[n]ot a lot, apart from big orchestras, was written and stuck to as if written in stone." Indeed, on one occasion, "[w]e even had one MD turn up with nothing and [he] shouted at us because nothing happened when he counted in!"

Obviously, not all recordings required an MD. By the time the Who arrived in the studio, the band had rehearsed Pete Townshend's music. They soon came to believe not only that they didn't need an MD, but that they could produce themselves, with Townshend relying on the members of the band and on Kit Lambert to help him shape and realize his musical ideas. Nevertheless, the producer, Shel Talmy, provided invaluable criticisms from outside the social circle of the band, even if the social circle prevailed. When John Cameron worked with Donovan as music director, he helped the folk musician to reimagine his music and its presentation. For Donovan and producer Mickie Most, Cameron facilitated a process in which the Scottish folk singer made the transition from an acoustic to an electric performer and from folk to rock.

Some artists and repertoire managers relied heavily on their MDs, as Columbia's Norman Newell did when he characteristically employed Geoff Love, crediting him on recordings. And even the musically adept George Martin used an arranger to help him with some projects, as when he brought in Johnny Pearson to assist in the recording of Cilla Black's version of Burt Bacharach and Hal David's "Anyone Who Had a Heart" (see Roberts 1964b: 10). However, most often the music director labored out of the public eye, with no acknowledgment on either the record label or sleeve. For example, despite his critical catalytic role in translating Donovan's ideas in "Sunshine Superman," John Cameron received no mention on the disk.

Most MDs began their careers doing arrangements for the bands in which they played, often gaining experience in London's numerous clubs and on tours. Some of the most successful music directors (e.g., Les Reed and John Paul Jones) came from musical families. Others, such as Charles Blackwell, arrived by way of personal volition. The root of the distinction between Les Reed and John Paul Jones lies in their births on different sides of a cultural divide, drawn in large part by national service. Reed came from a jazz background with an innate sense of how to voice horn sections. The rock 'n' roll generation that birthed Jones understood the power of the groove. Where Reed preferred the piano, Jones chose the electric bass. Moreover, the growth in the number of studios around London took some of the focus off corporate facilities: more studios meant more time to find the best tempo, rhythm, and ensemble feel. Reed's and Jones's differences were musical, generational, and vast, and yet they shared many of the same aesthetics. The shift from one generation to the next appears to have been less sudden revolution than gradual evolution.

Music directors and arrangers occupied a musical and social rank distinct from regular musicians, if by no other virtue than that they had the skills to organize music making. As such, this position professionally aligned them with producers. In a class-conscious context, being an MD placed one in a fluctuating social position. Sometimes, you were separate from the musicians for whom you wrote. Sometimes, you played with them in your musical arrangements. And sometimes, as a session musician, you played with them as a fellow contracted employee on someone else's gig. Indeed, music directors were often übermusicians, high achievers in a studio meritocracy. As one marker of that difference, Arthur Greenslade remembers that, when working for a studio like EMI, it calculated his fee as "15 guineas[2] for an arrangement," no matter how complicated or how successful the work. And Charles Blackwell recalls that he would commonly "invoice record companies in guineas and they would automatically work out the cheque payment in pounds and shillings."

Paul Lewis (2002) notes that the guinea constituted a traditional form of payment for artists and professionals that stood distinct from the pound, which functioned as the mode of payment for laborers. Thus, record companies financially interacted with arrangers (understood as professionals) in guineas, while they paid musicians (understood as craftspeople and whose rate the union had

---

[2] "Prior to decimalization the pound was divided into twenty shillings and each shilling was divided into twelve pennies or pence." A guinea had the value of one pound and one shilling (Lewis 2002).

negotiated) in pounds and pence. Les Reed notes, "It was a kind of class thing," recognizing that "the main man" received payment "in this fashion," whereas the musicians earned pounds, shillings, and pence: "Don't ask me why, but then, we were a class-conscious country."

Four individuals neatly illustrate different aspects of music directing and arranging in the sixties and how the tasks of the music director and arranger changed. Arthur Greenslade represents an older tier of arrangers and music directors who came of age during the heyday of 1930s dance band music; Les Reed, the jazz generation born before the war; Charles Blackwell, the generation born during the war, who gave form to rock 'n' roll; and John Paul Jones, whose "bulge" generation spoke the language of rock and pop fluently.

ARTHUR GREENSLADE

One of the most remarkable individuals to participate in the British pop and rock explosion, and who formed the mold for others, started as a pianist and became a session musician before moving on to arranger and music director. Older than most in this scene (he was in his forties when he played on the Kinks' first hit in 1964), Arthur Greenslade (1923–2003) evinced the motto "forever young." Like other music directors and arrangers, he often participated as a musician not only on some of his own sessions, but also on those of other MDs; however, his reputation grew from his work arranging, conducting, and directing music for artists such as Chris Farlowe, Shirley Bassey, and Dusty Springfield, among others. He also directed the house band—Arthur Greenslade and the Gee Men—on the BBC Light Programme's *Saturday Club,* from 10:00 a.m. until noon, an influential radio staple from 1963 through 1966. Where some credit their success to their determination and skill, Greenslade modestly believed that he was just a "very lucky guy" who "had opportunities all the way down the line."

When age four, he began to play piano at his widowed father's insistence: "Every Friday evening, I went to my music lesson for an hour. And here's the strange bit about it: I just was not interested." Like many kids, he was aware that his "mates would be waiting outside" and, consequently, would pitch his "music case in the corner," avoiding practice for the rest of the week. However, adolescence intervened, and his interest in music apparently erupted when his father (inspired by a scholarship his son had earned) informed him that schoolwork trumped piano lessons. By the time the war broke out, Arthur occupied the piano bench in a semiprofessional quartet: he was sixteen.

In the context of the jazz and dance bands with which he played, he developed his skills as an arranger for the next twenty years. His break into recording sessions as a musician did not come until around 1960, when contractors began calling him. His maturity and easy affinity with the new rock and pop of the age made him a natural leader on whom both contractors and producers felt they could rely.

Contractor and violinist Charlie Katz called first, and the two developed what Greenslade experienced as a long and productive, if sometimes stormy, professional relationship. Indeed, Katz and the other string-playing contractors became his instructors. Greenslade admits, "I'm lucky really. I never had lessons in arranging. I got advice." Arranging for bands came from his experience in those ensembles, but strings meant relying on the players he knew. "Luckily enough, I could hang with Charlie Katz and Sidney Sax. Anything I wanted to know about strings, I could ring them up and they would give advice." Consequently, producers came to know him as a strings arranger who understood jazz and called him when they wanted an orchestra to sweeten a recording.

Early Work

His first contracted arrangement for a recording came when Dick Rowe asked him to work on a cover by British crooner Ray Bennett of the Steve Lawrence American hit, "Go Away Little Girl." The arrangement imitated the original, and the recording flopped in Britain against Mark Wynter's version, but Greenslade's work attracted the attention of other producers. Like others, he worked with producers and artists to set keys and develop arrangements, but ultimately his responsibility was to work with everyone to maximize the musical potential of a session. One aspect of this process was to establish the nature of the arrangement from the beginning. When he arrived at the producer's office to routine a session, he would begin by asking, "Now, you want to tell me what to do? Or do you want an Arthur Greenslade arrangement?" He remembers, "It was either/or. And that always worked."

Reflecting the three-hour aesthetic of the fifties and early sixties recording industry, Greenslade expected to finish several recordings in one sitting. To this end, he complains that, although in about half the sessions the "producers would tell you what they wanted," the other half "didn't know," so "they'd keep us there, spending all that time on one blooming number." If a producer and/or music director had prepared the singer and had the arrangements complete, then they could "spend their time [getting] whatever they wanted out of the performance in the studio." For example, when working with Dusty Springfield on sessions such as "The Look of Love," Greenslade usually discovered that her producer, John Franz, had already planned most of the session: "John had perfect pitch and was a pianist [which would] save me mucking about finding the key." At the other extreme, in situations where the producer had undertaken little preparation, Greenslade would find himself testing the patience of the session musicians while trying to figure out what the producer wanted. With an eye on the clock and a signal from the producer, they sometimes simply had to make do with what they had. Ultimately, he would get the inevitable signal to call out, "Right, next title."

Of all of the artists with whom he worked, Dusty Springfield presented some of the most interesting challenges. Details mattered to Springfield, and the singer insisted on having a significant say in the recording. "I would get a call to go up to Philips Records, Johnny Franz's office and Dusty would be there. Dusty and John would have sorted out whatever numbers they wanted to record, and we would first set the keys and then discuss what was wanted with the arrangement." They "would go in with about four numbers" for each of "about three or four sessions" scheduled for the recordings. Out of the approximately sixteen recordings, "you would pull a single out." The problem for Greenslade (or any other music director in London at that time) was that Springfield insisted, as a singer, on having a say in the musical arrangement and the performance (singers usually had little say in the recording process), and she challenged expectations of what a woman could demand. Greenslade describes her as, although "a lovely girl," "a nitpicker."

Springfield's attention to detail and her determination to hear those details in the music could derail the already tight recording studio schedule. Commonly, she would single out a musician and demand the repeated performance of a passage until she found exactly what she wanted, no matter how many other musicians were sitting and waiting. In one instance, Greenslade remembers, "she kept us for about an hour. We're sitting there scratching our butts," such that the musicians considered finding others to take their places at the next day's session. The recording occurred at the old "Olympic Studios in a little mews, behind Selfridge's, and there was a bottle shop on the corner. At the end of the session, this chap from the bottle shop came in with a sap barrow and about six crates of beer for the boys, for us to turn up the next day." Springfield (taking the role of music director in a context where women had no previous standing) had sought to smooth the ruffled feathers of the old guard: "Dusty knew she'd upset us. She knew when she'd trod on somebody's foot." Negotiating attitudinal change in a male-dominated environment could involve invoking stereotypes of the master appeasing laborers with an offer of food or libations.

One of the fiscal realities of recording pop music lay in the resources available for hiring musicians, particularly orchestral players. A popular artist such as Dusty Springfield would expect significant musical forces and extended studio time for her recording sessions. However, with many productions, the budget could be quite conservative, as it had been with the Ray Bennett recording mentioned above: "that would have been an 'el cheapo,' about a nine-piece or something like that." Working within these parameters, Greenslade grew enamored of the luxury of writing for a full string ensemble. "In those days, I always used to have sixteen violins, four violas, and four cellos. That was the regular. That was beautiful to have in those days."

Given the expense of hiring an orchestra, some producers resorted to electronically expanding the ensemble by surreptitiously overdubbing and relying on orchestral musicians to play with considerable consistency: "If you went ten times, it still ain't going to be any better on the tenth one than what it was on the first run through." Relying on this ability, a producer would say, "Right Arthur, run it down," knowing that the initial "rehearsal" would be nearly perfect; however, while the producer "wouldn't put the red light on," Greenslade would know that the producer had nonetheless been taping. After the tape operator had cued the reel, the producer would signal with the studio's red light that the recording had begun and say, "Right, now we'll do a take," and double-track the second performance with the first to give the impression of a larger ensemble. Greenslade complains that this approach amounted to a contemptible way to give the impression of a larger ensemble, without the richness of a real orchestra. However, he would probably have known about the overdubbing: he would have had to cue the orchestra in sync with the original recording. But he had little choice. If he betrayed the producer's duplicity, he could lose his next commission.

Working with singers often proved to be one of a music director's most challenging tasks, as was negotiating with the Musicians' Union over the rule during the early sixties that "the vocal had to go on at the same time as the orchestral track." Those at the core of the session scene "were doing three sessions a day: morning, afternoon and evening, running from one studio to another." In this tight context, when a session ran overtime, other sessions felt the consequences. Vocalists represented the commonest cause for overtime. Ill-prepared or sick singers could "waste all the bloody time" because they "couldn't get it right." "Some of the takes would go on for ages and ages." The MU rule assured musicians of work whenever recording with a singer, but producers possessed a more economical magnetic approach: faking a performance, recording the accompaniment, and dubbing in voices later. Most commonly, they would put the singers in a booth in plain view of the orchestra, but not turn on their microphone. Then, usually at night, the singers would return and attempt their best performances over the previously recorded orchestral tracks.

In another common technique, the producer would select parts of different recorded performances and splice them together, an involved process that in the sixties meant cutting up lengths of tape and hoping that the edit would not be noticeable. For this splicing to be effective, every performance had to be at the same tempo and pitch; a good music director thus had to maintain very precise musical time from one take to the next (and sometimes one session to the next) and to keep everything in tune.

As an arranger, Greenslade created successful musical accompaniments for a variety of producers: "I used to do a lot of work with Andrew Oldham and I did some stuff for the Stones themselves, some string writing and put it on the Stones records." For example, when Oldham wanted Chris Farlowe to record a cover of the Jagger-Richards song "Out of Time," he turned to Greenslade to do the arrangement. After working with Oldham and Jagger on the musical structure, he created a score for a small string ensemble, which Oldham and Jagger then took into the studio to record. The rhythm section featured some of the most prominent session musicians of the day, including Joe Moretti (guitar), Eric Ford (guitar and bass), Reg Guest (piano), and Andy White (drums). The ubiquitous violinist Sid Sax (also a contractor) led the string section. Farlowe, however, had trouble delivering a convincing version of the song.[3] To assist, Jagger recorded a version over the same accompaniment to demonstrate how he thought the performance should go.[4] With additional coaching from Oldham, Farlowe found a convincing delivery and a hit record; however, the musicians had recorded the backing track separately from either of the sung versions.

Greenslade Interactions

The phenomenal international success of British artists in the sixties made British studios the destination for musicians and producers from all over the world. In this context, the music director's role paralleled that of a musical translator, converting other people's ideas into words and concepts musicians could understand. Notably, Greenslade recorded with Frenchman Serge Gainsbourg and American Rod McKuen. "Britain between the middle 50s and up to '68, because of the rock 'n' roll, we more or less took over the pop music world and all the continental people used to come to Britain to record, thinking that we were the geniuses behind all that stuff."

However, sometimes, the translation work between the musicians and a British producer might pose difficulties: "I would get my instructions through a

---

[3] The Stones had recorded the song a few months earlier, but with a dramatically different arrangement, which appears on the album *Aftermath* (1966).

[4] Decca would release this version after the Stones had severed their relationship with the corporation.

person like Dick Rowe, the A&R man, and I would tell [the musicians] what he wanted. You know, 'Drums, quiet down,' 'Play eight in a bar instead of four in a bar,' or 'Play the top cymbal instead of the high-hat.'" Sometimes, with the young bands that entered the studio looking for instant success, the music director needed to translate common musical and recording practices into terms they could understand. A member of the older studio generation, Greenslade's attitude toward rock musicians at times could be condescending: "they weren't musicians. Nothing was organized. All their stuff was by ear." Notably, his definition of "musician" (by which we presume he means "professional musician") hinges on the ability to read music. Musicians who could read music made his life easier.

Working with Oldham could also be challenging for Greenslade, who may have been sympathetic to rock, but clearly came from the establishment's generation. "Andrew used to come down to my house where we lived in Purley and we'd go in the dining room, chatting away." Unlike the traditional routine session, the artist would not be present at these sessions, which meant that setting the key for the singers could be, at best, difficult. Oldham would tell the arranger, "Oh, I want this," even though the producer "didn't know what he was talking about." Nevertheless, Oldham would demand, "Oh, I want an oboe in there." Greenslade figures that Oldham "hadn't got a clue what an oboe sounded like." Nevertheless, the arranger's approach was to have the producer "tell me what to do and you'll get it." More challenging, Greenslade found the drug use of the mid- to late sixties at odds with his ideas about decorum, especially in his home, where planning began: "Andrew would have his driver in there rolling him joints of marijuana. I didn't use that stuff. I used to say to him, 'Whoa, well blimey, if my wife comes in a minute, it will be murders!'"

Greenslade and contractor Charlie Katz came into conflict on one notable session for the American songwriter Rod McKuen, where the arranger also conducted the performance. McKuen—annoyed that some of the wind players continued to chat among themselves between recording takes—fired them. Outraged, Katz's wife, Lita (who had booked the session), complained, "I don't think much of you for not sticking up for the musicians." After that, Greenslade used another violinist-contractor, Sid Sax, to book musicians, working with Charlie Katz only when it was unavoidable (or when working with Dick Rowe at Decca, who used Katz exclusively as a contractor). Of course, McKuen had hired Greenslade, situating him firmly on the production side of the equation.

Producers also brought in music directors like Greenslade when they wanted to find ways to distinguish a recording from others competing for consumer attention. As the Clavioline had helped to draw attention to the Tornados' "Telstar," Art Greenslade purchased a Farfisa electronic organ and wrote its sounds into his arrangements, reaping income not only from the arrangement, but also for his performance services (or, for renting the instrument for the session). Unfortunately, Greenslade's instrument met with an unexpected end one day outside Lansdowne's basement studios. Guitarist Vic Flick witnessed the demise when "Arthur allowed John, the studio attendant, to carry his Farfisa up the two flights of stairs and leave it on the pavement for him to put in his car." Flick remembers the attendant

> [s]truggling up the stairs with the green monster and finally reaching the pavement [where] he leaned it against some railings. The trouble is, there's a right way and a wrong way to lean a Farfisa Organ against railings on a windy day, and, as Arthur's head came level with the pavement, he witnessed the horrifying sight of his money-making machine being blown flat on the unforgiving flagstones.

Flick heard "the clattering, crashing, and splintering sound" of the Farfisa's inner workings and the rattle when they "slid down to the bottom" as Greenslade picked up the instrument (Flick 2001). Thus ended the sound of the Farfisa in Greenslade's arrangements.

LES REED

One of the most prolific members of the mid-1960s London music scene, Les Reed (b. 1935) performed as a pianist on television shows and films, accompanied some of the best-known solo singers of the era, and functioned as a music director and arranger, helping rock artists and pop groups alike with everything from trumpet and sax accompaniment to song arrangements. Moreover, as a songwriter, he contributed some of the best-known pop songs of the sixties. He also provides an example of how talented individuals rose within the social ranks of British pop music culture, if not within British society.[5]

In an era of rapidly evolving musical tastes and technology, Reed functioned as a catalytic figure, facilitating some of the most successful British recordings of the sixties. His parents (both musicians) began his musical instruction early and supported him in his musical studies, including prepping him for entry into the London College of Music. As a child, he and his father performed on buses, earning money for the family, paying for his musical education, and developing a sense of audience taste. The teenage Reed performed professionally and, during his national service, learned the clarinet, which proved to be good training for his years on Denmark Street after the army demobilized him in 1956.

---

[5] He is now Les Reed, OBE (Officer of the British Empire).

Reed played piano in dance orchestras after his service, getting a chance to play with American jazz artists (including expatriate bebop trumpeter Alphonso "Dizzy" Reece) and meeting local musicians, such as guitarist Vic Flick. In the summer of 1958, Flick secured a Butlin's summer camp[6] engagement at Clacton-on-Sea, playing sets of "rock and calypso," reflecting the tastes of the time. For the jazz pianist, "that was the start of my intro into pops, because we were playing rock classics." Reed remembers that downstairs from them was a lounge where Cliff Richard and the Drifters played, which consisted of "Cliff with two of his players" (guitarist Ian Samwell and drummer Terry Smart). The trio apparently struck the owner as "too loud," and Richard and his band got "the sack after about six weeks." However, Richard had "just been into London to make 'Move It,'" which would move into the charts in September and become what many British musicians consider the first indigenous rock hit. Reed contemplates, "you can imagine [Butlin's] chagrin."

Back in London, Flick introduced Reed to a new colleague: trumpeter, composer, and arranger John Barry. "I was told to report on a Saturday morning at a place in Hammersmith for an audition, not only for the group, but for an upcoming TV series." The BBC broadcasted *Drumbeat* live on Saturday evenings, and for each show producer Stewart Morris "got together a lot of people like Adam Faith, Danny Williams, Marty Wilde—and lot[s] of rock stars. The Bob Miller Band and the John Barry Seven [were the] residents." Although the band sometimes played compositions like "Take Five," "our name was made basically on the sound of the John Barry Seven, which was so basic, but a good sound." However, Reed's reputation lay in being a jazz pianist and arranger, and the essentiality of rock and pop embarrassed him: "Coming from playing with some of the jazz greats, [rock] was based around three or four chords. I found this very, very intimidating, not to be able to put flattened fifths in here. I was looked at very strangely by John Barry if I did."

Barry's band environment provided valuable training for Reed as well as a context in which he could experiment with arrangements. Instead of dance-band jazz models, Barry emphasized simplicity and blending, which yielded clear and yet powerful recordings. A dance hall's sheer size required a big band (i.e., trumpet, trombone, and saxophone sections) to provide volume and rhythmic punch, but as amplification improved, the size and nature of musical ensembles changed

[6] Billy Butlin in 1936 built his first "camp," and subsequently many others, around entertainment venues where campers would stay in cottages or sometimes hotels from whence they could walk to the sea, rides, or evening dances.

over the course of a few years. Moreover, recordings depended on careful micro-phone placement for listeners who experienced music through a radio or from a turntable. Barry's band and arrangements captured this aesthetic.

In addition to the Saturday night broadcasts on *Drumbeat,* the John Barry Seven toured, often playing in converted cinemas, such as those of the Top Rank chain. In these venues, early rock and pop stars sometimes found themselves per-forming on the same show as comedians and to seated audiences rather than dancers. These contexts also demanded that they play in a variety of styles:

> There were times when we'd go out with Adam Faith, and the Honeys, and Larry Grayson, who was a great comic. And then on a Sunday, we'd probably do a concert with Eddie Cochran and Gene Vincent. Then another day, we would end up with Marty Wilde, and probably Joe Brown and these kinds of people. So, [the shows] were very varied in their makeup. We accompanied some of these guys if they didn't have their own bands.

He also got to work with artists who would later become well-known perform-ers, such as Dusty Springfield, whom Reed met when she performed with the Lana Sisters.

Accompanying different singers could be a challenge. Reed describes these concerts as "an integrated scene in a way, because, in the main, some of these guys had [written] music that you could play. But then some, like Dickie Pride, would turn up [and ask], 'You remember the record?' And I'd say, 'No,' so they'd get out a recording and in a rehearsal you'd learn it with them." Other times, the singers and featured artists "had their own dots,[7] which was great. Duane Eddy would come across and he'd have his own dots and we'd accompany him." In order to be successful in this environment, musicians had to be able to read music: "Vic [Flick] and I were very good readers as were the drummer, the bass player, and the tenor sax player. All very good readers." The combination of a good ear and musical lit-eracy allowed them to do well in a variety of performance environments.

Success on *Drumbeat* led to other television shows, including "*Thank Your Lucky Stars* (on Sundays with Brian Matthew), *Saturday Club, Easy Beat,* and *Top Gear,* all of those rock programs." In short, television, recording, and touring kept Reed and the other members of the John Barry Seven very busy, perhaps too busy. "It was just after [*Dr. No*]. We were doing a week in Swindon on tour when I decided I just couldn't take it any more. It was the touring and everything else." A compelling enticement to leave the road came in the form of an increasing number of requests to participate in recording sessions, which would leave him in London

---

[7] Notated music.

rather than on the road: "I'd been offered many jobs as a session pianist, so I thought I would cuff out of the Seven sort of late '62 or so [and] find my own way."

Reed Directs

Through television and film exposure, the musical and sonic imprint of the John Barry Seven had become the golden mean for some record producers who wanted that sound for their own records. Reed contributed to several early pop recordings, notably Adam Faith's early hit "What Do You Want?"[8] Songwriter Johnny Worth initially had asked Reed to create a demo he could use for Johnny Kidd and the Pirates: "I played it with a rock-type rhythm, but Johnny hated the song." Undaunted, they rearranged the song and "when we played it to John Barry for Adam Faith I changed the whole treatment of the song into a Buddy Holly, string-type treatment, and John Barry used this treatment for his arrangement." The recording became a number-one hit, and his work gained attention.

On one of Adam Faith's recording sessions, "I was playing piano and I remember Johnny Worth had a mate called Ray Horricks" (a producer for Pye and, later, Decca), who believed that Reed would make a good music director. "Ray heard me playing and he just came up to me afterwards and said, 'You really ought to be on record as a pianist, or an arranger, or something. You've got to do something on your own.'" Worth knew Reed to be a musician of considerable potential and proven reliability and, in the process, gave him work and advice on how to succeed in the London music scene: "Johnny was my first mentor in the business in the writing side along with Jimmy Kennedy. I learned so much from Johnny Worth it's ridiculous." In early 1962, Horricks brought the young pianist to Pye's Piccadilly Records as a musical director and gave him "a load of artists like the Countrymen." His first effort with that band, "I Know Where I'm Going," was a modest hit followed by bigger success when Joe Brown and His Bruvvers recorded "Picture of You."

At Pye, Reed learned that a music director served as a buffer between the studio and the musicians. Members of Brown's band had written "Picture of You" and had already rehearsed their arrangement. Reed stood as the only thing between them and the recording session. His primary interests lay in confirming that the song and the arrangement were satisfactory and that the recording stayed within the financial parameters set by Pye. Music directors routinely mediated between the producer and the musicians, listening to the concerns of each and

---

[8] Faith had been a regular on the television show *Drumbeat,* where he and Reed became friends. Indeed, Faith served as Reed's best man at his wedding in 1960.

arriving at a musical solution with which both sides could live. Reed recalls that, when Joe Brown and His Bruvvers first discussed the recording with him, drummer Bobby Graham had an idea: "I think we could do with a little timp roll on this." Reed agreed that such a musical touch would be nice, but when the band arrived at the studio, Graham looked around with regret: "Where are the timps? We agreed there was going to be a timp roll. You haven't brought your timps along." Reed had already determined that, as good an idea as a timp roll would be, he had no budget for it. "Look, I'm the musical director. I don't get timps for drummers."

The recording became a hit without the timpani, and Reed and Graham became friends as well as collaborators on a number of recordings, but Reed clearly asserted his role as the ranking professional. Reed remembers, "we did four titles on that one session. Three were hits": "Picture of You," "That's What Love Will Do," and "It Only Took a Minute." Reed believes that he "provided the musical knowledge on the session and indeed sang on it as well." With Horricks working as the producer, "I was there just to make sure that they were playing the right notes. It was an easy gig for me because I didn't have to do any arrangements."

Like other music directors, Reed would routine singers while working on an arrangement, first picking a key by asking a performer to "sing this out as loud as you can." Reed remembers that he did so "knowing full well that in the studio they wouldn't have to sing it so loudly because the microphone would pick it up." From hearing them sing this way, he "could deduce their top note pretty carefully, and their bottom note." From there, "you'd go into a key higher and, if they started to strain, you knew where you were." He maintained that "top and bottom notes were always the secret of a good recording," as well as knowing "where they felt comfortable." Another important part of a routine session was to look for the singer's strengths and to build those into the arrangement and the recording. His goal was to determine how a singer could be successful by studying "the way they phrased a lyric, the way they phrased a tune, and whether we could embellish on that phrasing." He then would "try and teach them the way I thought the song should be sung." This included working with singers who had a lisp or whose intonation might be less than accurate.

In Reed's opinion, "the worst thing for any producer or arranger is to hear the song being sung with a lisp, and I had many singers with a lisp. It's almost uncontrollable." One approach would be to select songs "where they don't have to lisp too much." If all else failed, he hoped that the engineers could fix the problem. Sometimes, singers would have mental blocks with particular melodic passages and difficulty singing specific intervals. Reed remembers how Australian Frankie Stevens had trouble with the interval "between G and A. He could hit a G, [but] he'd end up on either an A flat or a B. He couldn't hit a perfect tone on those two notes. Any other two notes were fine, it was just those two. So, we kept right clear of those two notes. Even taking it into another key or something for him to get away from it."

In working with Tom Jones, Reed remembers that he and songwriter/manager Gordon Mills tutored Jones in his phrasing and interpretation because "Tom used to sing a song very straight." He describes an early 1960s Jones performance: "he would just sing a song. There wouldn't be a lot of soul going into it even though we knew that he had the soul." In their minds, Jones's competition primarily included African American performers such as "Otis Redding and Marvin Gaye," and his problem lay in that "he didn't have those kinds of inflections." Jones's conservative Welsh choral voice needed assistance competing with Memphis and Detroit's gospel-inspired performances. Consequently, Reed and Mills coached Jones to discover an identifiable style of singing, fostering a more soulful approach in the Welshman. "Sometimes when you hear the inflections it's not Tom singing. It's either Gordon Mills or myself saying, 'Sing it this way.'" An illustration of this combination of "straight" and "soulful" can be heard in Jones's performance of "It's Not Unusual," which is sung with few ornaments but with a relaxed phrasing against the incessant beat. Reed's arrangement emphasizes a punchy brass section coupled with a driving rhythm section over which any shift in phrasing by Jones takes on added significance.

Reed and the Dave Clark Five

In 1964, the rise of the Beatles and other beat groups brought Reed's abilities as a music director to play with a group that the press briefly heralded as the successors to the fab four. The Dave Clark Five had won awards in 1963 on the London dance circuit and had served as a demo band for songwriters like Mitch Murray. The bandleader-drummer Dave Clark relied on singer and organist Mike Smith to drive the band musically; however, after a slow climb to the top of the charts, Clark must have been concerned about their longevity. Their early recordings on Pye's sublabels (Ember, Congress, and Piccadilly) had failed, but these (and demo recordings on Denmark Street) served as contexts in which Clark learned studio craft. Following the model of Meek, Talmy, and Oldham, Clark decided to gain control over his recordings, signing a lease agreement with EMI's Columbia label. Recording at Lansdowne Studios, Clark produced the sessions, double-tracking voices and instruments with some success—but he also sought musical advice. Over dinner, Clark's agent, Harold Davidson, approached Reed with the idea of becoming the Dave Clark Five's musical director. Reed had been successful with

Joe Brown and His Bruvvers and, to Davidson, the Dave Clark Five must have seemed in the same category. Could Reed work some magic with them too?

As an independent producer, one of Clark's first lessons had come in the areas of release timing and originality. Their initial Columbia single, "Do You Love Me" (a cover of the Contours' Motown single), reached into the top fifty; however, they released it weeks after a version by Brian Poole and the Tremeloes, whose version went to the top of the British charts.[9] Despite the power of the Dave Clark Five's recording and presentation, Brian Poole's version was already in the public's ear. Clark had been unsuccessfully asking British songwriters for material, so he prodded his singer and keyboard player, Mike Smith, into writing original material and established their first major success. "Glad All Over" replaced the Beatles at the top of British recording charts and led to the first of many premature proclamations of the Beatles' demise.

Reed's role with the Dave Clark Five involved both writing brass and saxophone arrangements (e.g., "You Got What It Takes" and "Red Balloon") and recommending musical changes. This assistance included choosing some of the best-known session musicians of the day, such as Vic Flick and Jimmy Page on guitars and Eric Ford on bass, to supplement the band. More controversially, Dave Clark and Les Reed also often brought in a session drummer, in part because of the written arrangements (Clark could not read music), but also possibly because Clark would have been preoccupied in the control room.

Bobby Graham had become one of the most sought-after session drummers in London, not only for his drumming skills, but also for his apparent imperturbability under pressure. Clark drummed on some recordings, but Graham (Harrington and Graham 2001) contends that he contributed regularly to Dave Clark Five sessions, including their first two hit singles, "Do You Love Me" and "Glad All Over." Indeed, many early DC5 recordings reveal a curious drum sound: one drum track laid over another. The phenomenon attracted notice even in 1963. For example, Dec Cluskey (1964: 13) of the Bachelors, in his review of "Bits and Pieces," complained, "There are two drummers on this and I wish they'd play together." Clark (1964: 1) responded with "I wish to make it quite clear that there was only one drummer—myself. Certain passages on the record were double tracked, and this might have given the Bachelors a wrong impression." The two drum tracks provide a fatter drum sound than was typical in Lon-

---

[9] Their success supports the notion that Dick Rowe and Mike Smith were at least partly correct when they turned down the Beatles in favor of Poole and the Tremeloes.

don at the time and, if Clark did agree to bring in Graham to muscle-up his recording, it proved a good decision.[10]

As with Joe Brown and His Bruvvers, Reed allowed the band members a substantial say in their sound, sometimes despite his advice. Notably, on the recording of "Bits and Pieces," Mike Smith's keyboard (a Vox Continental) clearly has a
different tuning than the rest of the band, which "used to go at my rattle because
he would insist in playing this damn thing." Reed recommended a session musician and/or a proven instrument:

> We had at our disposal people like Kenny Salmon, who had the most wonder-
> ful Lowrey with beautiful Leslie speakers. I said to him, "Let's use the Lowrey,
> for Christ's sake." But Mike would insist on playing this secondary kind of
> organ, which you wouldn't even look at on sessions. And, you couldn't hide it.
> That was the Dave Clark Five sound: out-of-tune.

In this case, Reed's contribution "did not involve doing a musical arrangement as
the group had worked out a routine." Instead, Reed "supplied a few extra musicians to help 'bump up' the sound in the studio." Reed remembers, "After the
[initial] recording [of "Bits and Pieces"], Dave Clark was anxious that the driving beat was not to his satisfaction, so we dubbed on a military sound (on the
beat) where the DC5 and myself stamped on a wooden panel throughout the
piece, which provided the sound that Dave was after."

Arranging by Reed

A year later, Reed contributed to the success of the Fortunes when their producer,
Noel Walker, asked him to arrange "You've Got Your Troubles." He began by listening to the demo recorded by songwriters Roger Cook and Roger Greenaway
and incorporating many of their ideas into his arrangement with "different instruments, all the secondary lines." Notably, "[t]hey didn't have trumpets on the
demo: they probably sang it, so of course I emulated that. 'If it works, then use
it'; that was my philosophy, and it did work." More obviously, the interlocking
melody and countermelody of the song were part of their composition, not part
of the music director's arrangement. However, in this way, Reed served as a facil-

---

[10] Reed limited his involvement with the Dave Clark Five to select sessions, but notes
that Graham appears on many recordings. The rumors of the involvement of a session drummer persisted into 1965, when Clark again claimed that there were only six in the studio
when they recorded "Glad All Over," including the recording engineer (Adrian Kerridge).
What he does not address is if they used a session musician to overdub any drumming. See
N.A. 1965a: 8.

itator for the recording: he took Cook and Greenaway's ideas and helped the Fortunes and Walker to realize a convincing recorded performance.

Music directors such as Reed were also often songwriters and thus well placed to promote their own material. Reed sold songs to the Dave Clark Five ("Everybody Knows"), Tom Jones ("It's Not Unusual"), Engelbert Humperdinck ("The Last Waltz"), and the Fortunes who, with a hit record, needed a successful follow-up recording. Reed teamed with Barry Mason to write "Here It Comes Again" and convinced producer Noel Walker to make this the next single. Reed even traveled to Germany, where the band was on tour, in order "to routine them and play them new songs. [When] they came back, we recorded in London." Reed achieved considerable success in the sixties as an MD (Wayne Fontana and the Mindbenders, "The Game of Love"), arranger (Wayne Fontana, "Pamela Pamela"), and songwriter (Herman's Hermits, "There's a Kind of Hush"). Eventually, he established his own publishing company and, in the process, climbed the musical food chain. He also helped to define the role of music director in the sixties, ensuring that artists in the studio had the best possible musical coach available.

Reed defines his role this way: "The job of an MD means that, from day one of the proposed recording, he is there to help select the material and, once this has been decided, takes the songs away to arrange and orchestrate them." Once completed, a copyist prepares the parts of an arrangement, "the date for the session is set, and everyone involved (orchestra, producer, MD, engineer, and group) meet for a three-hour session at the recording studio, where each song is rehearsed thoroughly, culminating in the actual recording." He asserts that the music director "literally directs the musicians, and conducts the pieces from his rostrum." The final part of the MD's role comes when they "overdub the lead vocals and backup singers." Fundamentally, "an MD's job is to work very close to the producer and engineer from day one of inception, to provide a very commercial entity for sale to the public."

CHARLES BLACKWELL

Had his parents not separated when the army stationed his father in Berlin, Charles Blackwell (b. 1940) might never have played the piano. While his mother sorted out her life, young Charlie Ramsey went to live with his grandmother and fell in love with her upright piano. "I'd moved to an area that was foreign to me [and] didn't have any friends, so I used to tinker on the piano" and "began to pick out melodies by ear." When his mother remarried, his new family could afford the luxury of piano lessons and thus began a period of musical experimentation and learning. He also acquired a new last name: Blackwell.

At sixteen, he took a chance and sent a few of his songs to the Denmark Street publishers Campbell Connelly. He remembers sitting "in this large room with a grand piano and trying to sing and play. They didn't want to publish the songs, but they thought they showed promise," and the company demonstrated its confidence by making him a stockboy. But, early the next year, another publisher—Barry Music—offered Blackwell work as a song plugger after hearing him at a Christmas party. Unfortunately, spring found him a stockboy again, this time for Essex Music, the licensee of much of Lonnie Donegan's skiffle tunes. Once more, the teen attracted attention, this time when arrangers with an office upstairs needed a copyist to produce parts for their weekly radio broadcasts. Part of the first generation exempt from national service, over the next few years, Blackwell copied parts for several arrangers, including Harry Robinson, the music director for the television show *Oh Boy!* which initiated his education in arranging: "I didn't have a clue basically. I'd had no training and I learned a lot from copying other people's scores [and] how they went about things. Mostly you learn as you're going along as such."

A different kind of opportunity arrived unexpectedly in the form of an eccentric and quixotic songwriter-producer who needed his services. Blackwell remembers that "while working in the office, I came across an engineer—a gentleman by the name of Joe Meek—who asked if I would like to write some songs with him." Denis Preston (Meek's patron in 1957) "shared offices with Essex Music, . . . so I would see Joe arriving and I think he heard me play piano, demoing one of my numbers" (Oldham 2000: 141). The musically illiterate Meek lacked the ability to fix the melodies in his head, to find suitable harmonic accompaniment, and to notate what he wanted. For his part, the ambitious and young Blackwell spied a way to have his songs recorded. He could still earn income from music copying and now Joe Meek provided the possibility of songwriting and arranging: "So I left Essex Music [and] went freelance."

Over a period of about two years, Meek produced several Blackwell songs and, when Meek set up Triumph Records, he officially brought Blackwell in as music director. Soon, Blackwell's career "snowballed because I was getting hits. Almost all of the other companies and other producers were interested in working with me. That's how things progressed." Working with Meek at RGM Sound on Holloway Road presented a set of challenges for Blackwell, particularly because the producer relied upon "younger musicians who didn't have a great deal of reading ability. He used to lay down the rhythm tracks with them, even though I used [to] write them out. It used to be quite hard work to get them to play what you wanted." Nevertheless, the musicians understood rock and pop, their phrasing, and their aesthetics and were eager to record. Blackwell, through his work with

Harry Robinson, had learned his craft with the musicians in the television house bands, including Eric Ford (guitar), Red Price (saxophone), Alan Weighell (bass), and Andy White (drums). "I really pinched [Harry Robinson's] rhythm section as such to use for my own means."

Unlike Greenslade and Reed, Blackwell instinctively oriented his arrangements to the recording studio, not the stage. During his time with Meek and others, he notes, "We were not really too interested in trying to achieve a really good orchestration with legitimate sounding instruments. We were more in the line of searching for sounds that might serve to catch people's ears, was fresh to people's ears, [and] thereby got their attention." In this role, the music director acted as a musical assistant to the producer and engineer in helping them to find new sounds from established instruments. And, like other songwriters of the era, they were deeply impressed by what they heard coming out of American studios. Blackwell describes the British as "very much influenced by the American [recordings], although we were doing things in our own way. Our era was very much leaning towards America all the time." Consequently, the rock rhythm section, not trumpets, trombones, and saxophones, served as Blackwell's musical model. Moreover, his musical sources more likely derived from Jerry Lieber and Mike Stoller than from Billy Strayhorn and Stan Kenton.

In his experimentations, Blackwell expected that some attempts would fail; however, he knew that the right performers could make a recording: "I often used to be worried about a certain orchestration, and I had no need to worry. It worked out very well. Obviously you're relying all the time on your musicians. I would hate to go into a session with problem musicians." To get good musicians, he had originally raided Harry Robinson's band, but with success, he came into competition with other producers and music directors, who were trying to hire the same musicians. Studios big and small competed for songs, musicians, and production crews, always aware that they could be outbid at any moment and yet perennially optimistic.

In preparing for a recording, building a solid rhythm section constituted Blackwell's first task. With the right musicians, he knew that an arrangement could be a collaborative effort in which artists exercised musical liberties within his parameters:

> It was certainly the fear in the arrangements. You could alter that very much so, and I did start to give my rhythm section more freedom for fill-in ad libs. I used to encourage them to put things in rather than write them down. Instead of trying to dictate to the drummer what he should play, I might add "put over half a bar fill," for instance.

Musicians often rewarded him with inventive accompaniments and memorable performances. Drummer Bobby Graham remembers that Blackwell was

> an exception to the rule because he was such a nice person to work with. Very laid back, and he's one of the boys. I always liked working on his sessions, always. There were people who I didn't like working with. But Charlie was never like that. He was such a good arranger and he let us have a little freedom. If we said, "Charlie, this passage here, what you've written, can we change that and do so and so?" he'd say, "Yeah, go for it."

Not coincidentally, Blackwell's age was closer to that of the musicians than many other arrangers.

To get these musicians, a music director needed to be ever aware of the Musicians' Union's rates and rules and the extent of its reach into the recording process.[11] In particular, the rules conflicted with what would become common practice: recording singers separately from the accompaniment. With the tradition of solo singers, whom studios marketed as commodities independently of their accompaniment, a recording session could mean considerable employment for instrumentalists, who played arrangements over and over while the director tried to get a convincing vocal performance. The union's representatives seem to have had little understanding of the notion of a unique performance, or an appreciation of double-tracking when their models were Frank Sinatra and Matt Munro. In the emerging world of rock and pop recording, a self-contained group like the Beatles possessed a distinct advantage: no musicians were out of work when recording accompaniment and solos separately, consequently the MU remained uninvolved. A producer like George Martin could record the basic guitar, bass, and drum accompaniment for a recording and then overdub (or bounce) guitar solos, hand claps, and, of course, the vocal parts.[12]

Blackwell remembers both how the MU prohibited studios from recording backing tracks separately from singers and how producers still managed to circumvent these prohibitions. Unfortunately for the production crew, some musicians (especially orchestral players) would report to the MU if they thought "something was amiss," at which point "somebody would sneak away to use the

---

[11] An example of the Musicians' Union's reach can be seen in how it enforced anti-miming rules in April 1965, mandating that musicians perform their music live on television rather than mime to their recordings.

[12] An MU agreement possibly nominally required Ringo to be present for the overdubbing, whether he was playing or not, and thus confirms his later claim that he learned to play chess during the recording of *Sgt. Pepper's Lonely Hearts Club Band*.

toilet and within fifteen minutes we had a union guy there. So we had to watch that." However, under special conditions, the MU would allow them to record a singer separately: "If something happened to an artist that we could prove was real, we used to phone the union and say, 'This artist can't make it. We've got a forty-piece orchestra. Can we go ahead?' And often they used to say that was okay."

Coach Blackwell

Like other music directors, the preparation of singers constituted one of Blackwell's most important tasks: "I would sit with them initially to try and fix the key, not to work with them at any depth, just enough to find out their top notes and their range, and fix the right key." However, the groundwork often ended there: "I wouldn't see them again until the actual session, so you're relying on them to learn the song." The only guides for the singer were his or her own instincts and the demo disk (which either the songwriter or Blackwell had recorded to show the arrangement). "Depending on whether it was a good demo with an orchestra, or just somebody singing with a guitar, they had to learn the arrangement, what intro you fixed and your routine. But quite often, I would sit in the studio afterwards and I would coach them." Even in the recording session, Blackwell would help them along by hitting "the note on the piano that they would hear in the headphones" but that would not appear on the record. In Blackwell's experience, the producer might discuss the material with the music director, but always in a consultative way: "I might be asked my opinion when I was visiting a producer and a singer to fix songs for the upcoming sessions. 'Do you think you could do something with this song?'" However, the core of the music director's role lay in finding an effective arrangement. Blackwell remembers, "I would hear the whole song in my head, and the whole feel of the arrangement. So, I probably would be looking for an overall package. I always find it very helpful to have some picture in my mind of what artist would be singing it. I think that helps a lot."

Like a theatrical director, Blackwell also worked with the producers to elicit performances from singers, beginning with their abilities and limitations and extending to tapping into their emotional strengths. Before the availability of eight- and sixteen-track recordings, one factor was whether a singer could give a compelling version of the song from beginning to end. "It's all difficult bounds. Sometimes you have singers that can sing the whole thing live. More often, you have to break it down in verses and drop in things. Certainly in those days, we were limited in what we could do, because there were a limited number of tracks." Blackwell puts the task down to a matter of "coaching a performance out of them, encouraging them, and giving them a parental lesson to say, 'That didn't sound quite right.'" In the process, he believed he had to be careful "because they're all very sensitive, these things. You have to try to do it very carefully." This might mean suggesting "some different phrases and actually telling them that there were certain notes that were out of tune."

Music directors often worked within very defined time constraints. When presenting music to performers, they knew that they needed to record as quickly as possible, often before someone else did. Musicians had to learn songs quickly and to find ways to plumb the emotional possibilities from their performance on command and without much preparation. Those who wrote their own material (e.g., Ray Davies with "You Really Got Me") could develop the song in concert before bringing it into the studio. However, when John Leyton recorded "Johnny Remember Me" (for which Blackwell acted as music director), he had almost no time to prepare. Of course, once a singer became familiar with the music, he or she could perform it much more effectively: "It always intrigued me that probably after two months on the road singing the same song, the singer would perform it much better if he were then to go back in the studio."

Perhaps the most musically demanding part of a music director's role came in developing the formal structure of a performance. Blackwell remembers that when "we used to sit and work out the key for the artist, that's one of the things we used to encounter, [when] we had to time the routine. How many verses and how many times? If it's a middle eight, after that, where do we go back through to finish at the right time?" Next in importance was "the intro, especially if you're intent on beginning something exciting. It can be very time-consuming and in turns very difficult to get into the score of the arrangement. I always tried to put a lot of emphasis on a strong introduction" so that the recording would catch the listener's ear immediately. Blackwell believes that his introductions to Tom Jones's "I'll Never Fall in Love Again" and John Leyton's "Johnny Remember Me" provide good examples. He describes the introduction to the latter as "very, very simple" with a "kind of an eerie choir."

Interestingly, he thinks that this intro might "not necessarily [be] brilliant from a musical point of view, but from an ear-catching point of view." An effective song ending also contributes to how an audience remembers a recording. Sometimes a "song lends itself to a strong ending and builds; then, it's the icing on the cake. Roy Orbison was the master of that." However, Blackwell observes, "most records used to fade, and that was the lazy way out," which gave the producer "some flexibility in the timing of the recording." Ultimately, the length of a recording ranked as "quite important" and came into the planning from the beginning.

In part, Blackwell learned, successful arranging reflects a pop fundamental: simplicity succeeds. "As I've developed as a musician, I've had to restrain my music ability and always think of the commercial ability of things." Consequently, rather than focus on "beautiful chords," Blackwell emphasizes that the recording should have "something that's going to catch your attention and at least [encourage you to] listen to the first half of the song." Paramount in recording is to "get people's ears."

Part of catching people's ears with an arrangement requires leaving room for interpretation: "I very much leave holes in my arrangements and that's a comment that I've had from Tom Jones. He said, 'I like your arrangements because you always leave me plenty of room to put in a phrase.' So that's important." The essence of this approach directs the arranger to provide only what the song absolutely needs: "Every time the lead melody finishes, you don't have to cram in lots of various figures and trumpets. If you've got a good rhythm section, that will suffice. It's a little-known fact that the biggest hits are the simplest things." Achieving this sparseness represents a challenge. "How many times have you heard a song and thought, 'Oh, that sounded simple!' But to sit down and write it is another thing." In this way, the MD facilitates one of the songwriter's goals: to create a vehicle for a memorable performance. Imperative in this process is "always getting the actual title of the song across. In whatever shape or form, I think it's very important on a pop record that you come to the end of the record and you know what it's called so if a song catches your ear you know what to go and ask for the next time you're in a record shop."

The music director also provides invaluable assistance to producers in helping them to select music. Indeed, in Blackwell's case, sometimes he was the producer: "The all important thing for me is always to choose the right song for your artist and to put together the right team. You'd be looking for the right orchestrator, the right rhythm section, an engineer you get on well with, that you can trust, [and a] good studio obviously." In that situation, the music director helped to make critical studio time productive. "Once you're in the studio, you're relying heavily on your arranger and hope he's done a good job." In London recording studios in the sixties, you did not often get a second chance: "You may have thirty musicians sitting there and you're trying to do three songs in three hours." In such situations, the arranger would be hard-pressed to make changes on the fly.

The music director also sometimes provided a score for the producer to help him keep track of the musical structure of the performance. Blackwell remembers in particular working with Peter Sullivan: "He always insisted that he have a lead sheet, like a conductor's sheet. We used to call it a 'control sheet' or a 'control-room sheet,' which was probably a double-stave, all the instruments coming in and out." Nevertheless, Blackwell notes that Sullivan sometimes ignored the notations:

> I can remember one occasion when I arrived at the studio and we didn't have this control-room sheet. So we head up to the meeting for the session [and]

I'm in for another ten, fifteen minutes while I did him [a control sheet]. Later in the session, when I was in the control room listening to playbacks, I had to remind him that he had the control room sheet upside down.

Ultimately, Blackwell supports the notion that a compelling performance trumps musical correctness. That aesthetic extended to the increased technological sophistication of recording in the sixties: "Everyone more and more became obsessed with separation, and you can't have any leakage across tracks. But obviously in the early sixties we had no option but to leak across tracks." As producers sought to control the sound of the recording and preserve the possibility of editing out mistakes, "[e]verything became a little bit colder, a little bit more clinical." In particular, Blackwell regrets the lack of spontaneity that began to emerge as producers and engineers had an increased number of tracks with which to play. He prefers in many ways the work of early producers, such as Jack Good: "He used to be one for atmosphere and feel." Blackwell remembers going "into the control room and saying, 'It's a great take, but the bass guitar's off a little bit.'" Good, however, had other priorities: "Oh, I don't care," Good said, "there's lots of hit records with mistakes on them."

JOHN PAUL JONES

Perhaps no music director exemplifies the final 1960s shift in the basis of pop music taste from jazz to rock quite as well as John Paul Jones (b. John Baldwin, 1946). Although best known today for his work with the band Led Zeppelin, Jones was a fixture of the mid-1960s London session scene as a contracted musician, arranger, and director who worked with a diverse catalog of performers, including Dusty Springfield, Tom Jones, Lulu, Herman's Hermits, Donovan, and the Rolling Stones.

Like Les Reed, John Baldwin came from a family of performers, his father (a big band pianist and arranger) and mother bringing him on stage as a child: "They were in variety—with a double act, a musical comedy thing. I've been on the road since I was two years old!" (Yorke 1990: 11). His father, Joe Baldwin ("who was a great Bill Broonzy fan"), taught him how to play piano, and John learned on his own the more portable "banjo-ukulele"[13] popularized by George Formby in the thirties and forties (Kryk 2002). His father wanted him to learn the saxophone, but, eschewing that advice, Jones found himself duplicating the bass parts of music he heard on the radio on his banjo-uke.

---

[13] Many know the instrument as the "banjolele."

In 1960, the Baldwins sent their fourteen-year-old son to a boarding school, Christ's College, Blackheath, in southeast London. The decision could not have been easy for the performers, whose incomes would have made sending their son to such a school difficult; however, entry into the school would have given their son broader opportunities for success than state schools generally offered. Perhaps as a way to earn spending money or to help pay for school, John took on part-time work for a local church as its organist and choir director. The teen eagerly continued his study of music, learning what the school had to offer: "I wanted to be an oboist at school. I really liked the sound of an oboe, but they said, 'Well we can't afford an oboe. You can play the clarinet instead.' And I thought, 'No, no, it doesn't sound right.' So I never blew—although I've played recorders" (Kryk 2002).

His penchant for learning musical instruments contributed to his careers as arranger, music director, and, eventually, producer. Jones told John Kryk of the *Toronto Sun*, "Some musicians will pick an instrument, love that instrument, and devote their lives to that instrument. I'm not like that. I started off playing piano, then I heard the organ and said, 'Oh, that's nice.'" Subsequently, he tried the harpsichord, guitar, and, of course, the bass. Eventually, he realized, "there's no way you're going to play all these instruments, to learn them to the point that you master them." However, with composing and arranging, he realized that, although one "can't play these instruments" with high proficiency, you can "write for them, and then hire people who can play them. Any exotic instruments you want, just write a part for it—book the guy."

With the growing popularity of rock 'n' roll, Jones became enamored with the idea of playing the electric bass, and in the early 1960s the most prominent electric bassist in Britain played with the Shadows: "I wanted to be the new Jet Harris" (Oldham 2003: 134). "My father had a ukulele, a banjo-ukulele, which is where I got my start in strings interest from. . . . The first thing I did was get the ukulele and tune it like a bass." However, Fender manufactured the best electric bass of the day, which had only recently become available in the United Kingdom: "When I realized there was a bass out there and I couldn't afford one, I just tuned anything I could in fourths. So immediately it wasn't a ukulele any more." Like guitarists, he found ways to amplify his instrument: "I took a telephone apart and jammed the mouthpiece underneath the tone bar underneath the strings, so I had an electric ukulele real soon, and it ran through my parents' radio" (Kryk 2002). At first, his father disapproved, thinking the electric bass guitar a fad; however, he seems to have relatively quickly come to the realization that good bass players always had work and, soon enough, his son was occasionally playing in his dance band.

In 1963, the determined young musician also knew from his father where London musicians congregated on Mondays to find work. Perhaps to his surprise, that's where he saw Jet Harris, who had left the Shadows the previous year for a solo career as a guitarist. "I walked up to him on Archer Street and asked him if he needed a bass player. He said, 'No, I don't, but they do,' pointing me towards the Jet Blacks. He was leaving them, so I auditioned and joined up" (Oldham 2000: 161). His stay with the Jet Blacks terminated abruptly when Harris drafted him to tour with fellow ex-Shadow Tony Meehan and to record their first single, "Diamonds." "I was seventeen and earning £30 a week with Jet and Tony, which was enormous" (ibid.). He began session life when contractors realized that not only did he play bass and keyboard (he had picked up work playing organ at the Flamingo club in Soho with John McLaughlin) and understand rock and pop, but, more important, he could read music. He had already tired of touring and was ready to leave the road: "I was 18 [and] I'd had enough" (Kryk 2002). The session work provided a semblance of domestic stability and a steady income that was less likely to evaporate in card games on the bus and in greasy motorway diners. Significantly, he took to the challenge of being a session musician: "Good training. . . . Good discipline. . . . You've got to get it together really quickly, you know. You sit down, they put the music in front of you, they pretty much count you in for a run-through, and then they go for a take, and that's it" (Kryk 2002).

Jones Arranges

His combination of abilities and natural facility with instruments, his affinity with rock and pop, and his long experience reading music made him a natural choice to begin contributing arrangements. "I discovered that musical arranging and general studio directing were much more interesting than just sitting there and being told what to play" (Yorke 1990: 14). His self-confidence and ambition overcame his fear that he might not be able to create satisfactory arrangements for sessions:

> The only real impetus I had for arranging was panic. I put me hand up. You know how it is—somebody asks does anybody do any arrangements and you say, "Yeah, sure." Then as the session gets closer, you get a book and try and work out what goes where. After a couple of these situations, you find you're an arranger. It happens that way for a lot of people. (Yorke 1990: 14)

He attributes some of his success as an arranger and music director to his preference for and experience with the bass. "There's a lot of composers who were bass players. You really have to understand rhythm, you have to understand harmony, and melody too" (Durkee 1994). In particular, he compares what a bass player does to guitarists, who "just have a different job. I think a good bass player is more of a composer, sort of on the fly, and an arranger. You've got to choose the right notes very carefully, or you ruin the whole thing" (Durkee 1994).

As his work gained notoriety, producers sought him out, and at least one of them thought he might have star potential. His looks and self-assurance attracted the attention of Andrew Oldham, who briefly attempted to make him a pop star—recording him covering the Astronauts' "Baja" and changing his name to give him a new identity, before making him his music director. Oldham explains:

> I got the name from a 1959 poster I recalled from Swiss Cottage for a Warner Brothers flick that died starring Robert Stack, *John Paul Jones*. I had no idea he was a real live controversial American hero. I just knew that John looked the part and could do the charts, and that I didn't want my arranger to be named after a piano. (Oldham 2003: 134)

Mike Leander, who had arranged Oldham's early productions (e.g., Marianne Faithful's "As Tears Go By"), had possibly been too old school for the young aggressive producer. Baldwin, now rechristened John Paul Jones, was young and in tune with Oldham's vision of music. "I started doing arrangements for Andrew when Mike Leander became a staff producer at Decca. Andrew Oldham established me as an arranger, which is what I wanted to do rather than just be a session musician" (Oldham 2000: 325).

What John Paul Jones possessed that others might have lacked was an understanding of how the core of the rhythm section—the bass and drums—could drive the entire performance in rock and pop. Thus, when he directed a recording on which he was also playing bass, he picked drummers like Clem Cattini, who could sync with his bass playing and around which other musicians could coalesce. Jones became integral to Oldham's musical machine and worked on many of his productions, especially at the tiny Regent Sound Studios: "Basically we just wanted to make records. I wanted to arrange, he wanted to produce, and neither of us was very choosy" (Oldham 2000: 326).

Located in Denmark Street, but working with the manager of one of the most popular groups in Britain at the time, Jones remembers that the recording sessions for which he wrote arrangements fell into two "different scenes." One he describes as "the group scene," which consisted of musicians who took the somewhat presumptuous stance, "Oh, we're a band, we write our own stuff and you'll want to record us" (ibid.). The other scene he describes as the "singer/songwriter/publishers," Denmark Street denizens who took a rather more freeform approach and whose motto Jones conjectures was "[l]et's get a bunch of people together, get a song, [and] make a record" (ibid.). He would work in both scenes.

Jones attracted the attention of other producers as well, notably Peter Sullivan, Robert Stigwood, and Mickie Most, who engaged him to do arrangements and direct studio performances. John Paul Jones made many of his best-known recordings with Mickie Most, scoring brass and strings in his arrangement of Geoff Stephens and Les Reed's "There's a Kind of Hush" for Herman's Hermits and strings for Lulu's "To Sir with Love." His sessions for Donovan, however, reveal an artist in transition. One of the first notable recordings that Jones arranged for the Scottish singer was his 1967 hit, "Mellow Yellow," for which he suggested a brass band reminiscent of Bob Dylan's "Rainy Day Women #12 & 35." At first, Donovan and other musicians seemed hesitant to accept the raucous trad-style arrangement, but "[t]hen Paul McCartney, who lived nearby, suddenly showed up, heard the horns and said, 'I really like that.'" The opinion of a Beatle "instantly changed everybody's mind" (Segal 2000). Jones describes himself as "pleased with the results: the record was different to what was happening in the general session scene" (Yorke 1990: 15).

Sometimes, the role of the music director simply consists of bringing the right musicians together and coaching them as an ensemble. "Hurdy Gurdy Man" represents one of the most often misidentified sessions of the era, some authors framing it as an unofficial Led Zeppelin recording. For example Ward, Stokes, and Tucker (1986: 436) claim in the popular *Rock of Ages: The Rolling Stone History of Rock and Roll* that both Jimmy Page and John Bonham are on the recording, and even Donovan gets the personnel wrong (Leitch 2005: 218).[14] Jones insists, "It was me, Alan Parker on guitar, and Clem Cattini on drums. Donovan played acoustic guitar." And for emphasis, he adds, "I booked the session" (Kryk 2002). Regardless, the performance-recording stands out as one of the signature artifacts of the era; Jones holds down the beat while Cattini provides flourishes around the drum kit. Cattini explains the style as of

> the era. I used to call it the "French Fill." I don't know, I always wanted to play semi-quaver triplets. Every French record you'd hear, "di-da-ly, di-da-ly, di-da-ly, di-da-ly." And half the time, it was a Mickey take, and that was the end of it. Basically, 99 percent of the time you were just there to play time easy. Just keep it going down the line.

To Cattini's embellishments, Alan Parker demonstrates why he was one of a small group of in-demand session guitarists of the time.

---

[14] Donovan places two drummers (Cattini and Bonham) and an additional guitarist on the recording.

Toward the end of this era, and shortly before he and Jimmy Page would form Led Zeppelin, John Paul Jones participated in one of the low points in the Rolling Stones' career. The internal conflicts within the band and between the band's leaders and their manager, Andrew Oldham, and the ongoing legal inhibitions to their operation contributed to a situation where no one took the lead in the recording studio. Jones remembers, "I did one session for Andrew and the Stones for *Satanic Majesties,* the arrangement of 'She's a Rainbow.' I just remember waiting for them forever. I just thought they were unprofessional and boring" (Oldham 2003: 365).

In the end, eager for change and, with improvements in equipment, the opportunity to play in larger venues with better accommodations, he considered joining a band, rather than playing for everyone else. The frustrations came "when I was doing sessions, which is what caused me to join Zeppelin in the first place." Ultimately, he decided "to give up the session world. Just to do something different and not to stagnate" (Durkee 1994). Fellow session musician Big Jim Sullivan describes the sentiment of the time: "All of us guys were at the top of the tree as far as sessions went, we couldn't do any more than we were doing. I said to the guys that we should get vocalists and a manager and go out on the road. At this time there was a lot of money to be made on live gigs" (Sullivan 2007).

In the end, John Paul Jones exemplifies the shift in the era from a generation raised on jazz to a generation raised on rock. While his background remains consistent with that of some of his predecessors, changes in technology allowed him both to become the music director for his own recordings and to continue touring as a musician on his own terms.

A CHANGE IN DIRECTION

While producers and engineers worked the recording side of the endeavor and songwriters and musicians the creative side, music directors negotiated between the two. An MD needed to mine the musical possibilities resident in the music and in the musicians and to place that gold in a form that could be recorded and sold. The four MDs profiled here exemplify how the task of putting together a performance—including arranging the music and coaching performers—evolved between 1960 and 1968. All four shared an uncommon musical intelligence and a willingness to embrace change. Each found his unique musical voice.

Art Greenslade—whether arranging for and leading a band for the BBC or enabling Dusty Springfield to realize the ideas she heard in her head—came to his task as a representative of a previous age. Born in the twenties, he represented the establishment in the studio, while remaining separate from it. He found joy in a balanced string orchestra and took pride in the Kinks' Ray Davies telling him how much he appreciated his playing. Greenslade's promotion to the status of music professional amounted to everything he wanted to be in life.

Les Reed arrived on London's music scene as an in-demand pianist who observed and learned the art of arranging from the musical world around him. Unlike Greenslade, Reed's ambition and talent catapulted him through the ranks in a postwar social climate where the barriers of class and age grew less important than one's accomplishments. Nevertheless, born in the thirties, his paradigm remained the big bands of the forties, and the powerful punch of brass and reeds mark many of his best-known recordings.

Of this quartet, Charlie Blackwell represents the phalanx of musicians born during the war. The first generation exempt from military conscription by the British government took to pop music as a way to distinguish itself from a generation that vividly remembered the war. These musicians also embraced improvisation and the beginning of a decentering of musical authority such that Blackwell's success hinged as much on his ability to make musical arrangements as it did on his recognition that he could draw upon the knowledge of musicians. Blackwell also found himself among those who first experimented with the possibilities of tape and electronic recording, and he incorporated these new ideas into his arranging.

Finally, John Paul Jones and the postwar baby bulge constitute the generation that came to musical consciousness in an era when rock pervaded the pop idiom. His specific family background provided him with a fluency in big band jazz, but his instincts were electric. Moreover, he understood the power of the groove. Where Greenslade, Reed, and even Blackwell defaulted to the piano as their vehicle for organizing an ensemble, Jones placed the rhythm section at the heart of his arrangements. His was a different world.

As weather vanes of musical change, Greenslade, Reed, Blackwell, and Jones listened for trends and incorporated new ideas into their arrangements. Producers relied on them to incarnate the quality of hip. Songwriters relied on them to finish their statements. And musicians relied on them to light the path to a successful performance. They were the surgeons of music, finding the heart of a song and sewing the patient up for show time.

5

The Write Stuff

Songwriting and the Articulation of Change

The songwriters who gravitated to London's Denmark Street in the sixties differed from the previous generation in that many primarily intended their songs for recording rather than for the theater. Indeed, one of the remarkable changes to take place in this era—the demise of sheet music as an important measure of a song's popularity—represented only a symptom of deeper differences. In the early 1950s, the *New Musical Express* routinely printed a ranking of sheet music sales, but by the mid-sixties, the weekly paper had dropped this measure of success. As the decade lurched forward, the paper's list of the top-selling singles grew longer and eventually a ranking of long-playing records (LPs) joined it.

Sixties pop recordings sought an undeniably youthful target audience and, predictably, personal independence emerged as an important theme. Songwriters sought to articulate the defiance of the bulge generation (consider Helen Shapiro's "Don't Treat Me Like a Child" by John Schroeder and Mike Hawker), but they also searched for a British or, more specifically, "English" identity in their music. Even more important, they wanted respect.

In the years before and during the war, British songwriters (particularly those associated with the music hall tradition) found a ready market in the United Kingdom. Notably, George Formby's films—all featuring songs like "When I'm

Cleaning Windows"—were great successes, not only in the United Kingdom, but abroad, and not just in the Commonwealth. For example, in 1946, Stalin awarded Formby the Order of Lenin for being the funniest man on screen and, in the fifties, the queen made him a member of the Order of the British Empire. However, in the 1940s, with the rise in popularity of American dance bands and their music, British musicians and composers took to imitating that model, leading social critics to complain about the Americanization of British life.

British pop music in the fifties and early sixties relied on a steady supply of songs, commonly from foreign sources. British artists picked up and anglicized songs that had been hits in the United States, Germany, and even South Africa for the domestic market, copying arrangements and presentation styles, while adhering to British tastes and the BBC's aesthetics. British songwriters eventually won the respect of the industry and British consumers, but for a long time the notion of a "British hit song" was an oxymoron.

"Covering" recordings (taking an existing record and recreating it with different musicians) constituted common British musical practice (as it was in the United States) with both advantages and disadvantages. In the days before multinational corporate global releases, songs and arrangements often had to prove themselves in local contexts before coming to the attention of national and international communities. Songs failing to register locally were unlikely to be successful globally.

Recordings from the United States and Europe often made their way to the United Kingdom either in the luggage of tourists or in the form of negotiated releases by companies in London. These releases had a degree of reliability and safety that a new song by an unproven songwriter did not have, but the British versions lacked originality, and recreating them drained British pop music of adventure and risk. British audiences tended to prefer British performers and that principle gradually extended to British songwriters, who often had one remaining and surprising obstacle: the British music-publishing establishment. George Martin (with Hornsby, 1979: 58) describes British publishers as being "a very strong force. If they took up a songwriter, or accepted one of his songs, it was their plugging to the record companies and the radio people, which gave it a chance of being a hit. If you didn't have a publisher behind you, you might as well not bother to write at all."

In the fifties, British songwriters worked in the time-honored Tin Pan Alley mode, approaching rock and pop songs as genres whose characteristics they could learn and imitate. For example, Lionel Bart, Tommy Steele, and Mike Pratt treated rock 'n' roll as a vehicle for comedic parody in Steele's 1956 recording, "Rock with the Caveman," and accidentally wrote Britain's first rock hit. Tommy

Steele's trio, which featured Bart and Pratt as "the Cavemen," "played country songs and comedy." Their "theme song," Steele recalled, was "Rock with the Caveman," "and it was a joke, a spoof, the sort of thing Monty Python might have done" (Leigh with Firminger 1996: n.p.). In early 1962, old-school songwriter Hubert W. David (1962: 10) prophesied the demise of straight rock 'n' roll songs and, in their stead, he saw two genres emerging: the "ballad-with-a-beat" (which "has to have a 'story'" and a "definite melody") and the "jingle song" ("a series of short verses all leading to one repetitive chorus"). Of course, his description could easily apply to George Formby's songs, but this comment does suggest that the British songwriting establishment felt that it could embrace (and perhaps undermine) rock and pop.

In the postwar years, British cover artists included one of the most successful performers: in 1953–1956, trumpeter Eddie Calvert performed discrete renditions of "Oh Mein Papa" (German), "Cherry Pink and Apple Blossom White" (French), "Stranger in Paradise" (American based on Russian music), "John and Julie" (British), and "Zambesi" (South African). All of these tunes were UK hits, and all—with the exception of "John and Julie" (the theme song of a popular British film celebrating the recent coronation of Elizabeth)—were covers of songs from outside the United Kingdom. In 1960, with some notable exceptions, English pop songwriters and recordings of their songs were popular almost nowhere else but Britain. The American producer Shel Talmy describes the British popular music industry that he encountered in 1962 as inconsequential: "They were strictly into cover records and what they were doing originally wasn't even hardly worth talking about." More specifically, he describes British songwriting as "terribly British and nobody outside of England was interested in hearing it."

The older generation of songwriters—those whom Rimler (1984) calls "show writers"—wrote successfully in the fifties for domestic artists. But a new generation of songwriters, born in the 1930s (too young to have fought in the war, but old enough to have done mandatory national service), began to emerge with instincts for the new musical style. For example, Jerry Lordan (b. 1934), who also had a brief career as a singer on Parlophone, brought an original mix of pop intuition and Tin Pan Alley sophistication to his compositions (e.g., the Shadows' "Apache"). Once he became a songwriter, he stayed on the production side of recording and seldom again performed in public. Similarly, Johnny Worth (b. 1931) connected with a song for Adam Faith, "What Do You Want?" that a number of other British songwriters found influential. Coming in the year of Buddy Holly's tragic death (on 3 February 1959), the recording features Faith's imitation of the Texas rocker's idiomatic style. "What Do You Want?" reached number one in the United Kingdom. Worth's song sounded like rock to British ears.

Worth recognized the changes that were taking place in British popular music, noting:

> [In] the early stages of the renaissance of popular songs, you had a kid singing with backing from pro musicians. He had to have it taught him by a pro. When Cliff [Richard] came along, for the first time we had a youngster backed by youngsters. Now there is no adult interference—the product is now 100 per cent teenager from the writer to the artist. (Roberts 1964c: 11)

He may have been overstating his case and misrepresenting the majority of recordings made in London at the time, but he did understand an industry in the throes of a revolution. The British songwriting community was shifting its mix of specialists (those who primarily wrote songs for others to perform) and singer-songwriters (who primarily wrote songs for themselves to perform). Naturally, the specialists sometimes performed and singer-songwriters sometimes composed with others in mind, and both proliferated and prospered through the sixties, but the latter became increasingly prominent.

British songwriting developed its own professional associations to reflect its growing self-confidence and success. The British Academy of Songwriters, Composers, and Authors (BASCA) even cooperated with other organizations (e.g., the Composers Guild of Great Britain and the Association of Professional Composers) to recognize and to support its members. BASCA, for example, annually offered its Ivor Novello Awards to recognize outstanding songwriters in its community.

In 1958, the first salvo of British individuality sounded when an obscure group of teens led by a dark-haired immigrant from India released a song written by their guitarist. Ian Samwell's "Move It" and Cliff Richard's performance of the song demonstrated that the British could indeed rock. Two years later, Johnny Kidd and the Pirates trumped Samwell's success with "Shakin' All Over." In both cases, musicians wrote songs to perform and record (perhaps setting an example for Lennon and McCartney), but the system seemed unable to grasp the idea of the performer-composer. Characteristically for the time, Richard's management almost immediately promoted Samwell from Richard's chief Drifter to producer and songwriter (where he had a number of successes). In contrast, although Johnny Kidd co-wrote "Shakin' All Over" with his bandmates the morning before their recording session (and even though he claimed sole authorship), his career as a songwriter was short-lived.

The connections between individuals and their musical communities, and their relationships with live performance and recording, defined this revolution in British songwriting. The continually shifting balance in how songwriters (a) worked by themselves, with assistance from others, or in teams, and (b) performed their own material or wrote for others outlines the trajectory of sixties British pop. The collaboratively written song—with two or more individuals contributing text and music and sometimes sharing authorship—occupies one facet. Another version, the self-motivated individual providing both music and text and possessing the ability to self-edit, provides an ideal for some forms of songwriting, especially the singer-songwriter. Songwriting teams ranged from exclusive relationships (e.g., Lennon and McCartney) to those temporarily formed with the specific purpose of composing a few songs (e.g., Geoff Stephens and John Carter's recurring partnerships).

The range of independent songwriters included the novices who served as benighted vehicles for flashes of creative genius and, at the other end of the continuum, seasoned professionals able to compose successful music on command through hard work, insight, and great skill. However, even in these contexts, individual songwriters often took advice from others and incorporated these ideas into their work. Thus, performing songwriters often picked up (and took credit for) ideas developed by the musicians with whom they worked and the audiences for whom they played. The romantic notion of the isolated and autochthonous composer generating the totality of a musical work (think Richard Wagner) remained alive in 1960s pop music, but a different reality contributed broadly and deeply in almost all cases.

The American pop industry in the sixties often emphasized relatively long-term exclusive songwriting team arrangements, notably husband-wife teams like Gerry Goffin and Carole King, Barry Mann and Cynthia Weil, or Jeff Barry and Ellie Greenwich. Detroit's Holland, Dozier, and Holland and Nashville's Everly Brothers provide other examples of families involved in songwriting. Individual songwriters (e.g., Neil Diamond) have had important roles to play in American popular music too, but teams were the norm. Men guarded the bastion of the British songwriting community. Very few women songwriters appear as part of the 1960s British musical community and, when women did participate (e.g., Jackie DeShannon), they were foreign.

British songwriters often worked both officially and unofficially in teams with other music professionals, but the kinds of exclusive relationships that Americans favored were less important. John Lennon and Paul McCartney's exclusive relationship was unique, perhaps reflecting their affection for American models. Notably, songwriting dyads and triads have both vertical and horizontal qualities expressed in terms of writing credit: not everyone who contributes to the creation of a song receives an ongoing share of the song's income. Regardless, this community produced some remarkably successful songs.

Two interlocking sets of variables describe the methods and goals of British songwriters. First, some worked by themselves, while others collaborated. Sometimes, this collaboration was discrete (as in a casually suggested and accepted modification to the music or words) and sometimes it was overt. In the case of overt collaborations, sometimes both individuals contributed to the music and words, and at other times one composed the music and the other wrote the words. Second, some songwriters composed material that they or their group could perform, while others were content (or preferred) to stay out of the limelight, writing material for others to perform. In both cases, they often (but not always) had specific individuals in mind for the song, with expectations that they would perform in a particular way. Most performers who wrote their own songs came from rock and folk music, where figures like Buddy Holly, Chuck Berry, and Bob Dylan—artists who performed their own songs—made a significant impression on aspiring British musicians. The dichotomy of "professional songwriters" and "performing songwriters" illustrates in part the generational evolution as one ideal replaced another. Moreover, throughout the era, issues of class, professionalism, and generation found expression in the music and its creation process.

London in the sixties witnessed the emergence of a number of successful songwriters. Les Reed followed the model of working with others, including Geoff Stephens (on Herman's Hermits' "There's a Kind of Hush"), Barry Mason (on the Fortunes' "Here It Comes Again"), and Gordon Mills (on Tom Jones's "It's Not Unusual"). Although Graham Gouldman composed music that he hoped his group, the Mockingbirds, could turn into hit recordings, he ended up as one of the most successful songwriters for other groups. The Hollies ("Bus Stop" and "Look through Any Window"), the Yardbirds ("For Your Love," "Heart Full of Soul," and others), and Herman's Hermits ("No Milk Today") all had success with Gouldman's songs. Donovan Leitch, on the other hand, wrote songs mostly for himself, his performances drawing on traditional British and American folk material and growing into surreal pop tableaux. Although he came to reject the pop industry (even going into extended seclusion at the end of the sixties), he came to success first on Denmark Street under the care of Geoff Stephens and Peter Eden, just as Terry Kennedy had mentored John (Shakespeare) Carter and Ken (Hawker) Lewis.

Numerous other British songwriters provided the stuff from which pop dreams were made. Steve Winwood, Rod Argent, Tony Hatch, George Harrison, Roger Cook, Roger Greenaway, Ken Howard, Alan Blaikley, and many others all left their indelible songs in the ears of the Western world in the sixties. They provided material for themselves and for others to interpret. Most of them worked in cooperation with others so that the songwriting process really did form a kind of extended community. Potentially, we could depict each song as the product of a network of musicians, poets, producers, music directors, and friends, all coming together in the studio to create a recording. This generation of British songwriters created something special. They championed youth and the working class, they challenged the war generation and the establishment, and, in the process, they helped to bring pride back to being British with their search for a distinctively British style of music. Indeed, one could argue that British songwriters helped to resurrect British pride in the post–Suez crisis world.

The first heterogeneous wave of British songwriters sought to capture and duplicate the excitement they heard in American pop songs. They found some success by evoking the excitement of rock and pop and inspired others to both imitate them and create something new and unique. Geoff Stephens and Mitch Murray loved the new musical style, but functioned as part of the old model in which songwriters were seen in Denmark Street's offices but not heard on recordings. John Carter and Ken Lewis, younger still, arrived to be songwriters only to find themselves swept up in the pop industry as performers. Lennon and McCartney flourished as performers but kept songwriting as their fallback occupation for when the Beatles might lose their popularity, an eventuality they originally predicted to be in months not years. Their music began as effective vehicles for making records and stirring up audiences, and became complex and layered testaments to a golden age. Always following behind them, Jagger and Richards came to songwriting reluctantly, but soon found the activity crucial to their survival as artists and their promotion to the status of the barbarians at the gates. Not until Ray Davies and Pete Townshend do we have unabashedly British songwriters who were proud to declare their identity on stage. In the course of a decade, from 1958 to 1968, British songwriting went from a local curiosity to an internationally recognized phenomenon.

GEOFF STEPHENS

The epitome of the Denmark Street professional, Geoff Stephens (b. 1934) provides an example of the artistically promiscuous craftsman on that short block. In the sixties, he co-wrote with John Carter, Roger Greenaway, Les Reed, Peter Callander, Barry Mason, Ken Howard, Alan Blaikley, Don Black, Mitch Murray, and Tony Macaulay and penned some of his most successful songs independently. Never a public performer, Stephens helped to manage, promote, and produce both Donovan (e.g., "Catch the Wind"), in the early stages of the Scottish singer's professional career, and one of the more unusual performance eccentricities of the sixties: the New Vaudeville Band. Although few outside the industry know his name, the sixties would not have been the same without him.

As a child and adolescent, Stephens had dabbled at an aunt's piano and "loved the sound that came from it," but received no formal musical training. When the war ended, his family moved to the mouth of the Thames: in Westcliff-on-Sea (near Southend-on-Sea), they opened a guesthouse. Perhaps most important, in addition to the BBC, their location on Britain's east coast enabled them to pick up American Forces Network broadcasts from Germany and Radio Luxembourg. This environment—music programs of jazz, American pop, and classical music on the family radio and in the resort town's cafes—left Stephens in love with music.

The catalyst for Stephens came in the form of an inspiring high school teacher: "From that point on, I decided I wanted to be a writer; [but] I didn't know what kind." After a two-year Middle East stint in the national service, Stephens steered his interest toward music and poetry, and began to seek ways to support himself and his young wife. He remembers that he "loved pop music: loved it to death," and set himself a goal of "three years to be a songwriter." First, however, he needed an income and found various occupations that allowed him "enough time to write the songs" and "to go to London and get them published, not to mention establishing contacts."

In an age when sheet music sales still constituted a significant part of a songwriter's income, and when publishers thought of music primarily in terms of the printed page, Stephens entered the fray at a distinct disadvantage: he had never learned how to read music. In the mid-1950s, the most common way for a young songwriter to bring material to a publisher's attention involved notation; consequently, Stephens engaged the assistance of musical professionals: "I used to take these musical journals and put an advert in saying, 'Songwriter wishes services of a trade musician.' I got guys to do that for me and I paid them, albeit what I could afford." His method consisted of singing to the musician, who would transcribe the music he heard. What Stephens could not sing was the harmonic structure of the song; that he left to a discovery process with the musician:

> There was a guy in the pit orchestra in the Palladium who used to take down my songs. I'd sing [and] he said, "What's the chord?" I said, "I don't know anything about chords. Play me something." And when he played the right chord, I'd say, "Yes, that's it." So I knew the harmony I wanted to go with that melody. I heard it in my head.

When Adam Faith recorded Johnny Worth's "What Do You Want?" Stephens remembers feeling empowered. He describes Worth as "brilliant. He wrote great pop songs! That man was Britain's first real pop solo writer to challenge the Americans. Johnny Worth was strictly pop, but very, very on the mark." However, even with musicians assisting him in the melodic and harmonic realization and notation of his songs, when he sent manuscripts to publishers, they politely declined him: "I used to get so many rejections and I thought they were mad, I had so much faith in myself." Like other songwriters, he countered disappointment with enthusiasm and attributes his survival to being both "young and confident" and willing to learn from his mistakes. Persevering in 1961, he had his first success. Stephens remembers, "[A] publisher picked up a song, some sheet music, and said he liked it." The letter read: "Mr. Poser[1] [the publisher] is very interested in your material. Could you please come up and see him?" Stephens (who still has the letter) saw the song "Problem Girl" picked up by Mike Leander and recorded by the Chariots. Poser also briefly employed Stephens as a song plugger (an awkward role for a nonperformer), promoting the publisher's material, which, in the process, helped Stephens to learn about successful commercial songs.

"The Crying Game"

In 1964 (when he was twenty-nine), at the crest of the beat boom, Stephens finally found success with the Midlands group the Applejacks, when they recorded a song he had co-written with Les Reed, "Tell Me When." Freddie Poser had impressed on Stephens the value of a catchy song title, and "Tell Me When" (as in "tell me when to stop pouring your drink" but applied metaphorically to a personal relationship) demonstrated the potential success of this approach. That same year, Dave Berry's recording of Stephens's song "The Crying Game" firmly put the songwriter on the musical map. For the composer, the attraction of the song lay in its premise: "I just loved the title, 'The Crying Game.' I think the title is brilliant." In this statement resides the central philosophy of his approach to songwriting. The title "seemed the perfect seed from which to grow a very good pop song," which for Stephens means a song that "touches a chord in many people's hearts. We all know what it's like to cry and the deep feelings which are attached to it."

He observes that the text lacks "perfect rhyming," but believes such conceits are relatively unimportant in a pop song. Stephens reads the lyric to this song as "more like prose—the opening lines in particular have a colloquial quality." More important, "the general tenor of the lyric was the thing that was instrumental in creating the tune and the harmonies." In other words, for Stephens, the song's sentiment inspired both the words and the music, and these arrived in his "head simultaneously." He remembers "no conscious effort . . . to match the two enti-

[1] Frederick Poser had been the general manager of the successful publishing firm Mills Music, but had left to start up his own company. In the mid-sixties, Poser established a relationship with the successful manager Eve Taylor, who represented artists such as Sandy Shaw. In the early sixties, Poser had one of the most respected British songwriters under contract: Johnny Worth.

ties." The premise of the song and its mood constituted the core of its success. In particular, Stephens identifies one phrase as particularly effective: "One day soon, I'm going to tell the moon, about the crying game." He describes the feeling of the line as "ethereal," amplified by his choice of melodic intervals (close together at the beginning and then wide apart as they fall awkwardly toward the end). His father inspired another telling phrase when talking about a skilled tradesman: "He knows all there is to know," inconspicuously gives the song a personal meaning: "I remember when I wrote it I thought, 'Well that's lovely.' I always remember my dad saying it, and I loved my dad. I thought, 'I know all there is to know.' It just says it, doesn't it?" The phrase takes up a common Stephens approach: seizing upon a popular colloquialism and reapplying it in a new context.

The recording of the song illustrates some of the ways in which London's sociomusical network functioned in the sixties. From his Southern Music studio upstairs at 8 Denmark Street, he arranged a session in the company's basement studio: "That was the place. There was no other place in the sixties. You went to Denmark Street." The demo of the song with fellow Southern Music songwriter John Carter singing illustrates an important part of the process. Publishers increasingly used demos for promotion, and music directors and producers commonly took their musical cues from these performances, often matching the arrangement, tempo, and style in their own interpretations. Stephens remembers that Carter "sang most of my demos, because I didn't have a real belief in my voice." Moreover, in the context of the demo, Stephens commonly got feedback from his fellow songwriters and from the session musicians about the value of the song. Carter's description of "The Crying Game" as a "great song" reinforced Stephens's self-confidence. Stephens believes that songs "either score with people or they don't. They either love them or they hate them." Indeed, Stephens prefers "songs like that, where some people hate them and some people love them to death, because I think in the end it's the love-them-to-deaths which will win through."

Songwriters like Stephens had a variety of avenues by which to bring their material to the attention of producers, who sometimes relied on unexpected critics to evaluate the songs. Indeed, an informal network of songwriters and producers (e.g., Mickie Most) often met over lunch and late at night to play darts and "sink whiskies." Stephens had given a demo of "The Crying Game" to Decca producer Mike Smith, who later, during a game of darts, told the songwriter, "Sandy [Smith's wife] likes that song." Stephens replied, "What song?" "The Crying Game," Smith responded. Thus, they began a dance that would lead to decisions about the production and the artist.

Stephens and Smith were both looking for opportunities. Smith would have known that the songwriter would interpret his statement as an expression of interest in production rights, and the relationship between a songwriter and pro-ducer possessed both personal and professional qualities. After all, as a Decca producer, Smith's responsibilities included unearthing both artists and reper-toire: songwriters relied on producers to record songs, and producers depended on songwriters for new material.

Parallel social contacts also facilitated the connections between songwriters and producers, such that Stephens felt "through my close contact with [Mickie Most] I was able to call him up directly any time of the day if I had a song I thought would be good for one of his acts. He'd see you the same day. You'd go round and without ado he'd put the demo on the turntable." Stephens notes, "If the first 20 to 30 seconds didn't grab him, it was thumbs down. If he played it all the way through, it meant he was going to cut it."[2]

In Stephens's approach, the musical materials grow from the words and the story. As a wordsmith, he believes that, with the right words, the melody comes easily. Consequently, his musical ideas can be both unusual and sometimes mun-dane. Stephens comments, "I know the great musicians like Les Reed say, 'I would never have done that,' because it doesn't follow a harmonic sequence. So, in a way, although I would dearly love to be able to know about harmonies, and their sequences, in that case it was a good job I didn't, because I might not have done it." Of course, the song does follow a harmonic sequence. The melody, how-ever, has some large leaps in it that a songwriter with a melodic orientation might have avoided. Indeed, Derek Johnson's (1964: 6) review of the song indicates that he thought the melody was weak: "The lyric is well-conceived, and the overall effect is warm and embracing. But its chances would have improved if the melody was a trifle stronger." And in an interview with Richard Green (1964b: 2), Dave Berry expressed initial unhappiness with the song, although his concern seemed more to do with the stylistic departure from his rhythm-and-blues preferences.

Stephens defends his aptitude, while at the same time expressing admiration for those with musical abilities: "There were times when I really wished I were a musician like Les Reed, who is a terrific, terrific musician, and can write great songs." Similarly, he admires songwriters like American "Burt Bacharach who knows all the rules of music and harmony" and how to "break them" because, in Stephens's opinion, "he broke them purposefully to create something original." Stephens reflects that he is "happy not to have that knowledge and skill, because I believe my deficiencies in that department could often take me to places a mu-sician dare not go from a creative point of view." Consequently, he describes his

---

[2] Not surprisingly, demo recordings could be quite short.

attitudes about music theory as "equivocal": he finds himself "speculatively believing [theory] to be creatively advantageous." He also finds his situation "extremely irksome from a practical point of view in having to place so much reliance on notators/arrangers, and not being able to play my own songs (and others) on the piano." Still, he notes the "self-evident" truth that "not all good musicians make good songwriters," suggesting that sometimes musical ignorance equals bliss.

Part of Stephens's success may lie in his willingness to listen to the opinions of others, perhaps deriving in part from his reliance on music professionals to notate and to perform his music. For example, demo sessions provided a context in which songwriters often resolved important musical issues. In the case of "The Crying Game," John Carter suggested a change in the chord structure of the song. Stephens remembers, "I had all the chords for it, except one. I didn't have the right chord, and John gave it to me at the demo session. He said, 'Why don't you try that chord?' I said, 'Yeah, that's better.'" This kind of recommendation and modification seems to have been common in London recording studios during this era, with songwriters making modifications to their songs on the fly, changing chords (and text) in the course of performance and recording. While not exactly improvisatory, the composition process nevertheless often seems to have been communal and fluid. Many of the most successful songwriters mastered the art of managing the evolution of a song over its creative stage, embracing the counsel of others as the work evolved. Indeed, these songs often changed right up to and during the moment of recording.

"Winchester Cathedral"

John Carter also played a pivotal role in another Stephens song, "Winchester Cathedral." By the summer of 1966, Stephens had dedicated two years to the promotion of Donovan's career and to the legal issues surrounding ownership of the Scottish singer's songs.[3] Now, he poured himself back into the creative comfort of Denmark Street. "Winchester Cathedral" was one of about six songs that came rather quickly in this period, and Stephens remembers laughing while writing it. Perhaps the experience of promoting folk music and of listening to the emerging fusion of folk and rock musical idioms had left Stephens with a new appreciation of style. While he would have been unlikely to attempt to write in the fashion of either Dylan or Donovan, he was no longer the same composer who had written

[3] As Donovan was a minor, Stephens and Peter Eden had negotiated the publishing rights for the singer's material with Southern Music, which in turn sold the recording rights to Pye Records.

"The Crying Game." And although he had not intended to write "something totally off the wall," as he sat "tinkling away at the piano," he "suddenly came up with the opening musical line, and simultaneously as if from nowhere, 'Westminster Cathedral, you're bringing me down, you stood and you watched as my baby left town.'" He thought he had written a "dummy lyric" and proceeded to finish the song in that vein "chuckling" to himself and intending to write a "proper" lyric later.

In this process, he balanced the need to be different with the parameters of what currently constituted a popular song. "Winchester Cathedral" combines aspects of British trad jazz (in the wind parts, if not the vocal timbre), pop (in the prominent electric guitar breaks), and "old records going back to the twenties and thirties," particularly the aspect where "the song was played through in its entirety instrumentally before the vocalist put in his appearance." A radio playlist in the sixties could be diverse, ranging from the Rolling Stones and the Yardbirds to Frank Sinatra and Bert Kaempfert. "Winchester Cathedral" came close enough to the contemporary idioms of 1966 to be acceptable, and was different enough to be novel. Still, Stephens was not immune to the social commentary of Dylan and others, and perhaps a subconscious resentment percolates through the coy text. Similarly, he may also have been inspired by Ray Davies' embrace of tuneful hymns to British society (e.g., "A Well Respected Man" and "Dedicated Follower of Fashion"). As he worked with the song, he came to the realization that, "although the lyrics may be silly, at least they're original," and hesitantly decided to go ahead with them.

While at first listen the lyrics seem conservative and evocative of a simpler age, Stephens admits that his "antiestablishment views" play into the song's interpretation and "maybe subconsciously that was my intention." The song effectively says something "against institutionalized religion, churches, the labor that's gone into them, and the people that got killed building them"; in other words, he takes on the establishment. As he wrote the song at the piano, he "found something which amused" him and that sounded "interesting and weird." His first line blames a church that can no longer hold relationships together, which consequently plays a role in the tragedy: "I lost my girlfriend because you didn't ring your bell."

The melody and singing style, on the other hand, betray a lack of great anguish at the consequences. Indeed, the prevailing sentiment might better be said to be either apathy or extreme emotional restraint (sometimes described as part of the English character). For such a devastating personal event, the singer's presentation is effectively dispassionate and perhaps even emasculated. The change from "Westminster" to "Winchester" came because Stephens sought a word "more widely known in America" (e.g., Winchester rifles), reflecting a conscious decision to appeal to "the biggest market for British songwriters." Stephens also came to understand that Westminster Cathedral had associations with the Catholic church, and he wanted a more direct hit on Britain's Protestant establishment: "I checked it out actually, Westminster Cathedral was Catholic. . . . Winchester was Protestant. Better." He sanguinely adds, "[T]here were just more Protestants than Catholics in England, hence a wider potential buying public."

His own first reaction to the song was that "it was so stupid, I wouldn't even demo it. I wouldn't bother." When he did preview this song (and the others) for a reaction, his friend Peter Eden advised him to "demo it. I think that's funny." In Southern Music's studio, Stephens contemplated how to present the demo. He had formed ideas about musical fills and the general ambience of the performance, but remained unsure how to create this atmosphere. Working with John Carter as his singer, he remembers: "We had these plastic coffee cups in the studio, and I said, 'Look, knock a hole in that and use it like a megaphone.'" Stephens insists that such ignorance often aids in writing and recording songs: "That's the way it should be done. It was only because of a lack of knowledge as to how it should be done and [because] there was a coffee cup in the studio, that I did it that way. It needed something else—because it's such a silly song—so we did that and, when we finished it, we all laughed." Carter, remembering the story slightly differently, claims he pinched his nose and cupped his hands around his mouth. No matter what the method, the acoustic effect created a narrow timbral window reminiscent of the pre-microphone age.

Now that he had a demo recording, Stephens began to shop the song to record companies and encountered an immediate positive response from the producers and music directors with whom he spoke. Stephens concluded that he should produce the recording himself. No doubt, his recent experiences with Donovan had emboldened him to pay for the studio time and musicians and to hire arranger Kenny Woodman to write the wind parts (with Stephens dictating). "When you're writing a song, you do generally get the whole thing melody-wise, even though there may not be lyrics for different parts." Contractor Charlie Katz recruited "all the good session guys," and Stephens initially sang the lead; however, he never "felt happy" about his singing. Having already invested a considerable amount in the recording and remembering the demo, he asked, "John, would you mind? I'll pay you a percentage. Would you sing it?" Carter wisely and graciously accepted.

Stephens called the assorted session musicians who recorded the song the "New Vaudeville Band" and leased the recording to Philips Records, which pressed it on its Fontana label. However, he wanted to be sure of the disk's success despite Philips's second-tier rank as a record company in London. When the record went into stores, he checked on sales. "I went around all the shops, and they said, 'Yeah, we had it, but we've sold out. We can't get any more records.'" Stephens then called up Leslie Gould at Philips and complained: "You have a hit record on your hand[s], but it's not in the shops." Gould responded, "Thank you for calling, I'll look into that." Stephens remembers Gould being good on his word.[4]

One theme recurs in a number of Geoff Stephens's comments about his life and music: class privilege. For example, he remembers that, during his national service "as a middle-class boy from working-class roots," he felt he would be "more at home in the company" of ranks other than officers. Although he remembers having the opportunity for scholarships, the "pointed questioning" about his father's occupation helped him to recognize that to be "the son of a mere butcher (and not even self-employed) was very definitely infra dig for Cambridge at the time." He remembers being "very angry about this," such that he "stubbornly refused to entertain the idea of further education." His songs reflect these attitudes. His celebration of the workman's qualification that "he knows all there is to know about something" bestows respect upon the labors of craftspeople. And his text for "Winchester Cathedral" challenges a British institution as a symbolic representation of the repression of the working class.

MITCH MURRAY

I knew I had found [a hit song for the Beatles] when Dick James brought me a number written by Mitch Murray called "How Do You Do It." After he'd played it to me I jumped up and said, "That's it. We've got it. This is the song that's going to make the Beatles a household name, like Harpic."[5] —George Martin, with Jeremy Hornsby, *All You Need Is Ears*

By late 1963, Mitch Murray (b. Lionel Michael Stitcher, 1940) had written hits for Gerry and the Pacemakers ("How Do You Do It?" and "I Like It") and Freddie and the Dreamers ("I'm Telling You Now" and "You Were Made for Me"). Indeed, the previous year, George Martin had told John Lennon and Paul McCartney that if they could write a song as good as "How Do You Do It?" then they could record their own songs. Of course, "Please Please Me" would meet the challenge, but Murray's songs set the standard.

Growing up in the Jewish community of Golders Green in north London, neither Murray nor his merchant parents had much of a musical background, al-

---

[4] Stephens also notes how the industry has changed: "You could never do that today. You could never get to them. Could you? There's no way. They'd put you through about a million secretaries."

[5] Harpic is a prominent brand of toilet bowl cleaner.

though his father did possess an impressive record collection. However, after seeing *The Affairs of Dobie Gillis* (1953),[6] in which Gillis (Bobby Van) serenades Pansy Hammer (Debbie Reynolds) with a guitar, the adolescent bought a ukulele, thinking this would be just the thing to impress girls. Learning chords from the fingering diagrams on the music, he developed a rendition of Lionel Newman's "Again"; however, unable to read the staff notation, he could only approximate the rhythm of the words and improvise the pitches of the melody. The performance bore a passing resemblance to Newman's song, but more significant, Murray realized that he had the basis of a new song and hatched the idea that, with a bit more effort, he too could be a songwriter. Learning that songwriters also earned royalties, he began to explore how he could bring his sales experience to bear upon this new career aspiration. The life of a songwriter presented a story line that the young Mitch found irresistible and, reassuringly, his parents supported him. Adopting the nom de plume "Mitch Murray," he created a separate identity from the salesman of ladies' handbags with a professional name that sounded "familiar" and "authentic."

Here again, technology played a role in changing songwriting. Without knowledge of how to put music into staff notation, Murray sang his attempts into a tape recorder that the family owned, sometimes accompanying himself on the ukulele. With growing confidence in his creations, he took them to Denmark Street and shopped them to the various music publishers. At first, most rejected him outright, and those that attempted to sell his songs (e.g., Leslie Conn) proved ultimately unsuccessful. However, many did give advice. Bobby Britton (at Southern Music) recommended finding songs that were currently selling to use as models. Referring to Murray's songs, Britton offered the critique that "they're alright, but they're not commercial. They're not gonna sell." He suggested, "Why don't you listen to the radio and hear what's selling." Today, Murray reflects that he had been writing to please himself and that what pleased others might be more valuable. Murray describes Britton's comments as "very basic information, but very useful. I started doing that; I started listening to [songs] from a commercial angle for the first time." He had been writing stuff that he "thought was tuneful and had little good ideas, but they weren't fitting into a formalized, salable item."

Like Stephens, Murray claims, "you can hear the influence" of Johnny Worth in his songs (e.g., "How Do You Do It?" and "I Like It"), in particular the quality of "constantly surprising yourself." However, searching contemporary music to hear good examples meant that Murray had to beware of a trap:

---

[6] The television series *The Many Loves of Dobie Gillis* (which premiered on CBS in America in September 1959) was not shown by either the BBC or ATV in the United Kingdom.

If you start feeling too comfortable, then you have to do something, because you have to catch people's ear and not make it too comfortable for them. [I was] being inspired by other songs, but not thinking too hard about it. [I was] just getting into the mood or just getting into the atmosphere of what was selling and what was about.

The balance he sought created songs that had both unique identities and worked well within the current repertoire: "You want your song to sound immediately familiar. When you write a song and it actually sounds like something else, you're haunted by it. You're wondering if you're going to get sued; but usually it's just a good sign that you've written something that sounds familiar and yet it isn't."

Untrained as a musician, but ambitious and comfortably verbal, Murray learned his craft intuitively, seeking to create songs that were organic melds of text and music. He never wanted to think about the structure of a song; rather, he wanted to compose songs in which one part grew and flowed from another without obvious attention to the melodic and harmonic structure. Murray still feels that thinking about the structure of a song is the wrong way to go about composing: "I felt [that knowing] structures and the word for this and the chord for that should come later, once you've identified it. It's like declining verbs instead of just getting on and talking, especially in pop music; it's got to happen much more spontaneously." That said, he describes songwriting as a trial-and-error experience:

It's like a jazzman improvising. You're improvising as you're writing; you're editing. So you're doing a little and you think, "Oh no, no, no. Try again." And you try it a different way and then you stretch the notes. And that's what you're doing: you're editing yourself and you're saying, "Yeah, that's good, I'll keep that. Now what's the next bit?"

Eventually, Murray argues, you develop the ability to hear and to know what will and will not work in a song. When asked in 1963 whether he thought there was a formula for hit songs, Murray replied, "If there was, pop music would be pretty drab stuff." Moreover, in such a context, a songwriter "would be a sausage machine: you pump in rhyming lyrics like 'Moon-June' and a few melody patterns at one end and wait for the result to come out at the other" (Williams 1963: 9). Nevertheless, Murray found a musical comfort zone in which songs materialized with little obvious effort.

Early Efforts

Murray's first successes reflect the advice he received, and his apparently uncomplicated songs resonate with the era. While not as simple as some other recordings of the era (consider the minimalism of Lennon and McCartney's "Love Me Do"), they follow the formula of contemporary American pop songs with predictable harmonic progressions and catchy, oft-repeated hooks. Murray's early songs exhibit straightforward lyrics and melodies, and arrangements with an energetic spark: "There's always humor there somewhere in what I do. Even when it's trying to be a serious tearjerker ballad, I really would like to do other things with it."

The compositional method he describes draws on both inspiration (ideas that come quickly and easily) and technique (revision). For example, Murray thinks the songs that "come all-at-once are the most successful, always the best. It's one of the nice things about songwriting, this spontaneity." Other songs, such as "The Ballad of Bonnie and Clyde" apparently took more work. "[T]he original tune was nothing like 'Bonnie and Clyde,'" and the bridge melody ("Bonnie and Clyde got to be public enemy number one") seems not to have emerged until after Murray knew who the singer would be: "I knew we [Murray and collaborator Peter Callander] had to have something interesting for Georgie Fame to do in the middle." Fame had earned his reputation singing challenging jazz lines (e.g., "Yeh, Yeh"), which meant that, for "Bonnie and Clyde," Murray had an opportunity to create something different.

Murray contends that writing songs comes in inspirational streaks: "When you're cooking, you can really do everything; you can come up with five or six real hit ideas in a day." However, "[w]hen you're dead, you can sit there, you can write perfectly professional songs, perfectly competent tunes, but they haven't got the magic." Murray contends that, after writing a few hit tunes, one begins to recognize what works:

> Once you become professional and you're able to tell the difference, it's wonderful: you can go and play poker or go to the films rather than have to work. Because you think to yourself, "Well it's a lousy day today, I'm not having it. Goodnight." Other times you don't; again, like gambling, [but] you just don't stop when you're on a roll.

His notion of "professional" suggests a particular kind of commitment and experience. Curiously, he claims that one can write "perfectly professional songs" that are otherwise lacking in magic. On the other hand, the ability to recognize a hit song comes once one has "professional" status.

Murray's description of himself as a professional projects a statement about the social rank of songwriters. Indeed, his and Stephens's self-identification as nonmusicians fundamentally separates them from a perceived tradesmen status for musicians. As a nonmusician, he holds the notion that musical knowledge can present an impediment to inspiration. Indeed, thinking about musical form, harmony, and melody would have been difficult for him without any training. Consciously or unconsciously, both of these songwriters position themselves socially as separate from and distinctly above the musicians who performed their music, in addition to many others in the music profession.

As artists and repertoire managers began selecting his songs, Murray applied some of the salesmanship he had learned working for his father, asking them to put his full name on songs: "I always wrote to the label managers and asked them if they could do it and wrote to thank them afterwards. I was a bit of a promoter. I also wrote anybody who played my records, any disk jockey, anybody who recorded them, any recording manager, I used to write and thank them." Other songwriters passively accepted their first initial and last name, sometimes even spelled correctly.

As an independent songwriter with no formal publishing affiliation, Murray realized that getting his songs recorded would not happen spontaneously. Although professional songwriters had remained traditionally and symbolically behind the studio curtains, if Murray wanted his songs recorded, he needed to promote them himself. "Non-performing writers weren't known in those days," so he became persistent with publishers, disk jockeys, producers, music directors, and others. "Generally, it was all good PR, and I became quite well known very, very quickly because of that."

His first commercial success came with a B-side. In the fifties and sixties, producers would often put their own songs on the B-side of a recording, knowing that if the A-side sold, they received royalties for the B-side too. Murray's opportunity came with a Mark Wynter release for which he earned £500. He had approached Mark Wynter's manager, Ray MacKender, and convinced him that "That Kind of Talk" could be a good B-side and, as inducement, he made Mac-Kender an offer. Murray said, "Look, if you record this with Mark Wynter, then you can publish it." Murray describes this approach as "quite a clever thing to do because it ended up on the B-side. It would have ended up on no side otherwise." MacKender profited from the sales of the disk, and Murray received royalties as the songwriter. That provided incentive enough for MacKender to use the song as the flip side to Wynter's cover of Goffin and King's "Go Away Little Girl." In his first year, Murray cared little who published his songs: "The idea was getting a track record so people would take me seriously."

Unlike songwriters with publishing contracts, Murray could not rely upon a staff and facilities. Publishing companies functioned as support structures, mini-communities dedicated to producing songs (hits or otherwise), and provided legal, promotional, and production assistance. Being independent, Murray lacked this safety net; however, it also meant that he could exercise his entrepreneurial instincts: "I was never signed to a publishing company, not even my own, and that made me a little unusual, because I was able to go from one publisher to another to let them fight it out, to entertain me, to woo me, to [do] all the rest of it." Nevertheless, "[f]airly quickly, you settled on a publisher who seemed to do all the tricks for you. So in the end, you tended to be with one publisher anyway," at least until the next one gave you a better deal.

He reasoned that signing an exclusive contract would diminish a publisher's need to be proactive on his behalf. He wanted to keep publishers interested so that they would "keep in with you and get your music" recorded. In the end, Murray had songs with Dick James, Feldman's, and Southern Music, among other publishers. "I had hits with all of them. Contracts of all kinds." Moreover, each publisher had special relationships (official, unofficial, personal, and institutional) with London's various artists and record companies. Consequently, when Murray had a song he thought appropriate for a particular artist, he went to the publisher that could best pitch his song: "Some publishers had connections in one area, other publishers had connections in another."

Murray presumed that he would always be able to come up with successful songs and that music directors, producers, and managers would want him. Publishers collected the fees for administering song use and the sale of sheet music and, as such, they were also responsible for selling the songs by sending people to knock on office and studio doors to pitch products in their catalog. Song pluggers were only as successful as their connections and the goods they plugged, so they had to be critically sensitive about the songs they pitched and to whom they pitched them.

Murray represents one of the earliest proponents of the tape recorder as a songwriting tool. Working with a small German machine, he began the habit of recording bits of songs in development—"I would have enough equipment so I could see whether it was worth making the demo"—and trying different styles. As he was unable to write music in staff notation, tape recordings and working one-on-one with someone who could transcribe his ideas allowed him methods to save musical ideas and to communicate them to others: "I would go to an arranger or a copyist and get them to put it down as sheet music, have them copy up just the top lines" (apparently with chords). Often, he would sing the song to the copyists and work with them to define the music.

Like other songwriters, Murray made demonstration recordings to promote his songs to A&R personnel, managers, and artists. As an independent songwriter, he did not have automatic access to a company studio, nor did he have fellow songwriters or an expense account to hire available musicians to perform his songs. He had to make these personnel and technical arrangements himself and pay for them. The best-known independent studio for demos, Regent Sound, provided the right combination of freedom and professionalism. For musicians, he hired one of the most popular London dance bands of the era to make his demos: the Dave Clark Five. "I used to pay them £12 for the whole group, for the whole evening, and I used to pay the studio about the same," says Murray, "to do two or three titles in an evening." The band consisted of a drummer (Dave Clark), keyboard player (Mike Smith), guitarist (Lenny Davidson), bassist (Rick Huxley), and saxophone player (Denis Payton), providing a variety of possible instrumental combinations. Murray comments, "They were certainly [competent] and the price was right. They were versatile enough in the instrumentation, certainly for demo standard. As far as musicianship was concerned, really, I thought they were good enough for me."

Murray would begin by either singing or playing a tape of himself to the DC5 to give them "the idea of the tune, and then we'd work out a head arrangement," including setting the tempo and rhythm and establishing the general feel. For their part, the Dave Clark Five took advantage of these sessions to learn about the recording process, to make valuable contacts, and perhaps to get a recording break. Indeed, Murray explains that, when the Dave Clark Five did his demos, they sometimes asked if they could record the songs themselves, which they eventually did ("I Knew It All the Time"), albeit without success.

A recurring "problem" for him entailed "always finding a singer" who could do more with the materials than simply be in tune and on time. Murray wanted someone who could convey the emotional potential and "put the song across. Usually it was Mike Smith," whose raspy voice would become one of the defining characteristics of the Dave Clark Five's sound, and his ability to present a song convinced Murray to continue using them. However, Murray also used other singers, including songwriters who were under publishers' contracts in Denmark Street, such as John Carter and Barry Mason.

"How Do You Do It?"

One of Murray's songs—"How Do You Do It?"—holds a particularly important role in the British pop music explosion of 1963, even though (or perhaps because) both Adam Faith (the intended singer) and the Beatles (the appointed singers) turned it down. Murray began writing the song in his parents' front room on 4 May 1962 with his ukulele and tape recorder. His initial start consisted of "strumming the chords," after which he "just sang and got this tune going and, at the same time, it sort of came along with the words. The whole thing started developing and I more or less finished it in an afternoon, feeling it was pretty good." He told a slightly different story in a 1963 interview, where he indicates that he was "soaking in the bath at home. You know, just sitting there humming to myself when I got an idea for a song. It sounded pretty good in the bathroom, so I went downstairs and worked it out with my tape recorder" (Williams 1963: 9). In the same interview, he states that occasionally "the tune comes first, and in fact that is what happened with 'How Do You Do It.'" However, he also told Williams that he usually started writing with an "idea for a title," and in 2001 he recalled that his first inspiration for the melody of "How Do You Do It?"[7] came from the opening words (the title of the song): "With a first line like that, the song starts writing itself."

After recording the demo, Barry Mason told Murray, "Look, I'm going up to see Ron Richards. Why don't you come with me and bring this and a couple of others?" Richards (an assistant to George Martin) had begun producing Adam Faith's recordings, and consequently scouted for new material. At some point in the summer of 1962, Richards brought the song to Martin's attention (possibly on tape), and Martin—having heard that the song did not as yet have a publisher—liked the song enough to contact Dick James. Martin probably hoped that by contracting Murray with James he could secure his permission to use the song. He might also have been steering a potentially successful song to a friend who, more specifically, had ties with Martin's label, Parlophone. Murray recalls, "Dick James phoned me up, and said, 'I was with George Martin [and] Ron Richards the other day, and I heard a couple of your songs, Mitch.'" He had liked what he heard. Moreover, James had apparently learned something about Murray from others in the publishing industry. He told Murray, "I've heard about you around the street, and I heard these songs, and I was very impressed."

The three songs (which also included "The Beetroot Song" and "Better Luck Next Time") had impressed James, but "How Do You Do It?" became contested material. That producers and publishers found his songs interesting reassured Murray; however, the idea of a relatively unknown beat group from Liverpool recording the song presented risk. He hoped for a more established performer, someone who already had name recognition and a ready audience likely to buy records (which would pay Murray royalties). The Beatles commanded no such recognition in London, forcing Murray to take a chance by allowing them to release the record: "I was a bit reluctant about a new group getting that song because I felt the song was a hit. I didn't want to waste it on a new group." Murray claims that he withheld

---

[7] The original title of the song was "How Do You Do What You Do to Me, I Wish I Knew," but Murray decided that the title was too long. He revised it to "How Do You Do" and then to "How Do You Do It?"

permission until he could hear the recording: "I wouldn't sign the contract until I'd heard the record, because it was a new group and I didn't want my song wasted. Now that was a very cheeky thing to do at that time, but I did it."

When he heard the Beatles' version, he remembers feeling that they had given it an anemic rendering. According to Murray, he reacted by declaring, "I'm not signing any contract!" Lewisohn (1992: 78) maintains that the Beatles significantly reworked the song's arrangement from the version that Murray had provided. He also cites Murray's diary for 5 September 1962, which indicated that Murray had heard from Ron Richards that, of the various songs that had been rehearsed, "How Do You Do It?" had "[c]ome off best last night." Two days later, Murray would have heard the Beatles' version (and rejected it). The Beatles' manager, Brian Epstein, then invited Murray to Liverpool to hear Gerry and the Pacemakers in order to convince him that they would be right for the song. They would be up to the challenge.

Publishers and Producers

Murray consistently maintains that he retained publishing independence, even while promoting his material and negotiating publishing and recording rights. Brian Epstein obviously continued to seek Murray's songs for his artists, including "By the Way," which the Big Three released in July 1963: "That was one that Brian picked out. He claimed the demo and said, 'I've got a group for that.' And, that was him. Again, it was a new group, but as it was him and he was getting quite hot, I thought, 'Yes. Go with this Brian.' If you're playing poker and you're on a roll, you just keep pushing, don't you." (The recording reached the lower twenties in British charts.) Murray describes the arrangement as a "gentleman's agreement" that assumed words exchanged between professionals constituted binding contracts. Nevertheless, control clearly remained an issue for Murray. Each time he promoted a song, he evaluated the interpretations, knowing that a poor performance could undermine the value of the song as a commodity. A song might have potential to be a hit, but a lackluster performance could taint how other performers and audiences heard it, thereby spoiling the possibility of future successful recordings.

Murray observes that producers usually kept songwriters "way out of the studio" with only rare invitations to be present. One such instance came during a Freddie and the Dreamers session at EMI, after they had made two previous hit records with Murray's songs. Perhaps the reason for this invitation (and the previous exclusions) finds an explanation in his reactions to the previous recordings. Murray complains that Freddie Garrity's performances and John Burgess's productions missed his intentions, describing both "I'm Telling You Now" and "You Were Made for Me" as a "fuck up!" Given his hopes for the songs, he remembers that listening to the recordings "really depressed me." Given the effort and expense he had put into the songs and the preparations, he wondered, "How can they ruin that? All they had to do was copy [my demo]." Notably, after he asked to be in the studio, Freddie and the Dreamers recorded fewer of Murray's songs.

Indeed, Murray admits that the time spent on the demo represented an attempt to control the song: "We were putting everything we could into the demo, getting the feel right, getting the timing right. Even the arrangement was more or less done for them to copy." However, even after these preparations, Murray found that the producer, music director, and artist could "sing the wrong tune" or take "the tempo too fast." Another explanation, of course, might be that the production staff and musicians believed that they were improving on what Murray had given them and that they had a right and obligation to create a more successful product. Moreover, they would have asserted that right in the studio, especially a studio like EMI. In a few years, especially as independent studios flourished, songwriters would begin attempting to produce the recordings themselves. Murray observes, "It wasn't for the extra percentage. It was for the control."

However, producers had their own problems and songwriters were often initially unprepared for the tangle of administrative details that went into a recording session. First, they seldom had big names to record their songs, and so had to develop their own talent: "You're risking it because you can't produce established artists. You have to go and find your own artists." At that point, the songwriter is back to the problem that Murray had when deciding to allow "How Do You Do It?" to be recorded by one of George Martin's Liverpool groups: "You're risking your best songs with new artists."

JOHN CARTER AND KEN LEWIS

Although many authors herald Lennon and McCartney as the first British songwriting team to perform their own material, they had a precedent in John Carter (b. John Shakespeare, 1940) and Ken Lewis (b. Kenneth Hawker, 1942). In 1959, the same year that saw Adam Faith achieve a British hit with Johnny Worth's song, these two young Birmingham songwriters traveled to London. They had discovered their mutual songwriting interests in school, and their skills meshed productively with Lewis playing piano, Carter playing guitar, and both of them singing. Moreover, Lewis had some musical training, which proved a valuable asset when the two became professionals in that "he could write single note melodies." A short while after graduating, they found work, but set their sights on Denmark Street. Carter remembers, "We had written six songs while we were in school, so we came down to London. We had both had enough of working."

Their optimistic attitude was, "Let's go to London. We'll go down to Denmark Street and someone will sign us up." Carter and Lewis believed that, if "you wanted to be in the music business, that was the place to be, that was the rule."

The bus from Birmingham brought them to London and soon, they were going door to door, pitching their songs. Most publishers gave them a polite dismissal; however, at Noel Gay Music, industry notable Terry Kennedy gave the two young songwriters a listen and some support. Carter and Lewis then wandered off to British jazz icon Ken Colyer's Studio 51 club in Great Newport Street to catch a matinee before returning to Birmingham. Kennedy found them and said, "Good news, we may want to sign you." Three months later, the two teens moved to London, where they stayed with friends of Kennedy's in east London while they established themselves, again with Kennedy's assistance.

In order to supplement their meager initial songwriting income, they began performing. Kennedy arranged for a BBC audition (required in the early sixties before a paid appearance on radio or television), and the BBC began billing them as the British Everly Brothers. They appeared on programs such as *Saturday Club* and *Easybeat,* helping to establish their reputation as performers, even if they were not at first plugging their own songs. "We got known as a kind of quirky group, because people didn't know what to expect," Carter recalls. The source of this quirkiness lay in their interpretations of existing material: "We'd take an old song, like a music-hall song, such as 'You Wore a Tulip,' and do it in a Buddy Holly style. We'd take folk songs and do [them] in a rock style." This appreciation for musical style would also pay off as they developed as songwriters, trying out different grooves on their musical ideas.

As they became better known, their own compositions began to attract attention, and Carter discovered the unexpected: a "John Shakespeare" already had a membership in the Performing Right Society (PRS). If he wanted to be sure to receive royalties from his songs, he needed a professional name. Again, Terry Kennedy, now with Southern Music (as were Carter and Lewis), helped in their transformation: he recommended they call themselves "Carter-Lewis" and, when they eventually needed a band, named them the Southerners, after Southern Music: "That again was a spin-off from the radio thing. We had done radio broadcasts as Carter-Lewis. We started pulling [together] a few musicians for the radio broadcasts, [and] Terry Kennedy said, 'Call them the Southerners.' So we became Carter-Lewis and the Southerners." The band at one point included Jimmy Page on guitar and Viv Prince (later of the Pretty Things) on drums. Carter remembers considering the Carter-Lewis performance identity to be "a bit strange," not only because of the names that Kennedy had seemingly pulled out of thin air, but also because the hyphenation seemed so totally unlike any other performing entity of the time. "And so I became John Carter, and Ken became Ken Lewis." Carter also observes, "Everyone changed their names in those days, and it just sounded better than 'Shakespeare-Hawker;' . . . nowhere near as clumsy" (Dopson 1997).

Unlike other songwriters and musicians who totally abandoned their birth names in favor of their professional names (e.g., Mitch Murray), "John Carter" became John Shakespeare's professional identity while "John Shakespeare" remained his personal identity: "I've always [been] John Carter in the music business, but I'm still John Shakespeare outside the music business. It's like a dual personality." His family accepted the new identity as a condition of being a professional, and at least "Carter" seemed not quite as faux as "Vince Eager" or one of the other Parnesian names. Carter accepted the new role, recognizing that "you can still be your real person if you like, but in the music business, you're playing a part."

Background

As a child, Carter remembers improvising harmonies together with his parents and siblings: "We were a very musical family. When we were on holiday or when we were on outings together, we'd always end up somewhere in a pub, singing." Almost as important, the family loved improvising accompaniment: "We'd all break into harmonies. My father was a lovely singer, and my brothers. We all just sat down and started singing very old folk songs; but we'd all burst into these harmonies. I don't know how that happened. I could just hear that there should be another note there." This experience would serve him well and many of his recordings—whether as a featured artist, as a backup singer, or as a songwriter—had harmonizing vocals. The young John Carter, possibly because of his adolescent voice, found his musical place in the high parts above his father and older brothers: "I always remember my father. He used to be a great harmony singer. We'd start up a song and my brother would take the lead and [my father would] do a bass harmony. I'd think, 'Gosh, you could sing this at the top.' So, I'd fly into this top harmony and you'd end up with three-part harmony."

These family musical gatherings clearly shaped how Carter heard songs and perhaps how he saw music making: a communal activity to which individuals contributed their melodic lines to create harmonic composites. He recalls, "Every time we had a party, it'd always end up in what we called a 'sing-song,'" and they would sing songs like "Sweet and Low" and "Down by the Old Mill Stream," as well as music hall favorites. Music making meant performing with other people, not soloing. Moreover, these experiences left him with a profound sense of intuitive musicality:

> It is a strange feeling when you first start singing harmonies, because you
> don't know where they come from. Then you start to get those run downs and

things which remind me of classical harmonies, church harmonies, whatever, and that sounds great, because if someone else is holding the harmony, and you sing against it, that feels really good, because I'm moving around rather than just staying stuck.

John Carter seems to have carried a model of communal music making into his role as a songwriter, eventually collaborating with some of the most successful composers on Denmark Street. Carter and Lewis, as a songwriting team, found various sources for song inspiration: "It was never a set routine. Every time we sat down, it was either me strumming a chord sequence, Ken thumping another chord sequence [on the piano], or one of us coming in with an idea for a title, or just a little bit of melody." Once they had seized upon an idea, they worked at expanding and adding to it. Sometimes, one of them would come in with a single harmonic combination and say, "I heard this great chord," to which the other would reply, "Oh yeah, we could develop that." Carter describes this as working "backwards" by posing the question, "How can we work up to this?"

For Carter, the guitar proved to be "a very good writing tool" on which he could "thresh" and "get quite a rhythmic feel" for a song "as well as a chordal structure. And that's what I loved doing." Working with an acoustic guitar, he preferred open fingerings to barre chords; the former are normally louder to compete with the piano. "I loved playing open chords when I was trying to write a song. Even if it were the wrong key, I would set the capo up to a nice open sound. If I felt that this really sounded great in D, but the key was wrong in D, I'd take the capo out and play it in E." Carter and Lewis's performance inclinations also shaped the way they wrote songs. When Perry Ford joined them (at Terry Kennedy's recommendation) and brought a more sophisticated piano technique, their songs consequently took on a more complicated quality, usually with "a few more [chord] changes."

Funny How a Song Can Be

Carter found that working with a partner gave validation to his ideas (or, reflexively, veto of unsuccessful directions), and the collaborative method proceeded with each member of the team sending the song down a slightly different path. Sometimes, as Carter indicates, the beginning would be a title: "What do you think of this? 'Funny How Love Can Be.' Isn't that a nice title?" The text would suggest a rhythm and cadence for the voice, a melodic line, leading to an incipient idea that they would then try faster or slower to achieve a desired effect. According to Carter, "it would just evolve." At this point, self-editing began, retaining the parts that worked and rejecting those that seemed less than engaging: "You would get to something where you thought, well, that's not very good is it?

But the first part is nice, nice for the melody." From there, they would try different chord sequences and melodic lines until they found something that worked for them. Ultimately, part of what proved valuable to Carter was working with someone who would say, "Great! That's worth working on."

Carter's choice of the guitar as his compositional aid also shaped his harmonic choices. For example, the suspended chords in the Ivy League's "Funny How Love Can Be" arise from a standard manipulation of the top string of an open D chord on a guitar. The figure recurs frequently in the song and is so apparent that one reviewer described the song as "Elizabethan" (Dawbarn 1965: 9). Carter comments, "[S]uspended chords have always been my favorite chords. A suspended chord just sounds so emotional to me." Similarly, he recalls that diminished chords grew important in his writing (notably in the songs "My World Fell Down" for the Ivy League and "Let's Go to San Francisco" for the Flowerpot Men) and that he discovered them while practicing guitar. "I was learning barré chords, stretching the fingers, and then I'd go [plays a diminished chord], which seemed to be in a completely different key, but I thought, 'That's a lovely, ethereal start for a song.' And that became 'My World Fell Down.' I used to love those diminished chords." As with the suspended chords, his use of diminished chords arose as a consequence of his choice of the guitar as his musical interface, the actual physiological interaction with the instrument suggesting musical choices. Carter's experiments with these musical ideas changed how he approached other aspects of songwriting: "When I started to learn diminished chords, I learned all sorts of things." His recollection of the harmonic feel of the diminished chords was that they "didn't quite resolve to anything. And so, even when you started the diminished, it still hadn't resolved into anything until you get to [the major chord of] that chorus, it goes all over the place." The symbolic feel of the harmonies for him was "airy-fairy," which he found gave the music a "mysterious feel."

Although Carter does not compose with traditional harmonic and voice-leading rules in mind, he does recognize a kind of direction to the changes as well as a metanarrative. He comments, "[T]hat's the reason emotionally I used diminished chords: because it set something that was up there somewhere, but not resolving until it got to the chorus, and so you went through a journey until it all kind of went, 'Yeah, that's the key!'" Carter also recognizes that the shape and direction of the bass line can influence this journey, although he does not think of them as inversions. For example, one of the common voice-leading techniques that Carter and Lewis employed consisted of "changing the bass root of the chord, so, if you're going from a G to a D [chord], [then] D would be the F sharp, basic things like that. A lot of pop writers do that I think. It's just a nice trick and it gives you some kind of difference to the normal root of the chord." They would record these ideas in the demos they made to promote their songs to producers, showing the bass players the lines they wanted, as they did in "Let's Go to San Francisco" for the Flowerpot Men, where a first inversion D major chord results from a descending stepwise bass motion from the tonic, G major.

Intuitively, Carter, Lewis, and Ford composed songs as vehicles for their vocal harmonies, emphasizing their three-part vocals as distinctive from the other sounds of the time, notably that of the Beatles. Carter reckons, "Our music was a lot sweeter, and a lot more, I don't know, from the heart somehow, rather than the straight in-your-face kind of hard-sounding chords." When compared to the stark open fourths and fifths that appear at important points in some of Lennon and McCartney's best-known early songs, the Ivy League does indeed go for full triads, perhaps reflecting Carter's early experiences with family singing, as well as his respect for Brian Wilson and the Beach Boys. Vocal harmonies for Carter were an intrinsic part of the musical experience rather than an addition to something else. His harmonic language drew distinctly from the ways in which voices move from one pitch area to another, and he experimented with harmonic relationships as one way to extend his musical ideas.

In "Funny How Love Can Be," Carter uses the commonest chords in British popular music that winter: D, G, and A (I, IV, and V). The song builds around the sequence IV–V–I–V–IV–V–I (G–A–D–A–G–A–D), which, he observes, was different because "it started on the subdominant"[8] rather than on the tonic. The chorus also starts on the subdominant and states the IV–V–I sequence three times before preparing the dominant for a return to the tonic (vi–II–V), even though the first chord of the verse is actually a IV. In terms of the vocal harmonies, the first line of the verse starts with a unison and moves to a three-voiced middle before returning to a unison. The second line starts the same but ends in a triadic treatment. The chorus utilizes vocal harmonies throughout, culminating with a suspension on the dominant. Carter's falsetto vocal lines variously double the main melody line and provide color to the vocal landscape.

Song Reason

If anything, Carter approaches songwriting straightforwardly. Where some musical choices worked because of the inherent quality of the musical materials (such as suspended or diminished chords), Carter and Lewis primarily worked with melody. For Carter, "a suspended chord is just very, very emotional"; how-

---

[8] Carter recognizes that, in the sixties, he did not refer to chords with terms like "subdominant." Instead, he recalls that they called chords by numbers in a key. Thus, a G major chord in the key of D would be a "4."

ever, he also recognizes that "the melody on top of that adds the emotion as well." He reasons that, with an effective chord sequence and "a bit of melody that you put over that," a song gains more of a chance to be successful. "If it doesn't fit, then there's something wrong and you would check it out." Similarly, the song structures favored by Carter had idiomatic constraints, such as AABA and its variants, which dictated the general form into which his suspensions, diminished chords, and complementary melody had to fit:

> You did verse one, verse two, middle eight, maybe a solo, went back to the middle again, and finish[ed] a verse. Then choruses came a little after that, when you did a build up, like a verse, or two verses, because you were wound up from chords. And I think that the structure we ended up with was the most commercial.

What made Carter and Lewis significantly different from most other songwriters in the early sixties (like Stephens and Murray) resided in their status as featured performers. They were not the first (consider George Formby or even Noel Coward), but they developed an instinctive feel for songs that could be successful in both stage performance and the recording studio. When they wrote "Can't You Hear My Heartbeat" for Herman's Hermits, they not only heard a song that the Manchester band could perform convincingly on stage, they also (through their demo recording) showed them how this could be a vehicle for a convincing recorded performance (right down to the "spontaneous" sighs). Moreover, not only did Carter and Lewis provide them with a demo that Mickie Most, Herman's Hermits, and the session musicians who recorded the song followed closely, they also performed on the recording as the backup singers. Apropos of Murray's previous comments, by working as musicians, Carter and Lewis gained more control over their material.

Perhaps not surprisingly, Carter remains unsure of the importance of a song's text for the target audience (teenagers). He remembers that when he was interviewed about some of his songs by a teen interviewer for the magazine *Disc,* she did not catch the sentiment of the text, but instead complimented him on the melody. She asked him to tell her about the song because "it's just a catchy tune isn't it? And in a nice poppy record, the lyric doesn't matter." She did not tell him, "Well the third line is brilliant, isn't it, the way [it] rhymes 'sunset' with 'hunter.'" Contrary to what Murray claimed about learning to write for specific audiences, for Carter, "the songwriter likes to know that he's writing at least something that satisfies himself."

He notes that, in the late sixties, in the "psychedelic age," lyrics started to "get heavy," and he really didn't "do things like that." In essence, the culture change of the era, which emphasized surreal, political, social, and sometimes funereal themes, did not suit his strengths. He had to find a different way to get songs into the market. Perhaps more important, the Denmark Street songwriting tradition that had nurtured Carter had always been much more conservative than the youth culture. Carter and his collaborators wrote unadorned and unapologetic love songs. Even in the song that Carter and Geoff Stephens co-wrote for Man-fred Mann, "Semi-Detached Suburban Mr. Jones" (or, in some versions, "Mr. James"), they couch their criticism of middle-class life as regret when the lover marries someone else.

Carter and his associates walked in the vanguard of an enthused British music industry and a suddenly confident class of British songwriters that he believed compared "very favorably" with American songwriters. In *Melody Maker,* the success of British songs in the United States reassured him that they had crossed a threshold. "I think there is a British approach to songwriting and it is different from the American," he told the writer. The difference, he believed, was that British songs were "more basic" and that, while they were not as "sophisticated" as the American competition, they were effective (N.A. 1965b: 7). Other British songwriters would sound similar opinions—and produce different results.

Like Stephens and Murray, songwriting represented for Carter and Lewis an escape from the predictable day world of shop and office. They sought a route that would lead them past a preordained hierarchy and give them control over their lives. The risks that loomed sometimes dwarfed them, but the rewards tempted them and others, including a couple of teens from Liverpool.

JOHN LENNON AND PAUL McCARTNEY

The songs and songwriting of John Lennon (1940–1980) and Paul McCartney (b. 1942) have received considerable attention, notably from authors like Everett (1999, 2001), who has conducted extensive research on the models and sources of this repertoire. Kozinn (1995) also introduces their songwriting, often comment-ing on the visceral effect of their music. Lennon and McCartney's success has at-tracted the attention of journalists and interviewers for decades, such that at least one writer (Dowlding 1989) has even attempted to determine the percentages of in-dividual songs written by each of the Liverpudlians. However, how these two song-writers correlate to others who were composing in the same milieu often remains unconsidered. How different and/or the same were they from other songwriters of the era? What was the role and nature of collaboration in their approach? What was the relationship between songwriting and performance in their work?

The songwriters thus far discussed had varying relationships with performance. Geoff Stephens worked exclusively as a songwriter and demurred from performing even his own demos. And although Mitch Murray dabbled in performance, his main interest remained songwriting. However, like Carter and Lewis, Lennon and McCartney worked as a team balancing songwriting and performance, composing material for themselves and offering perhaps less-effective songs to others. Writing songs since they were in school, these two duos were the same ages: Carter and Lennon were born in 1940; Lewis and McCartney, 1942. However, in 1959, while the soon-to-be Carter and Lewis went door to door, selling songs on Denmark Street, Lennon and McCartney were still playing in Mona Best's basement.

Geography certainly worked to Carter and Lewis's advantage in that living in Birmingham allowed them to make daytrips to London. Lennon and McCartney in Liverpool must have felt as if they were a long way from nowhere. Nevertheless, the orientation of these two teams appears early in their careers. Their focus on performance distinguished Lennon and McCartney from most Denmark Street denizens. Carter and Lewis (and especially the former) arrived in London intent on becoming professional songwriters, performing as a way to support their careers. At the first opportunity in 1966 (after a car crash during a tour), Carter fled the stage. In that same year, Lennon and McCartney concluded that they too had had enough of touring.

Lennon and McCartney arrived in London as performers looking for a recording contract and saw songwriting as an entrée to the industry. When Sid Colman at Ardmore and Beechwood Ltd. connected Brian Epstein with producer George Martin, he did so because Colman wanted Lennon and McCartney's songs. Lennon and McCartney wanted a recording contract. The Beatles' early repertoire prominently featured covers of American recordings, notably by the Isley Brothers ("Twist and Shout"), the Shirelles ("Baby It's You"), Chuck Berry ("Roll Over Beethoven"), and Little Richard ("Long Tall Sally"). As avid readers of the musical press, they would have also known that songwriting promised the potential for income. They knew they wanted to become music professionals and that their songwriting distinguished them from other musicians. What distinguished them from other songwriters came from their abilities as performers.

Lennon and McCartney wrote music that would be effective in their performances, even copying the "ooo's" from the Isley Brothers' "Twist and Shout" into songs like "From Me to You" and "She Loves You," simply because audiences reacted. With success, they began to compose for other people, especially when they felt that the songs were unsuitable for themselves. For example, although Lennon expressed disdain for McCartney's "World without Love" (recorded by Peter and Gordon), and especially the line "Please lock me away," at which he claims we "always used to crack up" (Sheff 2000: 173), the song still bore his name, and he profited from its sales.

One characteristic that distinguished Lennon and McCartney from most songwriters on Denmark Street came from an agreement early in their relationship to share credit on almost everything they did. Perhaps as a consequence, they relied extensively on each other for their primary songwriting feedback, with occasional input from their producer and friends. At the end of the decade, when Lennon told McCartney that he wanted a divorce from the Beatles, his description echoed the reality of their songwriting agreement. Most Denmark Street songwriters routinely teamed up with different partners to create songs in a growing market for British material. Lennon and McCartney always combined working independently with working together, and, as they gained confidence as songwriters, their independence seems to have grown. Ironically, perhaps if they had not entered into an exclusive agreement to share compositional credits on everything they wrote, they might have been able to survive longer as a viable team. Part of the Beatles' success lay in their ability to function as a music-making family, an advantage that dissolved as dysfunction emerged. The pressure of continually producing new songs forced them to rely on each other, as Lennon reminisced in 1980: "We worked together partly because the demand on us was *tremendous.* They'd want a record, a single, every three months, and we'd do it in twelve hours in a hotel or a van. So the cooperation was functional as well as musical" (Sheff 2000: 138).

McCartney's reflections on their career decisions illuminate how they represented a transitional model from professional publisher-based songwriters to self-supplying musicians. Britain had a long tradition of performers who wrote their own material, but they almost always had collaborators on the inside of the publishing industry. McCartney's recollections suggest that they aspired to be professionals, "real musicians," suggesting that performance motivated them. Indeed, looking at their early career, performance constituted the most important part of their professional lives, with the majority of their income accruing from concerts. On the other hand, they embraced what would have been relatively unusual for white pop musicians in the fifties: they were performers who composed some of their own material. When McCartney (1983: 66b) declares, "when you think of Lennon and McCartney it's Rodgers and Hammerstein because that's who we were emulating," what he is probably trying to express is their dedication to songwriting. Of course, Rodgers and Hammerstein seldom performed as a duo and primarily wrote for the dramatic context of Broadway musicals. More likely, Lennon and McCartney's models were "Chuck Berry, Little Richard and the rest," both in terms of style and the model of the rock musician who performs his own material (ibid.). The principal white American models for them were

Eddie Cochran and Buddy Holly (whose catalog McCartney would eventually purchase): musicians who performed their own songs.

Perhaps the best explanation comes in McCartney's (1983: 66) recognition that their songwriting owed not a little to Gerry Goffin and Carole King "because we were very keen on their stuff." Indeed, the husband-and-wife team serves as a good illustration of the aspirations and problems inherent in Lennon and McCartney's partnership. McCartney sought a balance between the respectable success of the musicals composed by Rodgers and Hammerstein and the energy of Little Richard. Carole King and Gerry Goffin provide an illustration of a songwriting team bringing that kind of sophistication to pop music. However, just as King and Goffin's marriage would end in divorce, Lennon and McCartney eventually began to resent their binding relationship, especially as McCartney's penchant for control wore on the entire enterprise. McCartney later explained, "I can see how that could get on your nerves" (Miles 1997: 579), and the film *Let It Be* (1970) documents some of the tensions between McCartney and Lennon (and Harrison), but the differences in their approaches and attitudes toward songwriting were apparent at the beginning of their careers.

Early Lennon-McCartney

Their individual approaches to songwriting emphasized their particular talents and in many contexts proved to be complementary. Lennon possessed an idiosyncratic (and biting) verbal agility that first emerged in the satirical poems he wrote as a teen and, later, in the lyrics to his songs. Even when he sought to defy the focus on and interpretation of his words (as in "I Am the Walrus"), he demonstrated an aptitude for twisting language that few of his peers could match. Lennon recognized his role in the team: "I can't leave lyrics alone; I have to make them make sense apart from the song" (Sheff 2000: 138–139). By comparison, McCartney's upbringing in a home where his father actively encouraged his sons to play music manifests itself in his facility at absorbing musical ideas, transforming and recombining them, and making them his own. Given their orientations, Lennon could still create surprising musical ideas and McCartney, inspired lyrical passages; nevertheless, their aptitudes expressed themselves early in their careers.

McCartney describes his earliest composing sessions with Lennon as three-hour afternoon sessions, "from two till about five" (Miles 1997: 107–108), which Lennon portrays as "one-on-one, eyeball to eyeball" in which they were "playing into each other's nose" for "hours and hours and hours" (Sheff 2000: 137–138). They would often meet in McCartney's front room, where they "would either plonk a little bit on the piano or most of the time . . . sit down opposite each other" and play their guitars (Miles 1997: 35–36). In a description of their early approach to songwriting,

McCartney notes that the physical interaction with an instrument constituted an important part of the creative process and that different instruments could produce different results: "One night, I was trying to write one with a guitar, and I couldn't get it on the thing. I tried it on piano and it worked" (Roberts 1964a: 11).

The working-class environment in which Lennon and McCartney grew up perhaps created one of their most important techniques. McCartney admits, "We had a rule that came in very early out of sheer practicality, which was, if we couldn't remember the song the next day, then it was no good. We assumed that if we, who had written it, couldn't remember it, what chance would an ordinary member of the public have of remembering it?" (Miles 1997: 37). Assistance came when they would "literally write the name of the note over each word, we didn't have any tempo, you'd just have to remember how it scanned and its metre" (ibid.). Early on, their songs were "always quite quickly written, they were never protracted affairs" (Miles 1997: 38). However, later, the songwriting process would in some instances stretch over months.

In a revealing *Melody Maker* interview with Chris Roberts (1964a: 11), Lennon talked about the importance of the harmonic content of their songs: "On the music side, as far as I was concerned, if I found a new chord, I'd write a song around it. I thought if there were a million chords I'd never run out. Sometimes, the chords got to be an obsession and we started to put all unnecessary ones in." Indeed, some Beatles songs of the era (e.g., "If I Fell") are quite harmonically complicated and adventurous. Nevertheless, McCartney agreed that some of their songs were getting "too complicated" and "chordy," by which he meant their compositions were "not like modern jazz, but just dripping with chords that weren't supposed to be there anyway." Lennon concurred in what seems a common thread in 1960s British songwriting. He and McCartney had "decided to keep [the songs] simple," describing the approach as "the best way." Curiously, Lennon suggested that the more sophisticated approach "might have sounded OK for us, but the extra chords wouldn't make other people like them any better. That's the way we've kept it all along." By way of illustration, within a few short years, McCartney would be writing essentially two-chord songs (e.g., "Eleanor Rigby").

As for the question of which came first, the music or the text, McCartney comes down on the side of "some kind of accompaniment" (Miles 1997: 148). That is, he remembers starting with a chord progression and a general sense of meter and rhythm, adding words later. Outtakes and demos of later compositions like "Strawberry Fields Forever" seem to indicate that they continued this approach for many years. Unlike Mitch Murray, they did not work from inspired bits of text or melody. Lennon states (perhaps thinking about Murray's preference for textual inspiration), "We don't sort of think of a catch phrase and write around it. It could be quite nice if a catch phrase comes to you, but it doesn't happen often." (That said, a few months later, Lennon efficiently and quickly turned a Ringo malapropism into the title song for their first film, *A Hard Day's Night*.) Ultimately, once they had established the general harmonic structure of a song, they focused on "the tune and the words and the feel of the song" (Roberts 1964a: 11). That is, they started with a harmonic sequence, but the most important and perhaps most difficult part of their work lay in finding a compelling melody and text.

In the fall of 1962, Lennon and McCartney wrote "I Saw Her Standing There," which provides an illustration of their approach to music and text in this era. First, the musical basis of the song may reside in a composition by one of their favorite rock performers, Chuck Berry, whose "I'm Talking about You" had been in their Star Club repertoire in Hamburg. The Beatles' faster variation has the same theme of meeting a young woman (in this case, at a dance) and new musical material, but the underlying bass part is very similar. McCartney confesses, "I played exactly the same notes as he did in ['I'm Talking about You'] and it fitted our number perfectly. Even now, when I tell people about it, I find few of them believe me. Therefore, I maintain that a bass riff doesn't have to be original" (Miles 1997: 94). The text, however, was a different matter.

McCartney remembers that he "had the first verse," and from that, he was able to generate "the tune, the tempo, and the key" (partly contradicting what he says above about starting with the accompaniment). However, the initial text proved unsatisfactory. The first version had "She was just seventeen, she'd never been a beauty queen." Lennon and McCartney determined that they "had to stop at these bad lines or we were only going to write bad songs." Discarding "beauty queen," they went in search of another rhyme, roaming "through the alphabet: between, clean, lean, mean." At one point, they came up with "She wasn't mean; you know what I mean," but soon realized that innuendo could be more productive. "Well she was just seventeen, you know what I mean?" became the text, with Lennon and McCartney relying on their audience to substitute "the implied significance" (Miles 1997: 93–94). Indeed, Lennon found numerous opportunities to push listeners to make sense of his lyrics.

Another early co-written song reveals both their collaborative process and songwriting strategy. "She Loves You" combines inspiration from a recording by Bobby Rydell (probably "Forget Him" penned by British A&R manager Tony Hatch)[9] and careful craftsmanship. McCartney remembers that they were on

---

[9] Adam Faith covered the song in the United Kingdom and released it as a single in Spain. Faith recorded on Parlophone, and George Martin or Faith's producer, John Burgess, may have given Lennon and McCartney a copy.

tour and stuck in a hotel room when they decided to "have a ciggy and write a song!" The personal innovation in this instance, which he describes as "a she, you, me, I, personal preposition song," comes from the conceit of a "message song." Unlike previous songs, which had lines like "I love you, girl" or "Love me do," "She Loves You" makes the protagonist an observer of a relationship rather than a participant. The story ("I saw her, and she said to me, to tell you, that she loves you") placed "a little distance" between the singer and the subject (Miles 1997: 149).

Returning home to Liverpool, they finished the song on 27 June 1963 in Paul's home, where they auditioned the new tune for McCartney's father. Interestingly, the language of the song revealed two issues about the relationship dynamics between the McCartneys: class and age. His father's reaction betrays his predilection: "That's very nice, son, but there's enough of these Americanisms around. Couldn't you sing, 'She loves you. Yes! Yes! Yes!'" The songwriters "collapsed in a heap," the son informing his elder, "No, Dad, you don't quite get it!" Paul McCartney describes the episode as his "classic story about my dad. For a working-class guy that was rather a middle-class thing to say, really. But he was like that" (Miles 1997: 150).

His father expressed his complaint at least partly in terms of nationalism and the son interprets the exchange as about class, but the issue also reflects generational differences. Indeed, we can argue that Britain's young adults embraced aspects of American culture in part as a way of distinguishing themselves from their parents. "She loves you, yeh, yeh, yeh" declared youth independence and pride in working-class aesthetics. Embracing correct English would have betrayed class ambition. Thus, Lennon and McCartney's choice of the word "yeh" manifested a conscious statement about class and generation.

Growing Separation

As their lives became increasingly separate, so did their songwriting, especially as Lennon came under the influence of Bob Dylan's introspective songs. The texts of Lennon's "Nowhere Man" and "Help!" place emphasis on his isolation and sense of loss of control. For example, Lennon declared, "It's just me singing 'Help!' and I meant it" (Badman 2000: 163). He admitted, "When 'Help!' came out, I was crying out for help," although at the time, the significance of the text was lost on him.

Their eventual phenomenal success as recording artists allowed them liberties that other songwriters could never have taken. In particular, many of Lennon's post-1965 songs evoke a kind of surrealism, perhaps because of his growing dependency on psychoactive drugs, but more likely because Lennon had been enamored of Lewis Carroll's poetry since childhood. That imagery now emerged in his writing. In songs like "Nowhere Man," "Rain," "Strawberry Fields Forever," "A Day in the Life," and "I Am the Walrus," one can almost imagine Alice observing the scene. Indeed, Lennon later admitted, "I always wanted to write Alice in Wonderland" (Sheff 2000: 142).

Similarly, McCartney increasingly isolated himself, not only from Lennon, but also from the rest of the band. Perhaps ironically (given his statement above about his father), McCartney seems to have been looking for respect. The telling composition for him comes from the same year (1965), when he dreamed the melody for the song "Yesterday." Working out chords for the melody, he went to the piano, where he "found G, found F sharp minor 7th—and that leads you through then to B to E minor, and finally back to E. It all leads forward logically." He remembers asking himself, "[W]here did it come from?" However, he retreated from that line of reasoning for fear that the inspiration for the song "might go away" (Miles 1997: 202). Like some other songwriters, McCartney seems to have had a fear of knowing too much about the musical process. The only words he had for the song were "Scrambled eggs, oh, my baby, how I love your legs" (Miles 1997: 203). "Yesterday" arrived later.

At this point, he seems to have been ready to routine the song with the other Beatles, but one-by-one they demurred from contributing either to the song or to the recording. And why not? McCartney had essentially composed something that allowed him independence from the "group." Martin read McCartney's aspirations and convinced him to add a string quartet, which they scored at Martin's house. However, with McCartney recording by himself and Lennon moving toward increasingly personal songs, the band and the songwriting team had reached a point of departure. With notable exceptions, the two would move increasingly toward independent songwriting, developing their own styles and conventions.

In 1966, Lennon and McCartney's songwriting further split and took new directions. McCartney's "Paperback Writer" and Lennon's "Rain" reflect both a simplification of musical ideas and a temporary abandonment of sentimental love songs. McCartney's letter from a desperate author functions as a two-chord plea with harmonic elaboration that veils the song's underlying simplicity. Like "This Boy," the arrangement takes advantage of both their adeptness as harmony singers and the growing sophistication of George Martin and their new engineer Geoff Emerick's recording techniques, piling on layers of vocal overdubs. McCartney compensates for the lack of harmonic movement during the verses by providing an elaborate and prominent bass line that, with new recording approaches, resides prominently in the mix. By comparison, Lennon's "Rain" continues his thematic descent into depression, but similarly simplifies the harmonic structure of the song, highlights the harmonies, and relies on recording technology to create a surrealistic atmosphere.

One classic way in which Lennon and McCartney continued to cooperate on songwriting came through their contributions of different parts to songs, notably one composing the verse and the other the chorus. For example, McCartney began the song "Michelle" while a student at the Liverpool Institute as an attempt to imitate the Chet Atkins finger-picking style of playing guitar. His musical goal was to "write something with a melody and a bass line," while his social goal was to evoke "that French existential thing" as a way to attract girls (Miles 1997: 273). In 1965, Lennon encouraged his partner to rejuvenate the song idea for their album. McCartney, however much he had attempted to imitate French as a teen, now drew on another childhood connection. Ivan Vaughn had been instrumental in introducing McCartney to Lennon, and now McCartney asked Vaughn's wife Jan (who taught French) to help with the lyrics. She and McCartney worked together, starting with the name "Michelle" and looking for rhymes. Like a Denmark Street professional, McCartney had found a collaborator.

However, the song demanded a chorus, so Lennon borrowed an idea from Nina Simone: "There was a line in it that went 'I love *you,* I love *you,* I love *you.*' That's what made me think of the middle eight for 'Michelle': 'I *love* you, I *love* you, I *l-o-ove* you'" (Sheff 2000: 136; emphases in the original). Lennon continued, "[M]y contribution to Paul's songs was always to add a little bluesy edge to them. 'Michelle' is a straight ballad, right? He provided a lightness, an optimism, while I would always go for the sadness, the discords, the bluesy notes" (Sheff 2000: 136–137).

Similarly, McCartney contributed significantly to some of Lennon's best-known songs, with perhaps the most often cited example being "A Day in the Life." Lennon began the song after reading the newspaper and focusing on two stories: the death of the Guinness heir, Tara Browne, and road repairs in northern England. Adding reactions to a film in which he had appeared, *How I Won the War,* he had the makings of a song.[10] However, he still lacked a chorus, at which point, "John asked Paul if he had anything to go into the middle part of the song, and Paul came up with 'woke up, got out of bed . . . ,' which is really a completely different song. But it merged into the other one, because it provided a sort of dream sequence" (Martin with Hornsby 1979: 208). However, in these edited patchworks,

---

[10] A friend, Terry Doran, helped him with the verb in the line "Now they know how many holes it takes *to fill* the Albert Hall" (Dowlding 1989: 180).

consisting of one part Lennon and another part McCartney, lay the seeds of the demise of their working relationship. By their last album, *Abbey Road,* they were piecing together medleys from separately composed songs, which relied more on tape splices than on collaboration for their continuity.

Only Some Northern Songs

Given the importance of publishers in the careers of other songwriters, the arrangement that Brian Epstein and George Martin worked out for Lennon and McCartney is particularly telling. After an unsatisfactory relationship with Sid Colman of Ardmore and Beechwood in which the publishers apparently provided little or no promotion for "Love Me Do," Epstein determined that they needed to find someone who would aggressively sell the songs. George Martin put Epstein in contact with his old friend Dick James. By late 1962, James had left Sidney Bron (coincidentally, the father of actress Eleanor Bron from the film *Help!*) as a song plugger to form his own publishing company, Dick James Music. Martin convinced Epstein that James would be a good promoter, that he was "hungry," and consequently would promote Lennon and McCartney's songs. The arrangement that James worked out with Lennon and McCartney may have seemed generous for the time, but it sustained a common industry deception. First, James suggested that he, Epstein, and Lennon and McCartney form their own company, Northern Songs, of which he would own 50 percent and Epstein, Lennon, and McCartney 50 percent. The apparent fairness of this arrangement lurked in a self-interested promise to aggressively promote their songs, something they would have been unable to do while touring and performing. He promised to push EMI to distribute their songs and to find producers who would be interested in having their artists record Lennon and McCartney originals. However, Northern Songs lacked total independence. Someone would have to operate the company, which Dick James Music offered to do for 10 percent off the top. Thus, Epstein, Lennon, and McCartney earned 50 percent of 90 percent of the company's profits (45 percent) or 15 percent each, and, of that, Epstein's portion came from the gross before expenses. Lennon and McCartney's 15 percent realistically produced only about a 10 percent return.

Martin (with Hornsby, 1979: 129) describes James's arrangement as "clever" because "in offering as large a slice as 50% he ensured that they would sign a contract for a long period of time, during which all their works would go to that company exclusively." However, by the time Allen Klein arrived to renegotiate the Beatles' contracts, Lennon and McCartney had come to realize that they had lost millions of pounds on the arrangement. Their solution in 1968 was to form a new recording and publishing entity in an attempt to regain control over their work. Ironically, the process would result in Lennon and McCartney losing control over their catalog and sealing the fate of an irreconcilable relationship.

MICK JAGGER AND KEITH RICHARDS

The award of the title "most reluctant songwriters in 1960s British pop" probably goes to the so-called Glimmer Twins. Keith Richards (b. 1943) and Mick Jagger (b. 1943) initially loathed abandoning Chicago blues for what they saw as ephemeral ballads and musical trivia. Having known each other since solidly middle-class southern childhoods in Kent, they came to memorize the nuances and articulations of the blues and rhythm-and-blues tunes on the American records they treasured. In their first years in London, the very idea of "professional songwriters" ran counter to their notion of authenticity. Perhaps the idea of songwriting smacked of craft, workmanship, and class pollution.

Soon after Andrew Oldham became one of their managers and an aesthetic guiding light, he began to push Jagger and Richards to compose their own material. Keith Richards remembers a conversation with Oldham that started them down the road to songwriting:

> It had never crossed my mind to be a songwriter until Andrew came to me and Mick and said, "Look, how many good records are you going to keep on making if you can't get new material? You can only cover as many songs as there are, and I think you're capable of more." We had never thought of that. (Oldham 2000: 250)

Indeed, from Oldham's perspective, the band had potential but, unless he could assure them a steady and exclusive supply of good songs, the Rolling Stones would remain essentially a compelling club band. Oldham's tradesmen needed to learn their craft. Lennon and McCartney had demonstrated how to meld performance and songwriting. Pete Townshend remembers, "The Beatles had set this trend—you had to write your own material. The Stones had not proven they could write; their first record was a Chuck Berry song, and I think there was a lot of panic that they might not be able to do it" (Oldham 2000: 249–250).

Perhaps the turning point came on 10 September 1963, when Oldham and the Stones were desperate for a follow-up to their first release, "Come On." Not far from their rehearsal space at Ken Colyer's Studio 51 on Great Newport Street, Andrew Oldham saw Lennon and McCartney emerging from a cab, cornered them, and quickly inquired if they had a song that would be appropriate for the Stones. Lennon (whom Jagger remembers as being an aggressive song "hustler") responded that they did, although it turned out to be not quite finished (Cott 1981: 46). Arriving at the rehearsal space with Oldham, Lennon and McCartney huddled for a few minutes and put some finishing touches on "I Wanna Be Your Man." Lennon described the exchange as beginning with an audition: "They wanted a song and we went to see them to see what kind of stuff they did." Oldham must have conveyed to the Stones that Lennon and McCartney might have something for them. The problem was "Paul just had this bit and we needed another verse or something." The "audition" seems to have consisted of Lennon and McCartney playing what they had of the song "roughly to them and they said, 'Yeah, OK, that's our style'" (Sheff 2000: 171).

Finishing the song quickly, Lennon and McCartney came back with the product "and that's how Mick and Keith got inspired to write, because 'Jesus, look at that. They just went in the corner and wrote it and came back!' Right in front of their eyes we did it" (Sheff 2000: 171). The impression that you could write a song more or less spontaneously and still have it consistent with blues aspirations must have suggested to Jagger and Richards that they could do the same. Jagger admits as much: "I think everyone got turned onto the idea of writing songs" as Lennon and McCartney had. "It was like, if the Beatles can write, we can write" (Wyman with Havers 2002: 98). If that were not enough, a few months later, a visit to their recording session at Denmark Street's tiny Regent Sound Studios by American producer Phil Spector reinforced that conviction. Again in need of another song, they began jamming on the structure of "Can I Get a Witness," which they had just recorded. However, the jam needed words. "Mick Jagger and Phil Spector headed for the staircase outside the studio reception, and in ten minutes flat they polished off the lyrics" for "Little by Little" (Oldham 2000: 283).

Oldham made the original prognosis, having heard Freddie and the Dreamers' record "If You Gotta Make a Fool of Somebody," which Columbia released in April 1963:

> Mick, Keith, and I all liked the James Ray original—I more than liked it; I thought it was royalty, an amazing recording and song. Full marks to Freddie or his A&R man John Burgess for unearthing this gem, but for me it meant Mick and Keith had better get a writin'. Even the rare gems were being unearthed and moved to the high street. (Oldham 2003: 306)

However, their first attempts at writing songs received less than a warm reception. Leaving their comfort zone of performing rhythm-and-blues covers also meant incurring criticisms from the music community that had nurtured them. Journalist Richard Green (1963: 2) pointed out to Jagger in an interview that, after their recordings of Chuck Berry's "Come On" and Lennon and McCartney's

"I Wanna Be Your Man" (which the Beatles had by now recorded too), many believed they had "deserted their r-and-b style and gone over to more commercial numbers." Jagger later disagreed: "We were blues purists who liked ever so commercial things but never did them onstage because we were so horrible and so aware of being blues purists" (Cott 1981: 46).

Nevertheless, Jagger and Richards would soon be sitting in their kitchen with a demand from Oldham that they come up with something. If they had not composed a song by the time he got back, he would not bring them any food. Oldham (2000: 251) remembers that, when he returned, he could hear them working in the kitchen: "I got back from my mother's, quietly let myself in the downstairs front door, tiptoed upstairs and listened outside the flat door. I was happy to hear that Mick and Keith were inside working. I could hear a guitar, a voice, and a conversation; to me that meant a song." When asked if he and Richards had written anything, Jagger responded, they had "written this fucking song and you'd better fucking like it."

The song was possibly "Will You Be My Lover Tonight," recorded by George Bean, a "hardcore Stones" fan and part of the original community that came to their performances, who had hoped to record another early Jagger-Richards song, "My Only Girl." However, American Gene Pitney (whom Spector had introduced to the Stones) thought the song had potential, changed the melody, renamed it "That Girl Belongs to Yesterday," and had a UK hit in February 1964. They were learning their craft and their songs were getting better. The first song to garner international attention began with the problematic title "As Time Goes By," which they changed to avoid confusion with *Casablanca*'s memorable tune (Faithful with Dalton 2000: 23). Oldham's newest charge, Marianne Faithful, recorded and had a hit with "As Tears Go By" in May 1964. Again, this song, like others, apparently had input from members of a community of people supporting Oldham and the Stones. For example, Lionel Bart claims to have contributed to the lyrics, describing his participation as part of "a family affair" (Oldham 2000: 317). However, their early songs were all ballads and atypical of the music for which they were becoming increasingly famous. Jagger and Richards needed to come up with material that sounded as aggressive and rude as the Stones, or at least as the public persona they had adopted.

Richards notes of their early work that he "wrote the melody and Mick wrote the words," but that "every song we've got has pieces of each other in it" (Greenfield 1981: 170). For him, becoming a songwriter "was a mind-bending experience." As a musician in the early sixties, he seldom thought about anything more than performing: "I had the mentality of a guy who could only play guitar; other guys wrote songs" (Oldham 2000: 250–251). Jagger considers himself to have "had a slight talent for wording," and thought "Keith always had a lot of talent for melody from the beginning." Moreover, in their earliest collaborations, Jagger admits that Richards wrote most of the material, but that the two of them "worked hard at it. We developed it. You need application," even if their first songs were "terrible" (McPherson 2006).

Like Lennon and McCartney's composing experiences, Jagger and Richards often found themselves writing songs while touring, stuck in hotels and constantly in contact with each other. Jagger claimed that touring represented "the best place to write because you're just totally into it. You get back from a show, have something to eat, a few beers and just go to your room and write." For him, working from home was "very difficult because you don't want to do anything really but read and things like that" (Cott 1981: 47). The claustrophobia of the tour, lodged in the same hotel, allowed for the possibility of co-writing, because "if you got an idea for a song, you just went two doors down the corridor and put it together" (McPherson 2006). Hotels also provided an undistracted context in which to write. Richards remembers penning one of the great anthems of the sixties, "Satisfaction" (described below), while on tour in Florida and concurs, "You can do some of your best writing in hotel rooms" (Greenfield 1981: 170a/b).

Nevertheless, by the end of 1964, Jagger and Richards still had not written a rock song that they believed was suitable for the Stones. They had recorded their "Tell Me" as a demo, to find not only that Oldham had included it on their first album, but also that Decca had released it as a single in the United States. However, in the fall of 1964, they may have gained inspiration from the Beatles release of "I Feel Fine." This John Lennon song with a rock-blues harmonic and rhythmic structure features a recurring guitar riff that drives the song along and provides a framework against which a conversational melody with a concluding harmonized refrain stands out clearly. Jagger, when asked his opinion on the song, replied, "I like the backing more than anything . . . , it's very good," even though he did not "like the lyrics that much" (Paytress 2003: 78). The musical materials that Keith Richards had thus far been spinning had focused on chordal strumming with melodic interjections (e.g., "Tell Me"). That was about to change.

Richards and Jagger Get Their Groove

In early 1965 with "The Last Time," Keith Richards introduced a recurring guitar motif that serves as a rhythmic and harmonic backdrop for Jagger's melody, with harmonies at the end of each line and a structure similar to "I Feel Fine." Another significant probable influence, Them's recording of Van Morrison's "Gloria," released by Decca in November 1964, has a parallel harmonic structure. Perhaps an even more important feature emerges with Morrison's vocal delivery.

Until early 1965, Jagger's vocal style reflected the diversity of the Stones' repertoire, imitating Chuck Berry, Don Covay, or Hank Snow. However, Morrison's nasal and shouted presentation style in "Gloria" offered an authentically aggressive style of singing that Jagger soon personalized. Another source for the song was American. Bill Wyman (with Havers, 2002: 173) claims that the song "wasn't written by Mick and Keith" and that they worked from a 1955 Staple Singers recording, "This May Be the Last Time." What Richards and Jagger specifically lifted from the Staples' gospel moan (or one of the numerous covers of their recording, first by gospel groups and, later, by rhythm-and-blues artists) was the last line along with its melody and harmony: "Maybe the last time, I don't know."

Richards in 1982 quips that he wrote "The Last Time" "because the Beatles didn't have another good one and we'd rifled everybody else's repertoire." More seriously, they now began "to believe we could do it" (McPherson 2006). Thus, even though the song seems to owe considerably to both contemporary and historic recordings, for the Rolling Stones, "The Last Time" actually constituted the first time they had a self-penned and self-appropriate song. Jagger remembers that with "The Last Time," "it became fun. After that, we were confident that we were on our way, that we'd just got started" (McPherson 2006). Oldham (2003: 178–179) believes, "In just one year Mick and Keith's songwriting had graduated from soppy ballads to commercial ballads to album material for the Stones and, with the two songs we were about to record, finally cleared that last hurdle—to a real, live single for the Rolling Stones." The two songs were "The Last Time" and "Play with Fire," which we can see as descendants of "Little by Little" and ballads like "As Tears Go By." What Jagger and Richards were "getting good at" was moving beyond cover recordings, internalizing other people's ideas, and reworking them as their own.

Without a doubt, the most important song that Jagger and Richards wrote and that the Rolling Stones recorded in the sixties was "(I Can't Get No) Satisfaction." Like "The Last Time," Keith Richards began "Satisfaction" with a guitar riff and a refrain and proceeded to build a simple song:

> I woke up in the middle of the night, there was a cassette player next to the bed and an acoustic guitar. I pushed record and hit that riff for about a minute and a half, two minutes. Then I fell back to sleep. I left the tape running, and when I woke up the next morning I played it back. Amongst all the snoring I rediscovered and found the lick and the lyrical hook I'd come up with to accompany it. (Oldham 2003: 197)

Richards developed most of the song, with Jagger writing some of the words for the third verse "by the motel pool the next day" (Oldham 2003: 198).

The simple, three-note motif—first on the beat and then syncopated—marches forward, aggressive and unstoppable. The structure essentially consists of alternating choruses and verses. That is, one set of music and text ("I can't get no, satisfaction . . . ") repeats, followed each time by a contrasting melody with new text each time. That much is not terribly new. However, Jagger's delivery of these verses—snarls and anger, followed by the quietly intense but building threat of each chorus—resonated with the summer of 1965. Jagger suggests that a Chuck Berry song, "Thirty Days," may have inspired Richards because it "features the line 'I can't get no satisfaction from the judge.'" Jagger suspects an American influence because "it's not any way an English person would express it. I'm not saying he purposefully nicked anything, but we played those records a lot" (Oldham 2003: 198).

As with many song texts in the sixties, fans of "Satisfaction" have felt free to interpret. Richards, when asked about the possible interpretation of one line, "smoke another kind of cigarette," and whether he meant the song's text to be clandestinely subversive, begins by discounting double entendre. "A lot of them are completely innocent," he claims. Nevertheless, the popular image of the Rolling Stones possesses, if nothing else, a significant element of stage fiction. Richards continues his explanation with a twist:

> I don't think that one is. It might have been. I don't know if it was a sly reference to drugs or not. After a while, one realizes that whatever one writes, it goes through other people, and it's what gets to them. Like the way people used to go through Dylan songs. It don't matter. They're just words. Words is words. (Greenfield 1981: 170b)

Like Richards, Jagger opines, "I don't think the lyrics are that important. . . . I used to have great fun deciphering lyrics. I don't try to make them so obscure that nobody can understand, but on the other hand I don't try not to. I just do it as it comes" (Cott 1981: 47b).

The importance (or relative unimportance) of song texts to Jagger and Richards's compositions seems to vary with their intended audience. Oldham's strategy for selling the Stones portrayed them as the anti-Beatles, and the Stones themselves embraced this identity. The approach shows up in their song texts, especially those directed at the perceived establishment. Commenting on Jagger's lyrical penchant for challenging the vested interests of British society, Richards notes:

> Mick's always written a lot about it. A lot of the stuff Chuck Berry and early rock writers did was putting down that other generation. That feeling then, like in '67. We used to laugh at those people, but they must have gotten the message right away because they tried to put rock & roll down, trying to get it

off the radio, off records. Obviously, they saw some destruction stemming from [it]. . . . they felt it right away. (Greenfield 1981: 172)

Like John Lennon's material, Stones songs began to echo Bob Dylan's resentments. The first two verses of "Satisfaction" largely rail against advertising in general, about "useless information" on the radio and about television sales pitches for products that will make one's shirts whiter. The last verse, however, changes the topic and complains about the inability to seduce a woman. Perhaps Jagger's contribution, the last verse takes "Satisfaction" into unfamiliar pop territory: the voice is sexually aggressive. Certainly, 1950s blues and rhythm-and-blues could have obvious sexual themes (consider the Dominos' "Sixty-Minute Man"), but mainstream media had relentlessly censored that material. Perhaps Jagger's sometimes unintelligible delivery allowed the Rolling Stones to slip past the gates.

Soon, Jagger and Richards set into a composing routine with Richards generating the core musical and textual ideas for a song, often developing the groove in rehearsal with drummer Charlie Watts. Jagger then supplied "an attitude or a phrase . . . to pick up on," generating the story and delivery (McPherson 2006) and writing a number of verses that they could edit for final use. As with Lennon and McCartney, Richards would critique Jagger's lyrics, letting him know which he thought were the best: "I might write five verses and we only need three. Keith will say, 'Oh, that's a great line, let's combine it with this'" (ibid.). As Peter Townshend would do for Roger Daltrey, Richards distills his approach as "I write songs for Mick to sing." Moreover, Richards felt that he needed to get the singer interested in a song: "And then once he gets interested and does it—BOOM, there you go" (ibid.).

In the mid-sixties, these songs (e.g., "Satisfaction," "Play with Fire," and "Mother's Little Helper") painted the establishment as shallow and hypocritical. "Play with Fire" (the B-side to "The Last Time") drops the names of London districts like social bombs, contrasting the good life of a "block in St. John's Wood" and posh Knightsbridge with working-class Stepney in east London. The song also plays up another of Jagger's themes: male domination of women. Filled with contradictions (the mother is an "heiress," but the father controls her possessions), the song asserts that men control the material world and the freedom that women were beginning to enjoy in the sixties.

Richards describes Jagger's influence in the creation of songs as residing in his ability to be "a preacher," particularly "in his method of delivery." He believes that Jagger's participation allowed him to "write on a more political level, a more social level, because he can deliver it that way. To me, when I get down to it, there's really not very much difference. A song about you and I is really about the same thing at a more intimate level" (McPherson 2006). Nevertheless, Jagger feigns not to have thought much about the political and social meaning of his songs: "I think I AM a frivolous person. That's why it's hard for me to talk about [the meaning of my songs]. I don't print the words on the record; if you can't hear them it's too bad. I don't think they're great works of poetry" (ibid.).

The balance here seems to be that first, Jagger and Richards chose topics that would challenge the authority of the establishment broadly and parents specifically. They spoke to the determination of adolescents to be independent of their parents and to question social and cultural norms that they perceived as limiting their freedom. Second, neither Jagger nor Richards claim to have put great stock in the meaning of the texts, nor to consider what responsibility they might have for how teens would interpret their texts:

> [W]e never sit around and ask ourselves why we wrote a song, although now that it's done we join everybody else in trying to analyze why we did it. I think images just come out; you haven't that much to do with it. If you like an idea that comes along, you sort of carry on writing in the hopes that maybe you'll eventually find out why. There are no answers in the lyrics. They really just raise other questions, which is maybe the point of it. (McPherson 2006)

RAY DAVIES

As British pop artists flourished in the sixties, establishing London as the temporary world capital of popular culture, many British songwriters sought to capture a national identity in their compositions. In part, they were reacting to the marketability of British culture in the United States, but British audiences craved self-celebration. After the embarrassments of the Suez crisis, the Profumo scandal, and other indignities, for once London seemed to be on a roll, if only in the arts. With British artists topping the charts in the English and often non-English world and huge audiences as far away as the Philippines, to be "British" had cachet.

Perhaps none found an English voice quite as distinctive as did Ray Davies (b. 1944), who infused many of his songs with an essence of suburban London working-class culture. Davies and his younger brother, Dave, with a school chum (Peter Quaife) formed one of the most influential British groups of the sixties: the Kinks. They began by playing covers of blues, rhythm-and-blues, and rock 'n' roll and, once they signed with Pye, made recordings of songs like Little Richard's "Long Tall Sally." However, in 1964, publishers were eager to find original songs, and if members of groups showed an inclination to write, then managers and producers encouraged them to do so. Ray Davies had already been dabbling in composition and, in that summer of excitement, found a voice.

Unlike many other rock stars of the era, who purchased either tony estates in suburbs like Weybridge (e.g., John Lennon) or homes in exclusive London neighborhoods like St. John's Wood (e.g., Paul McCartney), Davies stayed close to his family in the working-class row houses of north London's Muswell Hill. At one point, when Davies had retreated to his Fortis Green home, the management of the Kinks sent veteran American songwriter Mort Shuman to determine why their source of income had shifted away from the edgy rock of the band's early recordings. Shuman thought that Davies simply needed to discard his family and move into town where, he presumed, the young songwriter would be inspired by the hedonistic life of a rock star. Davies, characteristically, disagreed: "suburbia was and would always be a major influence in my writing" (Davies 1994: 266).

When he was growing up, his working-class family loved music enough to have a piano in the front room, a place of which the brothers have fond memories of seasonal gatherings with singing. Their father played banjo and their sister Rene took piano lessons (as did Ray briefly); however, both brothers took to the guitar, with Ray getting lessons from his brother-in-law. Mike Picker's instruction came from classical guitarist Louis Gallo in Finsbury Park, and each week Picker would come home to interpret his lessons for his wife's brother. Ray learned to read music of Ferdinando Carulli and developed enough skill to play duets with Mike. Brother Dave, who taught himself guitar, remembers, "Ray had a better hook on remembering notation and reading music" (Davies 1996: 14). As for many adolescents in the late fifties and early sixties, the guitar became both an identity marker and a medium for self-expression for the Davies brothers. When he began to venture into the alternative world of Soho, Ray Davies found his interests in music and the style of his playing beginning to evolve: "Experience changes the way you think about chords and the notes you play. You bend the notes differently" (Davies 1994: 53).

Partly because space came at a premium in the Davies home, Ray moved out to live with his sister Rosie and her husband, Arthur, who owned a Grundig tape recorder on which Ray and brother-in-law Mike would record imitations of their favorite American artists. The two would listen to Buddy Holly and other 1950s artists, internalizing the phrasing and projection of these records (Davies 1994: 64). They also listened to performers like Merle Haggard, Chet Atkins, and Hank Williams, the last of whom became a model for Davies, not only as a performer, but as a songwriter. In these songs, Davies heard "a crying quality" that summed up his "own darker doubts about the world" (ibid.).

Arthur's Grundig would soon record some of Ray Davies' earliest composition attempts, including songs that would become hits for the Kinks: a finger-picked version of "Tired of Waiting for You," possibly as a skiffle tune and evoking for Davies "images of black slaves toiling away in the cotton fields" (Davies 1994: 62). He also worked on a repetitive "two-chord shuffle" that would eventually become "You Really Got Me" (ibid.).

In the early sixties, songwriting for Davies expressed his "confused sexuality and confinement in the society" and served as a kind of therapy; nevertheless, one night in a personal epiphany, he understood composing as "a lightning-rod from the Gods" (1994: 71). Songwriting emerged as his escape from an art school existence looming ready to entrap him in a predictable future. Perhaps music provided a ticket away from normality, "an emotional outlet" and potential method of "earning a living." However, existing as a songwriter for Davies meant having an inspiration. Most pop songwriters in this era simply imitated other commercially successful love songs. Ray Davies wrestled with the problem of how does "a wretched art student living off a Middlesex grant in a suburb of north London find himself a fucking muse?" (1994: 70).

The things that commanded his adolescent attention, "soccer, music and art," seemed unlikely inspirations. The turning point for him came when he realized that, unlike painting (where he imitated others), writing songs came "from my own experience, my own enlightenment" (Davies 1994: 71). He rejected what he believed would have been a dead-end career in commercial art, painting signs. "That night," he remembers, "I saw the stars for the first time and wrote poems and lyrics until the cold morning air made my lips freeze" (ibid.).

You Really Got Songs

In 1964, the Kinks (like the Stones and many other British groups) recorded covers of American rock classics, with sporadic success. The Stones had successfully released "Little Red Rooster," but the Kinks' version of "Long Tall Sally" flopped. To be successful, they needed good original material. Dave Davies remembers the day when he first heard his elder brother play the riff for "You Really Got Me" on the family's front-room upright piano. He "thumped out these crude fifths" with his left hand and "Little Richard–style eighth note chops" with his right, lumbering into the two-chord shuffle begun at Rosie and Arthur's house. The text and melody came from the phrase: "Yeah, you really got me going, you got me so I don't know what I'm doing" (Davies 1996: 62):

> Ray called me over to the piano to listen to a riff he was playing . . . with his two fingers. F G G F G. I wondered what it would sound like as bar chords on my guitar with my new amp sound. So I tried it. It was as if something magical had descended upon us in that modest little room. Ray shifted the riff a

tone. G A A G A. Then he repeated the same riff in D. I blared out the chords on my guitar. It was wonderful, instinctual. (Davies 1996: 3)

Ray Davies remembers that lyrics apparently "just seemed to pop out of my head" while he sat in the parlor of his parents' home (1994: 146). As the Kinks seemed to be touring incessantly, Davies wanted a song that would directly appeal to their audiences, especially as they began by opening for better-known groups like the Hollies and the Dave Clark Five. In that context, he saw the power of musical repetition as a way to move an audience emotionally and physically. Davies reasons that audiences reacted to these patterns automatically because "they knew the dance before they were born" (ibid.). "You Really Got Me" accomplished this. The Kinks included the song in their stage program, honing its sound and quirks until Pye relented and let them record the song. However, the details continued to change until the last minute.

Hal Carter, whom their promoter, Arthur Howe, had hired to help them "improve" their stage presence, told Davies that he needed to be clearer in the song's opening declaration. Carter complained that the lyrics left him wondering whether Davies was singing to a male or a female. At the start of the song, he offered the recommendation that the text be to somebody, "Jane, Carol, Sue, bint, tart—even just plain 'Girl.' Whatever you do, you have to make it personal" (Davies 1994: 147). Davies took his suggestion: "'Girl' instead of 'Yeah' meant a lot to me, but no one in the studio seemed to notice the difference" (ibid.).

With the success of "You Really Got Me," Pye invited the Kinks back into the studio with the expectation that Shel Talmy would be able to duplicate the formula with another Ray Davies tune. Instead, Davies brought the other song he had recorded on Rosie and Arthur's Grundig[11] as an arpeggiated, finger-picking instrumental: "Tired of Waiting for You." The final parts of the composition and recording event were auspicious. The night before going into the recording studio, Davies and his girlfriend, Rasa, had consummated their relationship and this, as well as the determination not to record another cover or Shel Talmy invention, spurred Davies to finish the song he had begun. Arriving at the studio, he routined the song with his brother and Peter Quaife, showing them the chord progression, working out the rhythmic accompaniment, and ultimately recording it (Davies 1994: 174). However, Davies had yet to compose the lyrics and

---

[11] Indeed, when he visited his sister during a later tour of Australia (Rosie and Arthur had emigrated), she played him "old tapes of me rehearsing with my guitar when I had lived with her. She was shocked when I revealed that one of the little 'plink-plonk' country songs on her tape had turned out to be 'Tired of Waiting for You'" (Davies 1994: 208).

asked to delay recording the vocals until the next day, feigning a sore throat. His intention had been to be aggressive; however, a "gentle melody" emerged, and the words "It's your life and you can do what you want" (ibid.). His life provided the context. The words revealed the details.

Still, when he arrived back at the studio the next day, he only had some of the lyrics. He searched his memory and recalled a poem he had written from the perspective of an anxious teen. Quickly working through the rhythms in his head, he threw these words into the song, intoning how exhausting anticipation can be (Davies 1994: 175). These different ideas collide and amalgamate in the song's unusual tripartite structure. The opening builds on the arpeggio riff and the hook that defines the song, now less finger picking and more aggressive slides. The second part breaks the pattern and, like "You Really Got Me," rises in pitch while the singer declares his loneliness and exasperation. The third part breaks the guitar rhythm further, throwing the music into a freefall while the words, "It's your life and you can do what you want" hang before building to a climax as the singer reasons with his lover to make up her mind. True to Davies' description of the haste in which he created the text, the song starts again from the beginning and repeats both music and words rather than inventing new text.

Shel Talmy immediately declared "Tired of Waiting for You" to be another number one; however, he also deemed the song inappropriate as a follow-up recording. "Tired" broke some of the formula established by their first hit, although it kept Dave Davies's distorted guitar sound. Indeed, when they finally did release this recording, Derek Johnson in the *New Musical Express* noted in his review that "Tired of Waiting for You" amounted to a "[c]hange of character for the Kinks" and a "departure from their raucous broken-beat approach . . . more subdued—really it's a rock ballad with a slow shake-shuffle beat. Very nice it is too!" (Johnson 1965: 6).

However, Talmy wanted a variation on "You Really Got Me" that would be immediately recognizable as a Kinks song, evoking the same kinds of chord changes and aggressiveness that had attracted record buyers in the first place. Davies chose to imitate himself, building chords again on the blues-derived flatted seventh that had featured so prominently in "You Really Got Me" and on the flatted third. As with "You Really Got Me" and "Tired of Waiting for You," Davies seems to have started with the harmonic and rhythmic materials first, adding melody and text afterward. His publisher, Eddie Kassner[12]—standing next to Davies as he

---

[12] A Denmark Street legend, Kassner would purchase Regent Sound Studios at the end of the decade.

pounded out the chords and matched their rhythm with a song about loving "All Day and All of the Night"—found bliss in this moment of apparent inspiration and market savvy (Davies 1994: 178). Davies wondered whether he had just lost something very, very important.

My New Friends

With success came the desire to evolve as a songwriter and to find that elusive personal muse. Ironically, for the man who came to celebrate working-class suburban London, an Indian muse may have inspired him. In early 1965, the Kinks landed in Bombay, where they stayed overnight in a waterside hotel. With his biological (and psychological) clock on Greenwich Mean Time, Davies woke up early and listened while local fishermen sang and prepared their boats. Davies found the songs and the context incredibly moving, perhaps reflecting the period's fascination with orientalist stereotypes, but illustrating the power that music held for him (Davies 1994: 204–205).

London musical life in 1964 buzzed with many ideas, one of which arrived with guitarist Davy Graham, who had been experimenting with North African musical ideas and had been gaining an elite audience. In imitation of Graham's experiments, Davies creates a drone with overdriven electric guitars, starts the melody of "See My Friends" on the third, rises to the fifth, repeats this pattern, and descends to the third, essentially making the third his melodic root. After repeating that pattern, he starts on the fifth, keeping the shape true to the original trichord, flattening the seventh so that the second phrase exactly parallels the first.

The structure of the fishermen's song resonated with Davies in a metaphysical way and spurred him to consider the relationship between music and life, indeed to parallel life and musical structure: "[Y]ou have the opening, which goes into a verse, then a middle period, you bring back the verse and the chorus, have another crack at the middle, try to start the verse again." At this point, Davies says, you "realize that it's all over, so you usually sing one or two choruses that everybody's heard before, then it either comes to an abrupt end or you just fade out—and you've got only three minutes to do all that" (1994: 275). Comparing what he knew of the lives and music of the fishermen (which was not much) to his own life and his music, he wondered whether their apparently simpler lives might not be an answer to his own problems (ibid.).

Songwriting for Davies underwent a catharsis after "See My Friends," and he began to search for new directions. Perhaps echoing the trepidation he felt singing for Eddie Kassner, he was particularly unhappy with how he had rushed the song "Set Me Free": "There are not many songs I'm ashamed of writing, but that's one." The aspect of the song that he was most embarrassed about was the classic rhythm-and-blues harmonic formula of I–vi–IV–V in C, which had proved a (successful) cliché for many musicians: "I swore to myself I would never use this sequence, but I did and I failed dismally. It's used in hundreds of songs. But nothing else would go in. So it can't have been a good tune anyway" (N.A. 1965c: 14). Davies describes this experience as "hackmanship," which he defines as to "contrive and target an audience rather than write from an inward, subconscious flow." The experience of writing and recording "Set Me Free" had made him "feel like a whore," perhaps because everyone else seemed quite pleased with the song and recording (Davies 1994: 233–234).

Here, Davies separates himself from writers like Stephens and Murray, who consciously tried to write commercially. Davies wanted something personal, something expressive of his own experience: he wanted art. Davies retreated to his suburban heaven where brother Dave remembers that he, Ray's wife, Rasa, and Ray "would often stand around the white upright piano that Ray had in his back room and work out vocal parts, go over sections of songs, work out arrangements, exchange ideas." A communal model of songwriting materialized in which the composer took inspiration from those within his social unit. Dave remembers that his brother would ask his opinion when developing musical ideas. For the younger brother, this phase in their relationship was "full of unconditional creativity and love, a wonderful period where the music seemed to flow in and out of the house like air" (Davies 1996: 49).

Davies had the revelation that, to change the Kinks' sound, he had to abandon the way he had been playing the guitar; this shift helped Ray Davies to reimagine his songwriting. He embraced open, fingered chords. In an interview with the musically challenged Keith Altham of the *New Musical Express,* Davies declares, "After 'See My Friend' [*sic*] I said we would never go back to the old sound and I meant it. We used to play this type of chord." Davies then "covered the top strings on his guitar" and explained, "Now we play this" and "opened the strings." (Altham could tell no difference between the chords.) Davies wanted a change, elucidating, "I'm trying to take pop music a step further now" (Altham 1965: 10).

Davies' musical response came as a radical departure. Instead of a driving rhythm, "A Well Respected Man" begins with an open strum of an acoustic guitar and the beginning of a story: "Well he gets up every morning and goes to work each day." Davies takes as his subject (loosely based on the Kinks' accountant, Robert Ransom) conservative privilege and hypocrisy. After scandals involving establishment figures like John Profumo, Kim Philby, and Dr. Stephen Ward (all in 1963) and a general decline in Britain's political prestige in the world, Davies questions the automatic respect that his society gives such figures. Indeed, in an era influenced by Bob Dylan's assault on the American establishment, Davies takes aim at the British elite, simultaneously celebrating the aspirations of England's working class.

Around this same time, his exasperation with the British recording industry led him to contemplate walking away from his success. His father's reaction proved immediate and indelible when, in a barely controlled rage, he reached out and hit his son, sputtering his anger at Ray's contemplated surrender. The episode left Davies "ashamed." The only defense that Davies possessed against the class system that had condemned his parents to their existence was songwriting, and he was about to abandon it (Davies 1994: 232). In this story, Davies reveals how his musical abilities provided a challenge to the class hierarchy that had threatened to imprison him as an art student. That pop music in the sixties had the potential to challenge the fabric of British rank and privilege testifies to its symbolic power.

"A Well Respected Man" parodies the businessmen of "the City" (the oldest part of London and the center of the financial district) and their class in a fashion similar to that of George Formby. Davies seems to have relished the comparisons with Formby, whose films usually portrayed the triumphs of an honest and simple working-class man over the vicissitudes of life and the advantages available only to those born to privilege. When asked how he felt when people described the "new" Kinks as the "Formby Quartet," Davies took the statement as one of personal support: "I feel complimented when people say it sounds like Formby. . . . He earned a lot of bread!" More important for Davies, "A Well Respected Man" "proved we can do something completely different from our previous singles." Again, Davies describes a process that seems to have begun with the harmony and rhythmic/metric aspects of the song, with the words coming late in the process: "I worked out the rhythm on a guitar while traveling in a car and the words seemed to fall in naturally to the chords. I think it's important the words should fall in almost by themselves. I've been told that's the way the Beatles work" (Altham 1966: 3). Interestingly, he repeats the same idea that John Carter declared when he said that the British style kept music simple.

Davies' embrace of English working-class life became a primary feature of his music in the late sixties, resulting in two important albums that took Britain as their subject: *The Kinks Are the Village Green Preservation Society* (1968) and *Arthur or the Decline and Fall of the British Empire* (1969). The latter in part tells the story of an English expatriate in Australia seeking opportunities for his family, which Davies' brother-in-law Arthur (who had moved to Australia) saw as inspired by his life (Davies 1994: 211). In an era when pop musicians rebelled against the generation that had survived the war and against a class system that condemned the majority of the population to limited education and menial labor, Ray Davies barricaded himself in the neat little homes and back gardens of north London, where he celebrated the working family's home and hearth. He embraced rejection: rejection of ostentation, rejection of privilege, and rejection of artifice. Consequently, his music took on a degree of sarcasm and cynicism about the status quo. He wanted to liberate people to be happy with their lives and to judge others as people.

PETE TOWNSHEND

While Ray Davies found his inspiration in the north London suburban life of Muswell Hill, Fortis Green, and Finchley Road, Pete Townshend's (b. 1945) demons resided in the sprawling west London working-class suburbs of Acton, Ealing, and Shepherd's Bush. More specifically, where Davies took ideas from his domestic redoubt of family sing-alongs and pub favorites, Townshend celebrated the life of working-class clubs like the Goldhawk. In these havens, young men came on weekends to dance, fight, and display their latest sartorial treasures, inspiring Townshend's earliest compositions with an aggressive edge that sometimes bordered on anarchy. Where Davies' suburban life sought blissful retreat, Townshend's held violence in the shadows. That he represented an unlikely bard to this court attests to his abilities as a cultural observer, if not his status as the most intellectual songwriter of the era.

When a student, he did well as long as studies had his attention; however, like Lennon and Davies, puberty seems to have temporarily redirected his enthusiasm from academia. And like these and other musicians who became prominent in Britain's popular music industry in the sixties, he found the government channeling him into art school, the graphic arts, and probable underemployment. Nevertheless, Ealing Art School transformed Townshend, who arrived as a crest of change and modernism swept through the institution. In 1961 (the year the sixteen-year-old Townshend enrolled), Roy Ascott helped put in place a new curriculum that emphasized the interconnections among the arts, linking drawing, painting, printing, sculpting, and design. In particular, Ascott's theories about art education were "informed by the principles of cybernetics" and his experiences in the national service with Decca's radar technology (Mason 2005). Ascott encouraged students to welcome technology (including electronics) into the creation of art and to recognize the special possibilities these new media offered.

Ealing introduced Townshend to a number of important artists of the time, such as Bernard Cohen, Adrian Berg, Noel Forster, Ron Kitaj, and others, including Gustav Metzger, the "English cybernetician" Gordon Pask, and semiotician Stephen Willats (Mason 2005). Metzger and Pask (perhaps Ascott's counterweight) notoriously embraced the dystopian notion of technology as an agent of decay and went about creating works that contained the seeds of their own destruction. Willats encouraged students to think about the communication process and the artist's relationship with his or her audience. Each of these artist-teachers provided an interpretive piece of Townshend's artistic psyche and influenced his creative uniqueness.

Art school also provided a social context for Townshend's personal transformation. One of his first acquaintances was an American, Tom Wright, who not only had a flat across Sunnyside Street from the school, but a collection of important jazz, blues, rhythm-and-blues, and rock 'n' roll recordings with which Townshend would spend hours. He also introduced him to a decidedly non-mod drug: marijuana.

Unlike some other songwriters of this era who came from family backgrounds where music constituted an incidental (if not a slightly delinquent) diversion from life's most important crises, Townshend's parents were both musicians, and his father, Cliff, remained a working musician until the early 1960s. Moreover, jazz saxophonist Cliff gave his son encouragement in most of his musical experimentation, including rock 'n' roll. He brought him to gigs, notably to summer engagements at seaside resorts where the Squadronaires (the RAF's well-known dance band that continued touring after the war) played nightly dance programs. These summer engagements provided a context where Townshend routinely watched his father play a prominent musical role with an adoring audience in tune with the band's dance music. Perhaps even more important, Townshend's father foresaw the end of his own musical world: "Pete, the big band is finished. We just can't afford to carry a 26-piece band and a coach and 26 hotel bills every night. It's just absurd, and you guys are going to take over" (Resnicoff 1989).

While his father was playing on the Isle of Man in the summer of 1956, Townshend had his first experiences with rock 'n' roll when a local theater showed the film *Rock around the Clock*. His mother Betty remembered taking him and a friend to see the film, and he "wanted to see it the next day and the next day and in the end we were giving him the money or getting passes for them. They were seeing this film daily" (Marsh 1983: 17). Ironically, in his first major act of juvenile musical revolt, Pete took up the banjo to play in a trad band, an aesthetic decision that would have likely been at odds with his father's love of swing and modern jazz. However, rock 'n' roll would come to dominate Townshend's life, and in the late fifties and early sixties he found one particular artist inspirational: "I don't think it was until I heard Chuck Berry that I realized what you could do with words—how unimportant the music was, 'cause Chuck Berry always used the same song" (Marsh 1983: 28). Like Jagger and Richards, once Townshend discovered American blues and rhythm-and-blues, he lost interest in the pop music that his band (the Detours) had been playing. Slim Harpo, James Brown, Bo Diddley, Mose Allison, and Jimmy Reed would become the base of their repertoire. Moreover, in late 1963, as the Rolling Stones began to attract more attention and larger crowds, Townshend and the band began to see that they could take on this music and still keep their audience. Singer Roger Daltrey in particular preferred these hard-edged blues tunes for his voice, and Townshend would learn to write tunes that Daltrey delivered convincingly.

Townshend and schoolmate John Entwistle played together in a variety of bands performing trad, country and western, pop, and rock 'n' roll, eventually linking up with fellow west Londoner Daltrey. Surviving several management changes and limited success (as both the Detours and, briefly, the High Numbers), the band that called themselves the Who found their niche and sympathetic managers in Kit Lambert and Chris Stamp. Lambert in particular would push Townshend to write songs reflecting the band's strengths and Townshend's life. After opening for Johnny Kidd and the Pirates, the band stripped down to the same configuration of guitar, bass, drums, and a singer, which meant that Townshend's guitar playing needed to incorporate both accompaniment and melody.

The audience the Who attracted featured that peculiarly 1960s manifestation of working-class male assertion: the mod ("modernists"). Regardless of their origins, the west London mods for whom the Who performed embraced sleek modern clothing styles (not the retro hand-me-downs of rockers), amphetamines, and dancing. Other parts of London would produce their own versions of the clerk who dressed better than his boss, but towns like Acton birthed a particularly proud and reckless class of short-haired and defiant young men. Pete Townshend "especially threw himself into all things mod. He was fascinated by this almost invisible sect. He was the first of the group to start taking pills—mod fuel" (Barnes 1982: 10). Mod culture constantly and rapidly evolved, with small variations in clothing and dance steps emerging every weekend and, sometimes, from one night to the next *during* a weekend. Townshend "practiced complicated steps to the two main mod dances, the 'block' and the 'bang.' He rehearsed the mod way of walking and tried to pick up the correct mod way of standing around" (ibid.). By immersing himself in the details of mod culture, Townshend (perhaps subconsciously) aimed at absorbing its energy and power, qualities that he could transfer to his music.

Despite his study of mod culture, Townshend's personal lifestyle and musical tastes were more eclectic than those of his audience. The pot he smoked, the big American car he drove, and his tastes for rock 'n' roll and jazz would have been repellent to most mods of the era. However, while mods generally refrained from designing their own clothing, they did often dictate to tailors how they wanted their clothes cut. Townshend created leather jerkins as early as 1963 (perhaps a consequence of Ascott's integrated ideas about the arts) and, eventually, bright, bold, colorful designs à la Peter Blake.

He had been dabbling with songwriting, and his college friend Richard Barnes (1982: 8) remembers that, when Townshend heard Bob Dylan's first two albums, *Bob Dylan* (1962) and *Freewheelin' Bob Dylan* (1963), he returned to his flat "raving about them." But it was not until *Another Side of Bob Dylan* (1964) that Townshend became serious about songwriting: "Pete played it endlessly, especially the track 'All I Really Want to Do.' Dylan and particularly this track spurred him on with his own song writing." Barnes, who was nearly a resident of Townshend's Sunnyside flat, remembers, "After this he would sit down with a guitar and a notepad and play around with a few lines he'd written. He kept a book of odd bits of writing, possible lyrics" (ibid.). Townshend's instinct that mods would accept Dylan's music if presented as rhythm-and-blues was confirmed when in 1964 the Animals released electric versions of Dylan's covers of their "Baby Let Me Take You Home" and "House of the Rising Sun." Mod audiences went to the concerts and cheered.

Manager Kit Lambert arranged for the Naturals to record one of Townshend's first attempts, "It Was You"; like Jagger and Richards with their first creations, Townshend did not feel that the song was appropriate for his own group. According to Barnes, Townshend "knew that if he could come up with a commercial song to record, it would solve all their worries" (1982: 38). Accordingly, Lambert purchased tape recorders for his young charge, both to record his musical ideas and to create demos for the other members of the band. Townshend remembers coming to the realization that "the only way I was ever, ever, ever going to make myself felt was through writing." Consequently, he "really got obsessed with writing rock songs" and probably "concentrated far more on that than on any other thing in life. I just used to go back after gigs and write and write and write all the time" (Marsh 1983: 118).

Townshend began by playing his compositions for Lambert, who also introduced him to new musical ideas, particularly those associated with his father, composer-arranger Constant Lambert: "He played me a lot of music that his father had sort of unearthed. I listened to people like Purcell, Corelli, William Walton, and Darius Milhous [*sic*: Milhaud] and lots of Baroque stuff." Moreover, the art school student found in Lambert someone who spoke an artistic language he understood: "He had a great grasp of musical terms and was able to make a critique. He used to throw in a lot of ideas and make suggestions that seemed to be completely inappropriate, but whenever I tried them they used to work" (Barnes 1982: 39).

"I Can't Explain"

One of the first demos that Townshend was willing to share with his mates, "I Can't Explain" offered a minimalist blues riff in the spirit of Eddie Cochran's "Summertime Blues," underlining inarticulate expressions of incomprehension, à la amphetamine-addled mods. Lambert's secretary, Anya Butler, a friend of Shel Talmy's wife, brought the demo and Townshend to the attention of the independent producer. This interest came at the start of Talmy's successful recordings of the Kinks, and Lambert was eager to catch that train.

Released the same day as the Kinks' "Tired of Waiting for You," "I Can't Explain," the Who's first recording with Shel Talmy, breaks new sonic ground and forms part of a trend of other London groups that marks the end of a year dominated by the Beatles and their Merseyside accomplices. Talmy's highly compressed recording of Townshend's Rickenbacker electric 12-string guitar evokes George Harrison's twang, but provides a hitherto unheard punch to the instrument. Although Harrison's rockabilly sensibilities focused on blended plucking, Townshend pushes the amplification envelope with explosive chords that rip through the progression like bursts of gunfire. Bringing in a different influence, the backing vocals provided by John Carter and Ken Lewis emphasized a falsetto approach that echoed the Beach Boys. Derek Johnson's (1965: 6) review in the *New Musical Express* described the song as "insidious and insistent, with an arresting backing—a sort of blend of Mersey beat and surfing!"

Marsh (1983: 144) quotes drummer Keith Moon and bassist John Entwistle as believing that "I Can't Explain" represented "an answer to 'You Really Got Me,'" while Townshend only goes as far as to say that he took a "kind of a lift off the feeling" of the Kinks song. However, the similarities between "I Can't Explain" and other songs of the era reside in the chord progression, E–D–A (harmonically V–IV–I or I–^{b}VII–IV), which seems to have been in the air in late 1964. Decca released Van Morrison's song "Gloria" on 6 November with this chord sequence. The Who recorded "I Can't Explain" with these chords forming the core of the verse that same month. And Jagger and Richards would put together "The Last Time" with this chord progression at its core in January 1965. Assisting in the song's triumph, Lambert staged a mini mod riot on the television show *Ready Steady Go!* on 29 January 1965, catapulting the song up the charts.

Following the success of "I Can't Explain," the Who wanted to record something that sounded like a live show. Townshend pieced together "Anyway, Anyhow, Anywhere" after a regular Tuesday night session at the Marquee, one of London's prominent music clubs. Barnes (1982: 39) remembers, "Kit made Pete and Roger stay up writing it all night so that they would have something to record the next day when they had the session booked." Although Lambert may have been emulating Andrew Oldham's kitchen strategy with Jagger and Richards, clearly "Daltrey and Townshend" were not destined to be the next great songwriting team.

The experience speaks to how the songwriting for the Who differed from that of Jagger and Richards. In particular, singer Roger Daltrey—while effective at evoking an aggressive masculine image on stage (and off)—lacked Jagger's relative verbal agility. A London School of Economics student, Mick Jagger certainly had learned to navigate the educational system better than had Daltrey and, in the early stages of the Rolling Stones, he was a prominent and eloquent spokesperson whom the musical trades quoted before the band even had a recording. In contrast, Daltrey's education ended with high school, and he seldom had much to say to the press, unlike Townshend who in the late sixties even had his own column in *Melody Maker*. Perhaps because of his rejection of school and his embrace of street life, Daltrey learned how to project his masculinity dramatically and physically, but not how to create it with language.

Townshend recalls, "I found it quite difficult to write for Roger; songs like 'My Generation,' 'I Can't Explain,' 'Anyway, Anyhow, Anywhere,' and lots of songs I wrote . . . are *embarrassingly* macho, because I was trying to find things that he would feel comfortable singing" (Resnicoff 1989). The lyrics and music of "Anyway Anyhow Anywhere" evoke some of the aggression and violence of their shows, but even more important they declare that the protagonist will go "anyway, anyhow, anywhere I choose!" The lyrics give voice to the mods who came to the Who's shows at the Marquee, especially those loyal fans who came from west London and either rode their motor scooters home or had to wait for the first morning train back to Shepherd's Bush. Mobility constituted liberation.

With "The Kids Are Alright," the guitarist demonstrates how Lambert's record collection shaped Townshend's harmonic approach: "I actually started to use baroque chords, suspended chords. It did a lot to create that churchy feel" and ended up having "a lot to do with the way I play" (Barnes 1982: 39). Moreover, Lambert's willingness to engage the art school student in the construction of a philosophical base underlying the creation and performance of music shaped the direction not only of Townshend's writing, but arguably of British pop music in the mid- to late sixties.

Townshend employed ideas learned at the Ealing Art School to explain his use of feedback and his destruction of instruments. Metzger even showed up at a few performances, apparently watching approvingly as Townshend rammed guitars into speaker cabinets (Barnes 1982: 7). Townshend also drew directly from artist Peter Blake: "In 1962, when I was at Ealing Art School doing my second year of a Foundation course, I came across some early screen prints of his. I admired his gentleness and sense of humour, but most of all his quintessential Englishness" (Bennett 2002: 60). Blake and Ealing thus dramatically shaped how Townshend imagined rock and pop: "My art college experience led me away from fine art and graphics and towards semiology and cybernetic theory." He maintained that pop art represented a phenomenon not just limited to performances by the Who: "Even London's streets are making a massive anti-establishment statement, every Saturday night. This is what we are trying to do in our music: protest against 'showbiz' stuff, clear the hit-parade of stodge!" (ibid.). Less a definition of pop art than a manifesto, Townshend imagined that his music constituted a cultural revolution, in part against Denmark Street (which he also ironically embraced).

Their Generation

If "You Really Got Me" served as inspiration for "I Can't Explain," then the Stones' "Satisfaction" validated the tone that Townshend had set in "Anyway Anyhow Anywhere," which exploded in perhaps his most famous pop art manifesto expression: "My Generation." Townshend describes the change in musical aesthetics this way: "I used to think the Beatles were very old fashioned, even when they were new. I remember someone saying to me, 'Don't you like the new Beatles album?' I said, 'It's full of those fucking Italian[13] love songs'" (Oldham 2003: 261). His rejection of the traditional love song—the core repertoire of pop music—stems in part from Dylan, but he found inspiration in the attitude that Jagger and Richards brought to their songs:

> Because the Stones built the wall, they couldn't see that they'd built it and the Beatles hadn't. The rules were laid down: you do not sing about fucking love, you don't do it, you don't sing soppy love songs. There are songs about "I Can't Reach You," "You're Beyond My Reach," . . . "I Exhort You," "I'm Gonna Fuck You," but "We Are in Love" is a No. . . . "We Are in Love" . . . that was just ruled out. (Oldham 2003: 261)

"My Generation" (with its famous line "hope I die before I get old") challenged the values of the wartime cohort, which formed the core of the establishment, through pop art. "I wrote it with that intention," proclaims Townshend:

> Not only is the number pop-art, the lyrics are "young and rebellious." It's anti middle-age, anti boss-class, and anti young marrieds. I have nothing against these people really—just making a positive statement. The big social revolution that has taken place in the last five years is that youth, and not age, has become important. (Jones 1965: 11)

---

[13] Note the underlying ethnic condescension.

Like "You Really Got Me," "My Generation" starts with the chords G and F; but writing even more radically minimalist than the Kinks' song, Townshend essentially stays with these chords, changing them only when he modulates upward first to A, then B-flat, and finally to C.[14] In other words, the song has two chords (I and ^{b}VII), and, instead of extending the harmonic sentence, he modulates abruptly to each of these pitch platforms, where he maintains the I–^{b}VIII harmonic relationship. The recording also turns the pop song model on its head, first with a bass solo instead of the standard guitar or keyboard solo, and second, with Daltrey's affected stutter. Moon insists that this defining performance feature came about as a fluke in rehearsal: "Pete had written out the words and gave them to Roger in the studio. He'd never seen them before, he was unfamiliar with the words, so when he read them through the first time, he stuttered" (Hopkins 1981: 239b). Kit Lambert, who was overseeing the rehearsal, demanded that they leave the tick in the performance, and alternative takes of the recording have no stutter, suggesting that the stutter represents at least a potentially rational decision.

The year 1966 would prove to be problematic for both Townshend and the Who. First, Kit Lambert argued that, since he had been rehearsing the band for recording sessions, he was essentially fulfilling the function of producer. As such, he convinced the Who that all they needed was a qualified engineer, and so they attempted to break their contract with Talmy. Second, Lambert and Stamp decided that they should establish their own record company (Reaction) in order to release recordings by their performers. After all, why should they be paying Talmy to be a producer when they were preparing the bands, and why should Decca be reaping the profits from record sales? Unfortunately, the primary reward of these decisions came as a prolonged, costly, and very public international lawsuit that resulted in canceled releases, the withdrawal of records, competing records on both Brunswick (the subsidiary of Decca with which Talmy had contracted) and Reaction, and an agreement not to record until May. Ultimately, Talmy won income from almost all of their 1960s recordings. Their recording of "Substitute" floundered temporarily in the charts while the lawyers positioned their clients for a change in the contract.

Even with the Who's recording career in disarray, Townshend continued to develop as a songwriter, challenging the aesthetic norms of pop and exploring controversial topics, most notably with "I'm a Boy," a song about a child whose

---

[14] One could argue that the unaccompanied melodic material between the sections of guitar accompaniment implies other harmonic relationships, but Townshend's decision to leave these parts unaccompanied points to a nonharmonic interpretation.

mother insists on dressing and treating him as a girl. Late 1966 saw two exceptional pieces of music from him: "Happy Jack" and "A Quick One while He's Away." The former mixes nearly undanceable measures of 10/4 and 4/4 while telling the story of teens tormenting a man who "lived in the sand at the Isle of Man" (where Townshend had spent a memorable summer). The backing track for "Happy Jack" features a recurring instrumental theme and prominent drums that function less as standard accompaniment (where the drummer maintains a rhythmic and metric groove) and more as melodic counterpoint. Lambert and Townshend created "A Quick One" as a collage of different musical ideas spliced together to tell the story of a woman, seduction, and forgiveness. This nine minute and eleven second "mini-opera" represents Townshend's first attempt to extend his narrative ability and to combine different pieces of music into a single composition. In many ways, the suite comes off as clumsy and amateurish, far below the quality of craftsmanship demonstrated in previous and subsequent songs. However, he succeeds in bringing another Kit Lambert idea into a pop context: an extended dramatic work using pop songs. Townshend and the Who brought this ideal to fuller fruition with *Tommy* in 1969.

A BRITISH VOICE

The sixties saw the establishment of an identifiably British—and specifically English—pop songwriting tradition. The voices possessed many accents, drawing on creators and interpreters from the nooks and crannies of the northern urban centers of Liverpool and Manchester, the Midlands, and Northern Ireland. The voices came from Jewish, atheist, Protestant, Catholic, working-class, middle-class, educated, and uneducated mouths, each speaking to optimism and hope for something better and a return of British pride.

Like elsewhere in the British music and recording industries, songwriting began the decade imitating American models, competing at a disadvantage, and struggling to discover its authenticity. Songwriters of Geoff Stephens's generation, born in the 1930s, represent the first assault on American domination. Internalizing American models, they found ways to subvert the syntax, reshape musical expectations, and establish a professional platform from which others would make their departures. The beginning of the war signaled the birth of a generation of songwriters who turned twenty in, at, or near the beginning of the sixties. They entered adolescence as rock 'n' roll established a symbolic expression of their growing independence and emancipation. As likely to draw on Hoagy Carmichael as they were Chuck Berry, on George Formby as on Elvis, they represent the vanguard of change.

Mitch Murray tapped into the exuberance of the era, even as he remained tethered to the past's infrastructure. John Carter and Ken Lewis took a few steps more along this path, projecting an increasingly English musical sophistication into an amalgam of American surf and pop, all the while seeking the most direct and simple way of presenting these ideas. And John Lennon and Paul McCartney's songs exude the era's hybridization and optimism, taking musical cues from Bing Crosby and the Everly Brothers and reimagining them as the Shirelles accompanied by Carl Perkins.

But Britain's economic, political, and military denouement in the postwar era also bred resentment and anger, which found expression through the sympathetic vehicle of American blues. When middle-class bohemians like Mick Jagger and Keith Richards commandeered Howlin' Wolf's defiance and the Staples Singers' laments into critiques of women and marketing, they did so to reference the lives of British adolescent males. Being white and British worked in their favor with their audiences and enabled their continued appropriation of African American elements; however, they also transformed the idiom. Applying this approach to the establishment's hypocrisy in compositions like "Mother's Little Helper" did not prevent them from shifting their musical vocabulary to invoke "Englishness," as they did with "Lady Jane."

Herein lies an explanation for part of the success of British songwriting in the sixties. With multiple stylistic identities available to composers and musicians, and an atmosphere in which the rejection of establishment models found wide acceptance, British songwriters forged a new set of meanings. When Ray Davies equated failure with resorting to a I–vi–IV–V–I progression, his disappointment resided not with classic do-wop, but with his goal of finding an alternative solution, perhaps growing from his own very north London identity. Davies and others forged a new amalgam at once nostalgic and progressive.

And iconoclast Pete Townshend sought something entirely new. Like Davies, he fills his songs with humor and pathos, echoing Lieber and Stoller, as well as Gilbert and Sullivan. "A Quick One" comes off as musical comedy, pantomime, and parody, artistic pretension and juvenile jest. More important, Townshend brought a coherent intelligence ready to ruminate and speculate on the "art" of songwriting. Few in Tin Pan Alley had thought of what they did as art, nor did the wider culture encourage them to think this way. Thus, within a few years, in part due to a burgeoning decentered postmodern interpretation of the world, rock had gone from miscreant graffiti to inspired expression. Some of the change was perceptual: we saw the world differently. However, the world of popular music itself had grown much more complex.

6

Red-Light Fever

The Musician's Life

In the studio, separated from producers and engineers by a double pane of glass, the individuals whose voices, physical dexterity, and intuition realized 1960s British pop labored in the realm of performance. The social mechanisms that placed them in these recorded moments carefully calculated the most efficient ways to reap their talent and to maximize their value. Consequently, musicians could be the most celebrated individuals in the entire ecology and, sometimes, the most hidden. Their names, faces, and music often sold millions of records and concert seats, and yet, more often than not, performers ultimately garnered meager financial rewards.

Rock 'n' roll (and its stepcousin skiffle) promised young British teens that they could play like Elvis or like Eddie Cochran. Many cajoled their parents into buying guitars, amplifiers, and drum kits, prompting neighborhood complaints and compounding existing parent-teen tensions. With the Beatles' triumph in 1963, thousands of mostly teenage boys sought to emulate the Liverpudlians' feats, both real and imagined. The most successful among them graduated from church halls to social clubs and dance halls and then, by dint of effort and/or talent (or sometimes dumb luck), cohort after cohort had their shot at the big time, first opening for better-known names, then touring with them, and, sometimes, having their chance at recording. The infrastructure that both supported and exploited these musicians operated most intensely in the context of the recording studio, where managers, agents, and contractors scavenged whatever fleeting benefits could be had of a musician's possibly brief, blazing moment of fame.

The process by which individuals became musicians and by which musicians articulated "musicianhood" reflects some of the ways in which British popular music changed in the context of a generational attack on class and the profession of music. We can understand some of the musical changes of the sixties in terms of how a large group of amateurs demanded and obtained access to the recording process; however, the recording industry preyed on this enthusiasm. Most corporate directors, and many producers and engineers, at first scoffed at the ambitions of relatively untrained musicians, but soon they came to realize the financial potential of inexperienced youth (aided by technology). Publishers and recording corporations saw considerable profit potential in individuals with great energy but little discipline. If an aspiring pop icon could write a song and perform well enough to have a hit record, a publisher could glean royalties from sales of the record and sheet music. If that same performer failed on the next attempt, the publisher could drop him or her from its roster and move on to the next exploitation prospect. All that was needed was a system staffed with enough professionals to ensure a consistent product and a steady stream of would-be Lennons and McCartneys.

We have already noted how those whose backgrounds included a piano in the household often seemed to have a musical advantage, by virtue of both the presence of the instrument and the attitudes of the families who were ready to devote precious income to its purchase and maintenance. Families with pianos seem to have embraced music as an active part of their lives, individually and communally. For those would-be musicians in families without the means or tradition, the guitar offered a reasonable alternative, relatively cheap at the entry level and improvable as (and if) the adolescent developed. Drumming, on the other hand, demanded an entirely new paradigm for parental support. Not only were drum kits expensive (a number of individuals recall either building their own drums or beginning with a hodgepodge of equipment), but the sheer volume of a drummer practicing could test the notion of even motherly love.

Although Oldham paints a picture of a generational assault on the professional establishment, many young musicians in the sixties aspired to be professionals, marking the leap from amateur status with the abandonment of their day jobs and, sometimes, their birth names. Perhaps the Beatles provide the most notable example: following Brian Epstein's conditions, abandoning their leather jackets and pants for cloth suits, planning their set lists, refraining from swearing and eating on stage, and generally grooming themselves to appear more professional. The notion of "professional" in this context connotes engagement in a particular line of work, rather than a guild-trained skill. Most often, a gradual transition ensued, with tours and gigs reinforcing the decision to abandon the factory or shop. Perhaps even more significantly, the decision (or the requirement) to join the Musicians' Union resonated with an obvious working-class labor tradition. Becoming a musician substituted for taking up a trade.

During this era of remarkable and rapid musical evolution, numerous loosely connected social scenes of British pop musicians engaged in the continual conflict between change and stasis. These performers grouped themselves through a variety of overlapping parameters, notably including the instruments they played, the kinds of music they preferred playing, and, perhaps most important, the contexts in which they played. Some individuals specialized in particular instruments and musical styles (for example, the newly emerging ska music of Caribbean immigrants as heard in Millie Small's 1964 "My Boy Lollipop") while others were generalists; some toured, some played regular gigs (such as West End shows), and still others focused on recording sessions (the sessioneers). The complex structure of this musical ecology begins to emerge as we recognize that these scenes interconnected, with many musicians forming links and achieving fluency in different playing styles.

At the core of almost every ensemble in the popular music industry, the members of the rhythm section divided themselves into the kinds of instruments they played: guitarists, bass players, keyboardists, and drummers. Producers came to recognize guitarists for their reputations as good lead or rhythm players; however, although production teams expected London's session guitarists to be able to play in a variety of styles, they also knew that each musician had particular strengths. Consequently, they might call on Vic Flick for his bold anthem-like lines (e.g., John Barry's "James Bond Theme"), Jimmy Page for bluesy improvisations (e.g., Them's "Baby Please Don't Go"), Jim Sullivan for fluid country-tinged interpretations (e.g., Dave Berry's "The Crying Game"), or Joe Moretti for edgy surf sounds (Johnny Kidd's "Shakin' All Over"). The same seems to have been partially true for drummers, with Bobby Graham's solid rock (the Kinks' "You Really Got Me"), Clem Cattini's inventive flourishes (Donovan's "Hurdy Gurdy Man"), Andy White's solid sense of time (the Beatles' "Love Me Do"), or Ronnie Verrell's affinity for the jazz-pop aesthetic (Dusty Springfield's "I Only Want to Be with You").

All of these musicians began their professional lives playing in dance halls and clubs, in jazz trios, big bands, skiffle groups, country and western bands, or rock groups. They cut their musical teeth imitating recordings, internalizing the structure of a two minute and thirty second hit, the palette of delivery methods, harmonic and melodic syntax, and the characteristic instrumental timbres of classic and rare tracks. With the recording studio as their goal, they perfected their technique with home tape recorders and hoped for the future. However, for the few who eventually won recording contracts, the recording studio could be a bittersweet experience. Having a single to promote could mean larger audiences, but most studios demanded that a finished recording be hammered out in about an hour, which meant that producers commonly brought in session musicians to ensure that they had a reliable product. A band like the Beatles—relatively inexperienced as they were from just a few years of playing clubs, dances, and tours—amounted to neophytes when they arrived at EMI in June 1962. Martin's decision to let them attempt a recording session with Ringo Starr in September stands as a testament to his patience and willingness to honor their integrity, but the selection of drummer Andy White to supplement the band on their next attempt should have come as a surprise to no one. By all accounts, tension underlay the social atmosphere of studio two that day, as it did in every studio where a young musician arrived imagining he was about to be recorded for posterity, only to find a seasoned professional appointed to easily fill his innocent musical shoes.

Ironically, success plagued the Beatles and other popular British groups in the sixties. With the bulk of their immediate income oozing from live performances, they toured almost constantly between 1963 and 1966, consequently leaving them little time to rehearse and develop new material (which speaks to the ability of Lennon and McCartney to continuously create hit material). However, even groups who had built their reputations on live performances could find themselves replaced in the studio. Notoriously, the Belfast band Them (with singer Van Morrison) arrived at a number of recording sessions only to discover that their producer (either Dick Rowe or Bert Berns) had hired Jimmy Page to replace their guitarist, Billy Harrison. Page recalls, "It was very embarrassing on the Them sessions. With each song, another member of the band would be replaced by a session player. It was really horrifying! Talk about daggers! You'd be sitting there wishing you hadn't been booked" (Frame 1997: 31). Indeed, sometimes the band members might not even be present, as when session drummer Bobby Graham overdubbed Morrison's minimalist "Gloria." Listening to the record, one can hear both Ron Millings's basic drumming driving the original track along, while Graham's busy rolls and flams march in the foreground.

Singers occupied a particularly critical position in the recording process. Their ability to project a song on stage could help to gain a recording test or be the primary reason a producer rejected a group. The least likely individual to be replaced on a recording session, a singer usually retained his or her status simply because of an inimitable vocal timbre and unique articulation. Ironically, without reference to an instrument, singers were very often the least musically knowledgeable people in the studio and commonly relied upon others to determine the nature of the musical materials. Exceptions existed, of course. Van Morrison had played saxophone in an Irish show band and Georgie Fame made his reputation as a pianist; but Mick Jagger and Eric Burdon relied on their talent for compelling delivery and remembering lyrics.

Managers and agents had few common conventions such that, although some came from musical backgrounds (e.g., Eric Easton, who co-managed the Rolling Stones, had been an organist), others were just as likely to be clothiers (Larry Parnes), record retailers (Brian Epstein), or college lecturers (Peter Jenner). Some managers treated their artist clients as children who needed nurturing and protection, while others clearly saw them as sources of income. Johnny Rogan (1988) categorizes 1960s British managers into a variety of self-explanatory categories: the "autocratic manager," the "concerned parent," the "indulgent manager," the "neophyte," the "poachers and inheritors," the "neutered lackey," the "dilettante manager," the "fatalistic manager," the "overreacher," the "scapegoat manager," the manager who attempted to fill two roles (e.g., producer and agent), the team manager, and the "record company manager."

The confusion of managerial types illustrates in a limited way some of the Wild West mentality of London's music business in the fifties, sixties, and seventies. For small-scale operations, a manager could book engagements in local dance halls and clubs, but, for major theaters and tours, you needed an agent with a license who could write and sign contracts. Managers chose agents commonly on the basis of the quality and quantity of contacts with ballroom owners that they could offer. As in other areas, on the management side, "young" often meant unequal access. Andrew Oldham complains how his relationship with Eric Easton resulted in part because he was too young to have an agent's license (he turned nineteen in 1963, the year he met the Stones). Consequently, Easton drew up contracts that benefited his own pockets and directed profits away from both Oldham and the Stones (Oldham 2000: 205). Few seem to have had the kind of confidence in their agent that Dave Berry had in Manchester's Danny Batesh, forgoing a manager completely and trusting Batesh to function in his best interest.

Regardless of the kind of management musicians had, they generally occupied the lowest tier of the recording industry ecology. Moreover, record companies, management, and the musical press conspired to construct the Cinderella myth of the pop star. Everyone loves the modern Everyman story of a manager discovering an innocent artist in an obvious place and bestowing fame and fortune (as told, for example, in the play and film *Expresso Bongo*). More often than not, reality found enthusiastic, but naïve, kids having their moment of public exuberance, only to be discarded in the next release cycle. The winnowing process did select some notable individuals, and their lives as musicians illustrate some of the social changes that underlay the musical evolution of London in the sixties. The socioeconomic background of musicians, the ways in which they became professionals, and how they functioned in the studio reveal both the excitement and despair they encountered.

BECOMING A MUSICIAN

The numerous musicians who contributed to London's recording culture in the sixties emerged from different generations, social strata, and ethnicities. Many had clear working-class or lower middle-class origins, such that markers of minor differences in economic status (e.g., the availability of a piano) could have a significant impact on their careers. Perhaps an equally important developmental factor for British musicians in this era lies in whether the government conscripted them to serve in the war (or, in the postwar era, into the national service) or if they belonged to the generation born in and after 1940, which the government exempted.

Although Americans saw the British invasion as populated largely by long-haired young men, one of the most active musicians of the era performed as a quiet, unassuming, and balding bassist with a dry sense of humor. From near Newcastle in the north of England, Allan Weighell (1922–2002) unexpectedly became a musician in the thirties when a girlfriend's brother enlisted in the army, leaving an untended bass in a local dance band. His only experience had been watching, but then the musician he replaced "didn't play any real notes on the string bass; he made a lot of rhythmic thumping, yet very clean." Weighell proceeded to teach himself how to play and to read, picking up tips from other musicians and gaining experience performing in church halls until the war interrupted his musical life. In 1956, playing stand-up bass, he became a Steelman, touring and recording with Tommy Steele in one of the first successful British pop/rock bands. Significantly, while learning to operate radar in the navy during the war, he had dabbled with a guitar in his idle time, so a decade later, when a television producer asked who would be willing to take up the newly invented (and imported) electric bass guitar, he volunteered.

Like many British musicians, Jim Sullivan (b. James Tomkins, 1941) holds fond childhood memories of family music making. Growing up with his grandparents in suburban Hounslow (his mother died when he was two), Sullivan's grandfather played a concertina and could sing "a few of the old cockney songs." But apart from recorder lessons at school, Sullivan's musical education consisted primarily of being a good listener. His introduction to guitar came in the mid-fifties during a visit with his sister, who "had an old round-hole guitar sittin' in the corner." Inseparable from the instrument after a loan from his grandparents, he brought his proud possession to the nearby Eastern Command Headquarters, where the U.S. military put on shows for locals and where "kids used to go and get gum from the Yankees." On this particular afternoon, he sat on the grass, toying with the instrument, when an American approached him, took the guitar, "tuned it, and started playing," prompting the teen to ask, "How'd you do that?" After showing him a few chords, the American said, "I've got a book for you," and "about five minutes later came back with this Mel Bay book." Proximity to the military base perhaps also helped to make Sullivan's family into country music fans, and Sullivan thinks of himself as being "basically raised on Hank Williams."

The postwar American military presence in Britain contributed to an environment in which American musical tastes influenced British musical sensibilities. Whether the records that American servicemen brought with them, the short-distance broadcasts from their British bases, the more powerful broadcasts from their German bases, or even the gigs that all of the bases provided, American culture proved to be an important influence on many British musicians in this era.

Musicianship figures prominently in the families of a number of well-known pop and rock musicians: Paul McCartney, Ray Davies, John Paul Jones, Pete Townshend, and Les Reed all had family members who provided musical role models. However, for those from nonmusical working-class backgrounds, music offered a potential escape from the tedium of the factory or shop. Guitarists like Bryan Daly (b. 1932) and Joe Moretti (b. 1938) struggled and/or had parents who were willing to devote a portion of their hard-earned income to purchase an instrument.

Jim Sullivan self-assisted his guitar education with his "little Danset" record player, which he believes drove his family "absolutely mad." His interests were growing beyond country and rock when, at about age eighteen, he discovered "Segovia, John Williams, and Julian Bream" and learned a Bach gavotte by ear. However, Bach's chaconne "had such an amazing affect" on him that he took up music in earnest, learning how to "work it out from the dots." His ability to read music would prove to be a critical skill in recording sessions.

Aspiring drummers had issues simply obtaining kits. Carlo Little (1938–2005)—who played briefly with the Rolling Stones but more routinely with Screaming Lord Sutch and the Savages and with Cyril Davies' Rhythm and Blues All Stars—pulled his first kit together from "secondhand shops: maybe a snare drum here or a tom tom there. They were just a mix, a mismatch." Bobby Graham (b. Robert Neate, 1940) had his father make his first kit from "big old biscuit tins and stretching rubber over the top." And Clem Cattini's (b. 1939) interest in rock 'n' roll in general and drums in particular came after seeing the film *Blackboard Jungle*. Friends who played guitar seized upon the present as the perfect time to "form a rock 'n' roll group," and, not having a drummer, chose Cattini to keep time. His first hodgepodge kit cost him about "£25 for the whole lot," including "a bass drum that I kind of had to look over the top of. It was thirty-two inches!"

Like many others, Bobby Graham learned by playing recordings on "this old wind-up gramophone," listening in particular to big band drummer Ronnie Verrell by slowing down the 78s:

> I used to put a little piece of cotton-wool against the revolving plate and just slow it down enough to hear what he was doing. And then I would practice it and copy it, again, and again, and again. I got home from school at four o'clock in the afternoon and that was it, I just locked myself away until it was bedtime. I just practiced and listened to big-band music.

By comparison, Andy White (b. 1930) first learned drumming as a boy scout, the troop band providing him with the opportunity to play "marches at parades," which led him at fifteen to play in "a real pipe band: the Rutherglen Pipe Band was first-grade in those days." At first, he learned by rote, but he soon "started going to a drum-set teacher in Glasgow, basically to learn to read, and that was his forte actually; he taught people to read and play charts."

Singer and guitarist Joe Brown (b. 1941) formed his musical memories living over his mother's workplace, a pub in east London where a family of musicians routinely played. One of them, Charles Danse, sold Brown his first guitar. Brown also listened to the BBC, where the music had "nothing to do with rock 'n' roll, or blues, or anything like that. It was like variety music, bands, and things." He remembers listening each week for the "hit parade" and particularly the song "Davy Crockett." Not surprisingly, Brown's recording catalog includes a wide range of musical styles, from rock to covers of music hall songs and George Formby classics. His interest in more contemporary musics came from skiffle in general and Lonnie Donegan in particular: "When he brought all these Negro blues songs over, with the three-chord trick on the guitar, and started playing it, every kid in the country, one in nine of the male population, was in a skiffle group in 1957." However, almost as soon as skiffle became popular, "suddenly rock 'n' roll" hit Britain. Brown particularly remembers Little Richard: "And then skiffle literally died overnight in '57."

Margot Quantrell (b. 1942) began her musical career unexpectedly. Although her family made music informally, a musical career had not entered her mind. In 1960, she was working as a clerk for Vernons Pools in Liverpool, one of several British companies that collected bets on football matches. She remembers unexpectedly receiving an order to report to an administrator's office, where she began a process that would make her one of the most requested backup vocalists in London. Vernons Girls consisted of sixteen women whom the company used as a promotion by getting them on programs like Jack Good's *Oh Boy*. Her first "audition" consisted of a degrading visual inspection. They told her, "Turn around. Let's have a look at your legs and see what sort of shape you are, profile, and smile, see what your teeth are like." They wanted to see "how you walked, how you held yourself." A few weeks later, she sang a selection of songs for them and passed the musical part of the audition, making her one of the troupe from which they chose the sixteen Vernons Girls. The company then sent the women (and two reserves) "once a week to learn the theory of music." More specifically, the singers learned how to read music in order to rehearse quickly for broadcasts. She was eighteen.

When compared to most British musicians active in 1960s pop and rock, Matthew Fisher (b. 1946) took a different route to becoming a professional. The organist responsible for the signature theme of Procol Harum's "A Whiter Shade of Pale," he had a background that most rock and pop musicians lacked. However, Fisher warns against jumping to conclusions: "I think people get the wrong impression if you say I'm 'classically trained.' They assume that I did a certain number of years in some conservatoire and achieved all sorts of exams, and I didn't. The highest exam I took was grade four." His parents (his father had been an amateur trumpeter who loved jazz and occasionally played guitar) had required him to take piano lessons, even though he never recalls practicing. He describes himself as "always a terrible reader [and] much more interested in the theory of it all rather than learning my little pieces." Fisher found himself captivated by the "chords and harmonies" of music, rather than its memorization. He also remembers a running feud with the music teacher that culminated with him passing his exams, dropping out of school, and joining a band to play guitar, bass, and even a bit of drums. Nevertheless, his interest in music theory persisted, and he enrolled at the Guildhall School of Music to continue his studies. The year was 1965, and he was nineteen.

On another track to musicianhood, singer Dave Berry's (b. David Grundy, 1947) semiprofessional drummer father introduced him to the bands and singers of the forties and fifties through "many, many of the great American bands: Stan Kenton, Woody Herman's Herd, Lionel Hampton, people like that." In Berry's opinion, he "had a very, very good grounding," which he "didn't think was very important at the time." Hearing artists like Bill Haley, Buddy Holly, and (of course) Chuck Berry, he caught the music bug and formed a duo with a guitarist, playing drums and singing: "It was a very odd lineup: a harmony group that was guitar and drums. We were playing local bars and we didn't think anything of it." In 1964, his recording of Geoff Stephens's "The Crying Game" provided a unique and memorable musical statement of the age. He turned seventeen that year.

Compare this sampling of musicians—all of whom made important contributions to British rock and pop in the fifties and sixties—to the beginnings of one of the best-known performers of the era. John Lennon's earliest musical experiences seem to have been with an accordion (Spitz 2005: 37), but as he turned fifteen, he discovered rock 'n' roll and skiffle. His mother, Julia, not only lent him £5–10 to buy a guitar, but she also taught him his first chords and ran social interference for him with his guardian, aunt Mimi. And when he began learning and playing skiffle tunes, he continued to rely on his mother for assistance. Drummer Colin Hanton remembers when their band (the Quarrymen) was at a loss for a chord, Lennon headed "off to his mum's. Julia immediately got the banjo out and showed him everything he needed to know. If one of the riffs got too complicated, she'd sing things to emphasize what she was trying to explain" (Spitz 2005: 55).

His comrade in adolescent music making had even deeper family support for music. Paul McCartney's father had inherited a piano and some of his own father's musicality, which he passed down to his first son. Conveying as much as he knew about chords and melody, Jim McCartney instilled a deep love of music in Paul, as well as a fluent musicality that the son would bring to almost everything he did. In 1956, Paul McCartney managed to convince his father to allow him to trade his trumpet for a guitar. Both he and Lennon separately spent that summer learning to finger chords, building to the July day the next year when they would finally meet. Lennon retuned his guitar so he could play the banjo chords Julia taught him, and McCartney restrung his instrument so he could play it left-handed. What could have been impediments to their learning may have indirectly contributed to their unique musical development.

Another factor in musical life, ethnic discrimination underlay much of British social discourse. Although many ethnicities sat at the receiving end of English spite (including the Irish, Scots, and the growing population of Asian, African, and Caribbean immigrants), the significant musical contributions of the Italian British community make them particularly notable. As already mentioned, the British government incarcerated Clem Cattini's father simply because of his ethnicity. And Joe Moretti has bitter memories of taunts during the war years:

> In 1939, Britain was at war with Germany and Italy, so, when my daddy was in the British army, we were called what would they call you in those days: macaroni or spaghetti or I-tie, Wop, Spic and Wetback and stuff. There was a sort of underlying hatred, especially in the schools, about anybody with an Italian name. It was sort of a stigma.

And musicianship for young working-class youth, despite its parallels with the trade work of their fathers, represented a challenge to popular notions of masculinity and heterosexuality. Bobby Graham remembers his father's reaction when he announced that he wanted to be a musician: "When I left school and said I wanted to be a musician, he was utterly disgusted. He said to my mother, 'I had a feeling he was queer.' My father was from a hard part of the East End of London and being a musician was something you just didn't do. It was feminine." In some ways, Graham's father proved to be correct, as British musicians would come to offer numerous interpretations of gender and sexuality in the sixties, partially as a generational challenge.

FIRST GIGS

The transition from playing in one's bedroom or in a pipe band to playing pop or jazz for others marks the point at which casual music making becomes a potential source of income and, consequently, the first step on the road to becoming a professional musician. Like Allan Weighell, Arthur Greenslade found his first employment with a band when the government called up the regular pianist for service during the war, and he quickly moved through different bands until he joined the Vic Lewis Orchestra (with another future session musician, drummer Ronnie Verrell). When Jim Sullivan left school at fourteen to work for the pharmaceutical firm Parke-Davis, he "had probably been playing guitar for three to four weeks" and would entertain his fellow workers at lunchtime "playing an old folk song like, 'Pick a Bale of Cotton.'"

Armed with a repertoire of basic songs and adolescent enthusiasm, Sullivan took his abilities to Soho, where he ventured into a coffeehouse that "eventually became the Skiffle Cellar." As his repertoire grew, he formed a country group called the "Clay County Boys, complete with fiddle and everything" and played "American bases, as well as the dance nights where the trad bands used to play." Playing country music presented an advantage: "we were all equipped to bypass skiffle." Indeed, a few years later (ca. 1958), they were primed for rock 'n' roll and for Jim Tomkins to adopt a stage name: "I formed the 'Jim Sullivan Trio' and started doing country rock and all that sort of stuff, because by then, we had heard Bill Haley, Chuck Berry, and Carl Perkins."

As the fifties tumbled into the sixties, London's Soho and adjacent streets became a haven for many different kinds of music. Sullivan describes the scene as "more spread out. First, there were the folk people who stayed down [in] the Skiffle Cellar.[1] There were the jazz people who split to Ronnie's,[2] and so on like

---

[1] The Skiffle Cellar and Les Cousins both have occupied 49 Greek Street.

[2] Ronnie Scott's club moved from 39 Gerrard Street to 47 Frith Street, both in Soho, in October 1959.

that." However, the 2i's coffee bar at 59 Old Compton Street in Soho became "*the center*" for musicians to make contact with other musicians and to "be discovered" by a record company or promoter. "The hardened rockers used to go down [to] the 2i's, 'cause you could have a play down there." He remembers the premises as being "tiny" and "totally jam-packed. People used to queue up outside, 'cause you could hear it coming up from the basement, which is where we played." Sullivan had just begun accompanying singer Vince Eager, whom he had met in the 2i's, when "[t]hese two guys came up to me and said, 'Marty Wilde's heard you play. Would you . . . ?'" Wilde in turn had asked his band, the Wildcats, "What about this guy? I've heard he's good." It would be with Wilde that Sullivan would have his first experiences in the studio.

Bobby Graham's first performance experiences came through "a guitarist who was a neighbor, two doors away. He was about twenty years older than me and, when I was ten or eleven, he knocked on my parents' house door and asked, 'Could Bobby do a gig tonight for me? My drummer's let me down.'" Graham at this point had his "first real looking kit . . . a real mixture, a Heinz 57, really, but it looked OK." The gig was "a wedding and that was the very first paying gig. I think I got two shillings and sixpence." He remembers the experience of "sitting up there and playing" as "wonderful. I'd have done it for nothing." Like Sullivan, Graham's skill meant skipping skiffle such that, in 1960 when someone suggested playing rock 'n' roll at Butlin's summer camp in Yorkshire, he balked:

> I was a real jazz snob and said, "No way." He kept on and on and on. He told me it was going to be great and it was going to be wonderful and lovely girls there and still, I said, "No! I'm a jazz musician." I wouldn't lower myself. And then he said it was going to be £20 per week! And suddenly I became a rock 'n' roll musician.

Money for Graham made all the difference:

> That was the first pro gig that I ever did. I'd been around playing at jazz clubs and places like this and trying to get a career going as a musician. I had a good name in the jazz world, but there was no money and I was finding that for about five years after I left school to the start of the rock 'n' roll career, it was real hard going.

The well-known and documented event at which Lennon and McCartney met—the Garden Fete at Saint Peter's Church field on 6 July 1957— reflects how musical life in the north was not that different from what Jim Sullivan or Bobby Graham experienced in greater London. The Quarrymen played on a truck bed while a crowd of kids gathered around to watch the sixteen-year-old Lennon lead his skiffle group through their limited repertoire. McCartney had come with a mutual friend to see the spectacle and, before the evening dance, had a chance to show Lennon what he knew. About a month later, they were playing together and searching for engagements at dances and country clubs, building repertoire, honing their musical skills, and establishing a stage presence. Eventually, like Sullivan, Graham, and Cattini, they would accompany (briefly) one of Larry Parnes's singers. Although other factors contributed to their development, their base in Liverpool both sheltered and precluded them from the opportunities and challenges of London. If they were to have any chance of significant success, they would have to leave their cocoon and compete in the London market. Ultimately, they would transform the British music industry in ways that many traditional musicians would resent, even as they profited.

Matthew Fisher maintains that British pop musicians imagined themselves differently with the advent of the Beatles:

> We had all these bands, who would model themselves on Cliff [Richard] and the Drifters and they might even call themselves, "So and So and the Something Elses." But they weren't really. It wasn't really a singer and a backing group. They were actually a group. But they thought they had to present themselves as a singer and a backing group.

However, the "Beatles put an end to all that." The new model meant that musicians could do more than just play their instruments: they could also sing. "You start to get the feeling from the Beatles onward that the idea of having someone who sings who doesn't play anything is a bit redundant. [That is], he's only doing half a job."

BEING A MUSICIAN

Going Pro

The transition from amateur to professional could come suddenly (and be over almost as quickly), but most often, musicians gradually found themselves gaining enough sustaining work. A residency at a summer camp or a limited tour with the promise of regular income could be enough incentive to move one to declare professional status. The sociocultural markers of the transformation could include membership in the Musicians' Union, a move out of one's parents' home, the adoption of a stage name, and some sort of change in physical appearance, including band suits or even dying one's hair.

Andy White's move to professional status came in the early fifties. Between military conscription and parental inquiries, he felt the pressure to become something, and he chose to be a drummer. At "the first opportunity," he "turned pro in a town called Ayr in Scotland, a ballroom." The engagement only lasted "about a year and a half" before he had "the chance of a summer job down in southern England," playing in Vic Lewis's band. Clem Cattini's musical break may have come when he failed his military medical examination, allowing him in 1957 to go on tour with Terry Dene and His Dene Aces. Ironically, when the army conscripted Dene and quickly discharged him for "nervous exhaustion," it terminated his star status in what may have been a conscious attempt by some officers to discredit rock. Cattini's career, on the other hand, took to the road, as he traveled with Vince Taylor and Chas McDevitt before Larry Parnes chose him for the backup band on *The Beat Show,* which accompanied Billy Fury, Marty Wilde, Johnny Gentle, Duffy Power, Dickie Pride, and others. Although the twenty-year-old drummer found performing to be exciting, reality revealed touring as "ghastly" and "non-stop. We were the band, and the artists came on one after the other, a continuous rock 'n' roll show. The first guy came on and sang three songs. The next one to come on, three, and then the next one, and another one. It was like that for about two hours, non-stop." The tour allotted very little time for rehearsal, other than establishing keys and endings, and in the end, this draining ordeal left band members exhausted and ready to find other work.

Change came when Cattini joined Johnny Kidd. Unlike package tours, with every gig in a new town and theater, accompanying a series of sometimes indifferent singers, Kidd and the Pirates had their regular haunts, including one where they played for "nearly two years every Saturday night" to an audience of between "1500 to 2000 people." These fans "became like friends" who, "when it was your birthday, bought you presents." They also came to "see a rock 'n' roll show. Full stop. Whatever they were—mods, rockers, whatever they were—it didn't seem to apply. They went to see a rock 'n' roll show. For Johnny, it was an across-the-boards audience."

Jim Sullivan's transition from amateur to professional came when Marty Wilde's band, the Wildcats, asked him to join, giving him the instruction: "Marty said you got to get your hair dyed blond if you want to join the band." With his coiffure suitably bleached, the band embarked on a two-week tour; however, hair color did not ensure longevity for everyone, and Wilde summarily dropped two of the members, leaving Sullivan and guitarist Tony Belcher. When drummer Brian Bennett and bassist Brian "Liquorice" Locking joined, the band would become the best-known version of the Wildcats, accompanying Wilde on recordings, as well as supporting Gene Vincent and Eddie Cochran when they toured.[3]

Joe Brown, who became one of the best-known British rock musicians of the late fifties and early sixties, took a different route to rock success. Audiences at the

---

[3] Bennett and Locking would later join Hank Marvin and Bruce Welch to fill out the Shadows when Tony Meehan and Jet Harris left.

time expected bands to be able to cover everything, and Brown found himself going directly from a skiffle group to being "the lead guitar player with this big orchestra,"[4] where his charge was "to learn how to play the solos." The transition did not come easily: "All of a sudden I'm out of a skiffle group, I'm in a big orchestra, and they're sending me solos to learn by Jimmy Burton."[5] In particular, working from recordings, he had to guess at how Burton and other American guitarists achieved some of their effects, particularly bent notes. A few years later, an American would provide a solution when Eddie Cochran taught him to replace the upper strings with a lighter and more flexible gauge: "Eddie was great, because there were only a few of us guitar players around, like Jim Sullivan and Colin Green and all that. We all used to get together with Eddie. I mean he was a good, good player and he showed us all that, which we thought, 'Oh Christ, this is easy now,' and it was."

Brown's relationship with the older jazz musicians in the orchestra, however, did not improve: "When I first started, I didn't have good experiences. I was the lead guitar player, playing all the solo stuff, and they [didn't] like that. I am eighteen years old with all these hardened jazzers, and they didn't like me at all. I'm playing all the solos and jumping about enjoying me-self." In addition to the spotlight on the young blond guitarist, the band members "hated rock 'n' roll." In particular, he remembers saxophonist Benny Green making a habit of wearing sunglasses when he played with Brown, explaining that "he didn't want any of his mates recognizing him."

Brown's transformation from guitarist-in-the-band to star came when a guitarist in a Larry Parnes show took sick, and the contractor booked Brown to take his place. Jack Good, the television show's producer, "was in the audience auditioning singers for the new show, *Boy Meets Girl*," when he noticed the new guitarist. "Who's that guitar player there?" he asked. After consultation with an assistant, Parnes identified him as "Joe." But, when Good asked, "Who's Joe's manager?" Parnes quickly responded, "I am." The next day, Parnes attempted to get Brown to sign a contract and (of course) change his name;[6] but by now,

---

[4] Probably Lord Rockingham's XI, a thirteen-piece band which had the distinction of having on Hammond organ Cherry Wainer, one of the few women instrumentalists in the British rock scene at this time.

[5] American guitarist Burton accompanied Ricky Nelson, Elvis Presley, and Jerry Lee Lewis, among others.

[6] Parnes seems not to have known what to do with Brown. Breaking his pattern of names reflecting male potency (e.g., "Vince Eager") or tenderness (e.g., "Johnny Gentle"), Parnes attempted unsuccessfully to call him "Elmer Twitch."

Brown (who had observed the process from the safety of the bandstand) understood some of how the machinery worked. He stood his ground, refusing to
change his name and demanding that they find housing for his mother and take
on the payments for his car, demands that Parnes did not refuse, although he
eventually reneged. Brown evolved into one of the biggest stars of early 1960s
British rock and pop, touring almost incessantly and appearing in West End
shows: "The reason I could enjoy doing all those years of clubs is because I've always thought to myself [that] it's not enough to psych yourself up to go out and
do a gig. You've got to psych yourself up to go out and *enjoy* doing a gig. It's the
ability to do that, that keeps you going."

For less well-known musicians, touring dangled the promise of a better future, even as the situation left one at the demeaning end of the attention (or inat-
tention) of the tour's star. Bill Covington's band, the Rustics, had won a talent
show, a contract with Decca, and a management and production deal with Brian
Epstein. Unfortunately, Epstein perennially focused his management attention
on the Beatles to the exclusion of most of his other artists, and his talents as a producer were severely in want of expertise. A few years later, Covington found himself on a package tour with a well-known singer when the star pulled the drummer aside: "Who's smoking dope?" Covington's quick reply was, "I don't know."
The singer persisted, "You know who's smoking dope! You're smoking it, aren't
you?" After a pause, the singer announced, "I've got the tip-off that the police are
going to raid the tour coach tomorrow before we leave. You can tell them now,
whoever's smokin' it, get rid of it now." Covington duly informed the rest of the
show, and the bus was clean the next morning when the police arrived.

Joe Moretti's professional elevation came about through a combination of his
desperation to leave Glasgow and his self-confidence. At first, he, Alex Harvey,
and others who had been in a rock 'n' roll contest packed up and hit the road,
hoping that the publicity of the competition would start them on the road to
stardom:

> We bought an old, old Austin Princess car with a chauffeur's bed in the front
> with the window locking you off from the back: a nine-seater and you've got
> to speak through this hole to the driver. So nine of us were in there: six in the
> back, and three in the front, and we lived and ate and slept in that car.

Their strategy for transporting instruments and also having room to sleep was to
"leave the stuff in the hall overnight. We'd usually just park somewhere out in the
country and go to sleep and then in the morning we'd go back to the caretaker,
pick up the gear, and then move on again." But touring Scotland began to seem

like a dead end. He and his new bride packed "a couple of suitcases and a couple of pots and pans from my dad" and left with £11 on a bus for London.

His inspiration had come from "seeing Jet [Harris], Hank Marvin, and Cliff [Richard] on *Oh Boy*." Convinced that his musicianship equaled theirs, he determined that, if they could achieve success, he could too. The young couple "arrived in London at six or seven o'clock on a Sunday morning" and "found a bed-and-breakfast place in Victoria." Leaving her to unpack, he set off to "try and find this 2i's coffee bar and see what was happening. Off I went up to Old Compton Street with my guitar and there was the 2i's." After talking his way past the door (and owner and ex-wrestler Tom Littlewood), he went into the loud, dank room and got up on stage: "You had to either go for it or not. You gave it as hard as you could." He evoked an immediate response and left the next day with Clem Cattini on a tour of Italy with Tommy Steele's brother, Colin Hicks, after depositing a cash advance with his young, temporarily abandoned wife in London.

Around the same time in Liverpool, Margot Quantrell was about to become a Vernons Girls casualty. Having almost, but not quite, made the music director's cut to a trio version of the Liverpool chorus, she and three other former Vernons Girls formed their own singing group. Eleanor Russell had begun work with singer Emile Ford as one of four Fordettes and asked Quantrell, Vicki Haseman, and Betty Prescott to join her. In late 1960 (after getting parental approval), they went "on the road with him for a year of one-night stands." A year later and back in London, Quantrell, Haseman, and Prescott left Ford and began singing backup for Joe Brown (to whom Haseman had been engaged for almost a year) as the Breakaways (i.e., the singers who had left the Vernons Girls). But the dynamics and expectations of marriage and career played on the lives of these singers. Jean Hawker replaced Prescott when that singer married, and, with the success of Joe Brown's "Picture of You," Haseman left to become his personal secretary. At first, employment as a backup singer seemed less than steady to Quantrell and, with only one or two sessions per week, she regretfully returned to office work. However, the number of night and weekend sessions continued to grow, and soon she realized that she was "earning five times more than my office job." Moreover, producer Tony Hatch wanted to be able to use her and the other Breakaways in an increasing number of sessions. In 1963, Haseman and Hawker rejoined, and the three Breakaways began providing backing vocals for singers like Dusty Springfield and Petula Clark just as the British popular music industry exploded.

Meanwhile, Lennon and McCartney's transformation into professionals—as fleeting at first as that status might have been—came when Bruno Koschmider contracted them to play in Hamburg for what would be about four months of exhaustion and exhilaration beginning in August 1960. By all accounts, Hamburg proved a crucible for many British musicians, and Lennon, McCartney, George Harrison, Stu Sutcliffe, and Pete Best were no different. (See Clayson 1997.) Their conversion seemed to be well under way upon their return to Liverpool when they appeared at the Litherland Town Hall in January 1961, not only in their musical abilities, but also in their attitude. Their billing as "direct from Hamburg" partly indicates their new identity as traveled and experienced. Perhaps as important, their decision in December of that same year to accept Brian Epstein's offer to manage them—with all of the conditions he placed on their relationship, which primarily included gentrifying their stage behavior—would prove momentous. That they had also played with the idea of adopting professional names (e.g., Paul McCartney had adopted the name "Paul Ramon" during their brief tour with Larry Parnes's Johnny Gentle) paints them in this regard less as exceptional and more as typical of British musicians in this era.

Musical Literacy

The ability to read music served as a significant (albeit inconsistent) marker between professional and amateur musicians (if not between generations), eliciting considerable myth and malediction on the part of musicians and fans. Part of the success of British skiffle and rock during the second half of the fifties hinged on young guitarists learning music through a combination of observation, guitar-fingering charts, and the development of good musical ears. On the other side of the musical literacy fence, performers who played piano, bowed strings (violins, violas, cellos, and basses), or wind instruments (such as the saxophone or trumpet) were more likely able to read notation and, thus, to learn more music faster. In the studio or broadcast environment, producers and music directors relied on literate musicians to create successful recordings, take after take, week after week. However, to young rock- and pop-oriented musicians, music notation demonstrated a hurdle they felt they could ridicule, even as it blocked them from full studio participation. The increased prominence of musically illiterate musicians in the studio signaled a 1960s storming of the recording Bastille.

Jazz commonly emerged as the first destination for nonclassical musicians showing any artistic promise and training, and, in that context, reading was paramount. Jazz musicians also generally scoffed at rock and pop musicians and, in particular, at their inability to read music, equating illiteracy with ineptness and/or a lack of musical sophistication. Perhaps in reaction, rock and pop musicians complained that jazz artists had a limited musical feel and, in an Orwellian twist, singled out the ability to read as the limiting factor. Perhaps to counteract their musical ignorance, they focused on what they could do well, which involved memorization and improvisation, and, at the same time, claimed that reading musicians were unable to do the same. The musical reality of course was much more complicated on both sides.

The old guard, like Allan Weighell, learned to read music not through music classes, but by observation, imitation, and mentoring by fellow musicians. Drummer Ronnie Verrell (1926–2002) credits tenor saxophonist Tommy Whittle with helping him, "parrot fashion if you like," to become musically literate. Moreover, in a jazz context, the lesson would have included learning how to translate straight notation into swing, the saxophonist providing the drummer with mnemonic equivalents. Verrell found the experience transformative: "It gave me such joy when I found myself phrasing with the brass. 'God, I can read!'" The ability to read got him into one of the premier big bands of the day, Ted Heath and His Music, and eventually into the recording studio. But with the rising importance of rock 'n' roll and young musicians who played by ear, the musical scene in Britain changed. "We weren't getting so many customers as we used to get," he recalls of the late fifties. "They were now all flocking to see the Bill Haley type of stuff."

For a jazz aficionado like Verrell, rock 'n' roll provided sure evidence of the decline of civilization: "I hate[d] it. It was just rubbish to me, absolute basic rubbish. Nothing. It's just nothing. Anyone could do it." Nevertheless, his professional reputation required the ability to play almost anything, including imitating the recordings his daughter played: "When I was asked to do some sessions and to play this type of stuff, I just played as basic as I could, pretended to enjoy it, and they said, 'Hey, that's great Ronnie.'" A testament to his musical ear and abilities, his colleagues in music—the guitarists, bass players, and drummers—for the most part were unaware of how he felt. His well-honed abilities meant that artists like Joe Brown routinely requested him for their sessions and shows, believing him to be deeply in sync with their musical aesthetics: "That's what got me a good living for years and years, playing this rubbish." With the survival of his family on the line, he adopted the maxim "Don't fight it, join it, otherwise you don't eat." However, the practical solution took an aesthetic and emotional toll: "It's awful to do that. I was so busy in the rock days, working three times a day, seven days a week. I didn't get time to do anything. This went on for years and years. I went home crying one night; I was on the verge of a nervous breakdown purely out of frustration playing this rubbish."[7]

---

[7] For all of his expertise, Verrell's reputation late in life came to be tied to the Muppets character Animal, whose drumming was performed by him.

Before Joe Brown's promotion to star, his initial broadcast experiences came in house bands, where rehearsals to ensure successful weekly live broadcasts could be intense. Brown claims that the musicians in the bands had different strategies for dealing with the music: "What a lot of guys used to do, the trumpet players, if they've been on the piss the night before, they'd get in early and they'd look through the parts. If there was any little top silver Gs or anything like that they didn't think they could handle, they'd just swap it over and give it to the second trumpet."

The three guitarists on *Boy Meets Girl*—Brown, Eric Ford, and Bryan Daly—had specific roles. Brown played the classic rock solos, which he had memorized from recordings or had learned to improvise. However, sometimes, the music director would give him music: "I go in there one day, and I'm early, and I pick this piece of music up, and it is like fly shit all over it. And I thought, 'What the bloody hell is this?' I'm panicking, because they used to give me charts, chord sheets, which I could read. I see the MD and I said, 'What's this?'" After briefly looking at the music, the music director reassured Brown that he already knew how to play the music. "Jack asked me to do that for you," the MD told him. "I've got a recording of it [from] last week's show and there are a couple of solos in it that you played. Jack Good asked me if I'd write them out for you so you could listen to them on the tape and relate it with what you played." Brown gratefully acknowledges that this "helped me to learn to read." Bryan Daly remembers his role on the show, *Boy Meets Girl,* a bit differently: "That was where I met Joe Brown," who was already "sort of a personality." Daly believes that he "was brought in on that show because Joe couldn't read a note" and because "you've got to have somebody who can come in and read this week's charts. I got the gig." In other words, the relatively unassuming Daly walked the flamboyant Brown (known for his spiky blond hair) through the more difficult preparations for the show.

SESSION LIFE

In the studio, musicians constituted the raw physical and artistic labor that transformed the ideas of songwriters and music directors into a sonic reality that producers and engineers could capture and process and that corporations could sell. In this context, two groups of musicians encountered each other. One crowd held the studio as their natural environment. Indeed, they spent a significant number of their waking hours each week at EMI, Decca, Olympic, Lansdowne, IBC, and the other London recording studios. The intruders, the touring musicians, arrived at the studio ready for posterity.

With the unprecedented success of 1960s British pop music, thousands of young musicians dreamed of becoming the next big thing. In the group mentality, members expected and required collaboration on everything and shared most everything in their lives. Not only did musicians in groups contribute to arrangements, but they shaped the essential materials of the songs. They felt they owned the music and resented the incursion of others into their myth. Perhaps more important, when someone in the group began reaping more attention (e.g., the singer) or financial rewards (usually the songwriter), that balance began to teeter.

Perhaps the most cited story in this milieu of a session musician replacing a member of a group describes Ringo Starr showing up on 11 September 1962 at EMI's studios to find Andy White's kit already situated against the wall. White believes that George Martin's assistant, Ron Richards, booked him because of a scheduling conflict: "George arrived towards the end of the session. I think I was booked because I'd worked with Ron Richards quite a lot." In other words, he thinks that Martin left the choice of session drummer up to Richards, who chose someone on whom he knew he could rely. Unlike most inside the London session scene in 1962, White knew who the Beatles were: "I'd heard of them through my first wife, Lynn Cornell,[8] who came from Liverpool. It was a kind of run-of-the-mill session really, for me." Although White cannot recall saying anything to Starr, Emerick (with Massey, 2006: 51) claims the session musician complimented the Liverpudlian on the band's reputation before disappearing down the stairs to the studio. The disappointed drummer dutifully volunteered to play tambourine on "Love Me Do" and maracas on "P.S. I Love You," but has since expressed disappointment and a degree of resentment about the decision to replace him.

Into the Studio

A musician's admission into the session scene depended heavily on his or her reputation with the contractors, who combed their little address books for the names and phone numbers of guitarists, drummers, violinists, singers, and whomever else a producer might request. When Ronnie Verrell received his first call from fixer Harry Benson, the initial questioning began, "I've heard that you're a good drummer. Can you read?" Verrell's defiant response was "I wouldn't be with the Ted Heath band if I couldn't." After stressing the importance of the recording artist, Benson booked Verrell for a session at Philips. The first assignment focused on a written part for two tom-toms, which Verrell sight-read while the cigar-puffing Benson looked over his shoulder. When the music director congratulated Verrell for his accuracy and playing skills, the contractor responded, "I pick my men with care." After that, Verrell notes, "the word got round, and

---

[8] Cornell had been a Vernons Girl.

then I started getting all sorts of people phoning me to do sessions." Neverthe-less, Benson's reaction is telling: the musicians were tradesmen to be contracted and (by implication) discarded at the convenience of the contractor or the displeasure of the producer or music director. The model replicates the social structure of an upper-class home, with the master relying on his butler or major-domo to manage the staff, put them through their duties, reprimand them when they failed to meet his expectations, and take the credit when compliments ar-rived. More important, such systems held out little hope of mobility.

Musicians who were members of touring groups encountered no less pressure to conform and to perform. When Jim Sullivan arrived in the studio for the first time as part of Marty Wilde's Wildcats, he brandished "this echo unit—like Cliff Gallop and James Burton," which gave him a "kind of slap echo on the guitar." The band had rehearsed the music and was prepared for the session, but when producer Johnny Franz heard them, he told Sullivan "to take all of the echo off." Franz, who was more comfortable with Shirley Bassey and Frankie Vaughn than with rocka-billy guitar, had further thoughts on Sullivan's sound: "I had a bit of bite on the amp at a certain volume, a really good crunch and he told me to turn the amp right down so it was all totally clean." Franz probably had Bert Weedon's jazz guitar sound in mind, but for Sullivan, the resulting recording was "totally soulless, and if you listen that's how we did the whole album.[9] I nearly cried when I heard the sound back. No echo. Nothing. No imagination whatsoever." Of course, the pro-ducer had the final say on the material and the recording: "The man had never heard a rock 'n' roll guitar before. He'd never heard Burton. It just amazed me."

As contractors began calling him for other sessions, the young Sullivan en-countered a different kind of class hierarchy: his rank in the studio pecking order: "There was more prejudice against us young guys in those days. The professional musicians who had been playing for years and years had got the session business sewn up. There hadn't been any new faces in the session business for years." But while the young musicians insinuated themselves into the system, they recog-nized that their time as studio artists probably also had an expiration date. Clem Cattini remembers thinking that his playing constituted the "flavor of the month" and that the contractors would tire of him as soon as the next competent drum-mer arrived on the scene.

Nevertheless, like the others, Cattini found his days filled with session work, which allowed little time for preparation for or reflection on what he played. More-over, the industry treated the music he and others created as disposable. Repeating

[9] *Wilde about Marty* (1959).

a variation on an oft-repeated phrase, Cattini intones: "If I knew it was going to be that important forty years later, I'd have played better in the first place. When you're involved in it, you don't realize the importance of what you're doing at the time." Moreover, Cattini has come to recognize that, in the eyes of the studio, he was little more than a laborer: "All I was doing was earning a living. I was doing a musical navvy.[10] You know, we want to get some roads dug today, so we get a spade and a shovel. So that was the thing. Doing it and earning a living."

Generational and Technological Change

Joe Moretti observes that the role of the ensemble in the studio changed in the years he worked in London: "In the early days, you recorded things in a natural way, like you would do with a group. You'd go in the studio and play. If the engineer could handle it, well fine. But normally you would play sort of mezzo forte out there, trying to find an internal balance in the band." However, as the technology grew more sophisticated and engineers began playing with recording techniques, musicians had to adapt: "All that changed when the close miking came in and, then gradually, the separating screens came in, and everybody was using cans."[11] Indeed, fundamental shifts in recording technology increasingly isolated and subsequently alienated musicians. Of course, the musicians contributed to these changes, such as when drummers (the most likely to be acoustically isolated) requested headphones.

With the arrival of younger musicians and production crews in the studio, the intellectualism of the postwar jazz age gave way to the emotionality of rock. The shift in aesthetics and in standards for authenticity produced new attitudes toward music. Moretti muses:

> [M]ore of the older generation of producers would look, for want of a better word, for a sort of sedate, more moderate sound. It was only when guys like Jimmy Page came in and stuff like that that we actually started winding the amps up. The new producers [and] musicians were of a like mind. They realized that if you want to get a screaming sound on the guitar you cannot do that quietly. It took a lot of time for some people to learn something as obvious as that, but there you are.

In this context, the relationship between musicians and engineers could be in turns supportive and confrontational. Musicians thought about performances, production crews thought about recordings, and corporations thought about

---

[10] Colloquial British for an unskilled laborer.
[11] Headphones.

products. The aesthetic differences, Moretti contends, led to decisions that some musicians considered to be "absolutely stupid." Again, guitarists felt that, too often, producers required them to play at unnaturally quiet levels. Describing the work of a well-known guitarist, Moretti claims that "some of the things he did, they would be reduced to a whisper, and then they would blow it up in the box. I mean, you cannot work like that." Producers and engineers interviewed for this book, of course, deny that they demanded the damping of amps, but importantly, musicians felt that these requests had been made of them. In part, the differences represent the consequences of social rank, and musicians, occupying the bottom rung, felt the least empowered.

In Moretti's philosophy of music, the guitarist "must play as near as damn live as possible. What you would do live on a gig. Be natural. Play natural. That's the only way you can actually come across on the recording as being natural." By late in the sixties, the volume at which bands played in the studio had increased dramatically. Engineer Gus Dudgeon, commenting on Eric Clapton's debut with John Mayall on *Bluesbreakers* at a 1966 Decca recording session (e.g., "All Your Love"), asserts that "the guitar was all over everything, it was on every single microphone, it was everywhere. But it was bloody exciting and we were all going, 'Christ, I've never heard a sound like that on a record ever'" (Shapiro 1998: 92).

Fixing a Hole

In the early 1960s, as a younger generation of musicians entered the session world from touring, the apparatus that kept sessions running smoothly encountered the occasional bout of social turbulence. The contractors—self-imagined mediators between the stars of the industry and common musicians—sometimes found themselves in conflicted social positions. Even though Joe Brown had become a well-known theater and film artist, he continued to play on other people's sessions, consequently turning the fixer's neatly constructed social hierarchy on its head. Brown now chortles, "Charlie [Katz] would look at the star of the show and, whatever happened, Charlie would please him and sod the musicians. He was real hard on musicians. So when someone would ask and I was booked, and turned up, and I'm with the musicians, he didn't know how to handle it." When Katz would enter the studio, the other session musicians would go quiet, but Brown would announce the arrival, "Oh here we go; here comes Charlie," to which the other musicians would mutter, "Shut up. Shut up." But, with his position secure, Brown felt comfortable knowing that, for his show "at the Buckingham, [Katz was] booking thirty-six musicians every week" (and collecting a fee). The situation left Katz in the unenviable position of having Brown shift social rank, knowing full well that, in another context, that position would change.

Herein lay the temptation of musical stardom: one could leap from the bottom to a higher position. Brown had done it. Jimmy Page and John Paul Jones had tried and failed, but would eventually do it. Some (like Cattini) would pass back and forth across the veil, sometimes prominently in front of the camera (with the Tornados) and sometimes hidden behind the microphone. Those who could sing (like Brown) made the transition easily; Page and Jones needed to wait until pop culture broadened the notion of "rock star." However, no matter what the position, musicians needed a critical quality: creativity. Bryan Daly knew that, in the studio, "Each player was expected to give certain amounts of creative input. One thing for sure was that if one was not up to being creative, one did not last in the business very long. One was gone in a moment."

Entering the session world often meant knowing someone on the inside. Daly maintains that he "got into the record business because of Joe [Brown], because no one will book you for a session till they know what you do. No one will know what you do until they book you. So it's a Catch-22." In Daly's case, "Joe insisted that I do his recording," in which context he met producer Tony Hatch, who then informed Charlie Katz, "I want this guy to play on my sessions. I've heard him play and he's good." The situation suited Daly perfectly: "It saved me from going into the orchestra and playing outside of the session business. The only thing I wanted to be was a session player because session players worked in London. They didn't travel." Indeed, many session musicians expressed their preference for studio work over touring because it allowed them to have families, not to mention the comfort of sleeping in their own beds. Being a session musician functioned as Daly's goal: "If I'm not going to be a session player by the time I'm twenty-eight, I'm going to leave the business." Fortunately for Daly, sessions came his way.

A recurring theme among session musicians, humor seems to have preserved them against the knowledge that their careers could be over at the whim of a contractor. Percussionist Eric Allen (b. 1938), like Daly, knew that "a session musician was what I always wanted to be, and I found we were all kindred spirits." In particular, sessions presented situations where an "awful lot of laughing went on, and I mean an awful lot of laughing! The camaraderie was fantastic." Working three or four sessions a day, and seldom taking time off, he describes himself as "on a high: musicians, singers, songwriters, producers, sound engineers mostly in our mid-twenties all doing it for the first time." Residing at the core of this mirth, a new generation now occupied important positions in the studio hierarchy, contributing to the optimism and adventurousness of the milieu.

Work for those musicians who gained entry to the session scene could be plentiful. Percussionist Stan Barrett (b. 1929) went "immediately into perhaps twenty sessions a week" in the early sixties as probably the principal percussionist in Charlie Katz's little black book. The studio calendar offered the three standard primary sessions per day, with commercials recorded in the early morning and special late-night bookings. Weekends could be lighter, but contractors increasingly booked those sessions as well. However, no matter how exhausting the schedule, session musicians believed that their work mattered. Eric Allen contends, "We were creating a new music, a new feel. What we recorded on a Monday morning was in the shops worldwide Saturday and being played by radio stations around the globe."

When contractors could not get a particular individual, often musicians recommended their replacements. Andy White, for example, "used to sub for Clem [Cattini] because he used to do Herman's Hermits. He was their drummer, as it were, and I used to quite often dep [deputize] for Clem with Mickie Most, the producer." In those instances, the guitar, bass, and drums would "go in and just do rhythm tracks. It was like a session rhythm section and we'd do four tracks in about an hour, and after you'd finished, he'd bring Herman in to fit the voice-over." The session musos (as they often labeled themselves) commonly ignored union rules against vocal overdubs, recognizing that such sessions would occur whether they knew about them or not. Moreover, an independent producer like Most could avoid detection because he used small independent studios where union representatives were less likely to be present.

Joe Moretti complains that, to Katz and the other music contractors, musicians "were just really a musical convenience. I don't mean that as a putdown; but, you were just an item that he could use. Sessions were a commodity." In such a labor-oriented part of the industry, the Musicians' Union should have been looking out for the musicians, but most of those in the rhythm section felt that they were little more than an afterthought to the orchestral players. Moretti remembers that, "at times, we would get representatives coming around from the union, checking out that we were being looked after and not abused"; but they seemed to him to be primarily concerned "that everybody had paid their union fee." The catch came that "you couldn't work in the recording studios or anywhere of any note like ballrooms unless you were a member of the MU." But the contractors (who were predominantly orchestral players) seemed more interested in sessions that featured symphonic musicians, both because they preferred that music and because they made more money on larger sessions. Small sessions consisting primarily of two guitars, bass, and drums were both artistically uninteresting to contractors and relatively unprofitable. In practice, when possible, producers bypassed the fixers.

Nevertheless, musicians had to tread carefully lest they run afoul of the contractors. The last thing a session musician wanted was for a contractor to "put them on holiday," the euphemism for blacklisting. Musicians at the mercy of London's unpredictable trains recall how a delay could endanger your career. One spoke of nearly missing the beginning of a show because a worker on the Underground had died on the tracks. The contractor docked the musician's pay and informed him that he should have taken an earlier train. Several recounted the apocryphal story of a muso who failed to show for a session because he had died, and the contractor complained that the musician should have hired a replacement.

Consequently, contractors wielded considerable power and could coerce musicians for musical favors, often conditionally offering poorly paying gigs while dangling the possibility of booking them for recording sessions. Bryan Daly describes Charlie Katz this way: "He'd make you go and do broadcasts which paid very bad money, and he put you down for rehearsals for people that were associated with the recording. I hated all that." Consequently, Daly would find "a deputy [a subcontracted musician] because I had to be at a big session for a TV show. And I wouldn't have it. I thought, 'I'm not going to do this bloody rehearsal stuff. We earn our money.'" Perhaps what irked musicians like Daly most was the inordinate control that contractors held over them and the presumption of ownership. Katz apparently (like Benson above) informed a music director: "Don't worry about it. I can get those boys. They're for me."

One rhythm section member contemplatively reflects that he and his colleagues had tragically failed to understand their art as "a business" and the contractors as "businessmen." For most sessioneers, music was a vocation, an artistic calling bestowed upon them through the whimsy of genetics, serendipity, and devotion. As gifted individuals, they operated under the presumption that contractors primarily called them because of their musicianship. Contractors certainly did call on individuals whose skills meant successful performances; however, they also chose those whom they could control. Indeed, a contractor's continued success depended upon his or her ability to hire competent and responsible musicians who arrived punctually for gigs with the artistic tools to make the event a success. However, once musicians came to understand the hierarchical and manipulative nature of their relationships with contractors, they resented them deeply and bitterly.

Musicians who appeared to be currying favor with contractors could find themselves shunned by other musos. One remembers:

> [In] London, if you did as much as be nice to a contractor, never mind about taking them to lunch or sending them a Christmas card or whatever, the other guys would kill you. I mean, they would. If they thought for one moment that you were sucking up, they would just send you to Coventry, they would ostracize you. I'm deadly serious.

Musicians nicknamed one such individual "the Caterer" because he sometimes invited contractors to dinner.

Great Expectations

Being a successful session musician meant being able to walk into a studio and play whatever the producer or music director demanded. Eric Allen describes "being a session percussion player" as "all about playing music of any genre and style," such that "adaptability and a feeling for all music is the name of the game." The same held true for every rhythm section musician who entered the studio. When musicians showed up for a session, they seldom knew who they would be accompanying, who else had been booked, or what kind of music they would be playing. Joe Moretti believes he had to be prepared for anything: "The trick was to pull it out of a hat. That was really it. Most of the guys, the guitar players and stuff, you were in at the deep end in a lot of music that you had no real experience in. So, you were actually learning as you went along."

The population of London's session world underwent continual transformations, with seasoned pros lasting for a decade, and new people arriving in almost every role. Moretti observes, "Most of the MDs, the musical directors, they were as green as we were. Don't forget we were still copying a lot of American music and looking for that sound, so, you arrived at the studio in a state of high anticipation and not a little bit of anxiety because you could be into anything at all." Again, musicians seldom had any idea about what kind of music they would be encountering: "One session, you could turn up there, and you're with a nineteen-piece classical orchestra. The next session, you go along, they want country-western. The next session is bossa nova, etc. So you had no idea what they were going to hit you with, and you got through three sessions a day."

Cattini comments that the producer on a session constituted the key to how much musicians could contribute and how many limits on their playing they would encounter: "It was the producers who gave us the freedom a lot of the time to do what we wanted, especially Shel Talmy. You had a hell of a lot of freedom to do what you wanted." The musicians with whom you played defined part of that contribution. For drummers like Cattini, the "main concern was who the bass player was 'cause you were at the bottom end of the band. I used to love playing with John Paul Jones on bass and Les Hurdle and people like that because you knew that you could have a good session. You were going to enjoy it." The bass and the drums met in the groove, the tempo, and the feel of the accompaniment. "I've always been of the mind that every tune has its own tempo and, if you hit that tempo right, it works."

Unfortunately for session musicians in the sixties, they had little time to find that groove. Moreover, performers often had few templates to follow as producers, music directors, and songwriters sought to create unique musical soundscapes: "There's so many times when a songwriter would come in with a song and it would be like 300 miles an hour. And I say, 'Have you tried doing it like this?' And then slow it down and get a groove, and they go 'Oh yes.'" (Not surprisingly, Cattini was a consistent favorite of Denmark Street songwriters like John Carter, who sometimes could find musicians sitting in Julie's Cafe ready to pick up work.)

Musicians also needed to know how much to contribute during a session, evincing the adage in pop music that "less is more." Cattini remembers:

> When I started doing sessions, I tried to impress the producers and whatever. It never did. It was so wrong. But that's what you tend to do. You say to yourself, "I'm going to do a flash fill here." And I find it never works. I decided, "This is madness. I'm just going to sit here and play time. Just keep the groove."

Knowing when to put in a fill constituted an art form that drummers learned both by listening to other drummers and through experience. Bobby Graham picked up some of his approach to drum fills by listening to American Hal Blaine and to the vocalist: "My trick was to wait till the singer took a break and fill it in. It's really as simple as that. And that was the absolute truth. I used to wait for that singer to take a breath for a new phrase coming in and that would be my cue to do something."

As recording techniques changed, production crews sought to isolate musicians and indirectly challenged the sense of ensemble, the quality of playing together. If musicians only knew when to fill by listening to each other, then separation could be a detriment. Graham maintains:

> [I] was the first drummer in this country to ask for headphones and I remember on the first recording session, I said, "Can I have some headphones please?" They said, "What do you want headphones for?" I said, "because I want to hear what the singer's doing, and I want to hear what the rest of the band's doing because I can't hear. I'm in a little drum booth, completely isolated. I cannot get a feel going."

Session musicians had another distinct advantage over touring musicians in that their livelihood did not depend on their physical appearance. Image propelled the British rock and pop juggernaut, and the physical presence of touring musicians proved to be exceptionally important. The success of the Beatles depended in no little portion on their remarkable clothing and hairstyles, plus their youth. When an audience of teens went to see a group perform, they expected to see musicians who were relatively the same age as themselves. Indeed, in band profiles published in papers like the *New Musical Express,* management routinely shaved a few years off almost every musician's age.

At the end of the era, in 1968, the youngest of the session musicians—people like Jimmy Page and John Paul Jones—made the transition to stars in their own right. However, some of the session musicians were relatively longer in the tooth and their appearance could be disconcerting for those primarily concerned with looks. Vic Flick recalls how bassist Allan Weighell arrived for a session with a French producer—and was nearly dismissed because he was going bald. They were recording "in Pye Two and we did the first day without the producer there because he couldn't get across from France." The next day, "he got there early and was listening to the takes of the day before, and he was enthusiastic about it." However, when the musicians arrived for the day's recording session, the producer looked "down through the window of the box" and saw Weighell arriving "with his old amplifier, his [bass], his bald head, and his pipe." The producer asked, "Who's that?" When the music director described Weighell as the bass player, the producer exclaimed, "I can't have him. I don't want him. I want the fellow that was on yesterday's stuff," only to be told that this was indeed the same musician. And the French were not the only ones who distrusted the "follicly challenged." Flick also remembers Dusty Springfield throwing guitarist George Kish out of a session proclaiming, "I can't work with a baldheaded guitar player."

Mother's Little Helpers

Although for many musicians, entry into London's session scene constituted a life goal, the work could be incredibly taxing. Eric Allen describes their existence as:

> all about producing the goods. Fortunately, the word "stress" had not been invented at this time or else we would all have been going down with fatigue and nervous breakdowns. So all the laughing and carrying-on in the studio was a necessary release. Musicians have everything in common, we laugh and cry at the same things, but because we are in a competitive business (you are only as good as your last broadcast) we can be experts at putting on the hard-nose thing to cover up the sense of insecurity and the fact that we're more sensitive than most.

Tony Newman (b. 1943), who drummed with Sounds Incorporated (a band that both recorded instrumentals and accompanied others), acknowledges that the stress of never knowing what to expect in the studio could be debilitating: "Certain musicians get red-light fever. You put the red light on for a take and they can't make it. I mean, it can be terrifying in there. I've been through it myself. You get roasted. The charts are difficult, and there you go." No matter how well pre-pared a musician was, when confronted with a challenging score, a room of mu-sicians, and a limited time in which to finish a recording, some experienced con-siderable tension. Newman notes, if "you've got a full sixty-piece orchestra, and you're the only drummer, you can't afford to mess up."

Bobby Graham admits that his philosophy of playing for a number of years was

> generally speaking, to get as drunk as I possibly could, because I was so ner-vous. When you're twenty years old and you're thrown in with deep-end rock 'n' rollers [and] with guys I had admired all my life, I thought, "What am I doing here amongst this lot?" These were powerful jazz players and session guys, and they were pretty rough rides.

Indeed, in his first studio days, when he arrived to play, the senior musicians "wouldn't talk to me, or Jimmy Page, or Jim Sullivan. Really, they gave us a hard time because we were the young, fresh guys coming in and they didn't like it." In part, the exclusion would have been a result of Graham displacing one of their own, representing the tenuousness of their own positions. Moreover, Graham symbolized a music they abhorred. Alcohol offered Graham a coping mechanism for the pressure. Other musicians had their own addictions, including drugs and gambling. When Graham arrived for his first Alcoholics Anonymous meeting, he "was so surprised to see so many guys there. I mean, I could've put a band to-gether that night from the guys who were at the AA meeting. And I hadn't got a clue that they'd got trouble as well. I mean, these were trumpet players, and all sorts of guys from the industry."

Other session musicians simply labored on until the pressures of always being perfect and at the top of their game took their toll. Vic Flick recalls pulling his car over near Marble Arch:

> I just absolutely broke down in my car, for no reason. Exhaustion, and the continuous stress of having to do it right. It might have been a particularly stressful session or I might've had the flu coming on. I got to the next date, and of course people said, "What's the matter with you?" because my eyes were red. I said, "Oh, I just got a cold or something." It's something that wafted over me.

Flick also asserts that they worked whether they were sick or well:

> I remember sitting in the studios. I'd have an undervest on, a shirt, a pullover, a jacket, and a leather coat on over that, and be shivering. You [were] working with a temperature of 103 because you couldn't get anybody to do the job, and you were committed. You had to do it, and did it then and there. It was great, but it was a really stressful time.

IN THE COURSE OF PERFORMANCE

Not only did musicians have to be prepared to play in any style, they were also in the business of staying in touch with the most recent musical technology and stylistic trends, always looking to be ahead of the aesthetic wave, but never so far ahead as to lose their market. More important, the music that MDs distributed at sessions commonly required considerable creative contributions on the part of the performers. Although scores sometimes specified melodic lines and/or rhythmic figures, much of the music consisted simply of general directions about form and an outline of the chord structure. With minimal information, a producer could tell an ensemble to begin playing, expecting the musicians to create the music in the course of the performance. For example, pianist MDs often knew little about guitar chord voicings, the specific kind of amplification and guitar they wanted, or any of the bagfuls of special effects that guitarists were beginning to accumulate. And producers could notoriously make demands that left musicians scratching their heads. Despite these exceptional expectations, these same producers could also condescendingly dismiss a musician's work as soulless.

Vic Flick remembers driving into town for a morning session and hearing a radio interview with George Martin; the host asked the producer, "Mr. Martin, what do you think of session musicians?" Martin responded with something like, "Oh, session musicians are just robots. They've got no creative ideas. It's the artists, it's the producers, it's the musical directors that are the ones who have the ideas. These session musicians, they're far overrated." The comments startled Flick and several other musicians who also heard the broadcast. Coincidentally, a few days later, these same musicians had a booking with Martin to record a backing track for singer Cilla Black. Martin arrived with "the normal thing, like D7/// from G///, and all this other business." Martin turned to the musicians and began a quick routine of the material before recording it: "OK, well let's run through this, fellows. You know, it's a sort of Harvey thing, so one, two, three, four . . ." Flick describes their musical interpretation of this notation as "chunk, chunk, chunk, chunk," which elicited a stunned response from the producer: "What are you doing? What are you doing?" The musicians deadpanned their reply, "Well, this is what you've written, George." As the reality of the situation began to sink in, Martin, stepping back from his music, drew a breath and backpedaled: "Oh, I see. I didn't really mean what I said, you know" (Flick 2001).

Producers and music directors regularly expected session musicians to flesh out their musical ideas with minimal official recognition on the disk. In one of the most notorious examples of a producer's great expectations, the Tornados recorded Joe Meek's "Telstar" in 1962, a few weeks after the launch of the American telecommunications satellite of the same name. The demo that Meek gave to Clem Cattini and the other members of the band has only a distant resemblance to the music they recorded. Meek's approach was to sing his draft of the melody (out of tune and sometimes indistinct) over a preexisting recording. The Tornados did the rest:

> All we had was a melody on a tape, with him singing on a backing track that had nothing to do with the melody that he was singing. The actual rhythmic sound and the chord structure was done by us. We worked it out. The melody that he was singing had nothing to do with the actual chord structure that was on the backing track that he was singing to.

Despite their contribution to the composition, none of the Tornados received any recognition for a piece of music that dominated Western radios for almost a year. Cattini provides this bittersweet data point: "We were the first British group to get a number one in America."

To add insult to injury, the Tornados found themselves unable to capitalize on the success of the recording because their management saw them as a backing band for Billy Fury. American media outlets asked for a Tornados tour, but "Larry Parnes and Joe [Meek], who were managing us at the time, said 'You can't go without Billy Fury.' And [the Americans] said, 'We don't know Billy Fury. We don't want Billy Fury.' So that was the end of that. It was very bad management." Instead of America, Parnes booked the Tornados for a UK package tour as the backing band: "We were doing the rock 'n' roll shows with Billy. We were the biggest thing on the bill 'cause we were the band with the biggest hit. We had a number one record, and yet, we were only allowed to play 'Telstar.'"

The view that a band member constituted a disposable resource extended beyond management figures like Parnes. When Matthew Fisher answered an ad in *Melody Maker*, he found himself in rehearsal with Gary Brooker to form the band Procol Harum: "When I came down there for that first rehearsal, they already had a bass player and a drummer and a guitarist who presumably knew the stuff. So really, it was just a matter of them playing and me just joining in and gradually getting to know the numbers that way." In this context, he first heard a draft of the song "A Whiter Shade of Pale." In this early incarnation, the song "was more or less like the record (if you switch out the organ). I just sat in and started playing the ideas that came to me" (Barbé 1998).

As rehearsals progressed and Brooker and Fisher traded solos, they realized that the recording would be much too long for commercial release. Consequently, they eliminated Brooker's piano solos, leaving Fisher to realize the structure of the song: "With that in mind I went home and planned out a definitive solo that would be the same every time. In doing so, I decided to change the bass line and a couple of chords at one point. The rest, as they say, is history" (Barbé 1998). Or perhaps not. In 2006, Fisher brought a lawsuit against Brooker and lyricist Keith Reid to claim a portion of the royalties and, in December of that year, a judge awarded Fisher a share of the ownership of the song, backdating the payment of royalties so that the organist would realize some of the profits.

But Fisher's story is the exception. In countless instances where session musicians or music directors have made strategic changes to musical material, they have seldom received any legal recognition for their contributions. And the system continues to simplify the complexity of intellectual contribution so that only a few profit from the product of many.

IT'S NOT UNUSUAL

Between the time that transplanted rock 'n' roll took root in Britain in 1956 and the technological revolutions of 1968, the lives of many musicians underwent phenomenal changes, although some elements of British society and life persisted in this scene. The occasional but sudden elevation of a pop performer from juvenile delinquent to royal command performer can only be considered phenomenal. The most obvious case at the combustion point, the Beatles, took a relatively inexperienced gaggle of leather-clad working-class Scousers laboring in a Hamburg strip club in November 1960 to become the darlings of the British media by November 1963. They provide one of the iconic examples of how pop music could allow individuals to bypass the battles over person-to-person, family-to-family, and neighborhood-to-neighborhood social rank. Ringo Starr comments in the Beatles' *Anthology* that, even within his own family, his fame altered familial relationships; and yet, for most musicians, the celebrity candle burned relatively quickly, returning them to the realities of working life in Britain.

That crucible of fame, the recording studio, underwent some of the most remarkable changes of this era, as the technology of making a record continually evolved. In 1956, when Tommy Steele first rocked with the caveman, Decca and EMI still had engineers and producers who had learned their craft with lathes and warm wax as the primary means of capturing sound. By 1968 and the introduction of eight-track and sixteen-track consoles, the youngest engineers had only known magnetic tape as their medium. Similarly, microphones, condensers, compressors, reverberation plates, and of course mixing boards often revealed their obsolescence even before their owners had paid back the loans. The people who worked with this equipment—almost everyone described in this book—adapted to these changes, or abandoned ship.

This milieu relied on musicians to create the magic. The producer might know more about film than fanfares, the music director might arrive with under-prepared, sloppy notations, the engineers may have had a liquid lunch, and the songwriter might not know the chords, but if the musicians were on their game, the session could be successful. The ability to combine solid musicianship with inspirational spark separated the wheat from the chaff, and sustained some in the business even as it sent others packing, whether a featured artist on stage or a hidden session player. Session musicians operated in a preformed social network in that, when a drummer arrived at the studio, he expected others to take the roles of bass player, guitar soloist, guitar accompanist, and keyboard player. Contractors, music directors, and producers filtered who specifically would fill these roles, but the interactions between musicians determined the quality of the performance.

The quest on the part of producers for control drove engineers to isolate sounds for manipulation, increasingly isolating musicians. At the beginning of the decade, studio recording paralleled stage performance: everyone (including the singers) performed for the microphones at the same time. You heard what the others played and you reacted to them, phrasing to blend your sound with theirs, synchronizing your articulations with those of the musicians around you. However, as recording tracks multiplied and the technical skills of the engineers grew more sophisticated, producers asked musicians to come to the studio alone to insert music into another's recorded performance. The resulting asynchronous performance (made by performers at different times and compiled in the studio) grew to be the standard so that, by the end of the sixties, the "live" performance recording had become somewhat of a novelty. With the proliferation of independent facilities in and about London, studio time no longer represented such a challenge. Even the Beatles periodically abandoned Abbey Road.

For many musicians, the rise of the asynchronous performance and recording proved a watershed. Newcomers to the studio had more time and opportunity to perfect their playing, replacing mistakes until they and their producer were happy. Session musicians began picking up more work at odd hours, but without the camaraderie of the other sessioneers with whom they had recorded so many other disks. The lives of recording musicians grew increasingly artistically isolated and often simply less fun.

Some, like Page and Jones, reacted by setting out to become featured artists in their own right, balancing the isolation of recording with the intensely social world of the tour. Big Jim Sullivan joined Tom Jones's band, touring and performing on television as a featured part of the show. Some stayed in the studio and learned to negotiate both glitter and disco in the seventies while others decided to leave the sound stage with their dignity. *Plus ça change . . .* With the rare exception of those who found stardom, most musicians ultimately remained at the bottom of the studio social order. Unless they found ways to become producers or music directors, or to achieve success as songwriters, their value to the system lasted as long as a two minute and thirty second record. Contractors continued to pressure musicians to take gigs they did not want, very few women became session musicians, and studios seem to have been isolated from the cultural and racial diversity that flooded Britain in the sixties.

We began this chapter with Allan Weighell, and will conclude with him. In the late sixties, as British rock and pop music splintered into a sparkling shower of psychedelic blues, bubble gum, nostalgia, punk, reggae, and a myriad of other styles, a contractor booked Weighell to play a show with a cast of mid-sixties icons. Weighell had been active throughout the sixties, at one point appearing regularly in the house band for the popular television show *Ready Steady Go!* playing alongside guitarist John McLaughlin, music director Art Greenslade, and the Breakaways. But this nostalgia performance, in his mind, was at best unfulfilling. If this were to be the future, he wanted nothing of it. Packing up and moving to Southampton to be closer to the sea, he worked on boats, tended a bar, and hid his previous life as a musician from those around him. When asked if he was bored living there, he replied in typical Allan Weighell understatement, "Yes, but what a wonderful place to be bored."

7

Please Please Me

On 11 September 1962, when Andy White set up his drum kit in EMI's studio two, he had heard of the band he was about to assist, knew of their popularity in Liverpool, and had an inkling that the session might be interesting, if routine. His real musical loves lay in jazz and in the traditional rhythms of Scottish pipe bands, but he had also developed an instinctual feel for pop music, which made him a natural for this session.

Few British drummers owned American Ludwigs like White's, which he had smuggled into the United Kingdom: "I picked it up in the States when I came over with Vic [Lewis].[1] We went round New York, Manny's and all the stores, and I met a guy called Bill Mather who had a drum store. He was originally from Yorkshire." The two Brits conspired to exchange White's well-worn British Ajax kit for the Chicago-made Ludwigs by placing the new drums "in the old cases to bring them back." For some reason, the customs agent at the last minute declined to inspect the contents of the beat-up containers, and a historic set of musical instruments clandestinely entered White's very public world.

---

[1] They had toured the United States in a package with Bill Haley and His Comets.

The drums had a "diamond black-pearl" finish and a twenty-two-inch bass: "They were a great drum set actually. I don't know what happened to it, I sold it, but I wish I hadn't." Rather than the Mylar heads that Ludwig had begun marketing, the traditionalist White preferred calfskin heads. More important, this particular kit sounded great to him: "I've heard Ludwig drums since then that didn't sound anything like it. Why I don't know, because there was no finish inside the shell or anything. Oh, but it sounded great. Really nice."[2] A few months later, when Ringo Starr went to replace his decrepit Premier kit at Drum City (114 Shaftesbury Avenue), he was looking for Trixon drums (perhaps like Clem Cattini's kit), and he chose the new "oyster black pearl" Ludwigs.[3]

On this day, White would record three songs with the Beatles: "P.S. I Love You," "Love Me Do," and "Please Please Me." As Lewisohn (1988: 20) confirms, White had been a regular at EMI. His payment card shows that he had been in the studio on 26 and 30 April; 1, 2, 8, and 14 May; 3 and 19 July; and 23 August before this September date, for which he would receive the minimum fee of 5 pounds and 15 shillings. That year, he had thus far earned about £65 through sessions at EMI. On this day, his work on "Love Me Do" would arguably contribute to the recording's success, not to mention his deft work on the flip side; but he would also help the band to rehearse and reimagine another song, "Please Please Me," which would signal their arrival as cultural icons.

George Martin has suggested that he had deep reservations about the Beatles. In a *Mojo* interview (Irvin 2007: 36), he recalls having the impression that they sounded like "crap," despite their personal charisma. Adding to his reservations, they wanted to record their own material, turning down Mitch Murray's song, which Martin rightly believed would be a hit. Martin muses that the "best song I could find was Love Me Do—I didn't think it was a hit, but we put it out." The only other possibility, "Please Please Me," he thought sounded like "a horrible dirge."

The song, a combination of musical influences from Bing Crosby's "Please" (recorded in 1940 and a favorite of Lennon's mother's) to Roy Orbison ("Only the Lonely") with perhaps a touch of the Shirelles, needed more attention. The underlying rhythm of Orbison's "Only the Lonely" (with its syncopated accent on the second half of the second beat and opening descending melody) and the

---

[2] The kit would have been a late 1950s Ludwig. Note in the photo of White at the London Palladium the straight legs on the floor tom and the wrench-adjusted spurs on the side of the bass drum.

[3] Coincidentally, the owner of Drum City, Ivor Arbiter, negotiated the purchase of the kit with Brian Epstein and drafted the now-famous Beatles logo, giving it to sign painter Eddie Stokes to realize. (See Babiuk 2001: 86–89.)

architectural pitch arch of the bridge unmistakably underpin "Please Please Me." However, this rock ballad, while artfully constructed, relies on Orbison's penchant for high drama, an ability that Lennon alone of the Beatles could achieve on occasion (e.g., the chorus of "This Boy"). Martin suggested, "if you double the speed it might be tolerable, but right now it's awful" (Irvin 2007: 39).

On this third trip to EMI (and with Andy White drumming), they debuted a faster version that, although still lacking in many of the details of the final release (notably in the backing vocals) seems to have held promise.[4] Particularly striking about this version, they inserted a drum fill in the middle of the bridge instead of the vocal response featured on the final version recorded in November (although Starr, who plays on the final release, still prepares the passage with a fill). We do not know whether White learned the drumming for the 11 September version from Starr, or whether Starr copied what he did on 26 November from White. No doubt, some exchange of ideas contributed to the final recording of the song, which remained a work in progress even after they finished the recording.

"Please Please Me" encapsulates some of the interplay between individuals that characterized this era: the song drew upon previous models and performance experience, the producer heard the inherent possibilities and shaped an interpretation of the materials, and a session musician set in motion interpretive features that the touring musicians incorporated and emphasized. More metaphorically, these successful recordings emerged from an attempt to please someone—a fellow songwriter, a producer, an engineer, a music director, a contractor, a publisher, or a fellow musician—and drive home the notion of consensual rapid change in this environment.

An enduring Beatles mystery concerns George Martin's decision to sign the Beatles without an artists' test. Perhaps his self-assurance silenced those at EMI who might have questioned his resolution to contract an unknown beat group from Liverpool, let alone one that Decca had recently rejected. And perhaps Epstein's position as an important merchant of EMI wares placed pressure on the producer. In any case, Martin's sense of class superiority may have enabled the introduction of a potentially systemically disruptive element (i.e., the Beatles), even if he believed he could control them. His musical authority in the studio at first cowed even the usually aggressive John Lennon into revising his music. If we were

---

[4] This version appears on the 1995 release, *The Beatles Anthology I*. The tempo of this version comes in slightly slower than the released version, but not nearly as slowly as Martin and others (including McCartney) have described. They may have auditioned "Please Please Me" during their June 1962 appearance in the studio with Pete Best. Only an incomplete list of songs auditioned on that date exists.

to imagine Norrie Paramor or Joe Meek as the Beatles' producer, we would arrive at an entirely different and dysfunctional situation. In short, Martin was the right person for this specific task.

For Norman Smith's contributions, we can hear by comparing the different versions of "Love Me Do" that he experimented with the recording. Each of those unique soundscapes places the bass and the drums differently in their mixes, with the voices, guitars, and harmonica floating sometimes nakedly and vulnerably in the foreground. His innate musicality shaped how the musicians interacted in the studio and, consequently, how they sounded when he recorded them. Moreover, his comments to Martin may also have shaped how the producer instructed the Beatles at this critical point in their careers. Thus, Norman Smith also was the right person. That both he and Martin functioned as ipso facto music directors for these sessions (and others) underscores the importance of musical experience behind the glass.

As songwriters, Lennon and McCartney drew upon a variety of sources for their initial inspiration, discovering ways to repackage proven ideas in novel guises. Indeed, their music (and that of other British songwriters) gave voice to a phenomenon of the postwar era in Europe: the juxtaposition of old and new. Just as blocks of glass and steel rose in what had been bombed-out lots adjacent to London's Georgian homes, the Beatles, the Stones, the Kinks, and the Who harnessed the new energy of rock to pursue such established pop themes as love, deceit, power, and complaint. The later success of bands playing traditional music with guitar, bass, and drums (e.g., Fairport Convention) illustrates the power of this musical translation.

As performers of their own music, and as working-class youth from Liverpool, Lennon and McCartney willingly listened to the authoritative voice of Martin while at the same time having the self-confidence to promote their own material. Moreover, Martin proved to be a sophisticated foil to their rough edges. They too come off as the right songwriters and performers for the situation, the right combination of youthful exuberance and obedience.

Finally, musicianship played an obvious and important role in the success of the Beatles and other groups in the sixties. In the studio, the social dynamics of the four Beatles and Andy White drove the music of that event. More authors than can be enumerated here have commented on the shortcomings of Ringo Starr's drumming. Nevertheless, a kind of Occam's razor philosophy applies in much of pop music: the simplest solution produces the best results. Session musicians may have scoffed at early performances by the Beatles and the Rolling Stones, critiquing their lack of ensemble playing and their rudimentary musical skills, but these performances possessed energy. In part, the quintessentially English quality that propelled this music around the world may have been its essential simplicity. That Starr's version of "Love Me Do" served as the first British release supports its validity, just as the use of White's version on the album and international releases came appropriately as people listened more intently to the recordings.

By 1968, the proliferation of studios and studio time and the introduction of eight- and sixteen-track recordings had transformed the recording life of London. Not only had recording technology grown in complexity, but studios chose new and unexpected locations. Olympic relocated from its converted synagogue off Baker Street to Barnes to escape from noisy and parking-deprived central London, forcing musicians to drive out to its location. In a different strategy, George Martin, John Burgess, and Ron Richards located their Associated Independent Recordings studio on the top floors of a building adjacent to Oxford Circus, where almost no parking could be had even after someone had hauled instruments up several flights of stairs.

The new facilities came as a reaction to the international success of the British recording industry and the control exercised by the major corporations in the mid-sixties. With new studio complexes—each often flaunting several separate studios for recording and mixing—musicians had more time available to record. Attitudes about how much time musicians could and should spend recording shifted. Not only could someone like Paul McCartney now indulge himself and spend hours recording and rerecording passages (monopolizing EMI's prime recording facilities), hoping to get exactly the version he wanted, so could performers with considerably fewer musical skills. Producers who knew little about music, but much about how to flatter egos, flourished. The old guard did not disappear, but many certainly looked to greener pastures.

AS TIME GOES BY

Justin Fox (2007: 54) has commented that content providers "alone have never generated the huge, reliable profits that keep investors happy and pay for midtown-Manhattan skyscrapers. No, the big money in media has always been in distribution." For record companies in the sixties too, the big money came from selling records, millions of them, and from the corporate ability to put those disks in shops. If the "historical media play . . . is having privileged access to limited shelf space" (ibid.), then the control that companies like EMI and Decca had over local retailers (like Brian Epstein in Liverpool) was considerable. Some have claimed that the success of the Beatles' "Love Me Do" owed more to Epstein's ability to purchase records at wholesale prices than to any real popularity of the band. Epstein has countered by crediting the enthusiasm of Liverpool fans for the number of disks that passed through his store. Regardless, the sales got EMI's attention.

When the Beatles and other British pop groups attracted adolescent attention, record corporations sold them the dream with producers, engineers, contractors, agents, and managers helping to create and disseminate the product they culled from music directors, songwriters, and musicians. Like the "navvies" described by Cattini, corporations generally treated musicians and engineers as musical laborers. Their services had value at the point of recording and promotion, and ended there. And yet, the music retains its vibrancy in the satellite radio stations and Internet Web sites that still celebrate that era of change and optimism. This musical era fundamentally changed the way we think about popular music and artists, and that perspective remains with us globally.

The members of that community of music makers and producers have weathered the intervening years with varying degrees of success. In addition to the lawyers, stockbrokers, and accountants who ran the corporations and set the parameters, those who could claim copyrights on a part of the product have generally prospered from their creativity. Songwriters and independent producers seem to have fared the best. Those whose claims on the recordings reside in their having contributed as musicians often have little to show for their participation, except for occasional news footage and their scrapbooks. Often, they continue to perform, touring and playing as part of nostalgia shows, although the generation born in 1940 is now almost seventy. Some scattered to Australia (e.g., Arthur Greenslade) or South Africa (e.g., Joe Moretti) and most to the United States (Shel Talmy, Malcolm Addey, Vic Flick, Andy White, Tony Newman, and others). They also sometimes sought new lines of work that could provide the dependability that banks look for when issuing mortgages.

QUESTIONS

To what extent do the British pop music and recording industries in the sixties illustrate class issues? Despite the supposed emergence of a meritocracy, few musicians managed to break the glass window between performance and production, and many engineers never occupied the producer's chair. Individuals moving up in rank from musician to producer constituted a relatively small sample, even toward the end of the decade. More commonly, the professional capacity in which one arrived was where one stayed, although musicians Charles Blackwell and Les Reed became music directors and songwriters, and Norman Smith became an engineer (and eventually a producer). Engineers at EMI's

Abbey Road facilities sometimes moved upward through the arcane ranks of tape operation, disk cutting, mastering, and balancing (e.g., Geoff Emerick), but few became producers unless they escaped the corporate environment. Some remained engineers, but sought better pay and working conditions by emigrating.

With the advent and expanded availability of recording equipment, combined with the growing technical capacity of these machines, musicians—particularly those who had established their value to corporate Britain through their work as featured artists—sometimes became radically redefined versions of the artists and repertoire manager. Pete Townshend—who began by operating his own tape decks—ultimately learned to manage sessions by artists such as Thunderclap Newman. Jimmy Page, reflecting an American model, rose by dint of his musical abilities from touring musician, to session musician, and (with a brief stint as a featured artist)[5] eventually to independent producer, before bringing all of these skills to bear on Led Zeppelin's behalf.

A sure sign of arrival to an elevated class status in Britain comes in the form of royal appointments; the Beatles were some of the first pop artists to receive honors when the queen made them Members of the British Empire. The honor occasioned a number of protests from members of the establishment (particularly, decorated war veterans), perhaps indicating how politically significant the British saw this decision by the Labour government. Nevertheless, the Beatles as a group were hardly the last to receive such honors, and now we see Sir Cliff Richard, Sir George Martin, Sir Paul McCartney, and Sir Mick Jagger.

How much of a role did generational difference play in this era? In some parts of the recording and music industries, age mattered significantly, while in others, less so. The age difference between John Lennon and George Harrison may seem slight, but in the defining years of their relationship, the former functioned almost as an older brother figure, establishing their roles for decades. And George Martin, fourteen years older than Lennon, at first must have seemed like a father figure, both to be obeyed and then, eventually, to be challenged. Producers were clearly aware of age and often equated it with musical empathy, if not ability. When a producer almost removed a musician of Allan Weighell's abilities because of his apparent age (or when Dusty Springfield bridled at having a bald guitarist), age served as an important marker. On the other side of the coin, one suspects that the success of individuals like agent/managers Tito Burns and Eric Easton, or publishers Eddie Kassner and perhaps even Dick James came from

---

[5] Page released a single in early 1965, "She Just Satisfies." See the advertisement in the 20 February edition of *Melody Maker* (N.A. 1965d: 3).

their wielding adult experience over youthful exuberance. Certainly, when most of the individuals described in this book entered the industry, they saw themselves as challenging an older generation.

What role did professional status play in this context? The appellation "professional" carries considerable semiotic baggage in the context of 1960s British pop and rock. Ringo Starr, when complaining in the *Beatles Anthology* about Andy White replacing him on 11 September 1962, emphasizes the operative word when he utters the phrase "*professional* drummer." His intent seems to be to diminish the importance of that occupational status, perhaps deriding the validity of the category (and, consequently, validating his own performance). And yet, former session musicians identify with some pride the point in time when they became professionals. Membership in the Musicians' Union stood as one marker of professional status, but even in this context the idea of a "professional" musician carries with it the implicit presumption of rank. Starr would have been a member of the MU, but he never possessed the abilities to be a successful session musician in the sixties. For those wishing to climb the corporate ladder, organizations like the Freemasons served as their hierarchical opportunity.

Becoming a music director entailed financial and social promotion from the status of musician, as evidenced in the practice of billing in guineas, which symbolically represented the occupational elevation of the individual. And songwriters found themselves—in large part because of the financial rewards associated with copyrights—forming their own professional organizations, both formal and semiformal.

What role did gender, sexual orientation, and ethnicity play in this musical scene? Little hard data exist on the ethnicity of members of this community, and corporations would deny that these issues played any role in the recording world of the sixties. However, some characteristics are obvious. First, straight white males dominated the British session scene in the sixties. People of color, let alone women of color, had no obvious role except occasionally as a featured singer, and featured singers were almost by definition outsiders to this community. Individuals whom I interviewed did sometimes ethnically define themselves and others as "Italian" or "Jewish," but vaguely remembered only one individual of Asian descent whom they had met in those studio years. Even the status of "Jew" in this environment carries the modification (in the words of one individual) of "London Jew," implying that they preferred to blend in with British society. On stage, artists of color like Emile Ford or, later, the interracial group the Foundation represented rare British examples.

Backing singers like Margot Quantrell were usually the only females in the studio (again, except for featured artists and the occasional harpist or string player). No women joined the rhythm section at the studio core of British rock. And many of the most well-known artists from this milieu (e.g., Dusty Springfield) kept their sexual orientation out of their official professional lives. Sessioneers, engineers, music directors, songwriters, and producers were predominantly male, white, and heterosexual. The Joe Meeks of this environment sometimes found themselves ostracized and isolated, and stood as a warning for those who tried to enter this world. Thus, the session world of London in the sixties reflected a conservative pre-1950s Commonwealth-immigration Britain.

Not surprisingly, a confidence in technology to solve problems drove the introduction of increasingly sophisticated (and complicated) innovations, which fundamentally changed the way people played and recorded music. If anything, the genre of rock 'n' roll owes its existence to the amplification of guitars and the ability of tape to capture and transform the sounds. Individual producers, engineers, music directors, songwriters, and musicians hungrily appropriated new equipment as tools with which to gain advantage over their competitors. A better amp, mixer, tape deck, or lathe could mean the difference between being part of the future or the past. The need for investments in financial and human resources voraciously and incessantly consumed individuals and their fortunes. The fickle hand of fate tempted many with the promise of fame and wealth, and legions of optimists marched into the breech looking for success. A lucky and talented few struck gold.

Finally, the social network of corporate executives, publishers, journalists, producers, engineers, music directors, songwriters, contractors, and touring and session musicians formed a complicated web of continually evolving interactions, establishing fresh relationships and renewing old relationships to advance individual recordings through the system and onto the charts. Each recording represents a finely woven cocoon consisting of elements from the conception of the songwriter and the performance skills of the musician, through the studio's cathartic manipulation, to the promotion of the disk in print and on stage. The myriad connections among individuals and the supporting creative environment trace an active and adaptive system searching for art and fortune.

Sixties London Recording Studios

Advision, 23 Gosfield Street, London, W1

Decca Studios, 165 Broadhurst Gardens, West Hampstead, NW6

De Lane Lea Sound Centre, 129 Kingsway, Holborn, WC2 (1968; moves to 75 Dean Street, Soho W1, 1970s)

EMI, Recording Studios, 3 Abbey Road, St. John's Wood, NW8

IBC Studios, 35 Portland Place, Marylebone, W1 (opened 1940s)

Kingsway Recording Studio, 129 Kingsway, Holborn, WC2 (until 1968)

Lansdowne Recording Studios, Lansdowne House, Lansdowne Road, W11 (opened August 1958)

Olympic Sound Studios (1, closed 1966), Carton Hall, Carton Street, Marylebone, W1

Olympic Sound Studios (2, opened 1966), 117 Church Road, Barnes, SW13

Philips Recording Studios, Stanhope Place, Marble Arch, London W2

Pye Recording Studios, 40 Bryanston Street (ATV House, Great Cumberland Place), Marble Arch, W1

Regent Sound Studios (1), 4 Denmark Street, Soho W1

Regent Sound Studios (2), 164–166 Tottenham Court Road (University Street), W1

RGM Sound, 304 Holloway Road, Islington, N7

Sound Techniques Studio, Old Church Street, Chelsea, SW3 (opened 1964)

Southern Music (demo studio), 8 Denmark Street, London W1

Trident Studios, 17 St. Anne's Court, Soho, W1 (opened 1968)

Selected Discography

The following entries include essential information about recordings mentioned in this text. Studio and release dates and personnel appear when available. As the focus of this book is the British industry, I have prioritized British release information, with American dates where relevant. This information derives from a number of sources, notably including invaluable discographies (e.g., Lewisohn 1988; Hinman 2004; Elliott 2002; Campbell 2001; Neill and Kent 2002; Joynson 1995; Povey and Russell 1997; and Rice, Gambaccini, and Rice 1995). Record reviews in *New Musical Express* and *Melody Maker* have also helped to identify dates and personnel. Each of these publications (along with *Record Retailer*) provided their own chart rankings, which invariably differed. Thus, consider UK rankings as approximate. And finally, the memories of musicians have provided information on personnel.

Animals. 1964. "Baby Let Me Take You Home" (Bert Russell and Wes Farrell; EMI Music Publishing Limited). Recorded at Kingsway Recording Studios, February 1964. Released as Columbia DB 7247, March 1964 (UK #21). Eric Burdon (vocal), Alan Price (organ), Chas Chandler (bass and backing vocal), Hilton Valentine (guitar and backing vocal), and John Steel (drums). Produced by Mickie Most.

———. 1964. "House of the Rising Sun" (traditional; arranged by Bob Dylan, Dave van Ronk, Alan Price; K. Prowse Music Limited). Recorded at Kingsway Recording Studios, 18 May 1964. Released as Columbia DB 7301, June 1964. Charts 25 June 1964 (UK #1). Personnel and production as above.

———. 1965. "We Gotta Get Out of This Place" (Barry Mann and Cynthia Weil; Screen Gems/EMI Publishing Ltd.). Released as Columbia DB 7639, 8 July 1965. Charts 15 July 1965 (UK #2). Personnel and production as above.

Applejacks. 1964. "Tell Me When" (Les Reed and Geoff Stephens; Southern Music Publishers, Ltd.). Recorded at Decca, 12 January 1964. Released as Decca F 11833, February 1964. Charts 5 March 1964 (UK #7). Al Jackson (vocal), Martin Baggott (lead guitar), Phil Cash (rhythm guitar), Don Gould (organ), Megan Davies (bass guitar), and Gerry Freeman (drums). Produced by Mike Smith.

Astronauts. 1963. "Baja" (Lee Hazelwood; Atlantic Music Ltd.). U.S. release as RCA Victor 47–8194. Jim Gallagher (drums), Bob Demmon (trumpet, guitar, keyboard), Dennis Lindsey (guitar), Rich Fifield (guitar, vocal), and Stormy Patterson (bass). Produced and engineered by Al Schmitt.

Bachelors. 1963. "Charmaine" (Erno Rapee and Lew Pollack). Recorded November 1962. Released as Decca F 11559, December 1962. Charts 24 January 1963 (UK #6). Conleth Cluskey (vocal and guitar), Declan Cluskey (guitar and vocal), and John Stokes (guitar and vocal). Produced by Shel Talmy.

John Barry. 1962. "James Bond Theme" (Monty Norman; United Artists Music). Released as Columbia DB 4898. Charts 1 November 1962 (UK #1). Vic Flick (guitar) and studio musicians. Produced by Norman Newell with John Barry (music director) and Malcolm Addey (engineer).

Beach Boys. 1962. "Surfin' Safari" (Brian Wilson/Mike Love; Guild Music Company, BMI). Recorded 19 April 1962, Los Angeles. UK release as Capitol CL 15273, October 1962. U.S. release as Capitol T-1808, 4 June 1962. Brian Wilson (vocal and bass), Dennis Wilson (vocal and drums), Carl Wilson (vocal and guitar), Mike Love (vocal and percussion), and David Marks (backing vocal and guitar). Produced for Murry Wilson by Nik Venet.

George Bean. 1964. "Will You Be My Lover Tonight" (Mick Jagger and Keith Richards; Southern Music Publishers, Ltd.). Recorded at Regent Sound Studios, 7 December 1963. Released as Decca F 11808, 24 January 1964. George Bean (vocal) with unidentified studio musicians. Produced by Andrew Oldham with Bill Farley (engineer).

Beatles. 1962. "Love Me Do" (John Lennon and Paul McCartney; MPL Communications Ltd.). Recorded at EMI, 4 September 1962. Released as Parlophone R 4949, 5 October 1962. Charts 11 October 1962 (UK #17). John Lennon (vocal and harmonica), Paul McCartney (bass and vocal), George Harrison (guitar), and Ringo Starr (drums). Produced by George Martin with Norman Smith (balance engineer).

———. 1962. "P.S. I Love You" (John Lennon and Paul McCartney; MPL Communications Ltd.). Recorded at EMI, 11 September 1962. Released as Parlophone R 4949, 5 October 1962. Paul McCartney (lead vocal and bass), John Lennon (backing vocal and guitar), George Harrison (guitar), Andy White (drums), and Ringo Starr (maracas). Produced by Ron Richards with Norman Smith (balance engineer). [b/w "Love Me Do"][1]

———. 1963. "Please Please Me" (John Lennon and Paul McCartney; Dick James Music Ltd.). Recorded at EMI, 26 November 1962. Released as Parlophone R 4983, 11 January 1963. Charts 17 January 1963 (UK #1). John Lennon (lead vocal, harmonica, and guitar), Paul McCartney (backing vocal and bass), George Harrison (guitar and backing vocal), and Ringo Starr (drums). Produced by George Martin with Norman Smith (balance engineer).

———. 1963. *Please Please Me*. Released as Parlophone LP PMC 1202 (mono)/PCS 3042 (stereo), 22 March 1963. Production as above.

———. 1963. "Love Me Do" (John Lennon and Paul McCartney; MPL Communications Ltd.). Recorded at EMI, 11 September 1962. Released on *Please Please Me*, 22 March 1963. John Lennon (vocal, harmonica, and guitar), Paul McCartney (vocal and bass), George Harrison (guitar), Andy White (drums), and Ringo Starr (tambourine). Produced by Ron Richards with Norman Smith (balance engineer).

———. 1963. "Baby, It's You" (Mack David, Barney Williams, and Burt Bacharach; Ludix Music Ltd.). Recorded at EMI, 11 and 20 February 1963. Released on *Please Please Me, 22

---

[1] I have utilized a common discography abbreviation (b/w) to indicate that the recording being discussed appears on the flip side of another recording.

March 1963. John Lennon (lead vocal and guitar), Paul McCartney (backing vocal and bass guitar), George Harrison (backing vocal and guitar), George Martin (celeste), and Ringo Starr (drums). Produced by George Martin with Norman Smith (balance engineer) and Richard Langham (tape operator [11 February]) and Stuart Eltham (balance engineer) and Geoff Emerick (tape operator [20 February]).

———. 1963. "I Saw Her Standing There" (John Lennon and Paul McCartney; Northern Songs, Ltd.). Recorded at EMI, 11 February 1963. Released on *Please Please Me,* 22 March 1963. Paul McCartney (lead vocal and bass guitar), John Lennon (backing vocal and guitar), George Harrison (guitar), and Ringo Starr (drums). Production as above.

———. 1963. "Twist and Shout" (Bert Russell and Phil Medley; EMI Music Publishing Ltd.). Recorded at EMI, 11 February 1963. Released on *Please Please Me,* 22 March 1963. Re-released on *Twist and Shout,* Parlophone EP GEP 8882 (mono only) on 12 July 1963 (UK #1). John Lennon (lead vocal and guitar), Paul McCartney (backing vocal and bass guitar), George Harrison (backing vocal and guitar), and Ringo Starr (drums). Produced by George Martin with Norman Smith (balance engineer) and Richard Langham (tape operator).

———. 1963. "From Me to You" (John Lennon and Paul McCartney; Northern Songs, Ltd.). Recorded at EMI, 5 March 1963. Released as Parlophone R 5015, 11 April 1963. Charts 18 April 1963 (UK #1). John Lennon (vocal and guitar), Paul McCartney (vocal and bass guitar), George Harrison (guitar), and Ringo Starr (drums). Produced by George Martin with Norman Smith (balance engineer) and Richard Langham (tape operators).

———. 1963. "She Loves You" (John Lennon and Paul McCartney; Northern Songs, Ltd.). Recorded at EMI, 1 and 4 July 1963. Released in the United Kingdom as Parlophone R 5055, 23 August 1963 (UK #1). John Lennon (vocal and guitar), Paul McCartney (vocal and bass guitar), George Harrison (guitar), and Ringo Starr (drums). Produced by George Martin with Norman Smith (balance engineer) and Geoff Emerick (tape operator).

———. 1963. *With the Beatles.* Released as Parlophone PMC 1206/PCS 1206, 22 November 1963. Produced by George Martin with Norman Smith (balance engineer).

———. 1963. "Roll Over Beethoven" (Charles Berry; Jewel Music Publishing Company, Ltd.). Recorded at EMI, 30 July 1963. Released on *With the Beatles,* 22 November 1963. George Harrison (vocal and guitar), John Lennon (guitar), Paul McCartney (bass guitar), and Ringo Starr (drums). Produced by George Martin with Norman Smith (balance engineer).

———. 1963. "I Wanna Be Your Man" (John Lennon and Paul McCartney; Northern Songs, Ltd.). Recorded at EMI, 11, 12, and 30 September and 3 October 1963. Released on *With the Beatles,* 22 November 1963. Ringo Starr (lead vocals and drums), John Lennon (backing vocals and guitar), Paul McCartney (backing vocals and bass guitar), and George Harrison (guitar) with George Martin (organ). Produced by George Martin with Norman Smith (balance engineer), Richard Langham (tape operator 11 and 12 September) and Geoff Emerick (tape operator, 30 September).

———. 1963. "I Want to Hold Your Hand" (John Lennon and Paul McCartney; Northern Songs, Ltd.). Recorded at EMI, 17 October 1963. Released as Parlophone R 5084, 29 November 1963. Charts 5 December 1963 (UK #1). Paul McCartney (lead vocal and bass guitar), John Lennon (backing vocal and guitar), George Harrison (guitar), and Ringo Starr (drums). Produced by George Martin with Norman Smith (balance engineer) and Geoff Emerick (tape operator).

————. 1963. "This Boy" (John Lennon and Paul McCartney; Northern Songs, Ltd.). Recorded at EMI, 17 October 1963. Released as Parlophone R 5084, 29 November 1963. John Lennon (lead vocal and guitar), Paul McCartney (backing vocal and bass guitar), George Harrison (backing vocal and guitar), and Ringo Starr (drums). Production as above. [b/w "I Want to Hold Your Hand"]

————. 1964. "Can't Buy Me Love" (John Lennon and Paul McCartney; Northern Songs, Ltd.). Recorded at EMI Pathé Marconi Studios, Paris, 29 January 1964, and at EMI, London, 25 February 1964. Released as Parlophone R 5114, 20 March 1964. Charts 26 March 1964 (UK #1). Paul McCartney (lead vocal and bass guitar), John Lennon (backing vocal and guitar), George Harrison (guitar), and Ringo Starr (drums). Produced by George Martin with Norman Smith (balance engineer) and Jacques Esmenjaud (tape operator).

————. 1964. "Long Tall Sally" (Richard Penniman, Enotis Johnson, and Robert Blackwell; Peermusic, Ltd.). Recorded at EMI, 1 March 1964. Released as Parlophone EP *Long Tall Sally* GEP 8913, 19 June 1964. Paul McCartney (lead vocal and bass guitar), John Lennon (backing vocal and guitar), George Harrison (guitar), and Ringo Starr (drums) with George Martin (piano). Produced by George Martin with Norman Smith (balance engineer) and Richard Langham (tape operator).

————. 1964. *A Hard Day's Night.* Released as Parlophone LP PMC 1230/PCS 3058, 10 July 1964. Produced by George Martin with Norman Smith (balance engineer).

————. 1964. "A Hard Day's Night" (John Lennon and Paul McCartney; Northern Songs, Ltd.). Recorded at EMI, 16 April 1964. Released as Parlophone R 5160, 10 July 1964, and on *A Hard Day's Night,* 10 July 1964. Charts 10 July 1964 (UK #1). John Lennon (lead vocal and guitar), Paul McCartney (backing vocal and bass guitar), George Harrison (backing vocal and guitar), and Ringo Starr (drums) with George Martin (piano). Produced by George Martin with Norman Smith (balance engineer) and Geoff Emerick (tape operator).

————. 1964. "If I Fell" (John Lennon and Paul McCartney; Northern Songs, Ltd.). Recorded on 27 February 1964 at EMI. Released on *A Hard Day's Night,* 10 July 1964, and for limited distribution as Parlophone DP 562, 4 December 1964. John Lennon (lead vocal and guitar), Paul McCartney (backing vocal and bass guitar), George Harrison (guitar), and Ringo Starr (drums). Produced by George Martin with Norman Smith (balance engineer) and Richard Langham (tape operator).

————. 1964. "I Feel Fine" (John Lennon and Paul McCartney; Northern Songs, Ltd.). Recorded at EMI, 18 October 1964. Released as Parlophone R 5200, 27 November 1964. Charts 27 November 1964 (UK #1). John Lennon (lead vocal and guitar), Paul McCartney (backing vocal and bass guitar), George Harrison (backing vocal and guitar), and Ringo Starr (drums). Produced by George Martin with Norman Smith (balance engineer) and Geoff Emerick (tape operator).

————. 1965. *Help!* Released as Parlophone LP PMC 1255/PCS 3071, 6 August 1965. Produced by George Martin with Norman Smith (balance engineer).

————. 1965. "Help!" (John Lennon and Paul McCartney; Northern Songs, Ltd.). Recorded at EMI, 13 April 1965. Released as Parlophone R 5305, 23 July 1963, and on *Help!* 6 August 1965. Charts 29 July 1965 (UK #1). John Lennon (lead vocal and guitar), Paul McCartney (backing vocal and bass guitar), George Harrison (backing vocal and guitar), and Ringo Starr (drums). Produced by George Martin with Norman Smith (balance engineer) and Ken Scott (tape operator).

———. 1965. "Yesterday" (John Lennon and Paul McCartney; Northern Songs, Ltd.). Recorded at EMI, 14 June 1965. Released on *Help!* 6 August 1965. Paul McCartney (guitar and vocal) with Anthony Gilbert (1st violin), Sidney Sax (2nd violin), Francisco Gabarro (cello), and Kenneth Essex (viola). Produced by George Martin with Norman Smith (balance engineer) and Phil McDonald (tape operator).

———. 1965. *Rubber Soul.* Parlophone LP PMC 1267/PCS 3075, 3 December 1965. Produced by George Martin with Norman Smith (balance engineer).

———. 1965. "Nowhere Man" (John Lennon and Paul McCartney; Northern Songs, Ltd.). Recorded at EMI, 22 October 1965. Released on *Rubber Soul,* 3 December 1965. John Lennon (lead vocal and guitar), Paul McCartney (backing vocal and bass guitar), George Harrison (backing vocal and guitar), and Ringo Starr (drums). Produced by George Martin with Norman Smith (balance engineer) and Ken Scott (tape operator).

———. 1965. "Michelle" (John Lennon and Paul McCartney; Northern Songs, Ltd.). Recorded at EMI, 3 November 1965. Released on *Rubber Soul,* 3 December 1965. Paul McCartney (lead vocal and bass guitar), John Lennon (backing vocal and guitar), George Harrison (guitar), and Ringo Starr (drums). Production as above.

———. 1966. *Revolver.* Released as Parlophone LP PMC 7009/PCS 7009, 5 August 1966. Produced by George Martin with Geoff Emerick (balance engineer).

———. 1966. "Eleanor Rigby" (John Lennon and Paul McCartney; Northern Songs, Ltd.). Recorded at EMI, 28 and 29 April and 6 June 1966. Released as Parlophone R 5493 and on *Revolver,* 5 August 1966. Charts 11 August 1966 (UK #1). Paul McCartney (lead vocal) and John Lennon and George Harrison (backing vocals) with Tony Gilbert, Sid Sax, John Sharpe, and Jurgen Hess (violins), Stephen Shingles and John Underwood (violas), and Derek Simpson and Norman Jones (celli). Produced by George Martin with Geoff Emerick (balance engineer) and Phil McDonald (tape operator).

———. 1966. "Paperback Writer" (John Lennon and Paul McCartney; Northern Songs, Ltd.). Recorded and overdubbed on 14 April at EMI. Released as Parlophone R 5452, 10 June 1966. Paul McCartney (lead vocal and bass guitar), John Lennon (backing vocal and guitar), George Harrison (backing vocal and guitar), and Ringo Starr (drums). Produced by George Martin with Geoff Emerick (balance engineer) and Phil McDonald (tape operator). [b/w "Rain"]

———. 1966. "Rain" (John Lennon and Paul McCartney; Northern Songs, Ltd.). Recorded at EMI, 14 and 16 April 1966. Released as Parlophone R 5452, 10 June 1966. John Lennon (lead vocal and guitar), Paul McCartney (backing vocal and bass guitar), George Harrison (backing vocal and guitar), and Ringo Starr (drums). Production as above. [b/w "Paperback Writer"]

———. 1966. "Tomorrow Never Knows" (John Lennon and Paul McCartney; Northern Songs, Ltd.). Recorded at EMI, 6–7 April 1966. Released on *Revolver,* 5 August 1966. John Lennon (lead vocals and guitar), Paul McCartney (bass and guitar), George Harrison (guitar), and Ringo Starr (drums) with tape loops. Production as above.

———. 1967. "Strawberry Fields Forever" (John Lennon and Paul McCartney; Northern Songs, Ltd.). Recorded at EMI, November–December 1966. Released as Parlophone R 5570, 17 February 1967 (UK #1/2). John Lennon (guitar and lead vocal), Paul McCartney (Mellotron and backing vocal), George Harrison (guitar and bass), Ringo Starr (drums and percussion), with Tony Fisher, Greg Bowen, Derek Watkins, and Stanley Roderick (trumpets), and John Hall, Derek Simpson, and Norman Jones (cellos). Produced by George Martin with Geoff Emerick (balance engineer), Phil McDonald (tape operator), and Dave Harries (tape operator).

―――. 1967. *Sgt. Pepper's Lonely Hearts Club Band*. Released as Parlophone LP PMC 7027/PCS 7027, 1 June 1967. Produced by George Martin with Geoff Emerick (balance engineer) and various other assisting technical staff, including Malcolm Addey (balance engineer).

―――. 1967. "A Day in the Life" (John Lennon and Paul McCartney; Northern Songs, Ltd.). Recorded at EMI, 19, 20, and 30 January and 3, 10, 13, 22, and 23 February 1967. John Lennon (lead vocal and guitar), Paul McCartney (bass, piano, lead vocal in chorus), George Harrison (guitar), Ringo Starr (drums), with Erich Gruenberg, Granville Jones, Bill Bonro, Jurgen Hess, Hans Geiger, D. Bradley, Lionel Bentley, David McCallum, Donald Weekes, Henry Datyner, Sidney Sax, Ernest Scott (violins); John Underwood, Gwynne Edwards, Bernard Davis, John Meek (violas); Francisco Gabarro, Dennis Vigay, Alan Dalziel, Alex Nifosi (cellos); Cyril MacArther and Gordon Pearce (double basses); John Marson (harp); Roger Lord (oboe); Clifford Seville and David Sandeman (flutes); David Mason, Monty Montgomery, Harold Jackson (trumpets); Raymond Brown, Raymond Premru, T. Moore (trombones); Michael Barnes (tuba); Basil Tschaikov and Jack Brymer (clarinets); N. Fawcett and Alfred Waters (bassoons); Alan Civil and Neil Sanders (horns); and Tristan Fry (percussion). Released on *Sgt. Pepper's Lonely Hearts Club Band,* 1 June 1967. Produced by George Martin with Geoff Emerick (balance engineer) and Phil McDonald (tape operator) and Erich Gruenberg (contractor).

―――. 1967. "She's Leaving Home" (Paul McCartney and John Lennon; Northern Songs, Ltd.). Recorded at EMI, 17 and 20 March 1967. Released on *Sgt. Pepper's Lonely Hearts Club Band,* 1 June 1967. Paul McCartney (lead vocal), John Lennon and George Harrison (backing vocals), with Erich Gruenberg (lead violin), Derek Jacobs, Trevor Williams, and Jose Luis Garcia (violins); John Underwood and Stephen Shingles (violas); Dennis Pearce and Alan Dalziel (cellos); Gordon Pearce (double bass); and Sheila Bromberg (harp). Produced by George Martin with Mike Leander (arranger), Geoff Emerick (balance engineer) and Richard Lush (tape operator).

―――. 1967. "I Am the Walrus" (John Lennon and Paul McCartney; Northern Songs, Ltd.). Recorded at EMI, 5, 6, and 27 September 1967. Released as Parlophone R 5655, 24 November 1967, and on *Magical Mystery Tour,* Apple/Parlophone PCTC 255, 7 January 1968. John Lennon (guitar, piano, and lead vocal), Paul McCartney (bass), George Harrison (guitar), and Ringo Starr (drums). Studio musicians include Sidney Sax, Jack Rothstein, Ralph Elman, Andrew McGee, Jack Greene, Louis Stevens, John Jessard, and Jack Richards (violins); Lionel Ross, Eldon Fox, Bram Martin, and Terry Weil (cellos); and Neil Sanders, Tony Tunstall, and Morris Millier (horns). Also appearing are members of the Mike Sammes Singers, including Peggy Allen, Wendy Horan, Pat Whitmore, Jill Utting, June Day, Sylvia King, Irene King, G. Mallen, Fred Lucas, Mike Redway, John O'Neill, F. Dachtler, Allan Grant, D. Griffiths, J. Smith, and J. Fraser. Produced by George Martin with Geoff Emerick (balance engineer), Ken Scott (tape operator), and Sidney Sax (contractor).

―――. 1995. "Please Please Me" (John Lennon and Paul McCartney; Polygram International, Inc.). Recorded at EMI, 11 September 1962. Released on *The Beatles Anthology I* on Capitol Records as CDP 7243 8 34445 2 6 on 20 November 1995. John Lennon (lead vocal and guitar), Paul McCartney (backing vocal and bass), George Harrison (backing vocal and guitar), and Andy White (drums). Produced by George Martin with Norman Smith (balance engineer).

Ray Bennett. 1962. "Go Away Little Girl" (Gerry Goffin and Carole King; Screen Gems). Recorded at Decca, December 1961. Released as Decca F 11550, January 1962. Ray Bennett (vocal) with session musicians. Produced by Dick Rowe with Arthur Greenslade (music director).

Chuck Berry. 1955. "Thirty Days (to Come Back Home)" (Charles Berry; Jewel Music Publishing Co. Ltd.). Recorded at Chess Records, Chicago. Released as Chess 1610, September 1955 (U.S. R&B #2). Chuck Berry (vocal and guitar) with Willie Dixon (bass), Johnnie Johnson (piano), and Fred Below (drums). Produced by Leonard Chess and Willie Dixon.

———. 1956. "Roll Over Beethoven" (Charles Berry; Jewel Music Publishing Co. Ltd.). Recorded at Chess Records, Chicago. Released as Chess 1626, 14 May 1956. Personnel and production as above.

———. 1959. "Back in the U.S.A." (Chuck Berry; Jewel Music Ltd.). Recorded at Chess Records, Chicago. Released as Chess 1729, 1959. Personnel and production as above.

———. 1961. "I'm Talking about You" (Chuck Berry; Jewel Music Ltd.). Recorded at Chess Records, Chicago. Released as Chess 1779, February 1961. Chuck Berry (vocal, guitar), Jimmy Rogers (guitar), Johnnie Johnson (piano), G. Smith (bass), Fred Below (drums), Jerome Green (maracas). Produced by Leonard Chess.

———. 1961. "Come On" (Chuck Berry; Jewel Music Ltd.). Recorded at Chess Records, Chicago. Released as Chess 1799, October 1961. Personnel and production as above.

Dave Berry. 1964. "The Crying Game" (Geoff Stephens; Southern Music Publishers, Ltd.). Recorded at Decca. Released as Decca F 11937, 10 July 1964. Charts 6 August 1964 (UK #5). Dave Berry (vocal), Jim Sullivan (electric guitar), Vic Flick (acoustic guitar), Reg Guest (piano), Allan Weighell (bass), with drums, percussion, and backing vocals. Produced by Mike Smith with Reg Guest (music director).

Big Three. 1963. "By the Way" (Mitch Murray; Dick James Music Ltd.). Released as Decca F 11689, June 1963. Charts 11 July 1963 (UK #22). Johnny Gustafson (vocal and bass), Johnny Hutchinson (vocal and drums), and Brian Griffiths (vocal and guitar).

Cilla Black. 1964. "Anyone Who Had a Heart" (Burt Bacharach and Hal David; Carlin Music Corp.). Recorded at EMI, 15 January 1964. Released as Parlophone R 5101, 31 January 1964. Charts 6 February 1964 (UK #1). Cilla Black with studio musicians, including Eric Allen (percussion). Produced by George Martin with John Pearson (arranger).

Joe Brown and His Bruvvers. 1962. "Picture of You" (John Beveridge and Peter Oakman; Peermusic UK Ltd.). Recorded at Pye Records in 1962. Released as Piccadilly 7N 35047. Charts 17 May 1962 (UK #2). Joe Brown (guitar and lead vocal), Pete Oakman (bass), Tony Oakman (guitar), John Beveridge (guitar), and Bobby Graham (drums), with Vicki Haseman, Margot Quantrell, and Jean Hawker (backing vocals). Produced by Ray Horricks with Les Reed (music director).

———. 1962 . "It Only Took a Minute" (Mort Garson and Hal David; Universal, MCA Music Ltd., Shapiro, Bernstein, & Co. Ltd.). Recorded at Pye Records in 1962. Released as Piccadilly 7N 35082, October 1962. Charts 15 November 1962 (UK #6). Personnel and production as above.

———. 1963. "That's What Love Will Do" (Trevor Peacock; Jack Good Music Publishing Company, Ltd.). Recorded at Pye Records in 1962. Released as Piccadilly 7N 35106, January 1963. Charts 7 February 1963 (UK #3). Personnel and production as above.

Heinz Burt. *See* Heinz.

Eddie Calvert. 1953. "Oh Mein Papa" (Paul Burkhard, John Turner, and Geoffrey Parsons; Peter Maurice Music Ltd.). Recorded at EMI. Released as Columbia DB 3337. Charts 18 December 1953 (UK #1). Eddie Calvert (trumpet) and His Orchestra. Produced by Norrie Paramor.

———. 1955. "Cherry Pink and Apple Blossom White" (Louiguy [Louis Guglielmi] and Mack David; Chappell Music Ltd.). Recorded at EMI. Released as Columbia DB 3581. Charts 8 April 1955 (UK #1). Eddie Calvert (trumpet) and His Orchestra. Produced by Norrie Paramor.

———. 1955. "Stranger in Paradise" (Robert Wright and George Forrest; Warner Chappell Music Ltd.). Recorded at EMI. Released as Columbia DB 3594. Charts 13 May 1955 (UK #14). Eddie Calvert (trumpet) and His Orchestra. Produced by Norrie Paramor.

———. 1955. "John and Julie" (Philip Green; Photoplay Music Ltd.). Recorded at EMI. Released as Columbia DB 3624. Charts 29 July 1955 (UK #6). Eddie Calvert (trumpet) and His Orchestra. Produced by Norrie Paramor with Philip Green (music director).

———. 1956. "Zambesi" (Anton Dewall and Nico Carstens; Shapiro, Bernstein, & Co. Ltd.). Recorded at EMI. Released as Columbia DB 3747. Charts 9 March 1956 (UK #13). Eddie Calvert (trumpet) and His Orchestra. Produced by Norrie Paramor.

Chariots. 1962. "Problem Girl" (Geoff Stephens). Released as Piccadilly 35061–3, August 1962. Personnel unknown. Produced by Mike Leander.

Dave Clark Five. 1963. "Do You Love Me" (Berry Gordy; Jobete Music Co., Inc.; ASCAP). Recorded at Lansdowne Studios. Released as Columbia DB 7112, September 1963. Charts 3 October 1963 (UK #30). Mike Smith (organ and vocal), Lenny Davidson (guitar and vocal), Dave Clark (drums and vocal), Rick Huxley (bass guitar and vocal), and Denis Payton (tenor saxophone). Session musicians possibly included Bobby Graham (drums), Vic Flick (guitar), and Eric Ford (bass). Produced by Dave Clark with Adrian Kerridge (balance engineer).

———. 1963. "Glad All Over" (Dave Clark and Mike Smith; Spurs Music Publishing Ltd., Ivy Music Limited). Recorded at Lansdowne Studios. Released as Columbia DB 7154. Charts on 21 November 1963 (UK #1). Personnel and production as above.

———. 1964. "Bits and Pieces" (Dave Clark and Mike Smith; Spurs Music Publishing Ltd., Ivy Music Limited). Recorded at Lansdowne Studios. Released as Columbia DB 7210, 14 February 1964. Charts on 20 February 1964 (UK #2). Personnel and production as above with Les Reed (music director).

———. 1967. "You Got What It Takes" (Berry Gordy, Roquel Davis, and Gwen Gordy Fuqua; Leeds Music Ltd.). Recorded at Lansdowne Studios. Released as Columbia DB 8152. Charts 16 March 1967 (UK #28). Personnel as above with session wind players (Stan Roderick, Bert Ezzard, and Eddie Blair). Production as above.

———. 1967. "Everybody Knows" (Les Reed and Barry Mason; Donna Music Ltd.). Recorded at Lansdowne Studios. Released as Columbia DB 8286, 28 October 1967. Charts 1 November 1967 (UK #2). Mike Smith (vocal) with members of the Dave Clark Five and session musicians. Production as above.

———. 1968. "Red Balloon" (Raymond Froggatt; Chappell Morris Ltd.). Recorded at Lansdowne Studios. Released as Columbia DB 8465, 6 September 1968. Charts 18 September 1968 (UK #7). In addition to session wind players (Stan Roderick, Bert Ezzard, and Eddie Blair), personnel and production as above.

Eddie Cochran. 1958. "Summertime Blues" (Eddie Cochran and Jerry Capehart; Cinephonic Music Co., Ltd.). Recorded at Liberty Records, Hollywood, May 1958. U.S. release as Liberty F-55144, 11 June 1958. UK release as London HLU 8702. Charts 7 November 1958 (UK #18). Eddie Cochran (vocal and guitar) with, probably, Connie Smith (bass), Gene Ridgio (drums), and others. Produced by Jerry Capehart and Si Waronker.

Contours. 1962. "Do You Love Me" (Berry Gordy; Jobete Music Co., Inc.). Recorded at Motown, Detroit, Michigan. Released as Gordy 7005A, 29 June 1962. Billy Gordon (lead vocal); Billy Hoggs, Joe Billingslea, Sylvester Potts, and Hubert Johnson (backing vocals); with Hughey Davis (guitar) and the Funk Brothers. Produced by Berry Gordy.

Countrymen. 1962. "I Know Where I'm Going" (N.A.). Recorded at Pye Records. Released as Piccadilly 7N 35029, April 1962. Charts 3 May 1962 (UK #45). Produced by Ray Horricks with Les Reed (music director).

Creation. 1966. "Making Time" (Kenny Pickett and Eddie Phillips; EMI United Partnership Ltd.). Released as Planet Records PLF 116 June 1966. Charts 7 July 1966 (UK #49). Kenny Pickett (vocal), Jack Jones (drums), Bob Garner (bass and vocal), and Eddie Phillips (guitar) (possibly with Jimmy Page, second guitar). Produced by Shel Talmy.

Tony Crombie and the/His Rockets. 1956. "Teach You to Rock" (Freddie Bell and Peppino Lattanzi; Edward Kassner Music Co. Ltd.). Released as Columbia DB 3822, September 1956. Charts 19 October 1956 (UK #25). Tony Crombie (drums) with, probably, Jimmy Deuchar (trumpet), Ken Wray (trombone), Derek Humble (alto sax), Stan Tracey (piano), Lennie Bush (bass), and Wee Willie Harris (vocal). Produced by Norrie Paramor.

Bing Crosby. 1941. "Please" (Leo Robin and Ralph Rainger). Recorded on 27 July 1940. Released on Decca, January 1941. Bing Crosby with John Scott Trotter's Orchestra. Arranged by Scott Trotter.

Crows. 1953. "Gee" (William Davis, Daniel Norton, and Morris Levy). Recorded at Bell Sound, New York, April 1953. U.S. release as Rama Records RR-5, May 1953. Charts 6 March 1954 (U.S. #14). Daniel Norton (lead vocal), William Davis (baritone), Harold Major (tenor), Jerry Wittick (tenor), Gerald Hamilton (bass), Mark Johnson (guitar), and Lloyd "Tiny" Grimes (guitar) along with unidentified studio musicians. Produced by George Goldner with Allen Weintraub (engineer).

Spencer Davis Group. 1965. "Keep on Runnin'" (Jackie Edwards; Island Music Inc.). Recorded at Lansdowne Studios. Released as Fontana TF 632, November 1965. Charts 2 December 1965 (UK #1). Steve Winwood (lead vocal and guitar), Spencer Davis (guitar and backing vocal), Muff Winwood (bass and backing vocal), and Peter York (drums). Produced by Chris Blackwell with Adrian Kerridge (balance engineer).

———. 1966. "Gimme Some Lovin'" (Steve Winwood; F. S. Music Ltd.). Recorded at Lansdowne Studios. Released as Fontana TF 762, 28 October 1966. Charts 2 November 1966 (UK #2). Steve Winwood (lead vocal and organ), Spencer Davis (rhythm guitar and backing vocal), Muff Winwood (bass and backing vocal), and Peter York (drums and percussion). Production as above.

Dominos. 1951. "Sixty-Minute Man" (William Ward and Rose Marks; Delmonico Music). Recorded at National Studios, New York, 30 December 1950. U.S. release as Federal 108, May 1951 (U.S. R&B #1). Bill Brown (bass), Billy Ward, Clyde McPhatter, Joe Lamont, and Charlie White with unidentified studio musicians. Billy Ward (music director).

Lonnie Donegan Skiffle Group. 1956. "Rock Island Line" (Huddie Ledbetter; Tro Essex Music Ltd.). Recorded at Decca, 13 July 1954. Released as Decca F 10647, 6 January 1956.

Original release on Chris Barber's Jazz Band, *New Orleans Joy* (10" Decca LF 1198), 1954. Lonnie Donegan (vocal and guitar), Micky Ashman (bass), and Beryl Bryden (washboard). Produced by Hugh Mendl with Arthur Lilley (engineer).

———. 1957. "Cumberland Gap" (traditional). Recorded 24 February 1957. Released as Pye Nixa N 15087. Charts 5 April 1957 (UK #1). Lonnie Donegan (vocal and guitar), Micky Ashman (bass), Denny Wright (guitar), and Nick Nichols (drums). Produced by Denis Preston with Joe Meek (balance engineer).

Donovan. 1965. "Catch the Wind" (D. Leitch; Donovan Music Ltd.). Recorded at Southern Music (also known as "Peer Music"). Released as Pye 7N 15801, March 1965. Charts 25 March 1965 (UK #4). Donovan (guitar and vocal), with Brian Locking (bass) and unidentified musicians. Produced by Terry Kennedy, Peter Eden, and Geoff Stephens.

———. 1966. "Sunshine Superman" (Donovan Leitch; Donovan Music Ltd.). Recorded at EMI, January 1966. Released as Pye 7N 17241, 8 December 1966. Charts 19 December 1966 (UK #2). U.S. release, July 1966. Donovan (guitar and vocal), with Jimmy Page and Eric Ford (guitars), Spike Heatley (bass), Danny Thompson (bass), Bobby Orr (drums), Tony Carr (percussion), John Cameron (harpsichord). Produced by Mickie Most with John Cameron (music director).[2]

———. 1967. "Mellow Yellow" (Donovan Leitch; Donovan Music Ltd.). Recorded at EMI, 1966. U.S. release on Epic, November 1966. UK release as Pye 7N 17267, 4 February 1967. Charts 9 February 1967 (UK #8). Donovan Leitch (vocal and guitar) with session musicians. Produced by Mickie Most with John Paul Jones (music director).

———. 1968. "Hurdy Gurdy Man" (Donovan Leitch; Donovan Music Ltd.). Released as Pye 7N 17537, 24 May 1968. Charts 29 May 1968 (UK #4). Donovan (vocal, acoustic guitar, and tambura) with Alan Parker (guitar), Clem Cattini (drums), and John Paul Jones (bass).[3] Produced by Mickie Most with John Paul Jones (music director) and Eddie Kramer (balance engineer).

Bob Dylan. 1962. *Bob Dylan*. Released as Columbia LP PC 8579 (stereo)/CL 1779 (mono), 19 March 1962. Produced by John Hammond.

———. 1962. "Baby Let Me Follow You Down" (traditional; arranged by Gary Davis, Fulton Allen, Geno Foreman, Dave van Ronk, Eric von Schmidt, and Bob Dylan). Recorded at Columbia Studios, New York, 20 November 1961. Released on *Bob Dylan*, 19 March 1962. Bob Dylan (guitar, harmonica, vocal). Produced by John Hammond.

---

[2] Donovan cites the personnel differently in different sources. In his autobiography (Leitch 2005: 123), he names Cameron as the music director and Thompson and Heatley as the bass players (as noted here). In Oldham (2003: 234), he names John Paul Jones as playing on the session. Jones, in Yorke (1990: 15), claims that Most hired him as the bassist for the session but that he became the arranger.

[3] Donovan claims that John Bonham was also on the session, but, in May 1968, the future Led Zeppelin drummer had not yet moved to London. Perhaps more important, he was not a session musician and would not have known Jones or many other session musicians. However, Donovan names Allan Holdsworth (guitar), Jimmy Page (guitar), Clem Cattini (drums), John Bonham (drums), and John Paul Jones (bass) (Leitch 2005: 217). The singer is clearly mistaken about Bonham, and Jones (Kryk 2002) is quite adamant about Page not being on this recording.

———. 1962. "House of the Rising Sun" (traditional; arranged by Bob Dylan, Dave van Ronk). Recorded at Columbia Studios, New York, 20 November 1961. Released on *Bob Dylan*, 19 March 1962. Personnel and production as above.

———. 1963. *Freewheelin' Bob Dylan*. Released as Columbia CL 1986, 27 May 1963. UK release as CBS BPOG 62193, November 1963. Produced by John Hammond.

———. 1964. "All I Really Want to Do" (Bob Dylan; Warner Brothers). Recorded at Columbia Studios, New York, 9 June 1964. U.S. release on *Another Side of Bob Dylan*, Columbia CL 2193, 8 August 1964. UK release as CBS BPG 62429, November 1964. Bob Dylan (guitar, harmonica, and vocal). Produced by Tom Wilson with Roy Hallee and Fred Catero (engineers).

———. 1966. "Rainy Day Women #12 & 35" (Bob Dylan; Warner Brothers). Recorded at Columbia Recording Studios, Nashville, Tennessee, 10 March 1966. UK release as CBS 202307, May 1966. U.S. release on *Blonde on Blonde*, Columbia LP C2L 41, 16 May 1966. Bob Dylan (guitar and vocal) with session musicians, including Wayne Moss, Charlie McCoy, Kenneth Buttrey, Hargus Robbins, Jerry Kennedy, Joe South, Al Kooper, Bill Aikins, Henry Strzelecki, and Jaime Robertson. Produced by Bob Johnston.

Easybeats. 1966. "Friday on My Mind" (George Young and Harry Vanda). Recorded at IBC Studios. UK release as United Artists UP 1157, 14 October 1966. Charts 27 October 1966 (UK #6). Steve Wright (vocal), George Young (guitar), Harry Vanda (guitar), Dick Diamonde (bass), and Gordon Fleet (drums). Produced by Shel Talmy.

Adam Faith. 1959. "What Do You Want?" (Johnny Worth; Belwin Mills Music Ltd.). Recorded at EMI, 25 September 1959. Released as Parlophone R 4591. Charts 20 November 1959 (UK #1). Adam Faith (vocal) with studio musicians, including Vic Flick (guitar) and Les Reed (piano). Produced by John Burgess with John Barry (music director), Les Reed (arranger), and Malcolm Addey (balance engineer).

———. 1963. "Forget Him" (Mark Anthony [Tony Hatch]; Leeds Music). Released on *For You*, Parlophone LP PMC 1213, and *For You—Adam*, Parlophone EP GEP 8904, 1963. Adam Faith (vocal) with unidentified session musicians. Produced by John Burgess with Malcolm Addey (balance engineer).

Marianne Faithful. 1964. "As Tears Go By" (Mick Jagger, Keith Richards, and Andrew Oldham; Westminster Music). Recorded at Olympic Sound Studios, 28 May 1964. Released as Decca F 11923, 26 June 1964. Charts 13 August 1964 (UK #9). Marianne Faithful (vocal) with Jim Sullivan[4] (guitar) and unidentified musicians (violins and cellos). Produced by Andrew Oldham with Mike Leander (music director) and Roger Savage (balance engineer).

———. 1965. "This Little Bird" (John Loudermilk; Acuff Rose/Opryland Music Ltd.). Recorded at Olympic Sound Studios, 9 April 1965. Released as Decca F 12162, 30 April 1965. Charts 6 May 1965 (UK #6). Marianne Faithful (vocal) with session musicians. Produced by Tony Calder with Mike Leander (music director).

Georgie Fame. 1967. "The Ballad of Bonnie and Clyde" (Mitch Murray and Peter Callander; Intune Ltd.). Released as CBS 3124, 4 December 1964. Charts 13 December 1967 (UK #1). Georgie Fame (vocal) with unidentified session musicians. Produced by Mike Smith.

[4] Marianne Faithful (with Dalton, 2000: 34) recalls that Jimmy Page played on the session; however, given that Sullivan had played on Jagger and Richards's demo for Oldham, the likelihood is that they would have used Sullivan on Faithful's recording.

Georgie Fame and His Blue Flames. 1964. "Yeh, Yeh" (Roger Grant, Pat Patrick, and John Hendricks; Roar Music). Recorded at EMI, November 1964. Released as Columbia DB 7428, December 1964. Charts 17 December 1964 (UK #1). Georgie Fame (vocal and organ), Bill Eyden (drums), Tex Makins (bass), Speedy Acquaye (congas), Peter Coe (tenor saxophone), Colin Green (guitar). Produced by Tony Palmer.

Chris Farlowe. 1966. "Out of Time" (Mick Jagger and Keith Richards; ABKCO Music, Inc.). Recorded at Pye Studios, 27–30 April and 6 May 1966. Released as Immediate IM 035, 17 June 1966. Charts 23 June 1966 (UK #1). Chris Farlowe (vocal) accompanied by Jimmy Page (guitar), Joe Moretti (guitar), Eric Ford (bass), Reg Guest (piano), and Andy White (drums), with a string section led by Sidney Sax and unidentified backing vocal. Produced by Andrew Oldham with Arthur Greenslade (music director) and Alan Florence (balance engineer).

Flowerpot Men. 1967. "Let's Go to San Francisco" (John Carter and Ken Lewis; Carter Publishing Co. Ltd.). Recorded at Seven Seas (Denmark Street). Released as Deram DM 142. Charts 23 August 1967 (UK #4). John Carter (vocal), Ken Lewis (vocal), Perry Ford (vocal), Clem Cattini (drums), Mickey Keene (guitar), Ken Lewis (Mellotron), and Dave Winter (bass). Produced by John Carter and Ken Lewis.

Wayne Fontana. 1966. "Pamela Pamela" (Graham Gouldman; Hournew Music, Ltd.). Released as Fontana TF 770, 18 November 1966. Charts 8 December 1966 (UK #11). Wayne Fontana (vocal) with studio musicians.

Wayne Fontana and the Mindbenders. 1965. "The Game of Love" (Clint Ballard, Jr.; Skidmore Music Ltd.). Released as Fontana TF 535, 29 January 1965. Charts 4 February 1965 (UK #2). Wayne Fontana (lead vocal), Bob Lang (bass and backing vocal), Eric Stewart (guitar and backing vocal), and Ric Rothwell (drums), with session singers (probably the Breakaways) and musicians. Produced by Jack Baverstock with Les Reed (music director).

Emile Ford and the Checkmates. 1959. "What Do You Want to Make Those Eyes at Me For" (James Monaco, Howard Johnson, and Joseph McCarthy; Francis, Day, and Hunter Ltd.). Recorded at Lansdowne Recording Studios, October 1959. Released as Pye 7N 15225, October 1959. Charts, 30 October 1959 (UK #1). Emile Ford (vocal and guitar) with George Sweetman (saxophone), Dave Sweetman (bass), Ken Street, Pete Carter, Les Hart, Alan Hawkshaw, and John Cuffley. Produced by Emile Ford and Joe Meek.

George Formby. 1936. "When I'm Cleaning Windows" (George Formby, Glifford, and Cliffe). Recorded 27 September 1936. Released as Regal Zonophone MR 2199. Featured in the film *Keep Your Seats Please*. George Formby (vocal and ukulele) with orchestra.

———. 1950. "When I'm Cleaning Windows" (Formby, Glifford, and Cliffe). Recorded at Decca, 21 January 1950. Released as Decca F 9444, June 1950. George Formby (vocal and ukulele) accompanied by Harry Bidgood and His Orchestra.

Fortunes. 1965. "You've Got Your Troubles" (Roger Cook and Roger Greenaway). Released as Decca F 12173. Charts 8 July 1965 (UK #2). Glen Dale (guitar), Rod Allen (bass), Barry Pritchard (guitar), David Carr (keyboards), and Andy Brown (drums) with studio musicians. Produced by Noel Walker with Les Reed (music director).

———. 1965. "Here It Comes Again" (Les Reed and Barry Mason; Donna Music Ltd.). Released as Decca F 12243. Charts 7 October 1965 (UK #2). Personnel and production as above.

Freddie and the Dreamers. 1963. "If You Gotta Make a Fool of Somebody" (Rudy Clark; B. Feldman and Company, Ltd., EMI). Recorded at EMI, 21 March 1963. Released as Columbia DB 7032, 26 April 1963. Charts 9 May 1963 (UK #3). Freddie Garrity (vocal) with unidentified studio musicians. Produced by John Burgess with Norman Smith (balance engineer).

———. 1963. "I'm Telling You Now" (Mitch Murray; B. Feldman & Co. Ltd.). Recorded at EMI, 8 July 1963. Released as Columbia DB 7086, 7 October 1963. Charts 7 November 1963 (UK #2). Personnel and production as above.

———. 1963. "You Were Made for Me" (Mitch Murray; B. Feldman & Co. Ltd.). Recorded 26 September 1963 at EMI. Released as Columbia DB 7147, 1 November 1963. Charts 7 November 1963 (UK #3). Personnel and production as above.

Serge Gainsbourg and Jane Birkin. 1969. "Je t'aime . . . moi non plus" (Serge Gainsbourg). Released as Major Minor MM 645 (UK #1). Serge Gainsbourg and Jane Birkin with studio musicians. Produced by Jack Baverstock with Arthur Greenslade (music director).

Gerry and the Pacemakers. 1963. "How Do You Do It?" (Mitch Murray; Dick James Music Limited). Recorded at EMI, January 1963. Released as Columbia DB 4987. Charts 14 March 1963 (UK #1). Gerry Marsden (lead vocal, guitar), Les Maguire (bass guitar, vocal), Les Chadwick (piano), and Freddie Marsden (drums). Unidentified second guitar (perhaps dubbed when adding vocal track). Produced by George Martin and Ron Richards with Peter Bown (balance engineer).

———. 1963. "I Like It" (Mitch Murray; Dick James Music Limited). Recorded at EMI, 24 April 1963. Released as Columbia DB 7041, 24 May 1963. Charts 30 May 1963 (UK #1). Personnel and production as above.

———. 1964. "Don't Let the Sun Catch You Crying" (Gerry Marsden; Dick James Music Limited). Recorded at EMI, 9 December 1963. Released as Columbia DB 7268, 10 April 1964. Personnel and production as above with orchestral musicians.

Bill Haley and His Comets. 1954. "(We're Gonna) Rock around the Clock" (Jimmy De Knight, Max Freedman; Myers Music). Recorded at the Pythian Temple, New York City, 12 April 1954. U.S. release as Decca 9–29124, May 1954 (U.S. #7). UK release as Brunswick 05317, January 1955 (UK #1). Bill Haley (vocal and guitar), Danny Cedrone (lead guitar), Joey D'Amborsia (tenor sax), John Grande (piano), Billy Williamson (steel guitar), Francis Beecher (guitar), Al Reed (bass), and Billy Guesak (drums). Produced by Milton Gabler.

Jet Harris and Tony Meehan. 1963. "Diamonds" (Jerry Lordan; Francis, Day, and Hunter, Ltd.). Released as Decca F 11563, 4 January 1963. Charts 10 January 1963 (UK #1). Jet Harris (guitar), Joe Moretti (guitar), John Baldwin (bass), Tony Meehan (drums). Produced by Tony Meehan.

Wilbert Harrison. 1959. "Kansas City" (Jerry Lieber and Mike Stoller; Lieber & Stoller Music Publishing). U.S. release as Fury Records 1023. UK release as Top Rank JAR 132. Wilbert Harrison (lead vocal) with Jimmy Spruill (guitar) and other musicians. Produced by Bobby Robinson.

Heinz. 1963. "Just Like Eddie" (Geoffrey Goddard; Peermusic AB.). Recorded at RGM Sound, North London. Released as Decca F 11693, July 1963. Charts 8 August 1963 (UK #5). Heinz Burt (lead vocal) with Ritchie Blackmore (guitar), Geoff Goddard (piano and backing vocal), and members of the Outlaws. Produced by Joe Meek.

Herman's Hermits. 1964. "I'm into Something Good" (Gerry Goffin and Carole King; Screen Gems/EMI Music Publishing Ltd.). Recorded at Kingsway Recording Studios. Released as Columbia DB 7338, August 1964. Charts 20 August 1964 (UK #1). Peter Noone (vocal) with session musicians. Produced by Mickie Most.

———. 1965. "Silhouettes" (Frank C. Slay, Jr., and Bob Crewe; Francis, Day, and Hunter Ltd.). Recorded at Kingsway Recording Studios. Released as Columbia DB 7475, 12 February 1965. Charts 18 February 1965 (UK #3). Peter Noone (vocal), Jim Sullivan (guitar), Vic Flick (guitar), John Carter and Ken Lewis (backing vocals and hand claps), and others. Produced by Mickie Most.

———. 1965. "Can't You Hear My Heartbeat" (John Carter and Ken Lewis; Southern Music Publishers, Ltd.). Recorded at Kingsway Studios. Released as Columbia DB 7475. Personnel and production as above. [b/w "Silhouettes"]

———. 1965. "Mrs. Brown You've Got a Lovely Daughter" (Treavor Peacock; Brakenbury Music/Hill and Range Music). Recorded January 1965. U.S. release as MGM K13341, February 1965 (U.S. #1). UK release on *Mrs. Brown You've Got a Lovely Daughter*, Columbia EP SEG 8440. Peter Noone (vocal) with Keith Hopwood (guitar and backing vocal), Karl Green (bass and backing vocal), and Barry Whitman (drums). Produced by Mickie Most.

———. 1966. "No Milk Today" (Graham Gouldman; Hournew Music Ltd.). Released as Columbia DB 8012, 6 October 1966 (UK #7). Peter Noone (vocal) with studio musicians. Produced by Mickie Most.

———. 1967. "There's a Kind of Hush" (Les Reed and Geoff Stephens; Donna Music Ltd.). Released as Columbia DB 8123, 4 February 1967. Charts 9 February 1967 (UK #7). Peter Noone with studio musicians. Produced by Mickie Most with John Paul Jones (music director).

Hollies. 1965. "Look through Any Window" (Graham Gouldman and Charles Silverman; Manchester Music Ltd.). Released as Parlophone R 5322, 27 August 1965. Charts 2 September 1965 (UK #4). Allan Clarke (vocal), Eric Haydock (bass guitar), Graham Nash (guitar, vocal), Don Rathbone (drums). Produced by Ron Richards with Peter Bown (balance engineer).

———. 1966. "Bus Stop" (Graham Gouldman; Hournew Music Ltd.). Recorded 18 May 1966. Released as Parlophone R 5469, 17 June 1966. Charts 23 June 1966 (UK #5). Personnel and production as above.

Honeycombs. 1964. "Have I the Right" (Ken Howard and Alan Blaikley; Ivy Music Ltd.). Recorded at RGM Studios, May 1964. Released as Pye 7N 15664, 16 June 1964. Charts 23 July 1964 (UK #1). Denis D'ell (vocal), Martin Murray (guitar), Ann "Honey" Lantree (drums), John Lantree (bass), Alan Ward (guitar). Produced by Joe Meek.

Howlin' Wolf. 1962. "The Red Rooster"[5] (Willie Dixon; Bug Music, Ltd.). Released on *Howlin' Wolf*,[6] Chess LP 1469, 11 January 1962. Howlin' Wolf (vocal), Hosea Lee Kennard (piano), Hubert Sumlin and Willie Johnson (guitars), Willie Dixon (bass), and Earl Phillips (drums). Produced by Leonard Chess.

Engelbert Humperdinck. 1967. "The Last Waltz" (Les Reed and Barry Mason; EMI Music Publishing). Released as Decca F 12655. Charts 23 August 1967 (UK #1). Engelbert Humperdinck (vocal) with studio orchestra. Produced by Peter Sullivan with Les Reed (music director) and Bill Price (balance engineer).

---

[5] Recorded by the Rolling Stones as "Little Red Rooster."

[6] Also known as the "rocking chair" album by collectors for the photo of a guitar resting on a rocker.

Frank Ifield. 1962. "I Remember You" (Victor Schertzinger and Johnny Mercer; BMG Music Publishing, Ltd.). Recorded at EMI, 27 May 1962. Released as Columbia DB 4856, 29 June 1962 (UK #1). Frank Ifield (vocal) with session musicians. Produced by Norrie Paramor with Norman Smith (balance engineer).

Isley Brothers. 1962. "Twist and Shout" (Bert Russell and Phil Medley; EMI Music Publishing, Ltd.). Released as Stateside SS 112, June 1962. Ronald Isley, Rudolph Isley, and O'Kelly Isley (vocals) with an unidentified band. Produced by Bert (Russell) Berns.

Ivy League. 1965. "Funny How Love Can Be" (John Carter and Ken Lewis; Southern Music). Recorded at Regent Sound Studios. Released as Piccadilly 7N 35222, 29 January 1965. Charts 4 February 1965 (UK #8). John Carter, Ken Lewis, and Perry Ford (vocals) with Jim Sullivan (guitar), Dave Winter (bass), Mike O'Neill (keyboards), Micky Keene (guitar), Clem Cattini (drums), and other studio musicians. Produced by Terry Kennedy with Bill Farley (balance engineer).

————. 1966. "My World Fell Down" (John Carter and Geoff Stephens; Carter-Lewis Music). Released as Piccadilly 7N35348, 12 October 1966. Charts 14 October 1966 (UK #8). Personnel and production as above.

Dick James. 1956. "Robin Hood" (Carl Sigman; Memory Lane Music Ltd.). Recorded at EMI, 5 December 1955. Released as Parlophone R 4117, 20 January 1956 (UK #14). Dick James (vocal) with session musicians. Produced by George Martin.

John Paul Jones. 1964. "Baja" (Lee Hazelwood; Atlantic Music Ltd.). Recorded at Regent Sound Studios. Released as Pye 7N 15637, 1964. John Paul Jones (guitar) with session musicians. Produced by Andrew Oldham with Bill Farley (balance engineer).

Tom Jones. 1965. "It's Not Unusual" (Les Reed and Gordon Mills; Valley Music Ltd.). Recorded 14 December 1964. Released as Decca F 12062, 22 January 1965. Charts 11 February 1965 (UK #1). Tom Jones (vocal) with studio musicians, including Stan Roderick, Kenny Baker, Bert Ezzard, and Ray Davies or Eddie Blair (trumpets), Ronnie Ross (tenor sax), Harry Klein (baritone sax), Bob Efford (second tenor sax), Vic Flick (rhythm guitar), Joe Moretti (lead guitar), Andy White or Ronnie Verrell (drums), Stan Barrett (percussion), Kenny Salmon (organ), Eric Ford or Alan Weighell (bass), and John Carter and Ken Lewis (backup vocals).[7] Produced by Peter Sullivan with Les Reed (music director).

————. 1967. "I'll Never Fall in Love Again" (Lonnie Donegan and Jimmy Currie; Tyler Music Ltd.). Recorded 16 January 1967. Released as Decca F 12639, 21 July 1967. Charts 22 July 1967 (UK #2). Tom Jones (vocal) with session musicians. Produced by Peter Sullivan with Charles Blackwell (music director).

Johnny Kidd and the Pirates. 1960. "Shakin' All Over" (Frederick Heath; EMI Harmonies Ltd.). Recorded at EMI, 13 May 1960. Released as HMV POP 698, 10 June 1960. Charts 16 June 1960 (UK #1). Johnny Kidd (vocal), Joe Moretti (guitar), Alan Caddy (guitar), Brian Gregg (bass), and Clem Cattini (drums). Produced by Peter Sullivan with Walter J. Ridley (executive producer) and Malcolm Addey (balance engineer).

————. 1960. "Restless" (Teddy Wadmore, Dale Stanley, and Frederick Heath). Recorded at EMI, 5 September 1960. Released as HMV POP 790, 30 September 1960. Charts 6 Octo-

[7] Les Reed indicates that Jones recorded two different versions of "It's Not Unusual" with slightly different line-ups.

ber 1960 (UK #22). Johnny Kidd (vocal), Joe Moretti (guitar), Alan Caddy (guitar), Brian Gregg (bass), and Clem Cattini (drums). Produced by Walter J. Ridley with Malcolm Addey (balance engineer).

Kinks. 1964. "Long Tall Sally" (Richard Penniman, Enntris Johnson, and Robert A. Blackwell; SONY/ATV Songs LLC.). Released as Pye 7N 15611, 7 February 1964 (UK #42). Ray Davies (lead vocal, guitar), Dave Davies (backing vocal, guitar), Peter Quaife (backing vocal, bass), Mick Avory (drums). Produced by Shel Talmy.

———. 1964. "You Really Got Me" (Ray Davies; Ed Kassner Music Co., Ltd.). Recorded at IBC Studios. Released as Pye 7N 15673, 4 August 1964. Charts 13 August 1964 (UK #1). Ray Davies (lead vocal and guitar) with Dave Davies (guitar solo), Peter Quaife (bass), Arthur Greenslade (piano), Bobby Graham (drums), and Mick Avory (tambourine). Produced by Shel Talmy with Bob Auger (balance engineer).

———. 1964. "All Day and All of the Night" (Ray Davies; Ed Kassner Music Co., Ltd.). Recorded at Pye Studios, 23 September 1964. Released as Pye 7N 15714, 23 October 1964. Charts 29 October 1964 (UK #2). Personnel and production as above.

———. 1965. "Tired of Waiting for You" (Ray Davies; Ed Kassner Music Co., Ltd.). Recorded at Pye Studios, 25 August 1964, with guitar overdubs in IBC Studios, 29 December 1964. Released as Pye 7N 15759, 15 January 1965. Charts 21 January 1965 (UK #1). Personnel and production as above.

———. 1965. "Set Me Free" (Ray Davies; Ed Kassner Music Co., Ltd.). Recorded at Pye Studios, 13–14 April 1965. Released as Pye 7N 15854, 21 May 1965. Charts 27 May 1965 (UK # 9). Personnel and production as above with Rasa Davies (backing vocal).

———. 1965. "See My Friends" (Ray Davies; Ed Kassner Music Co., Ltd.). Recorded at Pye Studios, 3 May 1965. Released as Pye 7N 15919, 30 July 1965. Charts 5 August 1965 (UK #10). Personnel and production as above without Rasa Davies.

———. 1965. "A Well Respected Man" (Ray Davies; Ed Kassner Music Co., Ltd.). Recorded at Pye Studios, 5 August 1965. Released on the *Kwyet Kinks* EP, Pye NEP 24221, 17 September 1965 (UK #1). Ray Davies (lead vocal and guitar) with Clem Cattini (drums), Dave Davies (guitar solo), Peter Quaife (bass), and Mick Avory (tambourine). Produced by Shel Talmy with Alan MacKenzie (balance engineer).

———. 1966. "Dedicated Follower of Fashion" (Ray Davies; Ed Kassner Music Co., Ltd.). Recorded at Pye Studios, 7, 10, and 11 February 1966. Released as Pye 7N 17064, 25 February 1966. Charts 3 March 1966 (UK #4). Personnel and production as above.

———. 1968. *The Kinks Are the Village Green Preservation Society.* Released as Pye NSPL 18233, 22 November 1968. Produced by Ray Davies and Shel Talmy, with Brian Humphries and Alan MacKenzie (balance engineers).

———. 1969. *Arthur or the Decline and Fall of the British Empire.* Released as Pye NSPL 18317, 10 October 1969. Personnel and production as above.

Billy J. Kramer with the Dakotas. 1963. "Bad to Me" (John Lennon and Paul McCartney; Northern Songs, Ltd.). Recorded at EMI, 27 June 1963. Released as Parlophone R 5049, 26 July 1963. Charts 1 August 1963 (UK #1). Billy J. Kramer (vocal), Ray Jones (bass guitar), Tony Mansfield (drums), Mike Maxfield (guitar), Robin MacDonald (guitar), with George Martin (piano). Produced by George Martin with Norman Smith (balance engineer).

Steve Lawrence. 1962. "Go Away Little Girl" (Gerry Goffin and Carole King; Screen Gems). Released as Columbia 42601, December 1962. Charts 12 January 1963 (U.S. #1). Steve Lawrence (vocal) with studio musicians. Produced by Al Kasha.

Huddie Ledbetter. 1951. "Rock Island Line" (Huddie Ledbetter). Recorded in New York City, January 1942. Released on Folkways Records, Electra EKL Box B, 1951. Huddie Ledbetter (guitar and vocal). Produced by Moses Asche.

Donovan Leitch. *See* Donovan.

John Leyton. 1961. "Johnny Remember Me" (Geoff Goddard; Peer Music Ltd.). Recorded at RGM Sound. Released as Top Rank JAR 577, July 1961. Charts 3 August 1961 (UK #1). John Leyton (vocal) with Lissa Grey (vocal), Geoff Goddard (piano), and members of the Outlaws, including Bobby Graham (drums) and, probably, Billy Kuy (guitar), Reg Hawkins (guitar), and Chas Hodges (bass). Produced by Joe Meek with Charles Blackwell (music director).

Lulu. 1964. "Shout" (O'Kelly Isley, Ronald Isley, and Rudolph Isley; Wemar and Big Seven Music). Recorded at Decca. Released as Decca F11884, April 1964. Charts 14 May 1964 (UK #7). Lulu (vocal) with session musicians "Big Jim" Sullivan (guitar), Clem Cattini (drums), and others, including the Breakaways (backup singers, including Margot Quantrell, Vicki Haseman, and Jean Hawker). Produced by Peter Sullivan.

———. 1967. "To Sir with Love" (Mark London and Don Black; Screen Gems, EMI Music Publishing Ltd.). Released as Columbia DB 8221, 23 June 1967. Lulu (vocal) with session musicians. Produced by Mickie Most with John Paul Jones (music director). [b/w "Let's Pretend"]

Humphrey Lyttelton Band. 1956. "Bad Penny Blues" (Humphrey Lyttelton; Tro Essex Music Ltd.). Recorded at Lansdowne Studios, 20 April 1956. Released as Parlophone R 4184, June 1956. Charts 13 June 1956 (UK #19). Humphrey Lyttelton (trumpet), Johnny Parker (piano), Jim Bray (bass), and Stan Greig (drums). Produced by Denis Preston with Joe Meek (engineer).

Henry Mancini. 1961. "Moon River" (Henry Mancini and Johnny Mercer; BMG Music Publishing Ltd.). Released as RCA 1256. Charts 7 December 1961 (UK # 44). Henry Mancini (arranger and conductor).

Manfred Mann. 1964. "Do-Wah-Diddy Diddy" (Jeff Barry and Ellie Greenwich; Carlin Music Corp.). Recorded at EMI, 22 June 1964. Released as HMV POP 1320, 10 July 1964. Charts 16 July 1964 (UK #1). Manfred Mann (piano), Mike Hugg (drums), Paul Jones (vocal), Mike Vickers (guitar), and Tom McGuinness (bass). Produced by John Burgess with Norman Smith (engineer).

———. 1966. "Pretty Flamingo" (Mike Barkan; Shapiro, Bernstein, & Co. Ltd.). Recorded at EMI 18 March 1966. Released as HMV POP 1523, 15 April 1966. Charts 21 April 1966 (UK #1). Paul Jones (vocal), Manfred Mann (keyboards), Mike Hugg (drums), Jack Bruce (bass), Tom McGuinness (guitar), and probably Lyn Dobson (flute). Produced by John Burgess with Geoff Emerick (balance engineer).

———. 1966. "Semi-Detached Suburban Mr. Jones" (John Carter and Geoff Stephens; Carter-Lewis Music Publishing Ltd.). Recorded at EMI. Released as Fontana TF 757, 21 October 1966. Charts 27 October 1967 (UK #2). Mike D'Abo (vocal), Manfred Mann (keyboards), Mike Hugg (drums), Klaus Voorman (bass), and Tom McGuinness (guitar). Produced by John Burgess with Geoff Emerick (balance engineer).

John Mayall. 1966. "All Your Love" (Otis Rush and Willie Dixon). Recorded at Decca, July 1966. Released on *Bluesbreakers*, Decca SKL 4804, 22 July 1966. John Mayall (vocal and organ), Eric Clapton (guitar), John McVie (bass guitar), and Hughie Flint (drums). Produced by Mike Vernon with Gus Dudgeon (balance engineer).

McKuen, Rod. 1969. *The Prime of Miss Jean Brodie* (film soundtrack). Studio orchestra. Released as Twentieth Century Fox 4207 in January 1969. Arthur Greenslade (arranger, musical director, and conductor).

Garry Miller. 1956. "Robin Hood" (Carl Sigman; Memory Lane Music Ltd.). Recorded at Pye Studios, December 1955. Released as Nixa N 1504, January 1956. Charts 13 January 1956 (UK #10). Garry Miller with session musicians.

Jimmy Miller and His Barbecues. 1957. "Sizzling Hot" (Joe Meek and Charles Blackwell; Essex Music). Recorded at IBC Studios, August 1957. Released as Columbia DB 4006, September 1957. Jimmy Miller (vocal) with guitar, washboard, beer-barrel bass, and accordion. Produced by Joe Meek and Denis Preston with Charles Blackwell (music director).

Moody Blues. 1964. "Go Now" (Bessie Banks, Larry Banks, and Milton Bennett; Trio Music 1963). Released as Decca F 12022, 12 November 1964. Charts 10 December 1964 (UK #1). Denny Laine (guitar, vocal), Graeme Edge (drums), Mike Pinder (piano, vocal), Ray Thomas (vocal), and Clint Warwick (bass guitar). Produced by Alex Murray.

———. 1967. *Days of Future Passed* (Peter Knight, Sr., and members of the Moody Blues). Released as Deram 161, November 1967. Mike Pinder (keyboards), Ray Thomas (flute and vocal), Graham Edge (drums), Justin Hayword (guitar and vocal), John Lodge (bass and vocal). Executive producer Hugh Mendl with Michael Dacre-Barclay and Tony Clarke (producers), Peter Knight, Sr. (music director and conductor), and Derek Varnals (engineer).

Nashville Teens. 1964. "Tobacco Road" (John Loudermilk; Polygram Music Publishing Ltd.). Released as Decca F 11930, 20 June 1964. Charts 9 July 1964 (UK #6). John Hawkens (piano), Arthur Sharp (vocal), and Ray Phillips (vocal) with session musicians Bobby Graham (drums), Eric Ford (bass), and Big Jim Sullivan (guitar). Produced by Mickie Most.

———. 1965. "This Little Bird" (John Loudermilk; Acuff Rose, Opryland Music Ltd.). Released as Decca F 12143, May 1965. Charts 20 May 1965 (UK #35). John Hawkens (piano), Pete Shannon (bass), Arthur Sharp (vocal), Ray Phillips (vocal), John Allen (guitar), and Barry Jenkins (drums) with session musicians, including Jim Sullivan (guitar). Produced by Andrew Oldham.

Naturals. 1964. "It Was You" (Peter Townshend, Eula Parker, and Barry Gray; Dick James Music Ltd.). Released as Parlophone R 5202, 20 November 1964. Ricky Potter (vocal), Curt Cresswell (guitar), Bob O'Neale (guitar), Mike Wakelin (bass guitar), and Roy Heather (drums). Produced by Ron Richards.

New Vaudeville Band. 1966. "Winchester Cathedral" (Geoff Stephens; Peer Music UK Ltd.). Recorded at Peer Music Ltd. Released as Fontana TF 741. Charts 8 September 1966 (UK #4). John Carter (vocal), Roger Coulam (organ), with unidentified session musicians. Produced by Geoff Stephens with Ken Woodman (music director).

Roy Orbison. 1960. "Only the Lonely (Know the Way I Feel)" (Roy Orbison and J. Melson; Acuff Rose Music Ltd., Opryland Music Ltd.). U.S. release as Monument 45–421, March 1960. UK release as London RE-U 1274, 1960. Charts August 1960 (UK #2). Roy Orbison (vocal) with studio musicians.

Peter and Gordon. 1964. "World without Love" (John Lennon and Paul McCartney; Northern Songs Ltd.). Recorded at EMI, 21 January 1964. Released as Columbia DB 7225, 22 February 1964. Charts 12 March 1964 (UK #1). Peter Asher (vocal), Gordon Waller (vocal) with session musicians, including Vic Flick (electric 12-string guitar), Harold Smart (organ), Allan Weighell and/or Ron Prentiss (bass), probably Andy White (drums), and others. Produced by Norman Newell with Geoff Love (music director), and with Peter Bown and Malcolm Addey (balance engineers).

Pink Floyd. 1967. "Arnold Layne" (Syd Barrett; Magdalene Music). Recorded at Sound Techniques Studio, 27 February 1967. Released as Columbia DB 8156, 10 March 1967. Charts 30 March 1967 (UK #20). Syd Barrett (vocal and guitar), Roger Waters (bass), Richard Wright (organ and piano), and Nick Mason (drums). Produced by Joe Boyd and John Wood (balance engineer).

———. 1967. "See Emily Play" (Syd Barrett; Magdalene Music). Recorded at EMI. Released as Columbia DB 8214, 16 June 1967. Charts 22 June 1967 (UK #6). Syd Barrett (vocal and guitar), Roger Waters (bass), Richard Wright (organ and piano), and Nick Mason (drums). Produced by Norman Smith with Peter Bown (balance engineer).

———. 1967. *Piper at the Gates of Dawn.* Released as Columbia SCX 6157, 1 August 1967. Production as above.

Gene Pitney. 1964. "That Girl Belongs to Yesterday" (Mick Jagger and Keith Richards; Southern Music Publishers, Ltd.). Recorded at Olympic Sound Studios. Released as United Artists UP 1045, 29 February 1964. Charts 5 March 1964 (UK #7). Gene Pitney (vocal) with session musicians. Produced by Andrew Oldham with Charles Blackwell (music director) and Roger Savage (balance engineer).

Brian Poole and the Tremeloes. 1963. "Do You Love Me" (Berry Gordy; Jobete Music Co., Inc.). Recorded at Decca, July 1963. Released as Decca F 11739. Charts 12 September 1963 (UK #1). Brian Poole (vocal), Alan Blakely (rhythm guitar), Alan Howard (bass), Dave Munden (drums), and Rick West (lead guitar). Produced by Dick Rowe.

Mike Preston. 1959. "Mr. Blue" (Charles Blackwell; B. H. Morris Ltd.). Recorded at Lansdowne Recording Studios, October 1959. Released as Decca F 11167, October 1959. Charts 30 October 1959 (UK #12). Mike Preston (vocal) with session musicians. Produced by Joe Meek with Harry Robinson (music director).

Pretty Things. 1968. *S. F. Sorrow.* Released as Columbia SCX-6306, 20 December 1968. Produced by Norman Smith with Peter Mew (balance engineer).

Procol Harum. 1967. "A Whiter Shade of Pale" (Gary Brooker, Keith Reid, and Matthew Fisher; Tro Essex Music Ltd.). Recorded at Olympic Sound Studios. Released as Deram DM 126, 19 May 1967. Gary Brooker (piano and vocal), Matthew Fisher (organ), Ray Royer (guitar), and session musicians Allan Weighell (bass) and Bill Eyden (drums). Produced by Denny Cordell.

Lou Rawls. 1962? "Music in the Air" (information unavailable).

Johnny Ray. 1951. "Cry" (Churchill Kohlman; Mellow Music Publishing). UK release as Okeh 6840. Johnny Ray (vocal), the Four Lads (Corrado "Connie" Codarini, John Bernard "Bernie" Toorish, James F. "Jimmy" Arnold, and Frank Busseri) (backing vocals), and unidentified studio musicians. Produced by Mitch Miller.

Cliff Richard and the Drifters. 1958. "Move It" (Ian Samwell; Multiwood Music Ltd.). Recorded at EMI, 24 July 1958. Released as Columbia DB 4178, 29 August 1958. Charts 12 September 1958 (UK #2). Cliff Richard (vocal), Terry Smart (drums), and Ian Samwell (rhythm guitar). Session musicians included Ernie Shear (lead guitar) and Frank Clarke (acoustic bass). Produced by Norrie Paramor with Malcolm Addey (engineer).

———. 1958. "Schoolboy Crush" (Aaron Schroeder and Sharon Gilbert; MCA Music Ltd.). Recorded at EMI, 24 July 1958. Released as Columbia DB 4178, 29 August 1958. Musical and production personnel as above with session singers. [b/w "Move It"]

Little Richard. 1956. "Long Tall Sally" (Richard Penniman, Enntris Johnson, Robert A. Blackwell; SONY/ATV Songs LLC.). Released as Specialty 572, 1956 (U.S. R&B #1, Pop #6). Richard Penniman (vocal, piano), Lee Allen (tenor saxophone), and others. Produced by Robert Blackwell.

Rolling Stones. 1963. "Come On" (Chuck Berry; Arc Music). Recorded at Olympic Sound Studios, 10 May 1963. Released as Decca F 11675, 7 June 1963. Charts 25 July 1963 (UK #21). Mick Jagger (vocal), Brian Jones (harmonica, vocal), Keith Richards (guitar, vocal), Bill Wyman (bass), and Charlie Watts (drums). Produced by Andrew Loog Oldham with Roger Savage (balance engineer).

———. 1963. "I Wanna Be Your Man" (John Lennon and Paul McCartney; Gil Music Corporation). Recorded at Kingsway Sound Studios, 10 September 1963. Released as Decca F 11764, 1 November 1963 (UK #9). U.S. release 17 February 1964. Personnel as above with Brian Jones (slide guitar). Produced by Andrew Oldham.

———. 1964. "Can I Get a Witness" (Brian Holland, Lamont Dozier, and Edward Holland; Jobete Music). Recorded at Regent Sound Studios, 28 January 1964. Released on *The Rolling Stones*, Decca LP LK 4605, 17 April 1964. Mick Jagger (vocal and harmonica), Keith Richards (guitar), Brian Jones (slide guitar), Bill Wyman (bass), Charlie Watts (drums), Gene Pitney (piano), and Phil Spector (maracas). Produced by Andrew Oldham with Bill Farley (balance engineer).

———. 1964. "Not Fade Away" (Charles Hardin and Norman Petty). Recorded at Regent Sound Studios, 10 and 28 January 1964, and at IBC Studios, 4 February 1964. Released as Decca AT 15006, 21 February 1964. Charts 27 February 1964 (UK #3). Mick Jagger (vocal and harmonica), Keith Richards (guitar), Brian Jones (slide guitar), Bill Wyman (bass), Charlie Watts (drums), Phil Spector (maracas), and Graham Nash, Tony Hicks, and Gene Pitney (hand claps). Produced by Andrew Oldham with Bill Farley (balance engineer).

———. 1964. "Little by Little" (Nanker Phelge and Phil Spector; Southern Music Publishers, Ltd., Mother Bertha Music, Inc.). Recorded at Regent Sound Studios, 28 January 1964. Released as Decca AT 15006, 21 February 1964. Personnel as above. [b/w "Not Fade Away"]

———. 1964. "Tell Me (You're Coming Back to Me)" (Mick Jagger and Keith Richards; Southern Music Publishers, Ltd.). Recorded at Regent Sound Studios, February 1964. Released on *The Rolling Stones*, Decca LP LK 4605, 17 April 1964 (UK LP #1). Mick Jagger (vocal), Keith Richards (guitar), Brian Jones (guitar and tambourine), Bill Wyman (bass), and Charlie Watts (drums). Produced by Andrew Oldham with Bill Farley (balance engineer).

———. 1964. "Little Red Rooster" (Willie Dixon; Hoochie Coochie Music, BUG/Arc Music Corporation). Recorded at Regent Sound Studios, 2 September 1964. Released as Decca F 12014, 13 November 1964 (UK #1). Personnel and production as above.

———. 1964. "It's All Over Now" (Bobby Womack and Shirley Womack). Recorded at Chess Records, Chicago, 10–11 June 1964. Released as Decca F 11934, 26 June 1964. Charts 2 July 1964 (UK #1). Mick Jagger (vocal), Keith Richards (guitar), Brian Jones (guitar), Bill Wyman (bass), and Charlie Watts (drums). Produced by Andrew Oldham with Ron Malo (balance engineer).

———. 1965. "The Last Time" (Mick Jagger and Keith Richards; ABKCO Music Ltd.). Recorded at RCA Studios, Hollywood, January 1965. Released as Decca F 12104, 26 February 1965. Charts 4 March 1965 (UK #1). Personnel as above. Produced by Andrew Old-ham with Dave Hassinger (balance engineer).

———. 1965. "Play with Fire" (Mick Jagger and Keith Richards; ABKCO Music Ltd.). Re-corded at RCA Studios, Hollywood; January–February 1965. Released as Decca F 12104, 26 February 1965. Mick Jagger (vocal and tambourine), Keith Richards (acoustic guitar), with Phil Spector (guitar) and Jack Nitzsche (harpsichord). Production as above. [b/w "The Last Time"]

———. 1965. "(I Can't Get No) Satisfaction" (Mick Jagger and Keith Richards; ABKCO Music Ltd.). Recorded at RCA Studios, Hollywood, 12 May 1965. Released as Decca F 12220, 20 August 1965. Charts 26 August 1965 (UK #1). U.S. release as London 9766, 27 May 1965 (U.S. #1). Mick Jagger (vocal), Brian Jones (guitar), Keith Richards (guitar), Bill Wyman (bass), and Charlie Watts (drums). Production as above.

———. 1966. *Aftermath*. Released as Decca LP SKL/KL 4786, 15 April 1966. Produced by Andrew Oldham.

———. 1966. "Mother's Little Helper" (Mick Jagger and Keith Richards; ABKCO Music Ltd.). Recorded at RCA Studios, Hollywood, 8–10 December 1965. Released on *After-math*, 15 April 1966. U.S. release as London 45–902, 2 July 1966 (U.S. #8). Produced by Andrew Oldham with Dave Hassinger (balance engineer).

———. 1966. "Lady Jane" (Mick Jagger and Keith Richards; ABKCO Music Ltd.). Recorded at RCA Studios, Hollywood, 6–9 March 1966. Released on *Aftermath*, 15 April 1966. Mick Jagger (vocal), Keith Richards (guitar), and Brian Jones (dulcimer). Production as above. [U.S. b/w "Mother's Little Helper"]

———. 1966. "Out of Time" (Mick Jagger and Keith Richards; ABKCO Music Ltd.). Re-corded at RCA Studios, Hollywood, 6–9 March 1966. Released on *Aftermath*, 15 April 1966. Mick Jagger (vocal), Keith Richards (guitar), Brian Jones (marimba), Bill Wyman (bass), Charlie Watts (drums), and Jack Nitzsche (piano). Production as above.

———. 1967. "Let's Spend the Night Together" (Mick Jagger and Keith Richards; ABKCO Music Ltd.). Recorded at Olympic Sound Studios, 16 November and 6 December 1966. Released as Decca F 12546, 13 January 1967. Charts 19 January 1967 (UK #3). Mick Jag-ger (vocal), Keith Richards (guitar), Brian Jones (organ), Bill Wyman (bass), Charlie Watts (drums), and Jack Nitzsche (piano). Produced by Andrew Loog Oldham with Glyn Johns (balance engineer).

———. 1967. "Ruby Tuesday" (Mick Jagger and Keith Richards; ABKCO Music Ltd.). Re-corded at Olympic Sound Studios, 16 November 1966. Released as Decca F 12546, 13 Jan-uary 1967. Mick Jagger (vocal), Keith Richards (guitar and vocal), Charlie Watts (drums), Bill Wyman (string bass), Brian Jones (recorder), and Jack Nitzsche (piano). Production as above. [b/w "Let's Spend the Night Together"]

———. 1967. *Their Satanic Majesties Request*. Released as Decca TXS 103, 8 December 1967. Produced by Andrew Oldham and the Rolling Stones.

———. 1967. "She's a Rainbow" (Mick Jagger and Keith Richards; ABKCO Music Ltd.). Re-corded at Olympic Sound Studios, 18 May 1967. Released on *Their Satanic Majesties Re-quest*, 8 December 1967. Mick Jagger (vocal and conga drums), Keith Richards (guitar and backing vocal), Bill Wyman (bass), Charlie Watts (drums), Nicky Hopkins (piano), Brian Jones (Mellotron and tambourine), and unidentified orchestral musicians. Pro-duced by the Rolling Stones with Glyn Johns, Glen Kolotkin, and Gus Skinas (balance en-gineers) and John Paul Jones (arranger).

————. 1968. "Jumpin' Jack Flash" (Mick Jagger and Keith Richards; ABKCO Music Ltd.). Recorded at RG Jones Studios, 1–4 March 1968, and Olympic Sound Studios, 23–29 March 1968. Released as Decca F 12782, 23 May 1968. Charts 29 May 1968 (UK #1). Mick Jagger (vocal), Keith Richards (guitar and backing vocal), Brian Jones (maracas), Bill Wyman (piano and bass), Charlie Watts (drums). Produced by Jimmy Miller with Eddie Kramer and Glyn Johns (balance engineers).

————. 1968. "Street Fighting Man" (Mick Jagger and Keith Richards; ABKCO Music Ltd.). Recorded at Olympic Sound Studios, 13–18 May 1968. Released on *Beggar's Banquet*, Decca LP SKL 4955, 6 December 1968 (UK LP #3). U.S. release as London 45–909, 26 July 1968 (U.S. #48). Mick Jagger (vocal), Keith Richards (acoustic guitar and bass), Jimmy Miller (guitar), Brian Jones (sitar and tambura), Charlie Watts (drums), Dave Mason (śahanā'ī), and Nicky Hopkins (piano). Produced by Jimmy Miller with Eddie Kramer and Glyn Johns (balance engineers).

————. 1975. "Out of Time" (Mick Jagger and Keith Richards; ABKCO Music, Inc.). Recorded on 27–30 April and 6 May 1966 at Pye Studios. Released as Decca F 13597, 5 September 1975. Mick Jagger (vocal) accompanied by Jimmy Page (guitar), Joe Moretti (guitar), Eric Ford (bass), Reg Guest (piano), and Andy White (drums) with a string section led by Sidney Sax and backing vocals by Chris Farlowe and others. Produced by Andrew Oldham with Arthur Greenslade (music director) and Alan Florence (balance engineer).

Bobby Rydell. 1963. "Forget Him" (Mark Anthony [Tony Hatch]; Leeds Music). Released as Cameo C-280. Performance and production personnel unavailable.

Shadows. 1960. "Apache" (Jerry Lordan; Francis, Day, and Hunter Ltd., EMI). Recorded at EMI, 17 June 1960. Released as Columbia DB 4484, 21 July 1960 (UK #1). Hank Marvin (lead guitar), Bruce Welch (rhythm guitar), Jet Harris (bass), Tony Meehan (drums), and Cliff Richard (Chinese tam tam). Produced by Norrie Paramor with Malcolm Addey (balance engineer).

————. 1962. "Wonderful Land" (Jerry Lordan; Francis, Day, and Hunter Ltd., EMI). Recorded at EMI, 12 May 1961. Released as Columbia DB 4790, February 1962. Charts 1 March 1962 (UK #1). Hank Marvin (lead guitar), Bruce Welch (rhythm guitar), Jet Harris (bass), Tony Meehan (drums), and studio orchestra conducted by Norrie Paramor. Production as above.

————. 1964. "The Rise and Fall of Flingel Bunt" (Bruce Welch, Hank Marvin, John Rostill, and Brian Bennett; Escort Music/Carlin Music). Recorded at EMI. Released as Columbia DB 7261, May 1964. Charts 7 May 1964 (UK #5). Hank Marvin (lead guitar), Bruce Welch (rhythm guitar), John Rostill (bass), and Brian Bennett (drums). Production as above.

————. 1964. "It's a Man's World" (Malcolm Addey and Norman Smith; Shadows Music Ltd./Carlin Music Ltd.). Recorded at EMI. Released as Columbia DB 7261, May 1964. Personnel and production as above. [b/w "The Rise and Fall of Fingel Bunt"]

Helen Shapiro. 1961. "Don't Treat Me Like a Child" (John Schroeder and Michael Hawker; Lorna Music Co., Ltd.). Recorded at EMI, 16 January 1961. Released as Columbia DB 4589, 10 February 1961. Charts 23 March 1961 (UK #3). Helen Shapiro (vocal) with studio musicians. Produced by Norrie Paramor with Malcolm Addey (balance engineer).

Shirelles. 1962. "Baby It's You" (Hal David, Burt Bacharach, Barney Williams; Ludix Music Ltd.). Recorded at Bell Sound Studios, New York. U.S. release as Scepter Records 1227, 4 December 1961. UK release as Top Rank JAR 601, 1962. Shirley Alston, Beverly Lee,

Addie/Micki Harris, Doris Kenner (vocals) with studio musicians. Produced by Luther Dixon with Burt Bacharach (arranger).

Millie Small. 1964. "My Boy Lollipop" (Johnny Roberts and Robert Spencer [Morris Levy]). Recorded at Lansdowne Studios (?). Released as Fontana TF 449, February 1964. Charts 12 March 1964 (UK #2). Millie Small (vocal) with Ernest Ranglin (guitar), Pete Peterson (trumpet), Jimmy Powell and the Dimensions, with Red Godwin (guitar), Tony Lucas (bass), Alan Shepherd (saxophone), Duke Russell (drums), and Pete Hogman (harmonica). Produced by Chris Blackwell with Ernest Ranglin (music director).

Dusty Springfield. 1963. "I Only Want to Be with You" (Ivor Raymonde and Mike Hawker). Recorded at Philips Studios, Marble Arch, London, 17 October 1963. Released as Philips BF 1292, 4 December 1963. Charts 11 January 1964 (UK #12). Dusty Springfield (vocal) with the Breakaways (backing vocals) and studio musicians. Produced by John Franz with Ivor Raymonde (music director).

———. 1967. "The Look of Love" (Hal David and Burt Bacharach). Recorded at Philips Studios, Marble Arch, London, on 14 April 1967. Released as Philips BF 1577, 20 May 1967, as the B side of "Give Me Time." Dusty Springfield (vocal) with studio musicians. Produced by John Franz with Arthur Greenslade (arranger).

Staple Singers. 1954. "This May Be the Last Time" (traditional). Released as Sharp 603, ca. December 1954. Roebuck "Pop" Staples (vocal and guitar), Pervis Staples (vocal), Cleotha Staples (vocal), and Mavis Staples (vocal). Arranged by Roebuck Staples.

Tommy Steele. 1956. "Rock with the Caveman" (Tommy Steele, Lionel Bart, and Mike Pratt; Robbins Music Corporation, Ltd.). Recorded at Decca, 24 September 1956. Released as Decca F 10795, October 1956. Charts 26 October 1956 (UK #13). Tommy Steele (guitar) with Ronnie Scott (tenor sax), Major Holly or Benny Green (bass), Dave Lee (piano), and Kirk Dunning (drums). Produced by Hugh Mendl with Roland Shaw (music director).

Them. 1964. "Baby Please Don't Go" (Joe Williams; MCA Music Ltd.). Recorded October 1964. Released as Decca F 12018, 6 November 1964. Van Morrison (vocal), Billy Harrison (guitar), Alan Henderson (bass), Pat McAuley (keyboard), and Ronnie Millings (drums). Session musicians included Bobby Graham (second drum kit) and Jimmy Page (lead guitar). Produced by Dick Rowe with Arthur Greenslade (music director).

———. 1964. "Gloria" (Van Morrison; Carlin Music Group). Recorded at Decca, 6 April 1964. Released as Decca F 12018, 6 November 1964. Van Morrison (vocal), Billy Harrison (guitar), Alan Henderson (bass), Pat McAuley (keyboard), and Ronnie Millings (drums). Session musicians included Bobby Graham (second drum kit) and Jimmy Page (second guitar). Produced by Dick Rowe with Arthur Greenslade (music director). [b/w "Baby Please Don't Go"]

Thunderclap Newman. 1969. "Something in the Air" (John Keen). Released as Rack 604 301. Charts 11 June 1969 (UK #1). John Keen (lead vocal and drums), Andy Newman (piano), Jim McCulloch (guitar), and Peter Townshend (bass). Produced by Peter Townshend.

Tornados. 1962. "Telstar" (Joe Meek; Ivy Music). Recorded at RGM Sound, 16 and 17 July 1962. Released as Decca F 11494, August 1962. Charts 30 August 1962 (UK #1). George Bellamy (guitar), Heinz Burt (bass guitar), Alan Caddy (lead guitar), Clem Cattini (drums), Roger Lavern (keyboards), with Geoff Goddard (Clavioline and vocal). Produced by Joe Meek.

Who. 1965. "I Can't Explain" (Peter Townshend; Champion, BMI). Recorded at Pye Records, November 1964. Released as Brunswick 05926 and Decca 31725, 15 January 1965. Charts

18 February 1965 (UK #6). Peter Townshend (12-string Rickenbacker guitar), Roger Daltrey (vocal), John Entwistle (bass guitar), Keith Moon (drums), Jimmy Page (second guitar), and John Carter, Ken Lewis, and Perry Ford (backing vocals). Produced by Shel Talmy with Glyn Johns (balance engineer).

———. 1965. "Anyway, Anyhow, Anywhere" (Peter Townshend; Champion, BMI). Recorded at IBC Studios, 14 April 1965. Released as Brunswick 05935, 21 May 1965. Charts 27 May 1965 (UK #10). Peter Townshend (guitar, backing vocal), Roger Daltrey (lead vocal), John Entwistle (bass guitar), Keith Moon (drums). Production as above.

———. 1965. "My Generation" (Peter Townshend; Champion, BMI). Recorded at IBC Studios, 13 October 1965. Released as Brunswick 05944, 29 October 1965. Charts 4 November 1965 (UK #2). Peter Townshend (guitar), Roger Daltrey (lead vocal), John Entwistle (bass guitar), Keith Moon (drums). Production as above.

———. 1966. "The Kids Are Alright" (Peter Townshend; Champion, BMI). Recorded at IBC Studios, 13 October 1965. Released on *My Generation,* Brunswick LP LAT 8616 (mono), 3 December 1965 (UK LP #5). Released as Brunswick 05965, 12 August 1966. Charts 1 September 1966 (UK #41). Peter Townshend (guitar), Roger Daltrey (lead vocal), John Entwistle (bass guitar), Keith Moon (drums), and Nicky Hopkins (piano). Production as above.

———. 1966. "Substitute" (Peter Townshend; Fabulous Music Ltd.). Recorded at Olympic Sound Studios, February 1966. Released as Reaction 591 001, 4 March 1966. Charts 10 March 1966 (UK #5). Peter Townshend (guitar), Roger Daltrey (lead vocal), John Entwistle (bass guitar), and Keith Moon (drums). Produced by Kit Lambert with Glyn Johns (balance engineer).

———. 1966. "I'm a Boy" (Peter Townshend; Fabulous Music Ltd.). Recorded at Olympic Sound Studios, August 1966. Released as Reaction 591 004, 26 August 1966. Charts 1 September 1966 (UK #1). Personnel and production as above.

———. 1966. "Happy Jack" (Peter Townshend; Fabulous Music Ltd.). Recorded at Regent Sound Studios, 8–10 November 1966, with overdubs at CBS. Released as Reaction 591010, 9 December 1966. Charts 15 December 1966 (UK #3). Personnel and production as above.

———. 1966. "A Quick One While He's Away" (Peter Townshend; Fabulous Music Ltd.). Recorded at Pye, IBC, and Regent Sound Studios (Tottenham Court Road), November 1966. Released on *A Quick One,* Reaction 593002, 9 December 1966. Personnel and production as above.

———. 1969. *Tommy.* Recorded at IBC. Released as Track LP 613013–14, 23 May 1969. Produced by Kit Lambert with Damon Lyon-Shaw.

Marty Wilde. 1959. *Wilde about Marty.* Released as Philips BBL 7342, August 1959. Marty Wilde (vocal) with Jim Sullivan (guitar), Tony Belcher (guitar), Brian Locking (bass), Brian Bennett (drums), and others. Produced by Johnny Franz.

Danny Williams. 1961. "Moon River" (Henry Mancini and Johnny Mercer; BMG Music Publishing Ltd.). Released as HMV POP 932, 1961. Charts 2 November 1961 (UK #1). Danny Williams (vocal) with session musicians. Produced by Norman Newell.

Mark Wynter. 1962. "Venus in Blue Jeans" (Howard Greenfield and Jack Keller). Released as Pye 7N 15466. Charts 4 October 1962 (UK #4). Mark Wynter (vocal) with session musicians. Produced by Tony Hatch.

————. 1962. "Go Away Little Girl" (Gerry Goffin and Carole King; Screen Gems). Released as Pye 7N 15492. Charts 13 December 1962 (UK #6). Mark Wynter with session musicians.[8] Produced by Tony Hatch, perhaps with John Arthey (arranger).

————. 1962. "That Kind of Talk" (Mitch Murray). Released as Pye 7N 15492. Mark Wynter (vocal) with unidentified session musicians. Produced by Tony Hatch. [b/w "Go Away Little Girl"]

Yardbirds. 1965. "For Your Love" (Graham Gouldman; Hermusic Ltd.). Released as Columbia DB 7499, 5 March 1965. Charts 18 March 1965 (UK #3). Keith Relf (vocal, bongos), Eric Clapton (guitar), Paul Samwell-Smith (bass), Ron Prentiss (acoustic bass), Chris Dreja (guitar), Jim McCarty (drums), and Brian Auger (harpsichord). Produced by Georgio Gomelsky.

————. 1965. "Heart Full of Soul" (Graham Gouldman; B. Feldman & Co. Ltd.). Released as Columbia DB 7594, 28 May 1965. Charts 17 June 1965 (UK #2). Keith Relf (vocal), Jeff Beck (guitar), Paul Samwell-Smith (bass), Chris Dreja (guitar), and Jim McCarty (drums). Produced by Georgio Gomelsky.

Zombies. 1964. "She's Not There" (Rod Argent; Marquis Music Co. Ltd.). Recorded at Decca, 12 June 1964. Released as Decca F 11940, 24 July 1964. Charts 13 August 1964 (UK #12). Colin Blunstone (vocal), Paul Atkinson (guitar), Rod Argent (keyboards, vocal), Hugh Grundy (drums), and Chris White (bass). Produced by Ken Jones with Terry Johnson and Gus Dudgeon (balance engineers).

[8] The American version by Steve Lawrence (1962) reached number one on *Billboard* in early January 1963. His version did not succeed in the United Kingdom.

Bibliography

INTERVIEWS

Addey, Malcolm. Telephone: 5, 9, 10 October 2001; 21 February 2007; 16 May 2007. E-mail: 10 October 2001.

Allen, Eric. Telephone and e-mail: 10 May 2001. E-mail: 5 July 2005.

Baring, James. E-mail: 28, 30 July 2005; 1, 3, 6, 12, 18, 20 August 2007; 28 September 2007. London: 20 August 2007; 28 September 2007.

Barrett, Stan. Telephone: 9 May 2001.

Berry, Dave. Telephone: 24 March 2004.

Blackwell, Charles. Telephone: 19, 22 March 2001; 16 June 2003. E-mail 12, 22 January 2007.

Brown, Joe. Telephone: 8 July 2001.

Carter, John. London: 26 June 2000. Telephone: 16 May 2001. E-mail: 28 July 2005; 18 September 2006.

Cattini, Clem. Telephone: 22, 31 January 2001; 11 February 2001.

Covington, Bill. Liverpool: 1 July 2000. Telephone: 10 September 2001.

Daly, Bryan. Telephone: 25, 28 April 2001.

Dean, Roger. E-mail: 9, 19, 20 November 2006; 13 December 2006; 19 January 2007.

Efford, Bob. E-mail: 26 July 2005.

Fisher, Matthew. South Croydon, UK: 27 June 2000.

Flick, Vic. Telephone: 15, 28 March 2001; 14 July 2003. Saratoga Springs, New York: 12, 13 April 2006; Las Vegas: 1 July 2007. E-mail: 13 December 2006; 25 January 2007.

Flowers, Herbie. Telephone: 11 May 2001.

Foster, Mo. Telephone: 6 April 2001.

Graham, Bobby. Telephone: 14, 15, 20 March 2001. Hertford, UK: 19 July 2002.

Greenslade, Arthur. Telephone: 8, 15, 22 January 2002.

Harry, Bill. Telephone: 1 August 2003.

Jairazbhoy, Nazir. Telephone: 12 November 2000.

Jasani, Viram. Telephone: 3 April 2001.

Knight, Peter, Jr. Telephone: 26 August 2005.

Leigh, Spencer. Telephone: 9 March 2001. E-mail: 13 March 2001.

Lewisohn, Mark. E-mail: 19 January 2007.

Little, Carlo. Telephone: 30 March 2000; 4, 12, 18 April 2000; 24 September 2001. Wembly, UK: 20 July 2002.

Moretti, Joe. Telephone: 7, 18 July 2003.

Murray, Mitch. Telephone: 5, 7 April 2001. E-mail: 12 July 2003.

Newman, Anthony. Telephone: 8 September 2001.

O'Flaherty, Peter. E-mail: 24 April 2004.

Quantrell, Margot. Telephone: 11 August 2001.

Reed, Les. Telephone: 1 May 2001. E-mail: 3, 11 July 2003; 17, 23 January 2007.

Smith, Norman. Telephone: 17, 24, 31 October 2001; 29 July 2003.

Stephens, Geoff. London: 2 March 2001. E-mail: 3, 7, 8 July 2003; 26, 29, 30 May 2007.

Sullivan, Jim. Telephone: 22, 24 January 2001; 20 September 2002. Billingshurst, UK: 5 March 2001; 4 October 2007.

Talmy, Shel. Telephone: 14 February 2001. E-mail: 21 July 2003.

Verrell, Ronnie. Telephone: 4 July 2001.

Wedge, Pip. E-mail: 23 February 2003; 16 July 2003.

Weighell, Allan. Telephone: 26, 27 March 2001; 11 April 2001.

Weighell, Michael. E-mail: 21 May 2001; 3, 21, 26 August 2004. London: 23 August 2007.

White, Andy. Telephone: 10, 17 October 2001. Saratoga Springs, New York: 12, 13 April 2006.

PUBLISHED SOURCES

Altham, Keith. 1965. "New Sounding Kinks." *New Musical Express* (24 December): 10.

———. 1966. "Kinks Don't Mind 'Formby Quartet' Tag." *New Musical Express* (18 March): 3.

Ampex Corporation. 2006. *Corporate Background.* www.ampex.com/03corp/03corp.html# Chron (accessed 22 August 2006).

Appadurai, Arjun. 1991. "Global Ethnoscapes: Notes and Queries for a Transnational An- thropology." In *Recapturing Anthropology: Working in the Present,* edited by Richard Fox, 191–210. Santa Fe, NM: School for American Research Press.

Archer, William Kay. 1964. "On the Ecology of Music." *Ethnomusicology* 8(1): 28–33.

Arnold, Bruce. 2008. "Ketupa.net Media Profiles: BBC." Available at http://ketupa.net/bbc2 .htm (accessed February 2008).

Babiuk, Andy. 2001. *Beatles Gear.* San Francisco, CA: Backbeat.

Badman, Keith. 2000. *The Beatles Off the Record: Outrageous Opinions & Unrehearsed Inter- views.* London: Omnibus.

Barbé, Antonio Costa. 1998. *Procol Harum: Beyond the Pale.* www.procolharum.com/acb_mf 2.htm (accessed March 2007).

Barnes, David. 2006. *Digger's Interview with Shel Talmy.* www.retrosellers.com/features122 .htm (accessed November 2007).

Barnes, Richard. 1982. *The Who: Maximum R&B.* London: Plexus.

Beatles, The. 2000. *The Beatles Anthology.* San Francisco, CA: Chronicle.

Bennett, Andy. 2000. *Popular Music and Youth Culture: Music, Identity, and Place.* London: Macmillan.

Bennett, Andy, and Richard Peterson (eds.). 2004. *Music Scenes: Local, Translocal, and Vir- tual.* Nashville, TN: Vanderbilt University Press.

Bennett, Jon. 2002. "Respect." *Mojo* (March): 60.

Brand, Pat. 1962a. "On the Beat." *Melody Maker* (27 January): 8.

———. 1962b. "On the Beat." *Melody Maker* (3 February): 10.

Brown, Tony. 1958. "How Disc Stars Are Made." *Melody Maker* (15 March): 3.

———. 1960a. "The *Melody Maker* Scours Britain for the Truth about Teenagers." *Melody Maker* (12 March): 3, 8.

———. 1960b. "How about Tackling Adult Tastes?" *Melody Maker* (19 March): 3, 17.

Buskin, Richard. 2003. "Mickie Most: Record Producer." *Sound on Sound* (August). www .soundonsound.com/sos/aug03/articles/mickiemost.htm (accessed December 2006).

Campbell, Malcolm. 2001. *The Shadows at EMI: The Vinyl Legacy.* St. Andrews, Scotland: Idmon.

Charlesworth, Chris (ed.). 1994. *The Rolling Stones: A Visual Documentary by Miles.* London: Omnibus.

Clark, Dave. 1964. "Dave Hits Back: 'There's Only One Drummer—Me!'" *Melody Maker* (29 February): 1.

Clayson, Alan. 1997. *Hamburg: The Cradle of British Rock.* London: Sanctuary.

Cluskey, Declan. 1964. "Blind Date." *Melody Maker* (22 February): 13.

Cohen, Sara. 2007. *Decline, Renewal and the City in Popular Music Culture: Beyond the Beatles.* Aldershot, Hampshire, England: Ashgate.

Coleman, Ray. 1964. "George (the Shrewd One): It's Like Winning the Pools." *Melody Maker* (7 November): 7.

———. 1965. "Stars of Beat: No. 1: The Lead Guitarists." *Melody Maker* (27 March): 11.

Cott, Jonathan. 1981. "Mick Jagger." In *The Rolling Stone Interviews, 1967–1980: Talking with the Legends of Rock & Roll,* edited by Peter Herbst, 44–50. New York: St. Martin's Press/ Rolling Stone Press. (Interview originally published in 1968)

Cunningham, Mark. 1998. *Good Vibrations: A History of Record Production.* London: Sanctuary.

David, Hubert W. 1961. "Denmark Street Diary." *Melody Maker* (6 May): 4.

———. 1962. "Denmark Street Diary." *Melody Maker* (6 January): 10.

Davies, Dave. 1996. *Kink: An Autobiography.* New York: Hyperion.

Davies, Hunter. 1985. *The Beatles.* New York: Norton.

Davies, Ray. 1994. *X-Ray.* London: Penguin.

Dawbarn, Bob. 1956. "Rock-'n'-Roll Pays Off." *Melody Maker* (8 December): 3.

———. 1965. "Watch Out for the Ivy League." *Melody Maker* (6 February): 9.

Dopson, Roger. 1997. *Major League: The Collector's Ivy League,* compiled by Roger Dopson and Tony Rounce. London: Sequel Records (NEDCD 289).

Dowlding, William J. 1989. *Beatlesongs.* New York: Simon & Schuster.

Durkee, Arthur. 1994. "Master of the Low End of the Street: An interview with John Paul Jones." *Black Dragon Productions.* http://3.avatarreview.com:8081/BDP/stories/storyReader $229 (accessed January 2007).

Elliott, Martin. 2002. *The Rolling Stones: Complete Recording Sessions, 1962–2002.* London: Cherry Red.

Emerick, Geoff. 1983. "Recording Techniques." In *Making Music: The Guide to Writing, Performing, and Recording,* edited by George Martin, 256–265. London: Pan.

———. 2006. "Letters to the Editor: Response from Geoff Emerick." *Daytrippin Magazine* (8 March). www.daytrippin.com/letters.htm (accessed February 2007).

Emerick, Geoff, with Howard Massey. 2006. *Here, There, and Everywhere: My Life Recording the Music of the Beatles.* New York: Gotham.

Everett, Walter. 1999. *The Beatles as Musicians:* Revolver *through the* Anthology. New York: Oxford University Press.

———. 2001. *The Beatles as Musicians: The Quarry Men through* Rubber Soul. New York: Oxford University Press.

Faithful, Marianne, with David Dalton. 2000. *Faithful: An Autobiography*. New York: Cooper Square.

Flick, Vic. 2001. "Ringing Out Like a Bell." (unpublished memoirs, accessed courtesy of the author)

Fordyce, Keith. 1963. "Tips All the Hit Singles." *New Musical Express*, no. 835 (11 January): 4.

Foster, Mo. 2000. *17 Watts? The Birth of British Rock Guitar*, edited by Mark Cunningham. London: Sanctuary.

Fox, Justin. 2007. "Google Gooses Big Media: The Search Giant Rewrote the Rules of Distribution and Selling Ads: The Big Movie, TV and Print Outfits May Never Catch Up." *Time* (26 March): 54.

Frame, Peter. 1997. *The Beatles and Some Other Guys: Rock Family Trees of the Early Sixties*. London: Omnibus.

Green, Richard. 1963. "'It's Rhythm-and-Blues That's Booming Now,' Say the Rolling Stones." *New Musical Express* (27 December): 2.

———. 1964a. "The Animals Score Big Hit by Toning Down the Lyric." *New Musical Express* (26 June): 5.

———. 1964b. "Dave Was Unhappy about 'Crying Game.'" *New Musical Express* (28 August): 2.

Greenfield, Robert. 1981. "Keith Richards." In *The Rolling Stone Interviews, 1967–1980: Talking with the Legends of Rock & Roll*, edited by Peter Herbst, 156–178. New York: St. Martin's Press/Rolling Stone Press. (Interview originally published in 1971)

Harrington, Patrick, and Bobby Graham. 2001. *The Session Man: The Story of Bobby Graham, the UK's Greatest Session Drummer*. Raglan, Monmouthshire: Broom House Publishing.

Herman, Arthur. 2001. *How the Scots Invented the Modern World: The True Story of How Western Europe's Poorest Nation Created Our World and Everything in It*. New York: Three Rivers.

Hinman, Doug. 2004. *The Kinks, All Day and All of the Night: Day-by-Day Concerts, Recordings, and Broadcasts, 1961–1996*. San Francisco, CA: Backbeat.

Hopkins, Jerry. 1981. "Keith Moon." In *The Rolling Stone Interviews, 1967–1980: Talking with the Legends of Rock & Roll*, edited by Peter Herbst, 236–245. New York: St. Martin's Press/Rolling Stone Press. (Interview originally published in 1972.)

Hughes, David. 2004. "Large Green Tape Machines: The EMI BTR/2." *Old Radio Broadcasting Equipment and Memories*. www.btinternet.com/~roger.beckwith/bh/tapes/btr2.htm (accessed 22 August 2006).

Irvin, Jim. 2007. "Sir George Martin: The *Mojo* Interview." *Mojo* (March): 36–40.

Jagger, Mick. 1963. "The Rolling Stones Write for *Melody Maker*." *Melody Maker* (21 March): 3.

Johnson, Derek. 1964. "Bite and Punch from Billy." *New Musical Express* (17 July): 6.

———. 1965. "Derek Johnson Tips Six Chart Certs!" *New Musical Express* (15 January): 6.

Jones, Nick. 1965. "Well, What Is Pop Art? Who Guitarist Pete Townshend Has a Go at a Definition." *Melody Maker* (3 July): 11.

Joynson, Vernon. 1995. *The Tapestry of Delights: The Comprehensive Guide to British Music of the Beat, R&B, Psychedelic, and Progressive Eras, 1963–1976*. Telford, England: Borderline.

Kozinn, Allan. 1995. *The Beatles*. London: Phaidon.

Kryk, John. 2002. "John Paul Jones Transcript." *Toronto Sun* (17 March 2002). www.canoe.ca/JamJohnPaulJones/mar17_johnpjones1-sun.html (accessed July 2006).

LaborLawTalk. 2006. "Disk Jockey." *Dictionary*. http://dictionary.laborlawtalk.com/disk_jockey (accessed 17 September 2006).

Leigh, Spencer. 2004. "Obituary: Norman Newell." *Independent* (London) (7 December). www.findarticles.com/p/articles/mi_qn4158/is_20041207/ai_n12814939 (accessed March 2007).

Leigh, Spencer, with John Firminger. 1996. *Halfway to Paradise: Britpop, 1955–1962.* Folkestone, Kent, England: Finbarr International.

Leitch, Donovan. 2005. *The Autobiography of Donovan: The Hurdy Gurdy Man.* New York: St. Martin's.

Lewis, Paul. 2002. *What's a Guinea? Money and Coinage in Victorian Britain.* www.wilkie collins.demon.co.uk/coinage/coins.htm (accessed January 2007).

Lewis, Vic. 1958. "Stop Insults to Teenagers: They Deserve a Better Deal." *Melody Maker* (1 November): 3.

Lewisohn, Mark. 1988. *The Beatles Recording Sessions.* New York: Harmony.

———. 1992. *The Complete Beatles Chronicle.* New York: Harmony.

MacInnes, Colin. 1980. *Absolute Beginners.* Harmondsworth, England: Penguin. (Originally published in 1959)

Marsh, Dave. 1983. *Before I Get Old: The Story of the Who.* London: Plexus.

Martin, George. 1983a. "Record Production." In *Making Music: The Guide to Writing, Performing, and Recording,* edited by George Martin, 266–277. London: Pan.

———. 1983b. "Arranging Music." In *Making Music: The Guide to Writing, Performing, and Recording,* edited by George Martin, 78–83. London: Pan.

Martin, George, with Jeremy Hornsby. 1979. *All You Need Is Ears.* New York: St. Martin's.

Martland, Peter. 1997. *Since Records Began: EMI: The First 100 Years.* Portland, OR: Amadeus.

Marwick, Arthur. 1998. *Sixties: Cultural Revolution in Britain, France, Italy, and the United States, c. 1958–c. 1974.* Oxford: Oxford University Press.

———. 2003. *British Society since 1945.* London: Penguin. (Originally published in 1983)

Mason, Catherine. 2005. "A Computer in the Art Room." *Futures Past: Twenty Years of Arts Computing.* www.chart.ac.uk/chart2004/papers/mason.html (accessed October 2006).

McCartney, Paul. 1983. "Songwriting." In *Making Music: The Guide to Writing, Performing, and Recording,* edited by George Martin, 62–66. London: Pan.

McMichael, Joe, and Jack Lyons. 1997. *The Who Concert File.* London: Omnibus.

McPherson, Ian. 2006. *Time Is on Our Side: The Rolling Stones Forever.* www.timeisonour side.com/index.html (accessed October 2006).

Meintjes, Louise. 1990. "Paul Simon's *Graceland,* South Africa, and the Meditation of Musical Meaning." *Ethnomusicology* 34(1): 37–73.

Melly, George. 1970. *Revolt into Style: The Pop Arts in Britain.* Harmondsworth, England: Penguin.

Miles, Barry. 1997. *Paul McCartney: Many Years from Now.* New York: Holt.

———. 1998. *The Beatles: A Diary,* edited by Chris Charlesworth. London: Omnibus.

Morgan, Kenneth O. 2001. *Britain since 1945: The People's Peace.* Oxford: Oxford University Press.

N.A. 1956. "Club, Disc Boom as Rock-and-Roll Craze Spreads." *Melody Maker* (14 July): 2.

———. 1958a. "Not So Bad for England." *Time* (16 June). www.time.com/time/magazine/article/0,9171,863490,00.html (accessed February 2007)

———. 1958b. "Tommy Steele Forms His Own Disc Firm." *Melody Maker* (30 August): 1.

———. 1960a. "MU Orders Ban on Dates in South Africa." *Melody Maker* (9 April): 11.

———. 1960b. "The Short Busy Life of Cliff Richard." *Melody Maker* (12 November): 15.

———. 1961. "The MU Blacklists Mecca's 'Colour-bar' Locarno Ballroom, Bradford." *Melody Maker* (16 December): 16.

———. 1962a. "MECCA 'Rebels' to Form Rival Union." *Melody Maker* (20 January): 16.

———. 1962b. "The BFM Disbands, Members Join the MU." *Melody Maker* (8 September): 3.

———. 1963. "Merseyside a 'Closed Shop'? Midland Beat Groups Up in Arms." *Melody Maker* (6 July): 3.

———. 1965a. "Now It Can Be Told . . . , Dave Kills the Rumours." *Melody Maker* (22 May): 8.

———. 1965b. "Ivy League: Selling Songs to the Americans." *Melody Maker* (10 July): 7.

———. 1965c. "Music Has to Progress, Otherwise We'd All Still Be Doing, 'Rock around the Clock': Bennett? Williams? I Could Outsing Them Put Together." *Melody Maker* (21 August): 14–15.

———. 1965d. "Jimmy Page: 'She Just Satisfies'" (advertisement). *Melody Maker* (20 February): 3.

———. 2004. "Go Lonnie Go." *Guardian* (21 June). www.billybragg.co.uk/words/words1.php?word_id=2&cur_page=0 (accessed February 2007).

Neill, Andy, and Matt Kent. 2002. *Anyway Anyhow Anywhere: The Complete Chronicle of the Who, 1958–1978.* London: Freidman.

Neuman, Daniel. 1980. *The Life of Music in North India.* Chicago: University of Chicago Press.

Nichols, Roger. 2001. "I Can't Keep Up with All the Formats." *EQ Magazine* (August). www.rogernichols.com/EQ/EQ_2001_07.html (accessed September 2006).

Norman, Philip. 1981. *Shout! The Beatles in Their Generation.* New York: MJF.

Oldham, Andrew Loog. 2000. *Stoned: A Memoir of London in the 1960s.* New York: St. Martin's.

———. 2003. *2Stoned,* edited by Christine Ohlman (interviews and research by Simon Spence). London: Vintage.

Osborn, John. 1956. *Look Back in Anger.* London: Faber.

Palachios, Julian. 1998. *Lost in the Woods: Syd Barrett and the Pink Floyd.* London: Boxtree.

Palao, Alec. 1997. *Zombie Heaven* (sleeve notes). London: Big Beat Records.

Payne, Jack. 1957. "Showtalk." *Melody Maker* (19 January): 5.

Paytress, Mark. 1996. "'Aye, Eye, Cap'n!' Johnny Kidd Died 30 Years Ago This Month." *Record Retailer* (October). Reprinted at http://disc.server.com/discussion.cgi?disc=178299;article=1296;title=Johnny Kidd and The Pirates (accessed March 2007).

———. 2003. *The Rolling Stones: Off the Record.* London: Omnibus.

Portelli, Allesandro. 1991. *The Death of Luigi Trastulli and Other Stories: Form and Meaning in Oral History.* Albany: State University of New York Press.

Povey, Glen, and Ian Russell. 1997. *Pink Floyd in the Flesh: The Complete Performance History.* New York: St. Martin's Griffin.

Repsch, John. 2000. *The Legendary Joe Meek: The Telstar Man.* London: Cherry Red Books.

Resnicoff, Matt. 1989. "Godhead Revisited: The Second Coming of Pete Townshend." *Guitar Player* (September). www.thewho.net/articles/townshen/gp_89.htm (accessed October 2006).

Rice, Tim, Paul Gambaccini, and Jonathan Rice. 1995. *British Hit Singles,* 10th ed. Enfield, Middlesex, England: Guinness.

Rimler, Walter. 1984. *Not Fade Away: A Comparison of Jazz Age with Rock Era Pop Song Composers.* Ann Arbor, MI: Pierian.

Ritchie, Donald A. 2003. *Doing Oral History: A Practical Guide.* New York: Oxford University Press.

Roberts, Chris. 1963. "If You Want to Get Success—Get an Accent: The Way to Success in the Pop World." *Melody Maker* (22 June): 8–9.

———. 1964a. "Lennon and McCartney Tell You How to Write a Hit!" *Melody Maker* (1 February): 11.

———. 1964b. "Operation Hit: The Machinery That Took Cilla Black to the Top of the Chart." *Melody Maker* (29 February): 10–11.

———. 1964c. "Without a Song . . . : Three Top Songwriters Tell How to Keep Up with the Changing Pop Scene." *Melody Maker* (22 August): 11.

Rogan, Johnny. 1988. *Starmakers and Svengalis: The History of British Pop Management.* London: Futura.

Ryan, Kevin, and Brian Kehew. 2006. *Recording the Beatles: The Studio Equipment and Techniques Used to Create Their Classic Albums.* Houston, TX: Curvebender.

Scott, Ken. 2006a. "Letters to the Editor: Controversy Surrounding Geoff Emerick's New Book." *Daytrippin Magazine* (3 March). www.daytrippin.com/letters.htm (accessed February 2007).

———. 2006b. "Letters to the Editor: Rebuttal from Ken Scott Regarding Geoff Emerick's Response Addressing Criticism to His Book." *Daytrippin Magazine* (12 March). www.daytrippin.com/letters.htm (accessed February 2007).

Segal, David. 2000. "The Bassist Remains the Same." *Washington Post* (29 March). http://trublukris.tripod.com/inter/jpj99.html (accessed February 2007).

Shapiro, Harry. 1998. "The Wall of Sound: The Moment Eric Clapton First Plugged His Les Paul into a Marshall Amp, He Changed the Sound of Rock 'n' Roll and Became God." *Mojo Magazine* (April): 90–92.

Sheff, David. 2000. *All We Are Saying: The Last Major Interview with John Lennon and Yoko Ono,* edited by G. Barry Golson. New York: St. Martin's Griffin.

Slobin, Mark. 1993. *Subcultural Sounds: Micromusics of the West.* Hanover, NH: Wesleyan University Press.

Spitz, Bob. 2005. *The Beatles: The Biography.* New York: Little, Brown.

Steward, Julian. "The Concept and Method of Cultural Ecology." In *Readings in Anthropology,* ed. Morton H. Fried, vol. 2, pp. 81–95. New York: Thomas Y. Crowell Company. (Reprint edition, 1955)

Sullivan, Jim. 2007. *History of B. J. S.* http://bigjimsullivan.com/History.html (accessed February 2007).

Thompson, Gordon. 1995. *1960s British Rock and Popular Music: A Selective Chronology.* www.skidmore.edu/%7Egthompso/britrock/60brchro/index.html (accessed August 2007).

Tobler, John, and Stuart Grundy. 1982. *The Record Producers.* New York: St. Martin's.

Unterberger, Ritchie. 1985a. *Shel Talmy.* www.richieunterberger.com/talmy.html (accessed September 2006).

———. 1985b. *Shel Talmy Interview: Part Two.* www.richieunterberger.com/talmy2.html (accessed September 2006).

Ward, Ed, Geoffrey Stokes, and Ken Tucker. 1986. *Rock of Ages: The Rolling Stone History of Rock and Roll.* Englewood Cliffs, NJ: Rolling Stone Press and Prentice-Hall.

Wasserman, S., and K. Faust. 1994. *Social Network Analysis: Methods and Applications.* New York: Cambridge University Press.

Williams, Chris. 1963. "He Wrote Pacemakers' No. 1 in the Bath!" *New Musical Express,* no. 848 (12 April): 9.

Wyman, Bill, with Richard Havers. 2002. *Rolling with the Stones.* London: Dorling Kindersley.

Yorke, Ritchie. 1990. *Led Zeppelin: The Definitive Biography.* Novato, CA: Underwood-Miller.

Song Index

315

General Index